Ruderal City

**Experimental Futures: Technological Lives,
Scientific Arts, Anthropological Voices**
A series edited by Michael M. J. Fischer
and Joseph Dumit

BETTINA STOETZER

Ruderal City

Ecologies of Migration,
Race, and Urban Nature in Berlin

DUKE UNIVERSITY PRESS
Durham and London
2022

Printed in the United States of America on acid-free paper ∞
Designed by A. Mattson Gallagher
Typeset in Minion Pro and Futura Std
by Westchester Publishing Services

Library of Congress Cataloging-in-Publication Data
Names: Stoetzer, Bettina, [date] author.
Title: Ruderal city : ecologies of migration, race, and urban nature
in Berlin / Bettina Stoetzer.
Other titles: Experimental futures.
Description: Durham : Duke University Press, 2022. | Series: Ex-
perimental futures | Includes bibliographical references and index.
Identifiers: LCCN 2022026519 (print)
LCCN 2022026520 (ebook)
ISBN 9781478015963 (hardcover)
ISBN 9781478018605 (paperback)
ISBN 9781478023203 (ebook)
Subjects: LCSH: Urban ecology (Sociology)—Germany—Berlin—
History. | Human ecology—Germany—Berlin—History. | City
and town life—Germany—Berlin—History. | Nature and civiliza-
tion—Germany—Berlin. | BISAC: SOCIAL SCIENCE / Anthropology
/ Cultural & Social | SOCIAL SCIENCE / Human Geography
Classification: LCC HT243.G32 B475 2022 (print) | LCC HT243.G32
(ebook) | DDC 307.760943/155—dc23/eng/20220802
LC record available at https://lccn.loc.gov/2022026519
LC ebook record available at https://lccn.loc.gov/2022026520

Cover art: *Test 86* (Berlin, 2022). Photograph by
Vlad Brăteanu. Courtesy of the artist.

CONTENTS

This book's story began in the forest outside of Berlin. In the late 2000s, I embarked on a research project to study antiracist activism in Germany. This led me, quite literally, into the woods. In the formerly East German countryside surrounding the city, forest areas had become a transitory home to asylum seekers from Africa and the Middle East, who found themselves living in derelict military barracks. After remaining in legal limbo for years, many African refugees, together with advocacy groups, began to organize protests to draw public attention to the everyday racism, spatial isolation, and violence they experienced. The refugees' encounters with German forests were the result of a series of transformations in national and European Union (EU) asylum policies, as well as the heated nationwide migration debates following Germany's unification.

The fall of the Berlin Wall and the collapse of socialism ruptured and realigned Europe's political landscape. In the early 1990s, millions of people fled the war in former Yugoslavia (where my grandparents had grown up), while border conflicts and civil war increased in countries across Africa, such as Burundi, Mali, and Senegal. In 1992, close to half a million people sought refuge in Germany. Yet Germany's unification in 1990 also led to a resurgence in white nationalism: right-wing youth and neo-Nazis attacked refugee and migrant worker homes, setting them on fire in several cities. Soon after, EU and German asylum policies underwent sweeping changes that resulted in a sharp drop in the number of people seeking asylum and an increase in deportations. At the same time, local governments relocated many refugee homes to the peripheries of cities or to remote forest areas in the countryside. By the mid-2000s, refugee activists and advocates were organizing against everyday racism and the spatial isolation of asylum seekers, who now often lived in secluded forest areas in Brandenburg and other parts of former East Germany.

For decades, scholars, artists, writers, and activists of color have highlighted the persistent legacies of racism and colonialism in shaping European social life (Gelbin, Konuk, and Piesche 1999; Gutiérrez Rodríguez and Steyerl 2003; Hügel et al. 1993; Kelly 2019; Nghi Ha 2010; Oguntoye, Ayim, and Schultz 2007; Red Haircrow 2018; Wekker 2016). Yet despite this important work, public and academic discussion in Germany often continues to focus on racism as a phenomenon of the past or as something that occurs elsewhere (Yildiz 2020), while largely ignoring the struggles of people of color against racism in Europe as well as the country's own colonial history. Addressing this silence, my first book, *InDifferenzen: Feministische Theorie in der Antirassistischen Kritik* (2004), tracked twentieth-century feminist, transnational conversations on race and racism in Germany and showed how these conversations shed light on the blind spots, as well as the privilege and power of whiteness in Europe.

Drawing on this earlier research, my next and new project initially sought to map ethnographically how antiracist coalition work on refugee rights exposed the ways in which structural racism infuses social institutions and migration policies in Germany. Participating in and engaging with antiracist networks in Berlin and Brandenburg, I had wanted to trace how activist movements build alliances while retheorizing racism and social justice on the ground. Yet when I arrived in Brandenburg, the forests themselves demanded attention. The landscape—the forest, the ruined military barracks, and the lack of access to infrastructure—was at the center of people's stories about what it meant to become a refugee in this place. A Kenyan activist spoke about having no access to warm water, having to walk through the forest every day, and encountering wild animals at night, all while being stuck in legal limbo for years. This was neither a fairy-tale forest nor the industrial forest that helped lay the foundations for Germany's economic power. This was a forest haunted by nightmares of colonial and racial violence—a space in which Europe's racialized others were administered into a refugee/savage slot, from which they were forced to prove their worthiness to be integrated into European society.

While many German Berliners and tourists saw Brandenburg's forests as a place of nature and adventure, to the Kenyan activist, the forest—which she referred to as the German bush—was a space of unease and lack of possibility, crowded with uncanny creatures ranging from wild boars to bureaucrats to neo-Nazis (see also Stoetzer 2014b). Perhaps it is no surprise that people living in some of Europe's most notorious refugee camps have called upon images of the wild, invoking terms such as *the bush* or *the jungle* as they found themselves inhabiting the ruins of military barracks or shaky tents, dwelling on the edges of windy ocean cliffs, facing police violence, or having their temporary homes go up in flames. The so-called jungles in Calais, France, or Moria camp on Lesvos Island, Greece, are just two cases in point. As Deborah Bird Rose (2004) reminds us, racism makes for "wild country." The Kenyan activist's experiences thus provided a glimpse of how landscapes such as forests can become sites of nation-making, dehumanization, racial violence, and exclusion. Her stories offered testimony to the ways in which colonial legacies and contemporary racial injustices materialize not only in bodies but also in relations to land. Yet, as this book will illustrate, these landscapes of exclusion and violence could also become the very grounds upon which alternative futures are forged.

While I listened to people's accounts of feeling stuck in the forests of Berlin's peripheries, I realized that the figure of the wild followed a different path in the city. In the mid-2000s, the media frequently reported on the city's diverse flora and fauna. Many white Germans ventured out to explore urban nature in Berlin. Meanwhile, the country was riddled with public dispute over the presence of refugees and migrants of color. As parks became sites of debate over how migrant communities inhabit the urban environment, many urban gardeners created so-called multicultural gardens to cultivate plants and alternative communities across class and ethnic difference, thus hoping to escape increasing social divisions. These divisions and disputes over migration are certainly not unique to Berlin. Instead, they offer a window into the role that relations to urban lands and nature play in racialization processes in Germany and Europe. And they provide glimpses of what it means to live in hazardous environments of dehumanization—which is the central subject of this book.

In the 2020s, climate disasters have begun to wreak havoc across the planet, shaking a false sense of security held across the wealthy global North. The COVID-19 pandemic has laid bare and deepened the ways in which racial and economic inequalities affect whose lives become vulnerable and are exposed to risk. The Black Lives Matter movement has inspired protests across the globe. In Europe, these protests have reinvigorated the ongoing social struggle to confront anti-Black racism and police violence. The protests have also initiated a larger debate about structural racism within mainstream society and have given rise to demands for reparations for colonial crimes and for truly decolonizing Europe (El-Tayeb 2020). Yet in Germany, too often, public discussion continues to see racism as something that is always "elsewhere," contained as a phenomenon of the past or a problem of right-wing extremism. Although reflections of Germany's colonial history have begun to be more common in various public arenas, the question of how this history continues to shape whiteness, anti-Blackness, Islamophobia, and other forms of racism today is rarely addressed. This is especially true when it comes to understanding how colonial history has informed extractive practices that have led to the contemporary environmental crisis.

As Carolyn Finney (2014) and Malcom Ferdinand (2022) teach us, the legacies of colonialism, slavery, and ongoing racial injustice continue to shape destructive modes of inhabiting the planet—while nature spaces and environmentalism are often coded as white (see also Linke 1999a, 1999b, 1999c). Nature can thus become a resource for cementing the nation, white supremacy, and settler colonial power. But, as I learned in the forest at the edges of Berlin, it can also become a site for confronting the violence inherent in practices of racialization, administration, and exploitation that shape Western relations to nature. This book thus embarks on a journey through the forests, parks, rubble spaces, and gardens of Berlin to seek out these openings and the alternative modes of inhabiting the world that people craft in them.

ACKNOWLEDGMENTS

The labor, thought, and care of so many people contributed to the making of this book.

I am most indebted to my interlocutors in Berlin and Brandenburg, many of whom will remain anonymous here. Without their generosity in offering their time and sharing their experience and daily lives with me, this project would never have been possible. With their knowledge, creativity, and savvy wit, they taught me to see the world in new ways. Special thanks go to Maria and Eli (pseudonyms) and the people in Brandenburg who, despite having felt ripped off by *jambazi* ("bandit," "gangster," or "beggar" in Swahili; a.k.a. journalists and social scientists) in the past, offered me their trust and allowed me to write about their stories. In Berlin, many people humbled me with their hospitality, inviting me into their lives and families, spending time in parks, walking, gardening, and thinking with me about matters of ecology, home, and displacement. Many have become both teachers and dear friends. Special thanks go to the Kalın family and the woman I call Nursen in this book for their persistent engagement, storytelling, and kindness.

My project has been aided by several other individuals and public officials working for NGOs, advocacy groups, and Berlin's city administration. My gratitude goes to the Flüchtlingsrat (Refugee Council) in Berlin and Brandenburg, the Flüchtlingsinitiative Berlin-Brandenburg, the Grünflächenamt Mitte, the Senatsverwaltung für Stadtentwicklung, Bauen und Wohnen, the Senatsverwaltung für Umwelt, Mobilität, Verbraucher und Klimaschutz, the environmental organizations Naturschutzbund Deutschland (NABU) and Bund für Umwelt- und Naturschutz Deutschland (BUND), and the many connoisseurs of the Tiergarten and other green spaces in Berlin. Thanks also go to garden activists Andrea Geldner, Gerda Münnich, and Åsa Sonjasdotter, who have been important interlocutors throughout the years. Michaela Pohle, whose friendship has been with me since our teens, tirelessly sent me articles and kept me updated on Berlin's urban ecology news. Fatoş Minaz, Orhan Esen, Kathrin and Özgür, and several families in Berlin provided crucial guidance during my two trips to Istanbul. Ika Hügel and Dagmar Schultz were early friends and interlocutors whose work has had a tremendous impact. Conversations with Ingo Kowarik, Derk Ehlert, and Detlev Dahlmann were formative for my deeper understanding of the history of Berlin's urban landscapes. I am especially indebted to Herbert Sukopp for inspiring me to consider rubble plants and Berlin's unique history of urban ecology, as well as for offering his time, sharing photographs, and pointing me to relevant publications.

This ethnography has benefited tremendously from the wonderful intellectual communities and places that I have been fortunate to be part of in the past years. The Anthropology Department at the University of California at Santa Cruz (UCSC) was the most inspiring and vibrant intellectual home that I could have hoped for during my dissertation research, which laid the foundations for this book. I owe my gratitude to Lisa Rofel for her intellectual guidance, her critical close readings, and her enduring support over the years, and for teaching me when to let go. I thank Anna Tsing for her generous and careful engagement with key ideas in this book, for pushing and trusting me to become a better storyteller, and for walking, talking, and exploring ideas together for more than two decades. Hiking through the redwood forests in Santa Cruz in the 2000s, talking about rubble, forests, and urban ecology, from mushrooms to sticky goosefoot and other multispecies relations, long before some of these terms entered anthropological theorizing, will always be a reminder that academic knowledge is never produced in isolation but as part of a collective effort, a thinking together and thinking with. I thank Mark Anderson for the many conversations over coffee at Caffe Pergolesi, and for keeping things down to earth; and I thank James Clifford for inspiring key themes in this project early on and for his critical eye for ethnographic writing. Special thanks also go to Susan Harding for triggering several fruitful interventions at the beginning of my project. Hugh Raffles prompted me to think about Berlin's urban nature early on and taught me to attend more closely to the affective and methodological aspects of writing. I am deeply grateful to Donna Haraway for inspiring many questions that I explore in this project—even before I met her in person—and for sharing her expertise, feminist passion, and intellectual care throughout its development. I also thank Don Brenneis, Melissa Caldwell, Nancy Chen, Shelly Errington, Dan Linger, Carolyn Martin Shaw, Andrew Mathews, and Olga Nájera-Ramírez for being wonderful guides as teachers, and for their support throughout graduate school; thanks also to the staff at the UCSC Anthropology Department, especially Fred Deakin, Debbie Neal, Courtney Hewitt, and Allyson Ramage, who provided invaluable administrative support.

The Society of Fellows and the Anthropology Department at the University of Chicago became a lively intellectual home for several years while I revised the manuscript and did follow-up research. I thank all my colleagues and friends at the Society of Fellows, especially Fadi Bardawil, Greg Beckett, Nick Gaskill, Carolyn Johnson, Birte Löschenkohl, Benjamin McKean, Karthik Pandian, the late Moishe Postone, and Lauren Silvers. And I send special appreciation to my colleagues at the Anthropology Department, including Hussein Ali Agrama, Julie Chu, Shannon Lee Dawdy, Judith Farquhar, Michael Fisch, Susan Gal, Karin Knorr Cetina, Joe Masco, William Mazzarella, the late Nancy Munn, Stephan Palmié, and Kaushik Sunder Rajan. In Chicago, Zhivka Valiavicharska became an enduring friend, reader, and writing partner, and her always carefully crafted feedback was invaluable during the revision process. Several writing and reading retreats that included Amahl Bishara, Julie Chu, Michael Fisch, Eleana Kim, and Brian Larkin helped me rethink key theoretical questions in the book as they relate to the anthropology of infrastructure.

I also thank my colleagues at the former Department for Global Studies and Languages (GSL), my first home when I joined the faculty at the Massachusetts Institute of Technology (MIT). Special thanks go to Catherine Clark, Paloma Duong, Jeff Ravel, Emma Teng, the late Jing Wang, and Elizabeth Wood for their generous support and engagement. Ian Condry and William Uricchio carefully guided me with their mentorship in these first years. I am grateful for the many brainstorming sessions with Bruno Perreau, for his friendship, and wonderful advice as I jumped through the first hoops of the tenure process. Thanks also go to the German group in the former GSL, especially to Ellen Crocker, Kurt Fendt, and Dagmar Jaeger. Administrative staff, including Joseph Borkowski, Liam Brenner, Lisa Hickler, Elouise Evee-Jones, Olga Opojevici, Joyce Roberge, and the late Andrea Wirth, shepherded me through my first years at MIT. From the beginning, being in dialogue with and receiving feedback from faculty across MIT has been invaluable, and I especially thank Sandy Alexandre, Kate Brown, Rania Ghosn, Sally Haslanger, Caley Horan, Helen Lee, Jennifer Light, David Lowry, and Harriet Ritvo. Since 2019, the anthropology program at MIT has become my new intellectual home, and I couldn't ask for a more wonderful group of colleagues, mentors, and friends. I thank Héctor Beltrán, Manduhai Buyandelger, Michael Fischer, Jean Jackson, Graham Jones, Susan Silbey, Amy Moran-Thomas, and Chris Walley for their sharp minds and for our always lively and inspiring conversations. Special thanks go to Carolyn Carlson, Kate Gormley, Irene Hartford, Barbara Keller, and Amberly Steward for making things easy on an administrative level and for helping me navigate the everyday at MIT. Sharing key transition periods at MIT with Amah Edoh's friendship and humor has been, to use Amah's words, a beautiful surprise, especially in the global pandemic roller coaster that was 2020. And I am so grateful to Heather Paxson and Stefan Helmreich for their brilliant mentorship and generosity, for cheering me on, for closely reading multiple drafts, and last but not least, for fun summer afternoon joint work sessions in their backyard.

My students at MIT have been a delight to work with, and conversations both with individual students and students in my classes on environmental justice, urban anthropology, and race and migration have inspired me to reflect on and revise many aspects of this book. For assistance with research and translations, I thank Daniel Kraft and Serra Nur Sarıdereli. Elena Sobrino helped me with images, permissions, and finishing touches to the manuscript. David Darrow assisted with bibliographical work in the final stages of the production process.

I am grateful for having had the privilege to work with Kathy Chetkovich, Molly Mollin, and Micha Rahder, who provided amazing developmental and editorial feedback throughout different phases of this project. Special thanks go to Micha Rahder for her smart and careful edits that enabled this project to move across the finish line. Vlad Brăteanu's generosity and creative eye made all the difference for the cover image of the book.

I presented sections of *Ruderal City* at several conferences and lecture series, including at Syracuse University, the University of Chicago, Princeton University, the University of Toronto, the Universidad de Chile in Santiago, the Pontificia Universidad Católica de Chile, the Universidad Diego Portales in Santiago, UC Santa Cruz, Harvard University, the University of Michigan, Sarah Lawrence College, the Sanctuary for Independent Media and the Faculty of Arts and Science and Technology Studies (STS) at Rensselaer

Polytechnic Institute, and MIT. I thank my colleagues and listeners during these events for their engagement and productive feedback.

The material and arguments presented in this book also benefited tremendously from feedback during a series of workshops, including the STS Circle at Harvard University, the Matters of Urban Citizenship Workshop at Columbia University, the Military Ecologies Workshop at the University of California at Irvine, the Infrastructural Worlds Workshop at Duke University, the Anthropocene Campus at the Haus der Kulturen der Welt in Berlin, and the Chronopolis Symposium in the Department for Germanic Languages and Literatures at the University of Michigan. I would especially like to thank Nikhil Anand, Hannah Appel, Rose Cohen, Paulla Ebron, Cassie Fennell, Gökçe Günel, Kristina Lyons, Ramah McKay, and Austin Zeiderman for their wonderful feedback during some of these workshops.

Special thanks also go to Tomás Criado and Ignacio Farías, who invited me to discuss the framework of *Ruderal City* at the Institute of European Ethnology at the Humboldt University in Berlin. My gratitude also goes to the anonymous reviewers for their wonderfully detailed and productive comments on my manuscript, and for pushing me to develop some key ideas more deeply. At Duke University Press, I thank Joshua Gutterman Tranen, Liz Smith, and Ken Wissoker for their brilliant guidance throughout the revision and production process. Ken has supported the project with patience, intellectual wit, and enthusiasm since we began our dialogue many years ago. I am also grateful to Liz Smith for walking me through the final production process of the book and her flexibility during the last steps toward the finish line. My thanks also go to Mattson Gallagher for his fabulous work on the book cover. Andrew Ascherl provided crucial help with production of the index.

I would also like to thank the following interlocutors in anthropology and beyond for their engagement and feedback on my project: Dominic Boyer, Dorothee Brantz, Sandra Calkins, Mark Cioc, Jeffry Diefendorf, Matthew Gandy, Andreas Glaeser, Michi Knecht, Stephan Lanz, Uli Linke, Tobias Pieper, Eli Rubin, Avi Sharma, Nitzan Shoshan, Kathleen Stewart, Karen Till, Janet Ward, and Barbara Wolbert. Lissi Klaus, Ilse Costas, Ursula Apitzsch, and Brigitta Hauser-Schäublin were early mentors in Germany. Ghassan Hage has been a fun and inspiring interlocutor in the past decade.

In addition to their friendship, the following colleagues and friends provided critical feedback on drafts and key ideas that led to *Ruderal City*: Jason Alley, Patricia Alvarez Astacio, Nikhil Anand, Gretchen Bakke, Fadi Bardawil, Eunice Blavascunas, Kendra Briken, Nick Brown, Heath Cabot, Kim

Cameron-Domínguez, Zachary Caple, Rose and Emily Cohen, Lindsey Collins, Thomas Duveau, Bregje van Eekelen, Cassie Fennell, Malcom Ferdinand, Anna Higgins, Afsaneh Kalantary, Sarah Kanouse, Celina Callahan-Kapoor, Eben Kirksey, Sandra Koelle, John Marlovits, Andrea Muehlebach, Katy Overstreet, Damani Partridge, Jason Rodriguez, James Rowe, Daniel Salomon, Astrid Schrader, Alexis Shotwell, Cristián Simonetti, Aviva Sinervo, Susanne Unger, Suraj Yengde, and Armanc Yildiz. Nishita Trisal and Jason Alley have been dear friends and a crucial support network since grad school. Both generously offered many close reads and edits of drafts of this book. Noah Tamarkin has been a consistent writing partner since grad school and has cheered me on throughout different stages of this project.

For their companionship and support I want to thank my dispersed and yet nourishing community of friends and colleagues in Berlin and across Germany, the Bay Area, Chicago, Cambridge, Boston, Santiago, and elsewhere: Lionel Brossi; Ilker, Zoe, Filiz, and Ulrike Busse; Maggie Ervin; Wendy Farina; Luis Antonio Fraire; Cesar Glagos; Ben Carson; Rose and Emily Cohen; Alvaro Martinez; Ruth Müller; Juno Parreñas; Pep Serra-Diaz; Sandra Smykalla; Vivian Solana; Birgit Straehle; Mai Taha; Cynthia Taines; Barbara Oh; Michaela Pohle; Candace Roberts; and Suraj Yengde. Barbara Oh helped spark my interest in anthropology early on. I thank Laura Efron for the many joint writing sessions while she was composing a novel. In my first years at MIT, Alvaro Martinez and Pep Serra-Diaz reminded me of the witty and imaginative sides of my project by coming up with their own ruderal poetry and art, while my dear friends Lionel Brossi and Cesar González-Lagos opened up new ways of thinking about ruderal urban life and so much more in Santiago, Chile. A special thank-you goes to my former long-term housemates Michael Rasalan, Cynthia Taines, Mai Taha, and Aslı Zengin for their friendship, for their enduring support, and for reading many drafts of this project. Birgit Straehle and Luis Antonio Fraire offered the best distraction with speedy ping-pong matches, good food, and companionship at the beautiful Sprinkler Factory. Rania Ghosn, Taha, and El Hadi Jazairy were the most wonderful, supportive, and fun neighbors during a challenging time of the pandemic in Somerville. Finally, Gabriele Goszcz and her community of lovely critters, especially Winni, were lifesavers, offering a fun and nourishing home when I struggled with health issues in the last months of getting the manuscript ready for production.

Funding for various phases of this project has been provided by the Andrew W. Mellon/ACLS Foundation, a UC Santa Cruz Chancellor's Dissertation-Year Fellowship, the Wenner-Gren Foundation, the UC Regents, the Anthropology Department at UCSC, the MIT Office of the Dean of Humanities, Arts, and Social Sciences, and the German Research Foundation (DFG).

Earlier versions of portions of the text have also appeared in the following publications: pieces of chapter 4 appeared in Jeffry Diefendorf and Janet Ward's edited volume *Transnationalism and the German City* (2014); sections of chapter 6 appeared in *Ecologies of Socialisms: Germany, Nature, and the Left in History, Politics and Culture*, edited by Sabine Mödersheim, Scott Moranda, and Eli Rubin (2019); and parts of the argument that now appear in the introduction and chapters 1 and 2 were first published in *Cultural Anthropology*.

Unless otherwise noted, all translations in this work are my own.

Finally, I thank my parents, Brigitte Stoetzer and Bernd Eichstaedt; my brothers, Benjamin and Fabian; my late stepfather, Hans; my grandparents; and my extended family for their enduring support, love, and humor—and for keeping things in perspective. My mother always cheered me on and reminded me, as my great-grandmother would have said, to keep mind, body, and soul together. Without my family, this project would not have been possible. Special thanks go to my grandmother, who, a traveler and gardener herself, has inspired much of my work with her curiosity and keen sense for all plants and critters.

INTRODUCTION

On a chilly morning in the spring of 2017, I stood with Mehmet on the veranda overlooking his garden. As the sun began to peek through the clouds, he pointed out the garden's highlights: grape vines growing precariously on the side of the shack, the vegetable bed where cabbages would soon be thriving, his mother's cherry tree—just about to bloom—and a small pine tree that his father replanted after someone had thrown it away after Christmas. Built from scrap materials, the shack was crowded with odd objects: wooden and plastic panels, chairs, piles of tools, a colorful array of lamps, carpets, sun umbrellas, and a small sofa. But most impressive, with its trunk emerging out of the shack's front wall, was a five-meter-tall tree-of-heaven towering above the garden.

Mehmet's father, Osman Kalın, was a local celebrity. In the 1980s, when the Berlin Wall marked the boundary between East and West Berlin, he took advantage of a gap in state control and an "error" in precise territorial division. As local and family legend has it, it all started in 1983, when Osman left his job.[1] After working in construction for many years, he struggled with chronic back pain and was forced to retire early. Yet soon after retiring, he got bored and was ready for a construction project of a different sort. Living just a few blocks from the Wall, in Kreuzberg in West Berlin, he went on a stroll one day and discovered a small triangle of land in the Wall's shadow, littered with garbage. He began to clear it, and, after a few days, when nobody bothered to complain, he decided to plant some onions, a few tomatoes, and cabbage on the land. After a while, he added cucumbers, pumpkins, garlic, beans, sunflowers, and collard greens. His wife, Fadik, and he also planted several fruit trees, and they built a small shed that soon became a two-story house, cobbled together from metal sheets, old doors, wooden beams, grids from abandoned fridges, and other things they found in the streets. Soon, a neighbor joined their garden project and took charge of a small piece of the land. During summers, the couple's children, grandchildren, and other members of the family would work in the garden every day, enjoying the sun and eating fresh vegetables. The garden soon became a meeting place for passersby and neighbors, who came to help out, take a break, and socialize.

Struggling on a small pension, the Kalıns began to harvest the crops and sell them at the local weekly Turkish market. One day, just when the tomatoes began to ripen, two East German border guards knocked at Osman's door. Their garden, it turned out, was located on territory belonging to the German Democratic Republic (GDR). The East German government had constructed the Wall in a straight line to save money instead of following the zig-zag contours of the actual border, thus skipping the triangle of land on which the Kalıns' vegetables were now thriving. After long negotiations, the GDR government allowed Osman to stay—provided the sunflowers did not grow taller than the Wall.

In 1989, the Wall tumbled, and Osman's garden was no longer in an abandoned corner but at the center of the unified city. When the new district office protested the garden dwelling, Osman insisted that the East German state had entrusted the piece of land to him. In the end, the dismal state of Berlin's finances assisted Osman's cause, and plans to relandscape the former border zone into a green corridor stalled. Osman's garden was once again left alone. In 2004, the borough administration finally granted him the right to stay, recognizing the garden as a significant part of local history.

Today, people affectionately call the garden dwelling the Berlin tree house (*Baumhaus*), or *gecekondu*, in honor of the squatter houses that emerged at the peripheries of Turkish cities during rural-urban migrations from the 1950s onward. Gecekondu literally means "place built overnight," because such shelters often popped up overnight and people who built them took advantage of legal loopholes.[2] Many Turkish Berliners, like Osman, lived in such shelters before migrating to Berlin (Lanz 2007). Not unlike a Turkish gecekondu, Osman's Berlin version features a small orchard of apricot, apple, pear, and plum trees (fig. I.1). The shack has survived heavy storms, cold winters, and even a fire. A local priest helped Osman tap into the water infrastructure from the nearby church. And the large tree-of-heaven, once a small shrub growing in the cracks of the sidewalk, has become an impres-

FIGURE I.1 Berlin tree house. Photo by author.

sive part of the gecekondu's front wall. Each year, as the trunk expands, Osman and his son cut further into the wall to accommodate its growth.

The gecekondu is well known among Berliners, and as far afield as Istanbul, where news reporters have chuckled about Osman's clever dealings. Sometimes, on weekends, tourist groups stop by. In front of the shack, Osman put a few chairs and a table. One day, the chairs and table were stolen and the bench was burned by hostile neighbors. The next day, Osman quickly replaced them. The table's legs are now cemented to the ground, offering a place for neighbors, kin, and friends to gather and chat.

I open with the story about this small garden to introduce the notion of a ruderal city. Nestled in a small gap in the city's border infrastructure and built environment, Osman Kalın's gecekondu took advantage of the state's desire to create order, to simplify and to draw straight lines. Instead of fitting into existing boundaries, the garden's ecology was made possible by a gap, both in Osman's life and in the gray zones of the nation-state. Cobbled together from dreams, hard labor, edible plants, streetside trees, and cast-off furniture, the gecekondu embodies what I call a ruderal ecology in the city.

Ruderal comes from *rudus*, the Latin word for rubble. Commonly used in urban ecology (e.g., Del Tredici 2010; Sukopp 2008; Sukopp, Hejny, and Kowarik 1990), the term refers to organisms that spontaneously inhabit "disturbed" environments usually considered inhospitable to life: cracks in sidewalks, spaces alongside train tracks and roads, industrial sites, waste disposal areas, or rubble fields.[3] Unplanned worlds in the shadows of anthropogenic landscapes, ruderals are neither wild nor domesticated. Instead, they depend on "edge effects" and the juxtaposition of contrasting environments in one ecosystem.[4]

Ruderal ecologies can be found all over Berlin, and they entered my fieldwork in myriad ways. Yet it was Herbert Sukopp, a well-known urban ecologist, who drew my attention to their botany when I first met him in 2007. Surrounded by the Berlin Wall and cut off from their usual field sites in the countryside, Sukopp and other West Berlin botanists conducted research on plants growing in the bombed city's rubble after World War II. As he and his colleagues followed the city's rubble vegetation, abundant in unexpected newcomers from all over the world, they began to study plant migration and discovered a cosmopolitan ecology emerging in the city's "blasted landscapes" (Stoetzer 2011, 54; Tsing 2014)—an ecology that was the result of capitalist trade, displacement, and the destruction that nationalism had wrought across Europe. Through my subsequent conversations and interviews with Sukopp, I learned about ruderal plants such as sticky goosefoot (*Chenopodium botrys*) and tree-of-heaven (*Ailanthus altissima*), whose seeds had entered the city by hitching rides on the boots of soldiers and refugees, or via trains, horse fodder, and imported materials. These plants still thrive in Berlin today, including in Osman Kalın's garden. Attending to their ecologies and the stories people tell about them, I learned a new way of approaching "nature" in the city.

In this book, I offer the notion of the ruderal city as a framework for thinking about the heterogeneity of urban life in the ruins of European nationalism and capitalism. Exploring Berlin as a ruderal city (*Ruderalstadt*), I direct attention toward often unnoticed cosmopolitan yet precarious ways of remaking the urban fabric. Ruderal worlds emerge in the cracks of systems of urban governance and formal institutions. "Illicit" hitchhikers on infrastructural projects, they disrupt systems of human control and a social order in which only specific kinds of "human-environment relations" or "natures" have value and seem appealing.

Rather than constituting parallel cultures, wilderness, or cultivated nature, ruderal worlds thrive in in-between spaces and live amid inhospitality and relocation. Following them entails never telling a singular story about "urban nature"—a fraught term that refers to both shifting ecological imaginaries about cities and their physical transformation (Gandy 2022, 2006).[5] Like nature in the abstract Western sense, urban nature is built on histories of extraction, racism, violence, and colonization. Tracking ruderal lives in its place means catching glimpses of seemingly disparate worlds—to imagine urban ecologies otherwise, and to create an analytical lens that troubles environmental perspectives and combines them with an analysis of racism, migration, and social justice. Such a method of gleaning perspectives and thinking across registers is particularly salient at a moment when racism and capitalist exploitation are rendering much of the world inhospitable to many beings. Thinking with the ruderal, the goal is not to equate people with plants, but rather to ask how people, plants, animals, and other living beings are intertwined in projects of capitalist extraction and nation-making—and how they traverse these projects.

While scholars in the humanities and social sciences have written about ruderal plants or areas from the perspective of the history of science (Lachmund 2013) or by examining the aesthetics of and knowledges about urban nature and wastelands (Cowles 2017; Gandy 2013, 2022), I offer the ruderal as an analytic for ethnographic inquiry into contemporary urban life. Ruderal worlds are not utopian spaces of hope and cosmopolitan survival amid ruins, nor are they free from power. Instead, a ruderal analytic asks about the broader ecologies of human-built and social structures and the multispecies and often violent worlds they become part of. In short: ruderal worlds constitute an ecology of unexpected neighbors in the city.

Like other cities, Berlin has long been inhabited by diverse neighbors. And some have been more welcome than others. As concerns about climate change, environmental degradation, and species extinction have grown over the past decade, Berlin is often promoted as "Europe's Nature Capital." The city features a large diversity of plant and animal species, as well as many parks, lakes, gardens, and urban forests. Many local residents enthusiastically explore the city's nature and its nonhuman newcomers. Yet while Berlin is celebrated as a "Green City," its parks and forests have also become sites of contestation over migrant rights and appropriate relations to the urban environment. Amid intense political debate over migration, images of segregated, troubled neighborhoods abound.[6] At the same time, many Berliners seek out urban nature precisely to find refuge from the city's social divisions—for example by rediscovering allotment gardens or founding so-called multicultural or intercultural gardens.[7]

Based on fieldwork undertaken since 2007, *Ruderal City* offers an ethnography of the shifting racial politics of nature, migration, and the nation in Berlin and its hinterlands. Drawing on interviews and participant observation with migrant and refugee communities, as well as with ecologists, environmentalists, public officials, activists, and nature enthusiasts, the book illustrates that nature is a key register through which urban citizenship and belonging are articulated in contemporary Europe. *Ruderal City* takes readers on a tour of sites in and around Berlin that have figured prominently in German national imaginaries—urban wastelands, spaces of rubble, gardens, forests, and parks—to explore how racial, gender, and class inequalities are reconfigured in conflicts over the use, experience, knowledge, and management of the city's green spaces and urban nature.

The book's chapters show how projects of nation-making and racialization materialize in Berlin's ecologies and in people's relations to land and other beings. I direct attention to diverse but often unnoticed practices of remaking the urban fabric, including botanical research on "alien plants" in the city's rubble after World War II, contemporary urban gardening in migrant neighborhoods, "wild barbecuing" in parks by Turkish and Southeast Asian diasporic communities, and the experiences of East African refugees living in former military barracks in the East German forest at Berlin's periphery. These sites provide snapshots of social exclusions and practices that mark not only human bodies but also plants, animals, landscapes, and "things." In this sense, the book offers insights into shifting ecologies of racialization, migration, and nationhood and a cultural politics of race, nature, and difference (Moore, Pandian, and Kosek 2003): in the book's ethnographic stories, we can see how the nation's borders and boundaries are naturalized, and how multiple kinds of bodies become "matter out of place" (Douglas 2002), outside the recognized national body.

Yet, nature cannot be seen as a given, and it is much more than a metaphor. Whether mobilized as a category for urban planning or as a resource with which to racialize people's bodies or promote hope amid social conflict, nature becomes a way of assembling political order (Latour 2004) that always enlists multiple beings and is deeply fraught with histories of extraction and harm (Haraway 2008; Tsing 2012). Similarly, the scientific field of ecology has been entangled with the colonial encounter that has often rendered nature, or the environment, as an external and extractable resource (Ferdinand 2022; Hage 2017; Rajan 2006; Worster 1985). While attending to the ways in which relations to more-than-human worlds in the city are shaped by or rework racial, gender, and class inequalities, the ethnographic material presented in *Ruderal City* goes a step further: it points to ways of "being alive" (Ingold 2011) that are more complex than what existing analytical categories of migration, nature, and the environment— categories that are always also the products of administration, exploitation, and racialization—are able to capture. Instead, ruderal practices emerge from imploded power structures. Like the gecekondu, they exceed efforts to domesticate the world. Attending to such ways of being alive, and the more-than-human socialities they enable, can enliven urban analysis and broaden our understanding of relationality and politics (see also Haraway 2015; Kohn 2010; Myers, forthcoming; Raffles 2010; Tsing 2015). A ruderal analytic thus challenges cultural critique to trouble and rework common analytical distinctions—such as the distinction between culture and nature, matter and infrastructure, inanimate and animate, the nation and its "outsider" (the migrant), as well as the city and its countryside.

Gleaning glimpses of urban life in the ruins of racism and capitalism, *Ruderal City* creates a dialogue between environmental perspectives and the study of migration and racial politics in Europe. A ruderal framework goes beyond the usual kinds of stories told about cities—and about Berlin in particular—stories that tend to focus on buildings and people. Examining how people's relations to landscapes, plants, and other beings reshape urban socialities, I explore how to write about a politics of race and nation-making in ways that approach the city as a place of animate encounter. With this focus, *Ruderal City* speaks to the larger question of what constitutes cultural critique in a time of rubble—a time when the implosions of history, racism, colonialism, and capitalist modes of extraction render much of the world increasingly uninhabitable.

Anthropology as Cultural Critique in the Rubble of the Twenty-First Century

In the first two decades of the twenty-first century, a shift has occurred in anthropology and related fields. Keywords such as ontology, the Anthropocene, infrastructure, multispecies ethnography, new materialism, and the environmental turn have proliferated in numerous forums. A new kind of reflexivity has emerged as anthropology reflects on the vulnerability and earthly entanglements of its central subject: the (hu)man, or Anthropos.[8] In an era some call the Anthropocene,[9] humans have fundamentally changed the course of Earth's ecosystems (Chakrabarty 2012; Latour 2013) such that the modern fiction of nature/culture or human/nonhuman as ontologically opposed categories is impossible to sustain (de Castro 2012; de la Cadena 2015; Descola 2013; Haraway 1991, 2016; MacCormack and Strathern 1980). Instead, terms such as "naturecultures" (Haraway 2008) account for the ways in which ecological relations are always material-semiotic and people's relations to each other and the world are porous and deeply entangled.

This call for conceptual renewal carries a sense of urgency: in the face of climate change, social injustice, the global circulation of toxins and waste, and the destruction of habitats, anthropology, it seems, has become a science of ruins, examining the dynamics of life on a damaged planet (Tsing 2015; see also Dawdy 2010; Gordillo 2014; Harms 2013; Johnson 2013; Navaro-Yashin 2012; Stoler 2013, 2016). Responding to these developments and drawing on multispecies frameworks (Haraway 2015; Kirksey and Helmreich 2010; Kohn 2007, 2010; Raffles 2002; Tsing 2015) as well as longer legacies in feminist theory, science and technology studies (STS), environmental anthropology, and antiracist critique, many recent ethnographies model an anthropology that highlights the violence, vulnerabilities, and earthly entanglements of more-than-human worlds (Dave 2017; Govindrajan 2018; Helmreich 2009; Parreñas 2018; Weston 2017). Pushing beyond a framework of human impacts on the environment, these ethnographies place emphasis on "the effects of our entanglements with other kinds of living selves" (Kohn 2007, 4).[10]

With a similar interest in social-material relations, emerging anthropological scholarship on infrastructure directs attention to built environments and the physical networks of cities—such as roads, trains, water supplies, waste and sewage systems, or electric grids—to show how they enable social life and forms of urban governance (see Anand 2017; Boyer 2014; Carse 2012; Chalfin 2014; Fennell 2015; Larkin 2013; Schnitzler 2013). Anchoring analysis in the politics and poetics of human-built structures, this scholarship has opened up fresh perspectives on the relations between materiality, consciousness, and culture. This occurs at a historic moment when the limits of managing nature as resource and the toxic effects of late industrialism and of the (neo)colonial order become more visible (Fortun 2012; Liboiron 2021; Masco 2017). At the same time, the infrastructures of cities—specifically in the global North—are beginning to age and crumble and seem less reliable (as if they ever were). When the thing breaks, one notices its "thingness" (Heidegger 1970; Star 1999).

Approaching this kind of ruination as more than an impetus for aesthetic contemplation or imperialist nostalgia (Huyssen 2006; Rosaldo 1989; Stoler 2013), in which one mourns "what one has destroyed" (Rosaldo 1989, 107), anthropological reflections on ruins offer new sensibilities for grasping the spatial and temporal life of modern world-making projects—and their destructive effects.[11] Yet curiously, while abandoned factories, toxic dumps, weedy lots, and the gutted infrastructures of canals, roads, and schools appear as integral elements of urban landscapes, infrastructures and ruins are often theorized separately from one another.[12] In a similar vein, while crowded with images of rubble overgrown with weeds, scholarship on ruins rarely describes or theorizes the actual ecologies or animate worlds that emerge in spaces of ruination, even as some authors highlight the afterlife of ruins and its materiality.[13] As a result, focusing on infrastructure as substrate of human cultural systems risks assuming a vitalist dynamic, even when considering infrastructure's failures, highlighting its "experimental ontologies" (Bruun Jensen and Morita 2016), or showing how progress and ruination are intimately tied together (Johnson 2013). This vitalism depends on a deeply gendered and racialized binary distinction between technology, culture, and infrastructure as an active form of externalization, and matter, nature, or ruins as a passive, inanimate, or degenerate form (Le Guin 1989; Yusoff 2018, 13).

These dualities between infrastructure and ruins, or between active technology and passive "matter," also correspond with a nature/culture divide in urban scholarship. Although ecological metaphors played a formative role in understanding and managing twentieth-century urban human life (J. Light 2009; Mitman 1992), the lively presence of animals, plants, and other organisms in cities has long functioned as the constitutive outside, or other, of much urban analysis. With the development of industrial society and the emergence of sociology and anthropology, the city—specifically the European metropole—became the locus of culture, independent of the resources and labor of the countryside and the colony (Cronon 1991; Williams 1973). Whereas theorists such as Durkheim and Lévi-Strauss chronicled the (symbolic) role of animals and nature in rituals, myths, and everyday life, these are mostly absent (except in analogy) in the writings of many nineteenth- and twentieth-century theorists, such as Karl Marx, Ferdinand Tönnies, and Max Weber, who focused on "advanced" capitalist societies and their formal institutions (Jerolmack 2007, 875). Approaching the city as a solely human habitat, urban scholars have often reproduced a colonial and capitalist logic of urbanization that associates cities with progress and conquest over external nature (Wolch 1998, 119). Although recent scholarship has challenged this divide by examining various ecologies of urbanism (Anand 2017; Barua 2021; M. Bennett and Teague 1999;

Brantz and Dümpelmann 2011; Chalfin 2014; Gandy 2013, 2022; Heynen, Kaika, and Swyngedouw 2006; Rademacher and Sivaramakrishnan 2013; Wolch 1998), urban analysis often continues to treat nature as a background to urban life, "a physical place to which one can go" (Haraway 1992, 66).

Ruderal City offers an alternative to this binary approach to urban life. If we see urban environments as spaces built on the discursive, spatial, and material ruins created by racism, colonial exploitation, and dispossession—and if, as Anna Tsing (2014, 87) points out, "ruins are now our gardens"—then the questions become: What does it mean to live in these ruins, and who inhabits them? Whose natures materialize in today's cities and postindustrial landscapes? These questions set the stage for tracking the unruly heterogeneity that exists in the cracks of the urban fabric and its institutions.

It is with this focus on heterogeneous ecologies and unlikely neighbors that *Ruderal City* tackles the larger question of what constitutes cultural critique in a time of rubble. As Ryan Cecil Jobson (2020) and Savannah Shange (2019b) remind us, anthropology's field is quite literally on fire and has never been far from other fields of dispossession and violence such as the plantation. After all, the origins of anthropology were deeply entangled with the colonial encounter (Asad 1997) and early anthropological thinking contributed to the ascendancy of scientific racism (Burton 2015). The nature/culture dualism played a powerful yet ambiguous role in these developments. Throughout the twentieth century, one of the field's goals was to offer its mainly Western audiences a critique of Western culture, and to retrieve a sense of cultural heterogeneity amid the violence and destruction of colonization and global capitalism. For many anthropologists working in the early twentieth century, including Franz Boas and Ruth Benedict, the culture concept offered a challenge to European and North American biological racism and its ruinous effects (M. Anderson 2013, 2019)—especially in the wake of Nazi racism and anti-Semitism. Yet while these theories uprooted the idea that social hierarchies reflect natural, and hence inevitable, essential differences, some of the early twentieth-century liberal antiracist scholarship ultimately reinforced the modernist nature/culture dualism.

As Kamala Visweswaran (1998) argues, by splitting race from culture and assigning it to biology, major currents in anthropological thinking failed to trouble changing discourses of race, which in the postwar era increasingly drew on notions of culture instead of biology. Furthermore, by narrowly defining racism in relation to immigration, early antiracist scholarship sidelined more radical projects of repair—such as those articulated by William Willis (1972) and Diane Lewis (1973), who situated racism in the context of slavery and settler colonial violence. Challenging racial orders in ways that nevertheless minimized the structural features of racism while othering immigrants and people of color further normalized whiteness (M. Anderson 2019, 13). The racial contradictions of American liberalism and its inability to address white supremacy thus found their mirroring within the discipline itself (M. Anderson 2019).[14] The challenge for anthropology in the face of continued racism and accelerating environmental harm is therefore to trouble its "settled" liberal categories and fortify those more radical, feminist, Black, and Indigenous traditions that have opened pathways for tracing the persistent power of race and racism in their relation to other modes of exploitation (Harrison 1995; Hage 2017; Jegathesan 2021). Anthropology needs to account for the fact that it is not separate from the havoc that colonial exploitation of land and people wreaked and continues to wreak across the globe.

Decolonial, antiracist, and feminist critiques have challenged claims to scientific authority within anthropology and the discipline's reifications of culture for a long time (Behar and Gordon 1995; Clifford and Marcus 1986). In the 1980s and 1990s, feminists, activists, and Black, Indigenous, and people of color (BIPOC) scholars made visible the limits of the culture concept for understanding and explaining the social reproduction of power and inequality (Anzaldúa 1999; A. Davis 1981; Gilroy 1987; Hall 1992; Visweswaran 1998). Work published as early as the writings of W. E. B. Du Bois (1903) has shown that racism has biological and visceral effects resulting not only from physical violence but also from the slow violence of environmental injustice, or because of unequal access to health care, mobility, and housing (Burton 2015; Gravlee 2009). As Burton (2015) points out, the "common refrain that race is a social construct" often "fails to sufficiently explain what race is and how it impacts people's lives. In fact, the constructivist approach can obscure the dynamic relationship between race, politics, history, and biology."

This critical work has paved the way for an anthropology that tracks racism as a structural feature of nationhood in the global North and grapples with the intersectionality of social injustices in order to destabilize white supremacy and decolonize the social sciences (Beliso-De Jesús and Pierre 2019; Jobson 2020). Rupturing what Kathryn Yusoff calls "the racial blindness" (2018, xii) of planetary imaginings in the Anthropocene, it is necessary to center the unequal exposures of Black and brown bodies to harm and dehumanization in order to decolonize ecology (Ferdinand 2022) and also to better understand the "intersectional ecologies" (Guarasci, Moore, and Vaughn 2021) of urban life in Europe. As Heather Davis and Zoe Todd (2017) have observed, BIPOC communities have faced catastrophic end times and environmental devastation for centuries. The concept of the Plantationocene (Haraway 2015; Haraway et al. 2016) thus offers a critical alternative to the universalizing notion of the Anthropocene by centering slavery, colonialism, and racism as driving forces in shaping a "plantation logic" and extractive modes of relating to the world. Yet it is important to remember that Black, brown, feminist, and Indigenous scholars have put forward nonbinary approaches to human-nonhuman and environmental relations in the wake of colonialism, slavery, and the plantation for many years (Jegathesan 2021).

By turning to Europe, *Ruderal City* addresses the embodied effects of multiple forms of racism and the ways in which white supremacy and histories of violence and inequality inscribe themselves onto urban landscapes. Not unlike anthropological theory, post–World War II European political discourse delegitimized earlier, colonial, and fascist biological racisms while highlighting cultural difference in their aftermaths. Decades of antiracist scholarship and social movements based in Europe have shown how, with the rise of postcolonial migrations into Europe, seemingly insurmountable and static cultural differences have become the central theme of a new racism (Gilroy 1987; Ha 2014; Hall 1992; Hügel et al. 1993) that also shapes policy-making about who lives and dies at Europe's borders (Mbembe 2020; see also Balibar 1991; Balibar and Wallerstein 1991). While thousands of refugees have died seeking to cross EU borders, public discourse often frames migrants as bringing ruination upon European cities. Addressing these shifting racisms, *Ruderal City* asks how the ruins of European colonialism, racism, and capitalist extraction are challenged and remade in everyday relations to urban landscapes. What seeds does contemporary urban life contain for an ethnographic retelling of histories as iconic as the Berlin Wall or the Anthropocene, and for creating more livable futures? As the world deals with ongoing loss of hospitable environments due to increasing nationalism, racism, and extractive economies, anthropology can, with these inquiries in mind, reinvigorate its earlier question of what cultural critique might look like in a time of destruction.

In the Rubble of Europe

As literary scholar Fatima El-Tayeb (2008) has argued, the common narrative about the history of the European Union is that it constructed civil society in the ruins left behind by World War II. Yet this very project continues to be fraught with Europe's colonial legacies and the ongoing violence and exclusions at Europe's outer and inner borders. While the fall of the Berlin Wall held the promise of a less divided Europe, the decades since have been riddled with historical ruptures that radically altered the political landscape throughout Europe and the world. The collapse of socialism introduced intense cultural, economic, and political changes, opening up new possibilities and challenges to remake Europe's borders and rethink ideas about the homogeneity of Europe and the nation-state.[15] Migration and asylum have been at the center of these reborderings: as Cold War walls have fallen, new wars and nationalist movements have erupted across the world—and new border fences have gone up in the process.

These reborderings have been long in the making. The Schengen Agreement (first implemented in 1985) was aimed at eliminating border controls among its members while strengthening the surveillance of borders with nonmember states. This has had far-reaching consequences for EU immigration and asylum policies, temporary visa regulations, the implementation of cross-border policing, and judicial cooperation (Feldman 2011; Pieper 2008; Tazzioli 2019).[16] In the mid-2000s, when I began fieldwork in Berlin, asylum and migration infrastructures had been scaled down to a historic low in Germany and elsewhere in Europe in the aftermath of the 1990s so-called Asylum Compromise (Asylkompromiss) and the war in former Yugoslavia. Meanwhile border securitization became both increasingly militarized and outsourced to external territories. This dramatically changed in the wake of the so-called refugee crisis of 2015: as the war in Syria escalated, increasing numbers of refugees fled violence, ecological destruction, and poverty in the Middle East and Africa.[17] Making their way to Europe via the Mediterranean Sea and the Balkans, many people have continued to risk their lives on shaky boats or encounter violence at the border since then. Despite the fact that thousands of people die while attempting to cross the Mediterranean,[18] EU governments continue to assert control over migratory movements from the global South, claiming a state of exception and exacerbating refugee displacement and exclusion (Feldman 2011; Hess and Kasparek 2019; PRO ASYL 2020).

As the rise of right-wing nationalist movements, antimigration cam-paigns, and Brexit departures, as well as ecological crises and epidemics, unsettle EU political cohesion, the future of Europe and its political formation—as supranational entity, as region, or as composed of distinct parts—has become increasingly contested. These contestations pose a challenge but also offer possibilities for addressing Europe as more than a "looking glass" (Herzfeld 2010) for anthropology: they can serve as a cau-tionary tale not to assume the continent's or its nation-states' boundaries in advance but instead to provincialize whiteness and unsettle anthropological theory and knowledge production about Europe itself. Cross-disciplinary scholarship and social movements challenging Europe's exclusions can be a guide for once again reflecting on the status of Europe within the discipline (see also Asad et al. 1997). Scholars and activists of color have paved the way for decolonizing and rupturing the very concept of Europe: they have exposed white supremacy not only in right-wing groups but as an integral element of social life across European social institutions (Beliso-De Jesús and Pierre 2019, 47; Piesche 2017; Thompson 2018b) and as a structuring feature of extractive relations to land and nonhuman beings (El-Tayeb 2020; Ferdinand 2022).

Europe and its wealth emerged out of a *longue durée* of colonialism, capitalism, multiple racisms (including anti-Semitism; Islamophobia; anti-Black, anti-Asian, and anti-Latinx racisms), and their histories of plunder and expulsion. And yet, Europe is also shaped by histories of connection. Visual artist and cultural critic Hito Steyerl (2001) has invoked some of these perspectives of Europe in her work: they include stories about departures for a better life; the dreams of cleaning ladies, doctors, seamstresses, teach-ers, babysitters, mothers, and daughters; asylum seekers doing badly paid "labors of love"; intellectual traditions created in exile; and the travels of plants and their entanglements in histories of dispossession. Europe here is less an abstract idea than a dream: of equality, democracy, freedom, and prosperity. This dream can turn into a nightmare at any point and once again unleash violence, war, and exclusion. Keeping this juxtaposition in focus highlights the necessity of rupturing the very concept of Europe and the colonial order upon which Europe's wealth continues to be built—and instead foregrounding the heterogeneous lives of "European Others" (El-Tayeb 2011) who have inhabited and built Europe all along. The story of Osman Kalın's tree house captures this heterogeneity—a Europe in which the stories of people of color who become "migrants" or "refugees" (Thompson 2018) are at the center, laying bare its rifts. This sense of heterogeneity created in the *longue durée* of migrations, racism, and colonialism, as well as in Europe's collapsed and yet rigid boundaries, guides my analysis throughout *Ruderal City*.

While there has been considerable debate in anthropology and the social sciences over how to make sense of the politics of migration and race in Europe (Cabot 2014; De Genova 2017; Fassin 2011; Fernando and Giordano 2016; Giordano 2014; Kleinman 2019; Özyürek 2014; Silverstein 2005), it was not until the summer of migration in 2015 that there was a surge in analyses on the topic (Cabot 2019).[19] As a result, scholarship on mobility and migration today must reflect on economies of attention and be wary of erasing the long history of BIPOC and migrant activism and scholarship that has already troubled whiteness, racism, and ongoing colonial legacies within Europe for decades (e.g., Beliso-De Jesús and Pierre 2019; El-Tayeb 2011; Gilroy 1987; Gutiérrez Rodríguez 2018; Hall 1992; see also Stoetzer 2004).[20] It is thus crucial to look at the ways in which the very categories of migration, as well as the refugee and migrant, not only become subjects of scientific knowledge production but become racialized categories themselves, tied to state bureaucracies, to unequal distribution of wealth, dispossession of land, and disciplinary power (Brown 2005; De Genova 2017; Fernando and Giordano 2016; Gilroy 1987; Kleinman 2019; Malkki 1992, 498; Özyürek 2014; Silverstein 2005).[21]

In the aftermath of the Holocaust and decolonization, post–World War II European political discourse saw a shift that delegitimized earlier forms of fascist biological racism while highlighting "cultural difference." With increasing migrations into Europe from the Middle East and Africa, seemingly insurmountable and static cultural differences, as well as the entire field of migration, thus became the central theme of a new racism (Balibar 1991). Critical race scholarship and activisms have laid bare the historical breaks and continuities of these new racisms with anti-Semitism, anti-Black racism, and Islamophobia (El-Tayeb 2011; FeMigra 1994; Gelbin, Konuk, and Piesche 1999; Gutiérrez Rodríguez 1999; Hügel et al. 1993; Opitz et al. 1992; Otyakmaz 1995; Steyerl 2001). Others have developed critical analyses of the intersectionality of injustices (El-Tayeb 2011; Partridge 2012) or have ethnographically tracked the specters of nationalism and racism in Europe's urban fabric (Ha 2014; Linke 1999a, 1999b, 1999c). Racism here emerges as an integral feature of the structure of European life that is not limited to the past or to right-wing political movements.

Global protests against police violence and racism have more recently registered on the radar of European liberal publics. Yet political discourse often continues to situate migrants and communities of color as external to Europe (El-Tayeb 2008; Gutiérrez Rodríguez 2018). Challenging this narrative and a widespread downplaying of colonialism's destructive legacies across European publics, Black scholars and scholars of color have stressed the "coloniality of migration" (Gutiérrez Rodríguez 2018) to show that Europe's migration and asylum regimes perpetuate colonial and racialized hierarchies as they regulate movement across the continent's boundaries and determine who is seen as deserving access to Europe (El-Enany 2020).

Germany, as one of the most economically powerful European countries, is a desired destination for many refugees and migrants and has been at the center of much debate on migration in Europe (Mandel 2008; Partridge 2012; Shoshan 2016; Stoetzer 2018). Tensions around asylum in Germany's cities and their peripheries have grown since the summer of 2015, when increasing numbers of people fleeing war and violence in Syria and the Middle East embarked on the risky journey along the Eastern Mediterranean and Balkan route to Europe and Germany. As Noah Ha (2014) and others have shown (Zwischenraum Kollektiv 2017), racism, a key element of colonial power relations, continues to inform urban responses to migration: racialized practices of policing, planning, and memorialization shape the fabric of urban space in Germany.[22] As migrant labor is often delegated to informal sectors, and as European political discourse stresses disconnection and division in cities as a consequence of migration, the question of how to confront the spatial dynamics of racialized exclusion has become more urgent than ever.[23] Decolonizing migration and the European city thus includes confronting the ways in which exclusions of racism and the nation-state become tangible not only at Europe's outer borders but also within its urban centers. And most importantly, it involves centering the perspectives and struggles for self-determination of communities of color (Zwischenraum Kollektiv 2017).

Yet to address the complexities of multiple borders—old and new—and the ways in which people inhabit and actively remake Europe's cities and their margins, it is important to push beyond a focus on urban space and migration. Developing a ruderal lens in this book, I instead think across different communities and thematic registers of urban life and its ecology to explore how the governance of nature in the city and its peripheries becomes a key site in which racialized inequalities, borders, and the nation materialize.

In this spirit, *Ruderal City* begins from the insight that the pervasive rhetoric decrying a clash of cultures in contemporary Europe and the mononaturalism persistent in thinking about urban and rural environments are poor tools to think with. Rather than asking how to maintain order amid disorder, or stressing the disconnection between urban inhabitants and their environments, it is time to change metaphors. In a world of ecological destruction and a political context in which migration and cultural hybridity are perceived as problems, it is important to turn attention to how the ruins of colonialism, nationalism, and capitalism are inhabited in contemporary cities: Who is said to belong where? Who is racialized—and thus cast as less-than-human—with reference to nature or its ruination and thus rendered "out of place" in the city? By focusing on the ways in which urban socialities build alliances across species for more livable cities, the following chapters seek to capture the complexity of heterogeneous borders and the histories of rupture that constitute not only Berlin or Germany but also Europe and the world today.[24]

Berlin, Ruderal City

There is perhaps no better place from which to think about urban life in the rubble of European capitalism and nationalism than Berlin. Throughout Berlin's history, the city's ecology and physical environment have played a central role in the formation and reconstruction of German nationhood, empire, and the political transformation of Europe. The traces of Germany's imperial history, World War II, and Cold War divisions are still visible throughout the city's streets, buildings, and green spaces today. Berlin has been constructed as a city at the center of world history: it is saturated with narratives about the West and twentieth-century European history (Boyer 2001, 424).

Hence, for scholars in the humanities and social sciences, Berlin has been a city under constant revision. It has occupied an important location in studies of national identity, fascism, postsocialism, and the formation of European (post)modernity. This is reflected in the attention paid to the city's changing architecture, urban space, and intellectual culture.[25] The metaphor of Berlin's "shifting sands" (Boyer 2001) not only points to the fact that Berlin and its surrounding state of Brandenburg are built on sandy soils but also signals processes of becoming, historical erasures, and ruination that have been at the center of the city's physical and symbolic transformations. Yet while scholarship on Berlin has highlighted competing historical layers and overlapping cultural identifications, remarkably little has been said about Berlin's *shifting sands* themselves. Little do we learn about how people have inhabited the city's lands, or how other beings have been implicated in that.

A few scholars in geography, environmental and landscape history, architecture, and the history of science have tackled this gap (Brantz 2022; Rubin 2016). For example, Jens Lachmund (2003, 2013) examines the history of urban ecology in postwar Berlin, and Matthew Gandy highlights the aesthetic, cosmopolitical, and ecological dimensions of Berlin's urban nature and *Brachen* (fallow lands, wastelands) (Gandy 2013, 2022; Gandy and Jasper 2017).[26] In her book *Seeing Trees*, Sonja Dümpelmann (2019) shows us how street trees inspire politics, become aesthetic objects, reshape climates, mark urban space, and become instruments for remaking citizenship in Berlin and New York. Building on this scholarship, *Ruderal City* brings together diverging concerns with the built environment, memory, ecology, racialization, and nationhood. Rather than simply expand urban analysis to include nature and the nonhuman, I ethnographically trace how the intimate relations between people, landscapes, animals, and plants not only become sites of exclusion and racialization but also create new forms of solidarity, endurance, and healing in Berlin (see also Bauer and Bhan 2016; Hinchliffe and Whatmore 2006; Lee 2016).

Curiously, as I will discuss in chapter 1, Berlin became a field site for ecological research in the postwar period, generating new knowledge about "nature in the city." Botanical encounters in Berlin's bombed rubble landscapes traced the ways in which the city's very ecology was deeply entangled with the history of capitalism and empire. But even more than that, Berlin's very name tells us a story of nature in the making: signifying "a swampy place" or a "bend in the river," the city's making involved the straightening of rivers, the draining of swamps, and the domestication of many beings.[27] As Berlin expanded in the nineteenth and twentieth centuries, "nature spaces" such as parks and city forests provided important resources for "balancing" increasing class divisions, fostering social integration, and enabling other projects of social reform (Dümpelmann 2019; Hennecke 2011).

During fascism in the mid-twentieth century, urban life was seen as being in contradiction with nature: whereas the Nazis idealized the countryside as pure space of the German nation, they imagined the city as a site of ugliness, full of "social ills" and dangerous racial mixing. The Nazi regime, attempting to write its power into stone and carve a "living space" for the racial elite in a newly ordered Europe, sought to transform Berlin's built environment and rid the city of "foreign elements." The regime's industrial projects and closely related systems of death and work camps, some of them located just outside of Berlin, enabled this transformation (Till 2005). At the end of World War II, the city's experience of urban breakdown created an awareness of both the fragility of urban infrastructures and the city's ecologies. During Berlin's division, the city's infrastructure, its road and train systems, as well as its electricity network and water lines, were severed—though only partially.[28] At that time, Berlin's forests and parks offered a space of leisure for local residents who found themselves navigating dead-end streets, surrounded by the walls of the Cold War. As a forester in one of West Berlin's largest urban forests, the Grunewald, once told me: "The Berlin Wall would not have lasted if it hadn't been for the city's forests." This odd material-social history entered yet another chapter when, after the fall of the Berlin Wall and subsequent unification of East and West Berlin, the city's infrastructures were frantically restitched together.

Today, new regimes of urban and environmental policy-making have once again transformed Berlin's physical environment, reconstituting it as a national capital, a global city, and a new European cultural center. Urban nature and green space have played a key infrastructural role in these efforts to renaturalize the nation. For example, the city's post-1989 landscape program created a greenbelt as part of a plan for the unified Berlin (SenStadt 2014, 22). The remaking of the city's ecologies has thus aided in unifying the city and nation and helped it appear as part of a "natural order."[29] In addition, the city's nineteenth-century legacies of environmental conservation, experiences of urban breakdown in 1945, and the subsequent political division and deindustrialization during the Cold War, as well as Berlin's financial crisis since 1989, have generated an abundance of open spaces in the city and its surroundings.[30]

In 2022, even as many spaces are being paved over and lost to urban development, almost 40 percent of Berlin's urban space still encompasses forests, allotment gardens, parks, or urban "wastelands" (*Brachflächen*).[31] As part of a wider global trend of creating environmental agendas for cities and integrating a consideration of urban ecologies and biodiversity into urban planning, Berlin has thus widely been marketed as a flourishing Green City (SenStadt 2014, 3). Reports show an increasing number of plant and animal species in the urban area, at times outnumbering species diversity in the surrounding countryside. As a result of warmer winters, urban sprawl, increasing traffic, deforestation, and monoculture farmland, many animals escape the countryside and find new habitats in the city (Riechelmann 2004). For example, with an estimated population between four and six thousand, wild boar use the city's corridors at night and together with other critters have also crossed my fieldwork paths many times.

Intrigued by this diversity, a variety of publics tending to urban nature have proliferated: during Berlin's annual Urban Nature Day thousands of residents tour the city to discover nature's magic—they search for weeds on sidewalks, follow the tracks of wild boar in forests, listen to the songs of nightingales in parks, or tour the vegetation of urban wastelands. Similarly, TV shows, news reports, and documentary films with titles like *Wildes Berlin* frequently portray both the city and its peripheries' abundant wildlife, including foxes, praying mantes, and raccoons as well as plants like trees-of-heaven and black locust. Exoticizing metaphors abound in these reports, as they celebrate the "urban jungle" or engage a multiculturalist logic of welcoming new neighbors into the city.

Yet while nature returns in these celebrations of Berlin as a Green City, public policy and media concerns about immigrant segregation and unemployment also reframe urban spaces as harboring troubled neighborhoods or parallel worlds within the city's body. Cultural imaginaries about urban nature and green space thus not only divide urban space into abstract categories of nature versus culture or technology—categories that elide more complex historical divisions and ecological relations in the city—but also emerge as terrains upon which urban conflicts around racism and migration play out. Yet in the process, relations to urban land get remade and the ecology of the city is imagined otherwise.

Rethinking Migration and Urban Nature

Berlin's physical, economic, and social fabric is shaped by a layered history of empire, displacement, and exile. The city's contested history of migration spans across centuries, continents, and ethnic communities. In the seventeenth century, French Protestant Huguenots, impoverished traders called *refugies*, settled in what was then the Prussian Empire. In the eighteenth century, Jewish communities became naturalized citizens and yet were confronted with continuous discrimination (Lanz 2005), and together with Roma and Sinti people faced persecution and genocide during Nazism and throughout the twentieth century. During the height of colonization and before World War I, Berlin residents included people from Germany's colonies such as Togo, Namibia, Tanzania, Rwanda, Samoa, and Papua New Guinea (El-Tayeb 2001; van der Heyden and Zeller 2002).[32] In the post–World War II period, migrant workers from countries such as Turkey, Spain, and Greece in West Berlin, and from Vietnam, Mozambique, Cuba, and Angola in the East, reshaped the cultural and social life of the divided city.

In the aftermath of Germany's unification, nationalist movements gained traction and antimigration sentiments intensified. After an initial postunification euphoria and construction boom in the 1990s, Berlin plunged into a fiscal crisis, which coincided with deindustrialization and wide-ranging changes in labor market policies and welfare reform implemented a few years later. Unemployment rates and poverty rose among many Berliners, and the city's Turkish and Middle Eastern communities, comprising close to 10 percent of the population, were especially affected because many were employed in the manufacturing sector (Lanz 2007; Mandel 2008; Partridge 2012).[33] Yet, as in many other cities across Europe, public discourse and policy has often located the source of these inequalities in migrants themselves—especially in their presumed lack of economic productivity seen as leaving traces of dereliction across the urban landscape.[34] Middle Eastern and African migrants and asylum seekers in particular have been held responsible for local crime and for failing to integrate into German society—despite growing evidence that they become targets of racial profiling and policing (El-Tayeb and Thompson 2019; Thompson 2018b). In this context, the question of how Middle Eastern and African communities inhabit nature in Berlin has become a key site in marking people's status as strangers and as racialized others, irrespective of citizenship. While people are often stigmatized on the basis of their residence in certain neighborhoods, public discourse poses their supposed lack of belonging to the urban environment as a source of danger: the danger of fire breaking loose, of wildness imposing itself on the civilized city.

These debates echo ideas about what it means to be German: the notion of *Heimat* (home or homeland) conveys the idea that Germanness is rooted in the land and that racialized bodies are foreign and threaten the natural world.[35] In recent years, local and national media have painted a gloomy picture of the capital's migrant problem. They depict scenes of unruly gangsters wreaking havoc on the tranquility of green space, or of unemployed, wild barbecuers—pursuing a pastime popular among many of the city's Middle Eastern residents—filling Berlin's green lungs with smoke and littering its parks with garbage. Both the bodies of migrants and the environments they inhabit, as well as the smoke, meat, and litter they produce, figure as polluting "matter out of place" (Douglas 2002). Meanwhile, migrants are rendered almost animal-like, in need of containment (Stoetzer 2014c).[36]

Tropes of undomesticated wilderness also inform public policies—for example, in the form of EU-based integration projects aiming to undo racial segregation, poverty, and urban decay. Attempts to integrate migrants into German society through language classes, education, and neighborhood beautification projects follow the colonial logic of civilizing populations—cast as spatially and racially other—by forcing people to conform to national political, social, and economic norms (Silverstein 2006, 289; Stoler 1995). These policies and Germany's "integration industry" (Nghi Ha 2010) are directed not toward all migrants but toward migrants of color from the Middle East and the global South.[37] As Paul Silverstein (2006) points out for France, plans to reintegrate Europe's hot spots, such as the *banlieues* in Paris, recall the Marshall Plan for rebuilding war-struck Europe, drawing parallels between the ruins of war and Europe's racialized urban peripheries today.

By 2015, the numbers of people attempting to enter Europe while fleeing political conflict in the Middle East and North Africa soared to historic highs.[38] With Germany among the core destinations, Berlin's local bureaucracies scrambled to accommodate asylum seekers.[39] Initially, public sentiment seemed welcoming toward migrants and refugees, especially those from Syria. Yet a closer look at media coverage reveals that naturalistic metaphors abounded—of waves, rivers, tides, and tsunamis of people straining Europe's and the nation's resources, not unlike natural disasters.[40] These scenes of chaos, waves, and so-called hot spots (*Brennpunkte*) at and within Europe's borders infused political decisions to distribute and manage asylum seekers' arrivals. As a series of violent incidents occurred after 2015, such as the events during New Year's Eve in Cologne, narratives of especially male migrants and refugees as dehumanized crowds running amok and bringing ruin upon Germany's cities echoed across public discourse.[41] Subsequent reforms of asylum law, enabling faster deportations of those considered undeserving, have aimed at domesticating this seemingly natural force at Europe's gate.

Amid these intense debates about nature and migration, the city's green spaces—especially its gardens—once again provide spaces of hope for escaping social divisions. Since the mid-2000s, so-called inter- or multicultural gardens have proliferated across Berlin and other German cities. By cultivating plants, urban residents hope to overcome cultural barriers and create communities of care for urban lands. Meanwhile, planners and politicians advocate for gardening as an opportunity to "integrate" immigrants into society: by engaging with plants, people can identify with their surroundings and let "integration grow" (Der Beauftragte des Senats für Integration und Migration 2007). The hope is that these engagements with nature can create and sustain community, building the grounds for a "true" multicultural society to sprout in the city's gardens (C. Müller 2000). Whereas after the war, rubble plants formed an ambivalent urban ecology amid nation-making projects, in the gardens of today's Berlin plant cultivation involves dreams of unifying the nation.

While these efforts attempt to produce new socialities across difference, migration regimes and racism manifest differently at Berlin's peripheries. Since the mid-2000s, many asylum seekers fleeing persecution, political conflict, war, and economic precarity in countries such as Kenya, Cameroon, Iraq, Iran, Pakistan, and Turkey have found themselves living in isolated shelters in the forests near Berlin. This is a consequence of postunification asylum and migration policies that first erected new shelters in cities and then, as a response to xenophobic attacks on these shelters in the 1990s, relocated many refugees to rural East Germany or to the peripheries of cities. In the case of Berlin, these relocations were often to the grounds of former military barracks situated in the surrounding countryside in Brandenburg's forests. Struck by high unemployment rates and depopulation in the years following unification, this region has also been increasingly marketed as an ideal place of recreation for city residents and tourists.[42]

Refugee activists and advocates have mobilized for years against the invisibility, immobility, and isolation of migrants in the forests of Brandenburg. But it was not until the late 2000s that the countryside moved to the forefront of public attention. In response to several violent attacks on migrants, refugees, and citizens of color, the struggle against racial violence and the increasing presence of right-wing youth in rural regions in the former East (see Shoshan 2016) intensified. These developments illustrate that racism and exclusion are more than just urban problems. Whereas many nature spaces in the city are sites of hope for overcoming social divisions, Berlin's forests and urban peripheries have transformed into landscapes of exclusion in which refugees inhabit the ruins of socialism.

In the context of these uneven developments, we can see how the struggle for inhabiting the European metropole continues to be shaped by a colonial dynamic that divides populations into those deserving to have access to the city and to the possibilities of a flourishing life and those who do not. As decolonial scholars have shown, urbanization processes in European cities continue to depend on stigmatizing, criminalizing, and dehumanizing racialized subjects—while at the same time exploiting their labor (Zwischenraum Kollektiv 2017).

Thus, as we expand our analytic lens of urban life to consider urban ecologies, there is a pressing need to remain alert to the "sticky" and persistent colonial and ethnoracial politics at work in European cities. Indeed, images of ruins, unruly nature, and urban plight in the global North, as well as a widespread sense of embattlement and porosity of national borders in the context of Europe's "migration crisis," express fantasies of colonial reversal—at a time when various projects of governability of our global order, such as the nation's efforts to shore up borders and domesticate its others, as well as capitalism's extraction of natural resources, are coming undone (Hage 2016). Similarly, attending to a city's ecology, we need to ask how unruly forms of (bio)diversity can so easily be co-opted by neoliberal projects of profit making that celebrate resilience and cultural hybridity (Helmreich 2016; Moore, Kosek, and Pandian 2003) in the city. After all, in cities across the global North, including Berlin, an aesthetics of urban wastelands too often paves the way for gentrification and displacement, especially of migrants and communities of color.

Addressing what it might mean to decolonize the city and its ecologies, it thus becomes salient to examine the ways in which colonial and destructive modes of inhabiting the earth continue to shape contemporary urban environments. In this vein, *Ruderal City* explores how Europe's borders, including those of the nation and its racialized others, are reconfigured in conflicts over people's relations to the urban landscape. Rather than answer in advance *how* race matters, this book emphasizes the enduring power of racism *and* its historical specificity (Gilroy 2004). This means departing from a continuing and widespread insistence across Europe and Germany to narrowly define racism in relation to the biological racism that was operative during fascism, or is at work "elsewhere" (see also Yildiz 2020).[43] Rather, racism emerges as an "axis of power" and a "kind of body politic" (Brown 2005, 72) that, together with nation-making projects (Gilroy 1987), not only provides "a critical medium through which ideas of nature operate" but also "reworks the grounds of nature" itself (Moore, Kosek, and Pandian 2003, 3). Racial practices mark bodies, geographical territories, and environmental milieus with the force of their distinctions (Hartigan 2017; Moore, Kosek, and Pandian 2003). Terms such as *geographies of race* (Brown 2005), *intersectional ecologies* (Guarasci, Moore, and Vaughn 2021), *racial ecologies* (Nishime and Williams 2018), and *racialized ecologies* point to the ways in which experiences of racism, dehumanization, and inequality become embedded in people's relationships to other beings and to land. Moreover, as Deborah Thomas (2019) reminds us, racism structures labor regimes and modern capitalist production, creates hierarchies of value attached to different bodies, and thus continues to "provide the parameters of what it means to be human today" (41).[44] Rather than simply expand urban analysis to include nonhumans, *Ruderal City* thus traces ecologies of migration and race to show how urban nature becomes the very terrain onto which racializations and nation-making are mapped out in contemporary Europe—but also how these are challenged.

Gleaning Methods for a Ruderal Analytic

The stories of the Berlin tree house and other makeshift sites convey practices of endurance and care in the city. Centering the lives that persist in the ruptures of capitalist urbanization and racial inequality, they comprise the heart of this book. Together, these stories offer a view into everyday forms of ruination and harm that, like rubble, are often labeled as insignificant.[45] A ruderal analytic thus directs focus to the *connective tissue* that binds people's lives to particular, often degraded, environments and to a lack of access to urban infrastructure and social mobility. Ruination, from this perspective, is an active process that uproots and displaces lives and shapes "what people are left with" (Stoler 2013, 9), while some people are stigmatized on the basis of that very residue. Yet while ruderal stories begin with ruins and decay, they do not end with it. As feminist and BIPOC writers have pointed out (Haraway 2016; Tsing 2015; Tuck 2009), it is important to go beyond damage and to situate one's analysis in the desire to forge new alliances. Indeed, cities are abundant with emerging practices of "ecological care" (Puig de la Bellacasa 2017) and forms of living and dying and conspiring together (Choy 2011; Haraway 2016; Myers 2019; Parreñas 2018; Tsing 2015). By tracing the "nature work" (Jerolmack 2007) of various actors, including refugees, barbecuers, tourist guides, foresters, nature enthusiasts, scientists, media, policy makers, as well as rubble plants, rabbits, mushrooms, and trees in Berlin, I show how more-than-human relations can serve as sites of endurance, care, and alliances against harm (Elder, Wolch, and Emel 1998).

Taking ruins not as an end point of analysis but as a point of departure, *Ruderal City* calls attention to heterogeneous and unexpected lives amid inhospitable and often violent worlds. A ruderal perspective illustrates the gaps in modes of governance that seek to secure Europe's borders, exploit land and labor, and manage populations. By thinking with Berlin's ruderal ecologies, we can generate stories that are different from those narratives about cities in which mixing and cultural hybridity are either overlooked or seen as a problem. If we understand ruination (Stoler 2013) and rubble (Gordillo 2014) not as separate from but as central to the urban landscapes we inhabit, built on social exclusions, capitalist urbanization, and profound environmental change, then, I suggest, the ruderal can serve as a guide to explore lives in the midst of these landscapes. Inspired by approaches in feminist, decolonial, and critical race studies, the following chapters thus eschew what Kim Fortun (2014, 314) has called the "Latour effect" in anthropology and science studies—namely, a singular focus on practices of expertise and actor networks that does not take a closer look at *the material and social constitution* of the toxic environments that make up people's lives. This involves ethnographically exploring ways of knowing and inhabiting the city that depart from and, in fact, break down extractive and colonial modes of relating to more-than-human worlds (e.g., H. Davis and Todd 2017; Haraway 2016; Parreñas 2018; TallBear 2011).

Although ruderal worlds emerge in the cracks of cultivated landscapes and modern schemes of order, they are not free from power. Deeply fraught, they tell a story about the lives that persist in the face of racialized exclusions, violence, and environmental destruction. In dialogue with Haraway's (2016) notion of "staying with the trouble," a ruderal perspective highlights the ways in which cultural identifications and strategies of survival are never authentic or pure but instead are situated within histories of disturbance. The chapters follow the "roots and routes" (Clifford 1997)—and uprootings— of Berlin's urban ecologies. In a nation where racialized others are treated with suspicion and never fully belong, some actors are unwilling to wait for their assigned place and instead stage spontaneous takeovers to create spaces of hospitality for humans and nonhumans alike.

By gleaning stories from these spaces, I look for evidence of how people, plants, and other organisms coevolve and conspire in partial connection. Landscapes are always more than the "material evidence" of the past or present—and they are more ambivalent than people might want them to be. Taking ruderal ecologies seriously therefore means more than reinterpreting multispecies landscapes or digging for deeper meanings in the sedimented historical layers of a city's soils. Rather, it means "resituat[ing] and recombin[ing]" (Till 2005, 95) disparate stories in an attempt to do justice to the complexities of more-than-human relations in the city—and to imagine new possibilities for the future.

For this reason, *Ruderal City* is not immersed in the study of one particular community or bounded object. While multisited ethnography (Marcus 1995) follows a social group or practice across different sites, my analysis in contrast is both situated in several communities and locations in Berlin and works across and alongside sites. I seek out connections between sites and track how relations between people and other beings, both animate and inanimate, not only intersect with forms of racialization but also exceed them. Throughout, I am committed to piling up stories that might at first glance seem disparate—from makeshift urban gardens, to traces of sunflower seeds on a sidewalk, to the smoke that emanates from barbecuing in public parks.

In an era of pervasive loss of hospitable environments, it becomes paramount to develop methods that allow us to look across scales, shift analytic frameworks, and tell a "rush of stories" (Tsing 2015). Again, feminist and critical race thinkers have paved the way here methodologically (Ebron and Tsing 2017), sketching out narrative practices that, rather than adhering to a logic of mastery and generalization, gather seeds (Le Guin 1989) of chance encounters that contain future possibilities.[46] Anthropology's field is never outside or in any way separate from other fields of settler colonial dispossession and extraction (Shange 2019a, 2019b; Jobson 2020). Cultivating narrative practices of gleaning stories therefore also responds to instances of refusal (Shange 2019a; Simpson 2007; Tuck and Yang 2014a, 2014b; L. T. Smith 1999) by interlocutors in the field against ethnographic desires to document the "real lives" of migrants and refugees, to focus on suffering, and to benefit from the interiority of people's lives. Honoring refusal includes creating more fragmentary, patchy ethnographic accounts that acknowledge partial, situated knowledges and follow the lead of interlocutors rather than privileging narrative thickness or a holistic picture (Liu and Shange 2018; Shange 2019a).[47]

Instead of easily adding up, the stories in this book thus interrupt each other, "not to resolve differences nor to merely celebrate diversity, but to provoke encounters across differences" that produce new partial alliances, thick solidarities (Liu and Shange 2018), and collaborative strategies for survival (Fortun 2012, 455).[48] As Austrian artist Lois Weinberger has shown, ruderals call for modes of "precise inattention" (Kos 2004): if you are lucky, you catch a glance of them out of the corner of your eye. Indeed, walking along the city's streets is precisely how you come across ruderal plants such as a tree-of-heaven. In this book, I show that such peripheral perspectives and the multiple stories they generate are also necessary for acknowledging moments of rupture and refusal in the rubble of Europe today.

Ethnography, in this vein, becomes a practice of gleaning narratives and creating connections between disparate worlds that forge spaces for unlikely neighbors, often framed as intruders. These neighbors, introduced in the following chapters, include more-than-human actors and practices that are both real and imaginary: from plants growing in the cracks of sidewalks, to informal food economies, to encounters with uncanny creatures in the forest. In tracing these stories, I do not retain a hygienic distance from which to critique the failures of nationalism and racism in environmental narratives. Instead, I show how stories about the nonhuman and dehumanization in the city and at its peripheries bear weight on who and what lives get to flourish. This mode of storytelling is thus not only a "method" but also a strategy for forging alliances across different orders and "irreducible difference[s]" (Haraway 2003, 49). In other words, it is a way of reading stories against their grain, instead of discarding them as (ideologically) inappropriate.

In it all, my own positionalities—as a fieldworker returning "home" not *from* the field but *to* the field, as a German citizen, as a queer white woman, as a researcher from the United States, and as the grandchild of expellees from rural Serbia who were able to claim German nationality after World War II—are not fixed but come to matter differently in various encounters and in my writing about them. Throughout the book, I locate these positionings and reflect on the blind spots and limits as well as the connections, privileges, and mobilities they create.

Following such a method of juxtaposing and generating multiple stories, including my own, *Ruderal City* accounts for the fact that cities are full of wonders and horrors. Urban life is abundant with stories that are much more interesting and strange than the predictable outcomes of formal economies, infrastructures, and institutions that protect private property and segregated communities. Attention to specific instances in which lively beings ally and connect across the collapsed and yet rigid structures of European colonial and racial power (see also Simone 2016)—with open-ended outcomes— might reanimate not only urban analysis but also cultural analysis itself (Weston 2017).

Mapping the Terrain

Juxtaposing different ethnographic stories, the chapters that follow address a set of connected questions: What are the ecologies of belonging that bind people to particular environments and displace them from others? How do specific landscape practices not only create new forms of exclusion and harm but also forge new alliances and vital reciprocities? To what extent do these practices reimagine or reconstruct the nation? To put these questions more broadly: Who gets to define what counts as nature or the environment (*Umwelt*) in the city of Berlin and its peripheries? And who can inhabit and make these environments their home?

Chapter 1, "Botanical Encounters," sets up the historical and analytical framework for the chapters to come. It focuses on an instance in Berlin's history when the urban fabric was literally torn apart: the destroyed city after fascism. It was in that moment that the city emerged as a more-than-human habitat, abundant with unexpected neighbors. In the years after the war, many ruderal plants flourished in the city's rubble for the first time, prompting West Berlin botanists to study plant migration in the city. Tracing this history, chapter 1 illustrates how these botanical encounters inspired a way of approaching nature in the city that both spoke to and departed from postwar cultural imaginaries of nature and the nation. The city's rupture, I argue, gave rise to a view in which nature or the environment was not "out there," but instead an unwieldy and integral part of the city—a ruderal city in which many beings have coexisted (however violently) all along.

Moving from the ruins of war to the gardens of today's Berlin, chapter 2 examines how people's care for plants becomes sites of both exclusion and hope in a city anxious about the presence of racialized migrant bodies. I situate a variety of urban gardening practices, including institutionalized multicultural gardening, as well as less visible everyday practices of cultivating plants, within broader projects of nation-making. I argue that while gardeners often aspire to wall out history and solve social conflicts through the care for plants, past and present racialized and class conflicts keep creeping back in. Indeed, gardens do not always turn out the way people have intended (Myers 2019). Hence, there is no single story to be told about gardens: nature serves as a tool both to shape a concept of culture, neatly fenced in, consolidating the nation, and to create openings for other possibilities (see also Satsuka 2015).

The next two chapters consider how debates about multiculturalism materialize in conflicts over urban parks and how Berlin residents inhabit them. Several parks have been at the center of public controversy over illicit food consumption and production. Chapter 3, "Provisioning against Austerity," zooms in on the worlds of one of these parks—the Preussen Park (Prussian Park) in former West Berlin, often referred to as the "Thai Park." In this park, Southeast Asian immigrants create an informal economy by preparing, selling, and exchanging foods. Following the park's intimate economies, I show how the Thai Park picnickers inhabit urban green space while utilizing it as a resource to sustain livelihoods and tackle cultures of austerity through the provisioning and exchange of food.

Whereas people in the Thai Park rework uneven global forces by creating an informal economy and the performance of gender, race, and kinship, this is not the case at our next location. Chronicling different productions of the "Barbecue Area" in Berlin's largest green space, the Tiergarten, chapter 4 turns to another kind of food production, the grilling of meat as urban leisure. The chapter traces how barbecuing has become a charismatic practice that triggers ongoing anxieties and pleasures around multiculturalism in Berlin and beyond. Via the specter of fire, smoke, garbage, and pollution, municipal authorities, media, and local residents portray barbecuing as a savage practice—a practice that threatens the civilized order of the European city and its proper human and nonhuman inhabitants. Barbecuing here is framed as a Turkish cultural tradition, while the barbecue area is marked as an other space in which migrant bodies are racialized and cast as out of place on the basis of their ostensibly inappropriate relation to the urban environment. At the same time, for Turkish migrants and Turkish Germans, barbecuing can create connections to land in the city that enable people to breathe, thus offering a refuge from work and the toxicity of everyday exclusions. By challenging European notions of domesticated nature, the Tiergarten picnickers forge a ruderal practice that caters neither to ideas about Turkish culture nor to German moralities of how to inhabit the city. Instead, they open a breathing space in which questions of who belongs to the city and who gets to be what kind of natural citizen can be renegotiated.

The two remaining chapters take us out of the city and into the forest at Berlin's edges to explore how racialized geographies and ecologies manifest differently in the formerly socialist countryside. Here, outside the city, we see the flip side of the previous chapters: at the urban periphery, many migrants are locked out and relegated to forest spaces, where they live in the ruins of the Cold War. A postunification nature park, the Märkische Schweiz, is located in the March Oder region in the state of Brandenburg and just a few kilometers east of Berlin. The March Oder region suffered high unemployment and depopulation in the aftermath of German unification. Reconfigured as an ecotourist destination since the early 2000s, the region and the park have more recently become home to refugees from Africa, the Middle East, and Asia, who find themselves living in isolated, partially government-run and partially privately run shelters in the forest. Tracking refugees' experiences and stories about the "bush" in the park, chapter 5 describes a sense of the *unheimlich* (uncanny)—an affect of displacement and cognitive dissonance, a feeling of simultaneous strangeness and familiarity—that comes into being in the sensory stirrings of everyday racism, from being in limbo in the forest at the edge of a European metropole, and in a social-material landscape in which the value of objects, personal histories, and imagined futures has shifted abruptly.[49] The unheimlich, I argue, offers a window onto contemporary ecologies of nation-making and racialization, as well as the lively worlds that fall by the wayside of the ruins that these create.

Chapter 6, "Stories of the 'Wild East,'" explores these ecologies from a slightly different angle. Here, I look at how attempts to make nature matter in times of economic collapse and social-environmental change articulate not only with practices of exclusion and racialization but also with efforts to challenge these practices. I track narrative and embodied practices of making "wild country" (Rose 2004) that operate across different registers: as an economic strategy, as a reenactment of space, as efforts to create national unity, and as a racialized process of becoming alien or less-than-human. These practices emerge in the cracks of frail economies, scaled-down asylum infrastructures, and the ruins of socialist ecologies. As wildlife—including formerly extinct species—reenters the region and efforts at ecological restoration proliferate, local Germans reenact the East as a space of wilderness and colonial adventure. Meanwhile, refugees living in these zones and encountering various forms of racism narrate their lives as having spun out of control. Attending to these stories and reenactments sheds light on shifting ecologies of nationhood and race in a postcolonial and neoliberal world. Following them, we see how whiteness and the nation get remade through wilderness and nature, and how the lives of communities of color are dehumanized and situated outside the nation's body.

The disparate sites and communities that appear throughout *Ruderal City* provide snapshots of social exclusions that work through people's relations to plants, animals, and places in the city and its peripheries. But they also shed light on creativity not only in the cracks of the city's built structures but also in the gaps of the very categories through which to make sense of urban life. Attending to the ways in which people and other beings transgress bounded naturecultures, the chapters not only offer a fresh way of thinking about life in today's cities but also hope to contribute to cultural critique in the rubble of twenty-first-century Europe. This critique searches for the heterogeneity and persistence of life amid nationalism's and capitalism's destruction—and thus joins broader conversations about how anthropology can be accountable and build solidarities across injustices. If we want to imagine a future of social and environmental justice in contemporary cities (and thus envision what AbdouMaliq Simone, focusing on racial and class inequalities in urban Africa, has called the "City Yet to Come" [Simone 2004]), we need to think harder about how unlikely neighbors in today's cities and their peripheries—including barbecuers, food vendors, foresters, environmentalists, mushrooms, wild boar, antelopes, rabbits, safari guides, gardeners, bunker friends, and refugees—inhabit and traverse existing spatial orders and landscapes of ruination.

Rubble

1

BOTANICAL ENCOUNTERS

Walking along the banks of the Spree River crossing Berlin's Museum Island, you have a good chance of making a surprise botanical encounter. Here, in Berlin's city center, amid government buildings and construction sites, you can find a small, yellow-flowering annual plant with a peculiar history. This plant is called sticky goosefoot, or *Chenopodium botrys* (fig. 1.1).[1] Covered with sticky, glandular hair, the plant grows between 10 and 80 cm tall. It has a strong aromatic scent and can be used as a flavoring in cooking. Preferring a Mediterranean or sub-Mediterranean climate, sticky goosefoot usually grows in ruderal spaces—the sandy and rocky soils alongside canals, roads, and train tracks, as well as the cracks of sidewalks, on ruins and waste (Sukopp 1998, 9).[2]

In the sixteenth century, the plant was imported from Istanbul and was cultivated in gardens throughout Europe—mainly for use in controlling moths and medicinal purposes.[3] During the industrialization and urbanization of the nineteenth century, as ruderal spaces and their gravelly soils proliferated alongside transport routes in and between urban centers, sticky goosefoot spread beyond cultivated areas in warmer regions across southern Europe, Eurasia, and the Middle East. In colder climates, such as north of the Alps, the plant grew only sporadically.

Curiously, sticky goosefoot has prospered in chilly Berlin. After Berlin had been heavily bombed toward the end of World War II, large areas of rubble dotted the city and remained there for decades. Ironically, these "blasted landscapes" (Stoetzer 2011; Tsing 2014) provided a habitat where

FIGURE 1.1 *Chenopodium botrys L.* Tessie K. Frank watercolors, circa 1895–1935. Archives of the Gray Herbarium, Harvard University (gra00006).

sticky goosefoot—and other "nonnative" plants—could flourish and become part of the permanent urban flora. This proliferation posed a riddle to West Berlin botanists, prompting them to study plant migration and ruderal ecologies in the city. Doing so, they developed a way of attending to more-than-human worlds that both spoke to and departed from postwar cultural imaginaries about the city (as a space of culture, separate from nature) and the nation (as a homogeneous domestic entity disconnected from the rest of the world). The emergence of urban plants as a scientific object of study also triggered the rise of urban ecology and impacted environmental policies in a city reeling from the trauma of fascism and war (Lachmund 2013). In subsequent decades, this curiosity about urban plants and the ecological dynamics of the city would also foster new public cultures attentive to urban nature in Berlin.

What follows is a story of both ruination and wonder. Sticky goosefoot's story is tied to Berlin's history of urbanization, migration, and trade; but it is also tied to a global history of climate change and the catastrophe wrought by fascism and nationalism in the twentieth century. After the war, city planners and landscape architects were busy reconstructing the nation by transforming the built environment and greening over the traces of war. In this context, rubble plants were deeply ambivalent indicators for a city coming back to life.[4] Yet Berlin's historical and political situation—the division of the city and the persistent presence of huge areas of rubble in the city center—ironically offered an opportunity for a different mapping of the city. Ruderal plants, thriving in the bombed city center, stood in contrast to both Nazi and postwar desires for spatial ordering: they were unexpected newcomers and unsettled ideas about who or what belongs and which communities are considered "out of place." Tracing these ruderal ecologies, botanists developed "arts of noticing" (Tsing 2015, 17) that recognized nature or the environment not as external or separate from human life, to be managed, controlled, and incorporated into anthropogenic landscapes, but rather as a central and unruly part of the city—a ruderal city in which plants, animals, and other beings have lived together, however unequally, for a long time.

As I show in this chapter, botanists' encounters with Berlin's rubble plants opened up possibilities not only for urban ecology but also for an anthropological analysis that attends to the heterogeneity of cities—including a city's unexpected neighbors—without erasing the traces of exclusion and violence inherited in urban landscapes.[5] Following this history of botanical encounters with sticky goosefoot in Berlin's rubble, I offer the *ruderal* as an analytical framework for rethinking and ethnographically tracing the heterogeneity of urban life in the ruins of European capitalism and nationalism. Approaching ruins in the broad sense as the very urban worlds we inhabit, formed by racialized exclusions, capitalist urbanization, and profound environmental harm, I suggest that the ruderal can provide a lens to explore them. Thinking with the ruderal does not mean equating people with plants or nonhumans but asking how multiple beings and their habitats get entangled in projects of nation-making, capitalist extraction, and environmental destruction—and how they disrupt these projects.

Attending to ruderal worlds can redirect ethnographic attention toward often unnoticed, cosmopolitan yet precarious ways of remaking the urban fabric—and thus to the unintended consequences of anthropogenic landscapes and transnational connections. Neither cultivated nor pristine nature, ruderals emerge alongside urban infrastructures and in their cracks. Unplanned, they are the result of migratory movements and displacement. Following them means never telling only one story but rather thinking across different registers to understand broader ecologies of migration and racialization—and the social dynamics of what it means to live on an increasingly inhospitable planet.

A Natural History of Destruction

World War II's frenzy of military technology brought a nightmare of destruction upon many cities across the globe. For their part, Nazi Germans fought a war on all sides: in the East, the West, against Jews, and against anyone who did not fit their ideology of racial purity or support their imperial aspirations. In an effort to remove all its enemies from cities, the fascist regime segregated and killed in ghettos and created "cities of death" (Shaw 2006, 52) in the extermination camps, often located in the countryside or on the outskirts of cities. Throughout the war, area bombing against civilian populations became yet another common tool of urban destruction.[6] By 1942, as genocide was being committed across Europe, the Western Allies radically changed their initial condemnation of aerial bombings and responded with air raids indiscriminately bombing Japanese and German cities, sending firestorms through Dresden, Berlin, and Tokyo and dropping atomic bombs in Hiroshima and Nagasaki.[7]

Between 1943 and 1945, thousands of air raids turned many German cities into rubble. Like the German bombing of Poland, Allied bombings in Germany were aimed at train and road networks and were intended to impact the civilian population and its morale; later, such bombings increasingly targeted industrial production facilities in an effort to bring the Nazi war machine to a final halt (Orlow 1999, 200). In *On the Natural History of Destruction*, W. G. Sebald describes the trauma of death, genocide, and destruction inscribed onto cityscapes all over Germany during and after the war—thus challenging a removed history of destruction that, curiously untouched by its subject, makes suffering and "the real horrors of the time disappear in abstraction" (Sebald 2004, 50). In detail, Sebald chronicles the technology and impacts of the bombs dropped on German cities, as well as the multispecies lives and deaths that followed: walls of searchlights; roars of aircraft; hollow thuds of bombs; pressure waves; breaking windows miles away from the detonations; doors tearing from their frames; seas of flames and trails of firestorms raging through streets; air reaching the force of a hurricane, ripping out trees by their roots and driving "human beings before it like living torches" (Sebald 2004, 27). Housing structures collapsed, sewage lines burst, and the asphalt on the streets melted. People's bodies were torn apart and burned. During one of the bombings in Berlin, the water in the canals caught fire and smoke rose to eight thousand meters. People died and went mad from what they saw. In the Berlin Zoo—like many other European zoos, imagined as a sign of imperial power—a third of the animals died. Deer and monkeys escaped, birds flew away through broken glass roofs, and lions were rumored to be loose and on the prowl (Sebald 2004, 91–92), joining an exodus of human and nonhuman refugees throughout a city twisted in rubble.[8] In the end, as Sebald tells us, the rats and "huge and iridescent green flies, such as had never been seen before," moved into the city and became the "repulsive fauna of the rubble" (Sebald 2004, 35).

When the bombings and battles ceased and the fascist regime was put to a halt, piles of rubble became an integral element of the urban landscape in many German cities. In fact, cities became almost synonymous with rubble. As Sebald recalls, "Few things were so clearly linked in my mind with the word city as mounds of rubble" (2004, 74). Yet the inferno of death and fire, and the "necropolis" (35) that came with it, would only be remembered in order to encourage the will for reconstruction. Nobody seemed to notice how the smell of decay that lay over the city resembled the air emanating from the basements of the Warsaw Ghetto after its destruction and the murder of its Jewish inhabitants just a few years earlier (4).

City of Rubble

As the capital of Germany, Berlin was especially targeted for bombing between 1943 and 1945. Thousands of people died during the bombings, including civilians and soldiers on the ground, in the air, and on all sides of the war (Diefendorf 1993, 16–17). By the end of the war, Berlin lay in rubble.[9] Large parts of the city center's built environment had been destroyed, including much of the aboveground train system, roads and electricity networks, and parts of the sewage system. Many people lived among the rubble in the bombed ruins of houses, in makeshift shelters such as abandoned military barracks, or in temporary refugee housing supplied by the occupying Allies (Diefendorf 1993, 131). Trees in parks and urban woodlands had burned down—the ones that remained were cut down for firewood during the following winters due to a shortage of coal. Much of the Tiergarten (Animal Garden), Berlin's largest park, which had been covered with dense woodlands before the war, became an odd landscape of charred tree stumps and felled trees. Because food was scarce, many Berliners started to grow vegetables in open spaces all over the city—especially in the Tiergarten and other parks. Berliners also became savvy plant experts: they participated in community events like *Aktion Wildgemüse* (Action wild vegetables) and sought out edible plants like dandelions and chickweed—and perhaps sticky goosefoot—that grew in the rubble (Botting 2005, 171).

At the same time, images of occupied Berlin as a feral city abounded: "Wild boar 'ravaged' the city's outskirts in herds fifty strong, and were avidly hunted by hungry civilians with bows and arrows or by bored GIs with burp guns. Likewise, British Tommies volunteered to help Berliners (now subsisting on less than 1,000 calories a day) track the three species of starving deer that had taken refuge in the Spandau and the Köpenick forests. Hard on the heels of the deer were their ancient predators. Signs were hastily posted on the autobahn: BEWARE OF WOLVES!" (M. Davis 2002, 384). Amid these images of Berlin "gone wild," another sentiment unfolded: numbness. As Sebald points out, in the destroyed cities after the war, there was a kind of "taboo, like a shameful family secret," "a tacit agreement, equally binding on everyone, that the true state of material and moral ruin in which the country found itself was not to be described" (2004, 10). Sebald chronicles the social and natural life in the rubble of the ravaged cities, as well as the numbing of the senses after fascism, as integral elements of the time.[10] Instead of pausing to consider the catastrophes fascism brought about, reconstruction efforts sought to move on as quickly as possible. This sensibility is illustrated in many scenes in German cities, such as Alexander Kluge's story about Frau Schrader, a woman employed at a movie theater, who set out immediately after an air raid amid death and destruction "to clear the rubble away before the two o'clock matinee" (Sebald 2004, 41). These are scenes of apathy and anesthesia amid a population living in ruins: people walked through the streets "as if nothing had happened, and . . . the town had always looked like that" (Alfred Döblin, 1945, cited in Sebald 2004, 3). Millions of homeless people wandered aimlessly and sheltered in ruins reaching up several floors behind burned-out facades (Sebald 2004, 35–37, 47).

This numbness had already found its correlate earlier during the w; when Nazi officials schemed plans for reconstructing Germany's capital once the war ended: they imagined they would revitalize the urban landscape—and by extension the nation, imagined as a homogeneous ethnic community—through nature.[11] Hitler and other Nazi officials despised Berlin because of its crowded working-class tenements, multiethnic communities, and leftist political tradition. Within fascist environmental discourse, Germans' alienation from nature resulted from urbanization and the dense living conditions of multistory working-class apartment buildings (*Mietskasernen*), which were seen as a manifestation of a "Jewish spirit" (M. Davis 2002, 383). Furthermore, Nazi racism declared war not only against racialized people but also against undesirable forms of nature, "justifying racist ideologies as a form of ecology, a doctrine of blood and soil" (Ackerman 2007, 153). In this context, landscaping became a tool of ethnic and racial cleansing.[12] In fact, some "Nazi ideologues actually welcomed the thousand bomber raids and firestorms as a ritual cleansing of the 'Jewish influence' of big city life and the beginning of a mystical regeneration of Aryan unity with nature" (M. Davis 2002, 383).[13] Others, like Albert Speer, Hitler's key architect in Berlin, were fascinated by ruins and, in their imperial nostalgia, saw value in them, overgrown with ivy. They could be seen as traces of and monuments to the greatness of the German empire (Diefendorf 1993, 3–4). After the first bombings in 1943, officials already proposed regenerating the urban landscape by clearing the rubble and planting trees. These greened cities with forests and gardens would replace the crowded and what they considered the "decadent Jewish metropolis" and reestablish rootedness to the land and soil (*Bodenständigkeit*) (Diefendorf 1993, 3)—a concept that had shaped landscape sensibilities since the onset of industrialization and German colonial rule (Cupers 2016).[14]

During the war, the rubble—a sign of defeat—was quickly cleared from the streets after each bombing raid and piled up in heaps all over the city (often by forced labor) until the bombings became so frequent that it was impossible to keep up with the destruction (Diefendorf 1993, xvi). As the end of the Nazi regime came within reach, the occupying Allies formed various plans for Germany's reconstruction. The Morgenthau Plan, proposed by the US secretary of the Treasury in fall 1944, envisioned the "pastoralization" of the entire country in order to prevent Germany from ever regaining industrial power and starting another war (Orlow 1999, 208; Sebald 2004, 40). In Berlin and other cities, many initially doubted whether it would be worthwhile, or even possible, to reconstruct the destroyed cities. Some suggested building new cities underground to protect them from future wars (Diefendorf 1993, 11). Others thought that Berlin in particular could never be reconstructed because it was so badly damaged, and that its ruins instead should be preserved as a reminder of the insanity of Prussian militarism and the Nazi regime (Ladd 1997, 174). Still others suggested greening the ruins with trees and meadows, and rebuilding cities in the countryside (Schildt 2002, 145).

Greening the Rubble, Rebuilding the Nation

Soon after the war and the initial political reordering of Germany, plans for reconstructing Germany took a different turn.[15] In 1948, the Marshall Plan was launched to boost the economic recovery and political reconstruction of Western Europe. In the immediate years after the war, reconstruction efforts centered on rubble and its removal from many cities. With this focus, the management of urban nature became a central element in "reconstruction."

During this time, Berlin, like the rest of Germany, was divided into four sectors. The three sectors of the "Western Allies" (French, American, and British) formed West Berlin and the Soviet sector formed East Berlin. With the growing tension between the Western Allies and the Soviet government and the rise of the Cold War, West Berlin was increasingly cut off from the surrounding Soviet-controlled countryside. In 1949, the two German states of the Federal Republic of Germany and the German Democratic Republic were founded. Traffic between East and West Berlin was limited and highly regulated. In 1961, at the height of Cold War tensions, the Berlin Wall was built. The new border situation would complicate reconstruction, and the city's rubble remained longer than it did in other German cities.

Not unlike during the Nazi regime, public officials and urban planners considered the rubble an eyesore. Yet the destruction also provided an opportunity to redesign the city—to erase traces of Nazism and "open up" what many considered to be a too-densely-built city before the war.[16] Using biological metaphors echoing both Nazi and previous urban planning discourse, many architects and planners sought to create more "organic" and "healthy" cities, with lower building density that could accommodate increasing traffic and an expanded transportation infrastructure. As Karen Till (2005) points out, by 1947, "fears of the past were encoded in competing urban-planning designs for a 'new world class city' that demonstrated 'the inner necessity, after . . . Auschwitz and Stalingrad, to completely redefine Berlin'" (41, citing Howell-Ardila 1998). Like Frau Schrader attempting to clear the rubble before the two o'clock matinee, planners (in agreement with occupying powers) tried to erase the traces of the war as quickly as possible. Almost immediately after the war, the municipal administration set up by the Allies in Berlin created a "Plan for De-Rubbling" the city (*Enttrümmerungsplan*), hired thousands of workers, and asked volunteers to clear rubble from the streets. Many streets and buildings that were only partly destroyed were declared a "public hazard" and demolished in an effort to eradicate the remains of the fascist regime.[17] Remaking the built structures and parks, planners hoped to leave the past behind and move toward a brighter future.

In the following years, as the city split into two, both East and West Berlin developed complex infrastructures to clear the city of rubble. With them came a whole new set of rubble technologies and vocabularies. The city's canals and remaining train network—as well as its makeshift trains—carried rubble from the city center to "rubble clearance machines" that recycled it into construction material for new buildings and streets. A train in East Berlin was called "Rubble Express" (Keiderling 1999a, 40). During the Berlin airlift at the onset of the Cold War, rubble was used to build new runways at Tempelhof Airport, where Western Allied planes landed to bring supplies into the city as the Russians had cut it off from ground transport networks and the surrounding countryside (Diefendorf 1993, 27).

East and West Berlin planners and architects deployed different forms of land use and building strategies to make the political ideals of democracy and socialism come to life (Till 2005, 42). And yet on both sides of the border, the rubble was considered ugly—a "leftover burden" of the war—and its clearance was considered necessary for economic recovery (Keiderling 1999b, 39). In the early 1950s, both municipal governments created long-range reconstruction plans for Berlin, and "de-rubbling" became increasingly refined and mechanized. In East Berlin, the Soviet-led government introduced so-called Reconstruction Sundays, encouraging the local population to help clear the rubble. As part of its efforts, the city of East Berlin even challenged the city of Leipzig to a competition to see which city could get rid of its millions of cubic meters of rubble in the quickest way.[18] In West Berlin, unemployed Berliners—many of them women and from all social classes—volunteered or were hired by the Allied powers as cheap labor to clear the rubble (Keiderling 1999b, 39). Soon, these "rubble women" would enter the national imagination as heroic figures. In addition, the city initiated various campaigns to closely track rubble-clearing "successes" and to call on Berliners to help make room for reconstruction. Even the city's emblem, the Berlin bear, appeared on a 1952 poster urging Berliners to help clean up the city (fig. 1.2).

FIGURE 1.2 The caption reads: "It is not hard, grumbles the bear, thus keep pace and build with us—National Reconstruction Program, Berlin 1952. Our success in April: stacked up 4,376,130 rocks, obtained 702 tons of scrap metal, cleared 65,557 cubic meters of rubble." Landesarchiv Berlin.

Despite this success, the question of how to dispose of the rubble was challenging, especially in West Berlin. Here, it became a challenge to move rubble to the outskirts because the city was politically cut off from the countryside. Meanwhile, the rubble reminded people of the death and destruction of the war. Thus, piling up the rubble, greening it, and letting trees and meadows grow over it was an attempt to erase the traces of history and "regenerate" from the Nazi past. As Jens Lachmund has shown, the creation of new green spaces—especially in those areas that had been destroyed during the war—was a central element of urbanists' approaches to reconstruction after the war (Lachmund 2003, 238). Lachmund writes, "Greening . . . was a relatively easy way to regain some sense of order in the labyrinth of ruins and rubble. Ruins carried the burden of undesired memories of death and destruction. Greening, in contrast, resonated perfectly with the self-image of a society seeking to separate itself from its Nazi past and . . . to prepare itself for economic growth and wealth" (238). In fact, these landscaping practices of greening the rubble, as well as the cultural imaginaries that accompanied them, were on par with what the National Socialists had already envisioned after the first bombings of German cities. Maintaining this legacy and greening desire, both Eastern and Western municipalities had workers collect rubble into heaps and landscape them into so-called rubble hills (*Trümmerberge*) that could be integrated into existing parks and green spaces. Both city governments created rubble dumping grounds next to urban forests and parks and planted dense vegetation on them so they would eventually appear natural (239).[19] Buried beneath were not only the fragments of thousands of buildings, but also the material remains of Nazi militarism.[20] Visions of progress through greening materialized in a landscape of gloomy hills. As Berlin is situated in a former ice-age meltwater valley and is mostly flat, most of its elevations today are rubble hills. There are fourteen of them altogether. The highest is located at the edge of a large urban forest, the Grunewald, in former West Berlin; it is 114 meters high and contains 12 million cubic meters of rubble (Keiderling 1999a, 1999b). Perhaps appropriately so, its name is Devil's Mountain (Teufelsberg).[21]

After the war, the theme of new life emerging from the ruins became popular in narratives of national reconstruction, while rubble became an object of national nostalgia. The rubble women (*Trümmerfrauen*) were celebrated as new heroes of the nation, enabling German society to look away from the horrors of the war and the Nazi regime. "Rising from Ruins" ("Auferstanden aus Ruinen") became the East German version of the national anthem in 1949. In the 1950s, a kneeling woman stooping to plant an oak seedling was depicted on the West German fifty-pfennig coin (fig. 1.3)— thus commemorating the rubble women as well as the women who replanted the urban and rural forests that had been cut down during the war.[22]

In this context of anesthesia and urban breakdown, the cultivation of plants in Berlin served multiple purposes. Short of food, residents grew vegetables in the city's destroyed parks. In the late 1940s, West Berlin's mayor declared the bombing of the city's major park, the Tiergarten, one of the largest wounds suffered by the city and made its reforestation a top priority.[23] Thousands of oak and birch trees were donated from across the country and brought in by plane during the Berlin airlift. A new infrastructure of nature (Carse 2012) thus emerged as parks were replanted and rubble was landscaped into hills covered with dense vegetation and forests (Dümpelmann 2019, 144ff.). While greening the rubble became a major element in the cultural imaginary after the war (Lachmund 2003), it involved a form

FIGURE 1.3 Fifty-pfennig coin. Photo courtesy of Bernd Eichstaedt.

of greening that was carefully managed. Neatly ordered, rubble and the emerging landscapes disguising it became part of Germany's "economic miracle" and a sign of progress in which past violence and the exploitation of labor both during and after the war remained invisible (Sebald 2004, 12).

Yet despite all the management, clearance infrastructure, and determination to forget, the rubble had its own life. Many rubble fields were situated along the new border zone between East and West Berlin and thus were off-limits for reconstruction (Lachmund 2003, 238). Stubbornly, rubble fields dotted the city for decades. And unexpected lives grew out of them.

Botanical Encounters in Berlin's Blasted Landscapes

As we sat sipping tea in Herbert Sukopp's office at the Institute for Ecology at the Technical University of Berlin (TU Berlin) one summer in the late 2000s, I asked how he became interested in studying the ecology of rubble spaces. Sukopp responded by rephrasing my inquiry: "Since all of Berlin lay in rubble, . . . I think the question should rather be: How could I have studied ANYTHING OTHER THAN rubble spaces?"[24] Quickly, he reminded me that in the postwar years, rubble was everywhere in Berlin, especially in the city center, and could hardly be overlooked. Sukopp was born in Berlin in 1930 and grew up in a landscape blasted by bombs. The rubble fields formed an integral part of his childhood and adolescence.

As the city lay bare in front of everyone's eyes, plants flourished in the rubble fields. Their proliferation triggered the curiosity of Sukopp and other West Berlin botanists who, with the increasing political division of the city, found themselves cut off from the surrounding countryside. In fact, with the construction of the Berlin Wall in 1961, the botanists were literally walled off from rural areas in their vicinity. Whereas they used to travel to the Baltic Sea, the Brandenburg countryside, the Harz mountains, or as far as Brazil for research, paying attention to the city suddenly became worthwhile. Both scientists and hobbyists thus began to turn their attention to plant life in the city. This was neither nature "out there" nor nature neatly demarcated and domesticated in parks and zoos, but a rubble flora that was, as he put it, "new, unfamiliar, and fascinating" (*neu, unbekannt und spannend*).

Sukopp, together with a diverse network of hobbyists and academic botanists, including Hildemar Scholz and Alexander Kohler, began sporadically exploring rubble fields in the early 1950s. Inspired by reports from other botanists and ornithologists on unexpected plant- and wildlife in bombed German and Austrian cities (Kreh 1955; Merxmüller 1952; K. Müller 1950; Pfeiffer 1957; Wilmanns and Bammert 1965), they began to research many of the city's rubble areas more systematically.[25] For Sukopp, collaborations across political borders were crucial to this endeavor and often involved secrecy. While he and other scientists like Scholz, who first was a student at the Freie Universität in West Berlin, played an important role in initiating research, they closely cooperated with hobby-botanists who were fellow members of the local Botanical Association and often secretly exchanged information with East Berlin botanists.[26] Yet even beyond these secret exchanges, their research included other subversive elements: by turning their attention not away from but toward the rubble, they departed from official planning schemes that tried to cover up the traces of the war. Later, they would also bump up against bureaucratic views on nature conservation. When in the field, the botanists' activities were often not recognizable within existing conventions of how to move around in the city and around the rubble: most people ignored them or assumed they were homeless, looking for scrap metals, or picking herbs—all common activities in these spaces at the time. Only children, as Sukopp pointed out to me, were curious enough to ask what they were doing. Indeed, botanists, deprived of their usual field sites, were often mistaken for what Sebald described as gleaners, who "could be seen between the ruined dwellings, now deprived of their purpose, searching for buried remnants of household goods, here salvaging a bit of tin, or wire from the rubble, there picking up a few splinters of wood and stowing them in the bags they wore slung around them which resembled botanical specimen containers" (Sebald 2004, 47–48). Botanists indeed gleaned their insights from a world of rubble. Instead of seeing rubble as urban wastelands, they re-envisioned them as another world in a ~~[busy]~~ usy with national reconstruction and an urge to move on. This other ~~[world]~~ d was rich in botanical traces leading to a different, more weedy history ~~[of the]~~ he nation, nature, and the city. And it was plants like sticky goosefoot that incited botanists to notice such a world of rubble ecologies—a heterogeneous world of plant life, movement, and migration, but also a world of ruination and militarized destruction in the name of nationalism that far exceeded any single, tiny plant.[27]

As botanists followed these traces in the rubble, they gained insight into an array of historical and environmental shifts and a diversity of urban habitats that resulted from a history of global connection *and* destruction. With their spontaneous takeover, the rubble plants were not what the Nazis had dreamed of: they were unexpected and unlikely neighbors and they provided a glimpse of the contingency of life in cities—and on earth. Their stubborn presence inspired scientists to stop seeing the city as opposed to nature. Instead, they began to reimagine urban life. The rubble plants were indicators for urban ecologies that coincided neither with the borders of the nation, imagined as a homogeneous biological community, nor with (post-)war planners' desires for national reconstruction. Indeed, Berlin's ruderal ecologies were much more sticky and ambiguous than what urban-planning schemes wanted them to be.

Ruderal Plants

Researching the rubble flora, Sukopp and his colleagues discovered a city bustling with plants from all over the world. The rubble vegetation was abundant in "spontaneous newcomers," "alien" or "nonnative invasive species" (Sukopp and Wurzel 2003) from warmer regions in the Mediterranean, Asia, and the Americas. These newcomers—usually considered weeds—grew in unexpected places across the city and formed unlikely communities with other plants, animals, and insects. For example, one bombed area, the so-called Lützowplatz, turned out to be home to a rich diversity of plants and insects that included much larger numbers than in adjacent city parks (M. Davis 2002, 385). Intrigued by the rich diversity and lush vegetation developing in the rubble, the botanists created elaborate plant lists. For example, a tree from China, *Ailanthus altissima* (tree-of-heaven),[28] the North American tree *Robinia pseudoacacia* (black locust), and the herb *Solidago gigantea* (giant goldenrod) appeared widely in Berlin for the first time. The tree-of-heaven was imported from China during the era of Frederick the Great and

FIGURE 1.4 Herbert Sukopp in a young black locust forest at Lützowplatz, 1952. Photo by Alexander Kohler.

had been planted as a decorative tree in gardens and parks in Berlin since 1780 (Stoetzer 2020a). Yet it was only after World War II, 170 years after its introduction, that it could be found throughout the city center. Similarly, black locust, originally introduced to Europe in 1623, did not thrive in Berlin until after the war (Sukopp and Wurzel 2003, 68–69) (fig. 1.4).[29] Other plants like mugwort (*Artemisia vulgaris*);[30] two *Chenopodiaceae* of Eurasian origin; saltwort and wormwood (*Salsola collina, Artemisia scoparia*); and a grass species of North American origin, Lindheimer's millet (*Panicum lindheimeri*), also appeared widely in the rubble (Sukopp 2003a).

The seeds of these plants had found their way into the city via diverse transport routes. Some of them had crossed the city on the boots of soldiers or refugees during and after the war. Others arrived in packaging material for imported goods. Many seeds entered the city in bales of hay, brought on wagons by the Russian and Ukrainian armies for their horses. Other seeds' routes remained unknown. What all the plants had in common was that they were able to thrive in dry, gravelly soils with poor nutrients. Usually, their seeds would have remained dormant, invisible, and unable to sprout in the city's pavement. Yet the rubble spaces provided grounds for the seeds to take hold and germinate.

Sticky goosefoot was one of the plants that attracted the botanists' attention. Originally exported from Istanbul as a spice and medicinal plant, it had spread as a weed in Southern Europe's vineyards (Sukopp 1971). In Berlin, sticky goosefoot made a temporary appearance in the nineteenth century, when botanists noticed a few escapees from gardens and trade exhibits popping up in the city center. Yet the plant did not reappear on a larger scale until after the war, when it flourished widely and for decades across Berlin's bombed areas (unlike in many other German cities where much of the rubble was cleared by the late 1950s) (Lachmund 2003, 240). From the mid-1950s on, the plant's spontaneous growth lured the attention of botanists like Sukopp: studying its ecology in detail, they tried to explain the riddle of why sticky goosefoot, like many other ruderal plants, appeared so widely in Berlin and only sporadically in a few other places north of the Alps.

The botanists produced meticulous accounts of the plant's tissue production (its growth rate, sprouting strength, root growth, etc.), the moisture and composition of the soil (specifically sand versus rubble, as well as nitrogen and ash content), the effects of light on its growth, and its water regimes. Furthermore, they studied its habitats and associations, as well as the successional dynamic of the other vegetation it was part of (Sukopp 1971, 16). The habitat of sticky goosefoot—rocky debris, riversides, and sandy soils—turned out to be a very specialized environment with little competition due to its inhospitability (Sukopp and Wurzel 2003, 68). As the botanists tracked the plants' high seed production and its dispersal, they found the largest density of sticky goosefoot in the "dead eye" of Berlin—the area that had been the city's most densely built-up, but heavily destroyed, city center (fig. 1.5).[31]

On further study, sticky goosefoot's presence in the dead eye of Berlin's center revealed a secret. Increasing trade, migration, and traffic, as well as the war, had given rise to a diversification of habitats and had introduced new seeds to the city.[32] The proliferation of a unique urban vegetation thus gave further clues about the heterogeneity of the city's ecologies—a heterogeneity that was an indicator for intersecting environmental, social, and economic dynamics that opened up new possibilities for rethinking urban life.

Unexpected Neighbors

Tracking changes in the urban flora of postwar Berlin, Sukopp and his colleagues developed an eye for an ecology of disturbed places: rubble fields, ruins, waste areas, and the spaces alongside railways, roads, walls, and

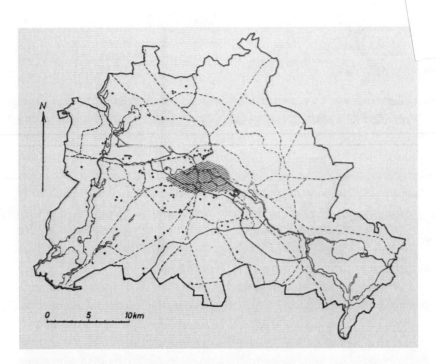

FIGURE 1.5 Distribution of sticky goosefoot, *Chenopodium botrys L.*, in the "dead eye" of Berlin, 1947–71. Map from Sukopp (1971).

ports. These spaces all hosted a surprising diversity of plant life. Describing his research and initial studies on urban flora at the beginning of the twentieth century, Sukopp argued that processes of urbanization did not necessarily lead to more uniform urban landscapes. To the contrary, he concluded that the development of ruderal flora "essentially runs parallel to the size and intensity of trade and industry; it is a direct standard of the technical culture" (Naegeli and Thellung 1905, 226, cited in Sukopp 2008, 84). This emerging sense of the diverse ecologies of ruderal spaces led the botanists to reconsider previous notions of the city as separate from nature. They began to challenge a dominant view—found not only in urban-planning schemes and cultural imaginaries of the time but also within the discipline of ecology—that separated cities from nonhuman life and saw cities as a controlled human habitat, and thus as a product of culture, not nature (Dierig, Lachmund, and Mendelsohn 2003, 11).[33]

The rubble plants not only inspired the botanists to unsettle nature/city divisions. They also pointed beyond nativist perspectives and beyond the boundaries of the nation-state by drawing attention to the global intercon-nectedness and heterogeneity of the ecology of cities. Although some of the botanists used vocabularies such as *foreigners, aliens, and guests,* thus engaging geographic imaginations that connected plants to a world of nations, borders, and immigration (Lachmund 2003, 245), they did not cast ruderal plants as unwelcome intruders. The first to inhabit disturbed lands, ruderals were not a nuisance: they could set the stage for other flourishing ecosystems—for example, by giving rise to spontaneous wetlands, attracting birds, or providing shade and organic matter for other species. Even more important, ruderal ecologies themselves pointed beyond seemingly distinct categories. Their composition, associations, and unpredictable succession schemes (Lachmund 2007, 248), as well as the rubble itself, did not easily fit into scientists' rectangular sample areas, nor did they always align with the classificatory schemes of adventive floristics and phytosociology.[34] In a dance of relating (Haraway 2008, 25), the botanists therefore had to adjust their frameworks and theorize the unexpected.[35]

At a time when immigration to Germany and West Berlin was increasing significantly, especially with the high demand for labor during the reconstruction period of the 1950s to 1960s, Sukopp and his colleagues thus began to see the ecology of cities as the outcome of global connection. They concluded that "modern cities are characterized by their worldwide connections and are uncoupled (disassociated) from the local surroundings with the consequence that the concept of a cultural landscape is only partly relevant" (Sukopp 2008, 87).[36] As a result, Berlin's urban ecosystems differed from those in the hinterlands. Indeed, in some urban areas, the botanists noted that species diversity was greater than in the surrounding countryside where monocultures of farming and forestry prevailed (Sukopp 1998, 9). Moreover, the ecological characteristics of a city were also shaped by other cities and rural landscapes across the world (Sukopp 2003b, 40). From this perspective, the city appeared as a new type of environment that was different from its surroundings but also challenged the rural/urban dichotomy altogether (Sukopp 1998, 4): its habitats comprised heterogeneous ecosystems that were not separate from technology, urbanization, trade, migration, and movement. "The cosmopolitan character of many urban plants," Sukopp and his colleagues concluded, "is a tribute to the ubiquity of humanity's modification of environmental conditions and to our efficiency as agents of dispersal" (Sukopp and Wurzel 2003, 68).

Yet ruderal ecologies also stood in stark contrast to persistent racialized geographies of the city versus the countryside, and to the kinds of native natures the fascist regime had imagined. Although the Nazis had been fascinated with wilderness, only certain kinds of wild things that were in line with the dominant racial ideology were allowed. Undesired aliens had to be weeded out (Zeller 2005). Nazis promoted wilderness (*Wildnis*)—defined as untouched nature, free from human contact and intervention—in their environmental policies, especially the protection of native wild animals and plants. In contrast, the city was imagined as nature's antagonist, full of social ills and a space of undesired, dangerous racial mixing. Similarly, the degeneration or destruction of the natural world was considered a product of urbanization, miscegenation, and human contact (Sax 1997, 13).[37]

With their abundance of nonnative plants, ruderal spaces turned out to be neither the native nature "out there" that Nazi planners had imagined for cities after the war, purged of all foreign influence, nor the urban nature of neatly landscaped imperial gardens, rich in exotic plants, that Europeans had dreamed up. Rather, ruderals were escapees from Europe's gardens of colonial and national landscaping, smuggled into cities via packing materials or taking a ride on the boots of refugees and soldiers. The botanists' research on ruderals thus also questioned a view of urban nature that read environmental degradation and urbanization through a nationalist lens and attributed ecological problems to the erosion of Germany's national character and the presence of foreign bodies (Lekan 2004, 4). Yet while ruderal worlds were indicators of ecological changes in cities, they were also reminders of war and the nightmare of ruination that fascism had brought across Europe. Thus, long before proclamations of an era of the Anthropocene, Berlin's botanists designated the ecologies of ruderal plants—these unexpected neighbors—to "be the prevailing ecosystems of the future" (M. Davis 2002, 385).

Cities as Heat Islands

Although ruderal plants served as indicators of global traffic and nature's entanglements with technology, they were also an indicator of climate change. Sticky goosefoot, tree-of-heaven, and black locust, for example, were only able to "naturalize" in the city because of microclimatic features (Sukopp 1971, 11): the distribution patterns of these plants gave clues about different temperature zones across the city. By tracking these plants' life cycles—the different starting points and phases of budding, leafing, flowering, and fruiting—one could determine different temperature regimes throughout the city, with flowering phases sometimes starting more than a week earlier in the city's center than at its edges.[38] From these distribution and flowering patterns, Sukopp and others concluded, "The dynamics of the plant mirrors the dynamics of the city" (Sukopp 2003b, 33).

From this perspective, cities came into view as heat islands on earth: they generally have a higher temperature than their surroundings, sometimes up to 12°C. This has the consequence of a greenhouse effect, which is enabled by the urban infrastructure (Sukopp 2003b). Due to traffic, power stations, industry, and heated buildings, temperatures are generally elevated, and levels of air pollution are higher in cities (especially carbon particles and trace gases). Because cities provide rough surfaces, like the walls of buildings, bridges, and narrow roads, wind speeds are reduced and solar radiation is less direct. In addition, humidity is lower in many urban locations. Because of the ubiquity of pavement, water tends not to trickle down into the soil but runs off quickly (Sukopp and Wurzel 2003).

This greenhouse effect also has a temporal dimension: over two centuries, and in the course of industrialization, Berlin, like other cities, had become hotter.[39] Sukopp and his colleagues thus concluded that the spreading of nonnative ruderal plants in Europe was promoted by the slow climate warming—on earth in general, and in cities in particular—beginning in the nineteenth century (Sukopp and Wurzel 2003). Indeed, since the 1850s, the effects of global climate change were intensified in larger cities by the ever-increasing urbanization and the resulting heat island effect. To analyze the interrelated effects of global and local warming, it thus became necessary to consider the time lag between a plant's introduction and its wider proliferation. For example, both *Chenopodium botrys* and *Ailanthus altissima* initially appeared in the late nineteenth and early twentieth century but did not spread on a wider scale until after World War II (Sukopp and Wurzel 2003, 69).

Ruderal Ecologies and the Unruly Heterogeneity of Urban Life

Chronicling the ecologies flourishing in Berlin's blasted landscapes opened up new possibilities for planning and conservation policies and changed the cultural imaginaries of the city. The botanists' curiosity about the vegetation of urban wastelands was not only at odds with the city administration's strategy of covering up the traces of war but with urban planning that did not take environmental concerns, such as species diversity and habitat destruction, into consideration. Instead, the botanists showed how rubble flora and fauna mirrored not only the history of Berlin and the effects of its trade, transport, migration, and connections across the globe but also its histories of destruction and environmental change. Berlin's unexpected inhabitants were thus a constitutive and active element of the urban fabric. They enabled new ecosystems to flourish and provided shelter for people and multiple other beings.

In the 1970s, botanists began to join forces with citizen groups to rally for the conservation of former rubble spaces or wastelands across the city. Although these alliances were not always immediately successful, they had a lasting impact on urban policy-making (Lachmund 2013).[40] Sukopp took on a role as adviser for the State Office for Environmental Protection and became the commissioner for nature conservation (*Naturschutzbeauftrag-ter*) in West Berlin in the mid-1970s (fig. 1.6). Developing the first maps of biotopes in Berlin,[41] he paved the way for their inclusion into the Berlin Landscape Plan as well as the Species and Biotope Protection Program—which ultimately led to the creation of expansive lists for endangered ferns and flowering plants.[42] Illustrating the heterogeneity and vulnerability of urban worlds, these biotope maps opened up possibilities for incorporating ruderal sites and urban wastelands (*Trümmerflächen und Brachen*) in conservation policies, and thus for a "greening design that does not accentuate the contrast between nature and the city" (Sukopp 2003a, 308) but instead "provide[s] insights into the uniqueness of cities, in which plants and animals play a big role" (Sukopp 2003b, 43).

Although these botanical encounters with ruderal plants shed critical light on modernist planning that aimed to dominate nonhumans (see Wolch 1998), their emerging views on urban nature were not immune to governance and commodification. Indeed, as Sukopp conveyed to me in several of our conversations, there is a risk of romanticizing urban nature and turning it into yet another category of administrative surveillance—similar to the term *green*. Historian of science Jens Lachmund (2013) picks up this very question in his book *Greening Berlin*. Lachmund shows how post–World War II ecological research in Berlin, with its elaborate mapping practices, produced urban nature as a new object of scientific knowledge. In particular, the biotope mappings introduced by West Berlin botanists wielded immense imaginative power because they visualized the heterogeneity of urban ecologies as an outcome of historical practices. This enabled a shift in conservation and planning that included rubble spaces or abandoned urban land in policy-making (Auhagen and Sukopp 1983; Lachmund 2013; 2004b, 232; Sukopp 2003b, 30). Yet Lachmund concludes that the original potential of this view was integrated into new forms of urban governance and lost "much of its initial political momentum" (2013, 6) because urban policies created new hierarchies of value by differentiating urban habitats

Naturschutz
in der Großstadt

BERLIN

FIGURE 1.6 "Nature Conservation in the City," brochure, published by Sukopp when he was West Berlin's commissioner for nature conservation (Sukopp 1980). The image on the brochure's cover features *Tussilago farfara*, also known as coltsfoot (*Huflattich* in German), a common ruderal plant. Photo by author.

according to their degree of closeness to nature. Maps, graphs, charts, and drawings of plants and their habitats thus helped create "a new epistemic and political order of urban space" (Lachmund 2004b, 232)—an assemblage in which environmental expertise, science, and administrative practices joined and coconstructed expert knowledges about urban nature that could be classified and governed.

From a slightly different perspective, Matthew Gandy (2022) points out in *Natura Urbana* that while Berlin botanists' research on ruderal plants departed from earlier nativist perspectives, they ultimately remained close to systems-based approaches, failing to integrate a broader analysis of human agency and politics into their view of urban ecology (129–30).[43] Furthermore, Gandy contends, in the 1970s, popular references to urban ecology—expressed in various social contexts from documentary film to political party campaign agendas—celebrated "urban wilderness" as icon of an emerging multicultural German society (137).

Despite these obvious complicities, sociopolitical blind spots, and incorporations of ecological research into urban governance or liberal multiculturalist agendas, I argue that the encounters between botanists and ruderal plants created an opening for the study of cities and for cultural analysis more generally. To consider these analytical and political possibilities it is necessary to think in registers in addition to science and discourses of expertise. If we read Berlin's postwar plant ecology against the grain, or alongside its own logic, and consider instead the affective ecologies (Hustak and Myers 2012) that the botanists' observations entered into, we might find alternative models to understand and respond to the horrors and wonders of urban worlds.[44]

Sticky goosefoot's ruderal ecologies are, in fact, more sticky and unwieldy than scientific or urban-planning schemes might want them to be.[45] With their sticky presence, ruderal plants challenge us to account for the interrelatedness of life in the city exceeding the value regimes of urban nature or culture, as well as a deeply racialized and gendered notion of the environment as an external, passive scientific object. Neither wild nor domesticated, sticky goosefoot and its ruderal companions dwell in the cracks of urban infrastructures, including the fissures of the categorical units of nature and culture through which we make sense of them. They are their unsolicited hitchhikers and invisible ecologies. Their presence demands a broader conversation about the unexpected consequences of anthropogenic landscapes, capitalist trade, war, imperial power, migration, and displacement and their effects on urban lifeworlds. Exceeding systems of human governance, ruderal worlds are not passive but have their own lives—these cannot be grasped by a universalizing and distanced language of science or cultural critique alone. Ruderal worlds capture a sense of both wonder and horror amid violence, war, and dislocation. In this sense, they constitute the layered—and transnational—ecologies that make up urban life today. Rather than search for pristine, second (Cronon 1991), third, or fourth nature (Kowarik 1992), ruderals direct attention to previously unnoticed cosmopolitan ways of remaking the urban fabric. In this ecology of unexpected neighbors, the story is never singular but always consists of multiple strands. And one does not know beforehand whether it will be a story of destruction or flourishing.

∿ ∿ ∿

In postwar Germany, new life emerging from ruins became an integral element of the national narrative. Yet ruins, as well as the memories and traces of violence, war, and destruction that are embedded in them, do not necessarily have to cater either to a nationalist story of victimization or to one of heroic reconstruction (Sebald 2004; Stoler 2013, 2016; Yoneyama 1999). Instead, the unpredictable life of ruins and ruination can lead us to question the automatism of progress and attend to the traces of histories of nationalist violence and exclusion in the present (Yoneyama 1999, 81). In this sense, the ruderal landscapes of postwar Berlin do not necessarily have to become a site of capitalist value-production or forgetting and greening over the traces of a violent past—nor do they have to become a site of multiculturalist and ultimately depoliticized nostalgia. They can instead be seen as spaces from which to contemplate displacement on an increasingly inhospitable planet shaped by racism, war, and environmental destruction. The weedy lives of ruderals do not attest to an urban environment (*Umwelt*) rendered as external; rather, they are witnesses to the very webs of living and dying in which organisms are implicated (Haraway 2008). And they are certainly more than mere side effects (Masco 2013) amid the "progress" and growth of capitalist production and nation-making.

W. G. Sebald's account of the fragile and open-ended lives amid ruins can serve as one of our guides here. Playing among the weedy blasted landscapes of the war, Sebald remembers a sense of uncanniness—a sense of never being quite sure whether one will stumble across death amid the flowering rubblescape: "By the 1950s the plot of land, where a few handsome trees had survived the catastrophe, was entirely overgrown, and as children we often spent whole afternoons in this wilderness created in the middle of town by the war. I remember never feeling at ease going down the steps to the cellars. They smelled of damp and decay, and I always feared I might bump into the body of an animal or a human corpse" (Sebald 2004, 76). As Sebald points out, even the flowers and trees making their way through the rubble shared traces of destruction. Indeed, you could tell the date of a building's destruction from the plants growing among the ruins: "It was a question of botany. This heap of rubble was bare, naked, all rough stones and recently shattered masonry . . . with not a blade of grass in sight, whereas elsewhere trees were already growing, pretty little trees springing up in bedrooms and kitchens" (Sebald 2004, 39). After the war, the chestnuts and lilacs had a second uncanny "flowering in Hamburg in the autumn of 1943, a few months after the great fire" (Sebald 2004, 40). Rather than perpetuate the anesthesia that capitalism and racism have cultivated in the face of their own destructive force (Buck-Morss 1992), these second flowerings might teach us to exceed a detached mode of scientific or cultural analysis and instead respond to the animate, ruptured, and, indeed, unhomely qualities of life amid destruction.[46]

Modes of Attention

Recent anthropological attention to ruins and infrastructure has offered an opportunity for grounding social analysis in built environments and material structures. Yet if we understand ruins and rubble (Stoler 2013; Gordillo 2014) in a broad sense as integral elements of urban worlds—built on capitalist urbanization, nationalism, racism, and profound environmental change—then Berlin's ruderal ecologies can provide a lens through which to capture the complexity of lives in their midst. As the planet has been and becomes increasingly inhospitable to many beings, the question is: Which lives thrive and which lives fall apart?

This question takes us past a view of formal institutions, large-scale planning, and expert discourses about ecology, geography, nature, migration, or the environment—toward more tangible forms of inhabiting and relating to more-than-human urban worlds. Seen from this perspective, ecology emerges not only as a field of scientific expertise, or as the "naturalization of politics," but as "the recognition of the immense complexity involved for any entity—human or nonhuman—to have a voice, to take a stand, to be counted, to be represented, to be connected with others" (Latour and Weibel 2005, 458–59).

As climate change, capitalist exploitation, neocolonial formations, war, and racial and sexual violence continue to rupture and rearrange the fabric of life, different creatures are pulled into new connections to one another (Weston 2017, 4). Addressing these connections between unexpected neighbors and the lives that thrive or fall into ruin thus involves thinking across seemingly different registers of power.[47] In order to keep these different scales in view, it is necessary to open engagements with citizenship, science, and urban space to wider fields of relating—including across species. Ruderals thus demand the sharpening of one's peripheral vision and thinking across registers. As Austrian artist Lois Weinberger reminds us, ruderals call for modes of "precise inattention" (Kos 2004): if you are lucky, you catch a quick glimpse of them on your way to somewhere else. Perhaps it is no surprise then, as Sukopp told me, that he and other botanists like Scholz first came across sticky goosefoot and other ruderals while riding their bikes to work, or walking near their homes, catching a glimpse of them out of the corners of their eye.

As feminist writers and critical plant studies scholars have shown, capitalist and colonial practices of extraction have profoundly shaped botanical knowledge production and the relations between plants and people—rendering both as resources, exploiting their labor in plantations (Chao 2022; Haraway 2015; Haraway et al. 2016; Li and Semedi 2021) or reducing plants to mere objects of study and classification (Foster 2019, 2). These forms of simplifying and extracting life and doing ecology—embedded not only in plantations and modern science, but also in the grids of urban life—erase the complexities of people's relation to land and to other animate worlds (Myers 2017b, 7). Disrupting colonial and extractive ways of knowing and relating thus requires being attuned to the vulnerabilities of life and cultivating modes of perception that reach across scales and social categories. It also means shifting the view from a notion of technology or urban built environments as forms of mastery over nature to forms of embodiment and internalization, to webs of living and dying—and the unrealized potentials and futures yet to come in contemporary urban worlds (Haraway 2016; Le Guin 1989).[48]

Inspired by feminist and decolonial approaches (Ferdinand 2022; Kimmerer 2015; TallBear 2011) of "doing ecology otherwise" (Myers 2017b), a ruderal mode of analysis is rooted in (attention to) urban lands and yet committed to gleaning glimpses of the disparate more-than-human communities that inhabit them. This means more than simply adding plants and animals to previously human-centered analyses: it also means accentuating the ways in which human and vegetal worlds have coevolved and coconspired (Myers 2020; Szczygielska and Cielemecka 2019) to reshape urban life. The story of ruderal plants illustrates the persistence and labor of plant life and other life in the city—despite efforts to reduce other beings to resources for extraction, ornaments for anthropogenic land use, or matter that helps raise urban property values. Yet as capitalist urbanization and Europe's legacies of colonialism and racism dispossess people and continue to make urban worlds inhospitable to so many, it is important to account for the fractures in the midst of urban landscapes and to work against the notion of being rooted in the land as the basis for claims to national belonging, private property, and ethnic purity. A ruderal lens thus approaches urban life by gleaning, collecting, and capturing the "things that fall away" and yet may carry "the political seeds [of] an alternative future which already exists in the form of devalued social modes of experience" (Tadiar 2009, 9).

Reprise

Although the war's blasted landscapes have largely disappeared, their more intricate traces are still present throughout Berlin today. In my fieldwork, rubble landscapes were tangible not only in Herbert Sukopp's stories about botanical encounters but in countless other ways. When I took a stroll in the Hasenheide park, in Neukölln, or the Teufelsberg in Grunewald—one of the city's rubble hills—I walked on piles of debris, now carefully landscaped into the controlled nature of urban greenery. Digging into the soil, you soon touch traces of debris—shards of tiles, bricks, porcelain, broken glass. The bombed landscapes of the war were also an integral element of many elderly Berliners' memories. One of my neighbors, Adam, who had grown up in Berlin and witnessed the end of the war, remembered the night the streets "melted" during a bombing raid while his family was hiding from Nazi persecution. In Neukölln I often sat on a balcony with Nursen, who had migrated to Berlin from Istanbul in the 1970s. As we talked, we looked at the grenade holes that dotted the wall of the building next door. Each spring, birds nested in them. Walking in that same neighborhood, along the canal, one passes nineteenth-century apartment blocks perched right next to 1950s- and 1960s-style "modern" buildings—as well as a few open lots, now landscaped as little parks or gardens, or cemented over and converted into parking lots. Attending to these spatial gaps and layers of time, you get a sense of what the immediate postwar landscape might have looked like.[49]

In other parts of the city, the traces of the war's rubble are less subtle, and ruins have become a key element of official memory cultures and tourism; for example, tourists flock to search the ruins of the war symbolized by the bombed tower of the memorial church (Gedächtniskirche) in former West Berlin, or they search out the remnants of the Nazi past in the razed foundations of the former administrative Gestapo headquarters, first landscaped over in the 1950s, then excavated in the 1980s, and now called the Topography of Terror.[50] Beneath the city's surface, there is yet another layer of the history of war. Several times a year, construction workers stumble across unexploded bombs. As Brian Ladd (1997, 175) points out, unexploded ordnance threatens to make a mockery of "metaphors about an 'explosive' past."

Since the unification of East and West Berlin, many open spaces have been paved over and turned into private property. Some ruderal plants such as sticky goosefoot are thus becoming less widespread, their seeds remaining dormant. And yet there has been a renewed appreciation for urban nature flourishing in the city's derelict landscapes and postindustrial urban lands.

Berlin's ruins and abandoned lots have become tourist attractions, offering a playground for a flourishing underground music scene and urban dwellers indulging in the city's nightlife (Schwanhäußer 2010). Amid a widespread global fascination with ruins, wastelands, and green spaces, Berliners once again venture out to search for the unruly vegetation of abandoned lots in the city.[51] Captivated by the city's natural diversity, community events, outings, and groups have turned their attention and care to urban nature across the city. During Berlin's annual Urban Nature Day (Langer Tag der Stadtnatur), thousands of Berliners, together with environmentalists, conservationists, foresters, ornithologists, wildlife specialists, and other nature lovers, tour the city to explore the wonders of nature: they search for weeds on sidewalks or in abandoned lots, seek out foxes, follow the tracks of wild boar in the city's forests, or listen to the songs of nightingales and starlings while touring the city's parks at night. TV shows, books (Riechelmann 2004), news reports, and documentary films titled *Wildes Berlin* (Gockel and Koch 2013) or *Natura Urbana* (Gandy and Jasper 2017) feature the city and its peripheries' abundant wildlife, chronicling the lives of raccoons, wild boars, foxes, praying mantes, or ruderal plants such as trees-of-heaven, as permanent urban inhabitants.

Since unification, citizen initiatives have allied with city officials to transform formerly abandoned patches of land into public nature parks, such as the Schöneberger Südgelände (a former switchyard for trains), or the Gleisdreieck (an abandoned railway junction in an industrial area). More recently, the Tempelhofer Feld, once a municipal airport in West Berlin, was converted into a public park. A great diversity of wildlife, especially birds, have made the former airport their new home, and Berlin's human residents often take a stroll on former runways. This appreciation of urban nature and the wild is also institutionalized within city planning and conservation programs for urban habitats: with more than forty protected nature areas in Berlin, the city administration has been hoping to improve the quality of urban life by fostering a "diversity of nature" and heterogeneous landscapes in the city (SenStadt 2014). When I initially met Sukopp in 2007, we were attending a conference called "Sundew and Tree of Heaven" (Sonnentau und Götterbaum) in appreciation of Berlin's rich ruderal plant life. Since then, the city has organized an abundance of events promoting urban wilderness as an integral feature of the urban environment.

Yet as tourist brochures promote Berlin as a flourishing Green City and as Europe's Nature Capital, debates about immigrant segregation and unemployment have highlighted so-called troubled neighborhoods, parallel worlds, and ghettos in the city. After unification, unemployment rates and poverty rose among many Berliners, especially among the city's Turkish and Muslim immigrant communities. In the process, public discourse and policy has increasingly located the source of inequality and precarity in migrants themselves. Debates about the arrival of refugees in Europe and Germany have further fired up a language of social hot spots that stresses disconnection and invokes a sense of danger and nature becoming out of control: the danger of fire breaking loose, or of wilderness encroaching on the civilized city. In this context of intense national debate about migration and asylum, the city's green spaces—its urban forests, parks, and gardens—become sites of refuge and of hope for the creation of a more cosmopolitan city.

The question that remains is whether, not unlike after the war, contemporary efforts to rehabilitate urban ecologies will turn into yet another version of reconstructing the nation through nature that glosses over past and present racisms, exclusions, and destruction, or whether these will take steps toward forging alliances across differences and remain alert to the inherited histories of violence and exclusion in the urban landscape.

This question will guide my analysis in the following chapters.

Gardens

2

GARDENING THE RUINS

Berlin—a green city? Everyone loves to say it these days. But what is it? It's just a pile of concrete after all.
—Hakim, gardener in the Hasenheide park

Berlin is a city abundant with gardens. Arriving by train from any direction, you pass hundreds of rows of green plots rich with flowers, trees, and vegetable beds. Neatly landscaped bushes are interspersed with patches of grass and trails. Small garden shacks can be found in the middle of each lot. Perched alongside train tracks or tucked in between five-story-high apartment buildings, these gardens are usually fenced in and feature short, neatly mowed lawns. Here and there, a German flag rises above a garden shack. If you look closely, you might also find small clay or plastic figurines with bright red hats peeking through the bushes: the "garden gnome," a constant inhabitant, has been an icon of these gardens for the past century.[1]

In Berlin, as in many other German cities, these so-called allotment gardens (*Schrebergärten* or *Kleingartenkolonien*) are plentiful: as of 2022, there were around 880 allotment garden sites with ca. 71,000 individual garden plots spread across the city (SenUVK 2022b).[2] Since most of these garden plots are state property (i.e., of the state of Berlin), most residents lease them, paying both an initial fee (2,000–5,000 euros) and an annual fee of approximately 500 euros. Regulation of these plots tends to be very detailed—including prescriptions on the size and design of garden shacks and fences; restrictions on how often one can stay overnight in a cottage; regulations on the diversity and composition of flowers, vegetables, "weeds," and trees; and guidelines on the height of the grass. Nevertheless, these gardens are also spaces of diversity. They are not only abundant with flora but also rich in animal diversity, providing a habitat for various bird species as well as insects, amphibians, and vertebrates such as foxes, mice, gophers, and rats. Sometimes, a sounder of wild boar makes its way through the gardens' gates, in search of food.[3] Moreover, as allotment gardens are scattered across Berlin, they make an important contribution to cooling the city's temperatures and thus mitigating urban heat island effects (Fenner 2020).

Since the turn of the millennium, local and national newspapers have reported a "revival of the gardens," and allotment gardens have become increasingly popular in Berlin and other German cities. Journalists, politicians, and urban planners have rediscovered the allotment gardens—once considered an icon of German national identity—as important spaces of "social integration": the hope here is that working together in gardens fosters social relations across ethnic and racialized divides and mediates what is perceived to be immigrant isolation from German society (A. Wolf 2008).[4] In this context, "multicultural" or "intercultural" gardens, containing communal plots of land (in contrast to allotment gardens' separate fenced-in plots), have become especially popular. For example, the Berlin Senate adopted a measure that allows district authorities to allocate land specifically for multicultural gardens and to provide equipment to facilitate their start-up (C. Müller 2009). In addition, the urban planning department, neighborhood associations, and programs like the Quartiersmanagement (a city development and integration initiative partly funded by the Social City program of the EU and the federal German government, discussed below), as well as environmental groups and church organizations, have promoted gardens as important sites of integration. Politicians praise gardening and people's engagement with plants as opportunities to overcome language barriers and cultural differences: the hope is that nature will provide a refuge in the city and not divide communities. In 2007, for example, Berlin's Representative for Integration and Migration (Beauftragte für Integration und Migration) advocated for the gardens as an opportunity to let integration "grow":[5] "There is more than just fresh air in a garden. There is exchange, people take up responsibility and shape their environment; and you can see people's initiative, identification and integration grow" (Der Beauftragte des Senats für Integration und Migration 2007).[6]

Thus, since the mid-2000s, many multicultural community gardens have been founded across the city. These gardens are often located in neighborhoods where migrant communities reside. They are situated on abandoned railway yards, torn-down apartment building lots, and other vacant pieces of land. Located in different parts of the city, the gardens are diverse in participant structure and scope, and many are members of (or at least linked to) the nationwide Intercultural Foundation (Stiftung Interkultur) or other local intercultural initiatives.[7] The Stiftung Interkultur aims at fostering intercultural contact and ethnic integration through gardening and leisure activities; it also provides logistic support for gardens all over the country. The foundation has been recognized by many government agencies as a paradigm for projects of "integration," civic engagement promoting "tolerance," and environmental education.[8] Among its participants, there is a sense of being part of a social movement, and emerging scholarship has evaluated and promoted these gardens as promising "social spaces of micro-integration" (Werner 2008; see also Meyer-Renschhausen and Holl 2000; Rosol 2006).

Early in 2000, Christa Müller, one of the cofounders of the Stiftung Interkultur, suggested that while politicians and media proclaimed multiculturalism to have shattered long ago in neighborhoods like Kreuzberg, the beginnings of a "true" multicultural society were sprouting in intercultural gardens (C. Müller 2000). In these gardens, people exchange seeds, share recipes, cook and barbecue together, and bake bread in a communal oven. By sharing knowledge, preparing food, and growing vegetables—including those that people know from home—gardeners literally "grow roots" (C. Müller 2000). Thus, many people see intercultural gardens as "successful integration projects because they encourage participation and provide scope for formative action. Not only the soil but also the heterogeneous social community, the neighborhood where the garden is situated, must be turned over and refashioned" (C. Müller 2007, 55).

From this perspective, urban agriculture provides a wide range of possibilities: it creates a sense of belonging and freedom, and it puts people in touch with nature. The hope is thus that urban agriculture and nature allow people to move past judgment, commodification, and social division and instead create home and a sense of connection to community (C. Müller 2009) in a world dominated by a capitalist market, industrial agriculture, and loss of biodiversity. With their community orientation and explicit goals of self-empowerment and socio-ecological change, intercultural gardens thus differ from both allotment gardens—privately used plots, with clearly fenced-off boundaries—and public parks, in which care for land is handled by the local Office for Green Spaces or is privatized.

Since the fall of the Berlin Wall, public debate about migration has been subject to recurring moments of intensification across Europe. In this context, political discourse has highlighted integration as the dominant framework for understanding and approaching migration. Assuming a lack of integration into German society, imagined to be homogeneous and white, planners, media, and politicians have often equated urban spaces inhabited by migrants and communities of color with wastelands, blaming them for deteriorating urban environments and the emergence of so-called social hot spots (*soziale Brennpunkte*), ghettos, parallel societies (*Parallelgesellschaften*), or problem districts (*Problembezirke*). In contrast, seemingly pristine urban nature is often coded as a white space in which racialized people are absent. As cultural geographer Carolyn Finney (2014) has shown for "the environment" and the "great outdoors" in a US context, these cultural imaginaries assume urban nature to be cared for and accessed by mainly white people.[9] Challenging these practices and imaginaries, multicultural garden projects attempt to offer space for all Berliners to create a more cosmopolitan city. As local residents work the soil, trade seeds, and grow vegetables, it is hoped that they will create new forms of solidarity and inspire others to look beyond and across hedges, fences, and social boundaries (A. C. Wolf 2008).

Gardens can be sites of magic and transformation (Munn 1992), and as Lesley Stern (2017, 2020) reminds us, they can be a window into the world: the neighborhood, the country, our present time. In gardens, nature and culture, the foreign and domestic, and the fictitious and the real meet. Moreover, gardens signal the "provisional nature of modern definitions of culture" (Hartigan 2017, xviii). Indeed, the very term *culture* was derived from an engagement with the domestication of plant life (cultivation) before it came to signify a solely human domain of action. In Berlin and beyond, the history of people-plant relations is fraught with violence, colonial power, and racism. Western scientific knowledge production about plants and their economic uses has too often followed an extractive logic, fortified by the history of colonial botany and the plantation. Yet gardens do not always adhere to human schemes of order. As described in the previous chapter, plants are both followers and fugitives of culture. Gardens can therefore be seen as a stage for redefining people-plant relations (Myers 2019) as well as people's relationships with one another. With this in mind, the gardens in this chapter offer a terrain from which to explore forms of care for more-than-human worlds. Guided by a ruderal lens, I am specifically interested in those practices of care that do not approach urban lands and other beings as resources or governable entities, but sow seeds for future alternatives.

As people turn the soil and sow seeds, how do their gardening practices match up with or intervene in existing forms of urban governance and in racialized imaginaries about urban neighborhoods? How do different meanings of *culture* and *integration*—key terms shaping debates about migration and the urban environment in Germany and Europe today—become alive in gardening practices? By addressing these questions, we can see how caring for plants and other beings not only articulates with experiences of harm and displacement (Tironi and Rodríguez-Giralt 2017) but also offers new possibilities for collaboration and coconspiracy (Choy 2011; Myers 2019) in remaking urban worlds.

Attending to different gardens in Berlin, this chapter traces the contested and racialized meanings of migration in political discourse and everyday life in Germany. In the stories of three gardens—a multicultural garden, a secret garden between bushes in a public park, and a woman's courtyard garden—we see how local gardeners produce ecologies and socialities that do not neatly fit into (neo)liberal models of migration and multicultural diversity. Rather than adhere to the courses of action that migration policies, urban planning, and local authorities carve out for migrants (see also Çağlar 2001), gardeners create everyday forms of "ecological care" (Puig de la Bellacasa 2017) that are not easily recognized as political within the expert apparatuses of planning, policy-making, media, and science.[10] While they might be deemed irrelevant, these practices are embodied ways of knowing, rehabilitating, and acting upon harmed landscapes and people (Tironi and Rodríguez-Giralt 2017) in the ruins of Europe's racial and class inequalities.

While the history of gardening is deeply entangled with a politics of nationhood and race in Germany and Europe, there is no single story to be told about gardens. Gardens provide heterogeneous tools for connecting to a place and to others, as well as strategies for disrupting existing forms of belonging to the nation and to Europe. Although Berliners may hope to wall out history and social conflict through caring for plants and urban nature, history keeps creeping back into gardens. The garden stories I present are crowded with fences, bureaucracies, economies, and conflict. And yet they also forge unexpected solidarities and ways of being (and staying) alive in a context in which many migrants face racialization and are often seen as out of place or as potential threats to urban order. Growing roots in the cracks of the state's spatial ordering, in formal economies, and urban policies, gardens can produce new political pathways that do not easily align with (neo)liberal or multicultural efforts to govern difference (see also Hale 2005; Povinelli 2002). Juxtaposing seemingly different garden stories can thus help sharpen our attention on exactly those encounters across difference that disrupt existing forms of belonging and forge openings for less harmful urban relations.

A Brief History of Gardens

The popularity of urban gardening in Berlin emerges from a longer history of gardening as a key element of nation-making in Germany. In Berlin, gardeners' care for plants has historically been closely entangled with the governance of urban space and its residents, as well as the management of class, gender, and race inequalities in the city. Yet European gardening practices have also been linked to colonial legacies. With the onset of European imperialism, the collection and circulation of seeds and plants from the colonies helped consolidate "imperial landscapes" in both the metropole and the colony (Foster 2019; Grove 1995).[11] Indigenous knowledges about plants were often exploited and erased in the process (Schiebinger 2004). Adorning English and French gardens, as well as cities and colonial plantations in the Americas, many plants were utilized to build European cultural and economic hegemony at home and abroad (Casid 2005; Stoetzer 2020a). As part of the larger trend of what Jill Casid (2005) has called "imperial landscaping practices," the cultivation and global circulation of plants in Europe's "gardens"—ranging from the plantation to the city, to botanical gardens, or to parks—thus both symbolized and materialized imperial power throughout the eighteenth and nineteenth centuries.

As they proliferated throughout Europe, botanical gardens became sites of scientific inquiry, conservation, and public pedagogy in which multispecies relations reshaped the contours of nation and empire (Hartigan 2015). Moreover, with increasing industrialization, plantation agriculture extracted the labor of plants, soil, and people into "resources" for building the wealth of the global North (Tsing 2015). Vast exploitation and ecological destruction have been the lasting effect of this. Landscaping therefore became a colonial practice for both transforming the European metropole and conceiving "national borders, contact zones, and colonial peripheries" (Casid 2005, xxi–xxii). Transplanting vegetation from the metropole served as a key tool in making claims to land and enabling a future in the colony—a practice that always also contained the seeds for alternative futures (Casid 2005, xix).

Yet by the mid-nineteenth century, German cities hosted not only botanical but also other gardens. Alongside so-called paupers' gardens in other European countries, the idea for *Kleingärten* (small gardens, allotment gardens) originated with political leaders, municipal administrations, welfare organizations, and wealthy factory owners and landowners as a means by which to confront and control poverty, hunger, illness, and social conflict. Replacing welfare and financial support for the poor, paupers' gardens (*Armengärten*) and alcove colonies (*Laubenkolonien*) aimed at promoting self-sustenance for urban workers by allowing them to grow fruit and vegetables in the city (Lorbek and Martinsen 2015; SenUVK 2022a). In Berlin, the city administration created the first *Armengärten* as early as 1833. As Berlin expanded into a metropole and became the imperial capital of Prussia by 1871, more and more people moved from the countryside to the city. In this context, gardens offered a refuge for the working class and the poor from the crowded and dusty tenement apartments (*Mietskasernen*) in which they lived (Bodenschatz 1987). By the turn of the twentieth century, there were more than 40,000 garden lots in the city (Hilbrandt 2021, 34). Yet a wide array of agendas and rationales were at work in the gardens throughout this time, ranging from factory owners leasing out land for profit and increasing property values, to health organizations such as the Red Cross seeking to confront disease outbreaks at the beginning of the twentieth century, to residents claiming unused lands to grow their own vegetables and sustain themselves.[12] With urban infrastructure increasingly fragmenting urban lands, the *Deutsche Reichsbahn* (German Imperial Railway) also, for example, allowed its employees to garden alongside train tracks, thus utilizing the gaps in the city's fabric that had opened up (SenUVK 2022a).

While gardens offered space for workers to both recreate and grow their own vegetables, they were also a state strategy to ensure the continuation of the labor force, to strengthen white European moral sensibilities, such as the heterosexual family, and to distract workers from going to taverns (SenUVK 2022a; see also Stoler 1995). Often referred to as colonies, some of the urban gardens carried the names of actual German colonies at the time, such as "Togo" or "Kamerun" (van der Heyden and Zeller 2002)— and many still do so today, despite repeated protests by antiracist groups.[13] Colonial aspirations for ordering nature and human desire thus shaped both the design of these gardens and the intimacies between plants and people cultivated in them. By providing spaces for exercise and education, gardens also strengthened a sense of national belonging: the aim was to pedagogically harmonize class relations through recreation and bodily exercise. This form of urban nature thus became a refuge from workers' living conditions—conditions that were deemed to make workers prone to "moral decay" and deteriorating health (Rosol 2012), thus threatening to undermine the order of the "civilized" metropole.[14]

These national and colonial legacies of gardening intensified in Berlin and other German cities when the Nazi regime made gardening a privilege reserved for "honorable comrades of German blood," barring all Jewish people from allotment gardens (Stih and Schnock, cited in Mandel 2008, 123). This shift occurred at a time when concepts of nativeness and home (*Heimat*) had high currency: many landscape architects and garden designers followed the ideology of "blood and soil" and used the concept of nativeness to build gardens, echoing the Nazi imperative to cleanse the "German landscape" of foreign elements (Gröning and Wolschke-Bulmahn 1992).[15] Gardens and "natural" ways to eat and farm were thus promoted as expressions of the cultural superiority of the "Germanic people" and of an assumed mastery of white people over nature (see also Treitel 2017).[16] And yet despite these attempts, some of Berlin's gardens also provided an important refuge for Jewish people to hide from persecution during this time (Grossmann 2009, 88).

Allotment gardens also served important economic functions: during the economic crisis after World War I, and again after World War II, they provided food to an impoverished and displaced urban population (Hilbrandt 2021). When much of Berlin was destroyed after the bombing toward the end of World War II, many people also used them as permanent residences (SenUVK 2022a). During the Cold War, allotment gardens were encouraged by the state in the 1980s as a supplement to collectivized farming in East Germany (Fleischmann 2022; Fulbrook 1991, 236). Throughout the twentieth century, the popularity of gardens attests to their role as "scenes and products of a network of social, physical and symbolic orderings" of space—gardens became an "amplification of the house" (Gröning and Schneider 1999, 150). Accessible to large parts of the population, they became sites of "habitual reordering," everyday homemaking strategies, and "intense personalization" (Gröning and Schneider 1999). Throughout Germany's history, gardens thus rearticulated different yet related dimensions of *oikos* (from which stems the English prefix eco-, as in eco-logy, but also eco-nomy, which can both be understood as involving the study of homelife and homemaking strategies; see also Paxson 2013, 32). By caring for plants and land in the city's gardens, residents made kin, and intimately entangled the care for plants with gendered and racialized notions of home, belonging, and moralities of nationhood. At the same time, gardens became both an integral element of urbanization and its antidote.

While the recent popularity of urban gardens is situated within this longer historical background, it certainly cannot be explained by this history alone. As Moore, Kosek, and Pandian point out, the couplings of particular racisms, naturalisms, and other politics of difference articulate in historically contingent ways and cannot simply be "'read off' from an underlying structural logic" (2003, 3).[17] Instead, we have to ask about the political stakes of the mobilization of people-plant relations and other more-than-human relations for remaking the social at particular historical moments.

Keeping this in mind, the popularity of gardens in contemporary Berlin is entangled with a series of social and political conjunctures: changing conservation policies, Germany's self-fashioning as one of the most environmentally oriented countries, and the rise of global social movements demanding political solutions to the climate crisis and industrial agriculture's destructive effects all make gardening in cities increasingly desirable to so many people. In addition, as Marit Rosol (2006) points out, civic engagement in green spaces appears at a time of a "crisis of green space" in Berlin and elsewhere. This is a time of neoliberal policy-making, when the maintenance and care of public green space is often transferred from the state to the responsibility of individual volunteer citizens or private companies. This development can be traced back to Berlin's fiscal crisis in the 1990s, as well as to a more general retreat of the social welfare state in Europe and Germany (Rosol 2006, 2012).

Dreams of urban gardens in today's Berlin also reveal changing national anxieties centered on migration, race, and "urban decay." As Michael Bennett and David Teague remark, in the North American context, urban desires for "nature" and appeals to "urban wilderness" often engage racialized ideas of spaces of otherness (framed as "savage") and white fears of the "ghetto" (1999, 6).[18] Indeed, Berliners' desire for urban nature and the popularity of gardens occur at a historic moment in which migration policies and urban planning practices seek to integrate and govern migrants in the city. In a climate of intense public attention to migration and the presence of Middle Eastern and Black migrants in Europe—in the aftermath of unification, 9/11, and the so-called refugee crisis of 2015—the two Berlin boroughs of Kreuzberg and Neukölln moved to the center of national concern about the impact of migration on the urban landscape. Thus, in order to better understand Berlin's gardens, it is important to first consider this city's shifting ecologies of migration and the racialization of some urban environments as troubled wastelands.

The Racialization of Urban Nature in Berlin

Brennpunkt: *combustion point, hotbed or hotspot, skid row, or troubled neighborhood*

hotbed: *an environment conducive to vigorous growth or development, especially of something undesirable*

hotspot: *an area in which there is dangerous unrest or hostile action*

—Definitions from LEO German–English Dictionary (http://dict.leo.org/)

Kreuzberg and Neukölln are two adjacent boroughs in southeastern Berlin with a long history of shifting borders and migrations. In the seventeenth century, Huguenot Protestant refugees sought asylum from persecution by French Catholics in Kreuzberg, building elaborate "French" vegetable gardens and orchards (Düspohl 2009). From the early nineteenth century, when the area was mostly meadowlands and orchards outside of the old city walls, both districts expanded and became the crossing point for the flow of goods, people, and livestock soon to be incorporated into the expanding city. In the nineteenth century, immigrants from Silesia, Pomerania, and East Prussia who had lost their land settled in the area in search of work (Mandel 2008, 151). Since the beginning of the twentieth century, when Berlin's population had grown to almost 2 million (from about 200,000 in the early 1800s), both Neukölln and Kreuzberg were inhabited by many working-class residents who moved to the city from the countryside in search of work (Mandel 2008).

After World War II, the two districts lay within the American sector, along the edges of the Berlin Wall which divided the city into two halves and cut off West Berlin from the surrounding countryside. Because of the proximity of the Berlin Wall, almost all the streets in the northeastern parts of both districts were dead ends. In the 1970s and 1980s, many neighborhoods in these districts became the new home of so-called guest workers from Turkey, Greece, and Spain, largely because of their low housing costs. Impacted by this history, the northeastern part of Kreuzberg became especially well known for both its multicultural population and a bohemian lifestyle shaped by the Berlin punk rock movement and alternative subcultures in the 1970s. Attracted by the cultural scene and low living costs, many young West Germans also moved to the divided city in order to avoid military service (which was not mandatory for West Berlin residents).[19]

Today, many Turkish Germans and other (first-, second-, or third-generation) Middle Eastern immigrants own small family businesses in the area—from vegetable stores and bakeries to electronics shops, cafés, and popular Döner kebab stands.[20] One Kreuzberg neighborhood that is often referred to as "Little Istanbul," the so-called SO36, centers on several large apartment buildings surrounding a local underground train station near the Kottbusser Gate (the former southern, pre-twentieth-century city gate, often referred to as the Kotti). During the city's division, the area was just a few blocks from the Berlin Wall. Affordable rents attracted many migrants who had come to the city, while squatters moved into the area's abandoned buildings and lots, creating a lively music and anarchist scene. A nearby "Turkish market" marks the edge of both Kreuzberg and Neukölln. This was also the area in which I lived during my research stays from 2007. It is situated along one of the few green spaces in the area—the Landwehrkanal, designed in the mid-nineteenth century by Prussian gardener and landscape architect Peter Joseph Lenné.[21] On weekdays, the market bustles with vegetable stands, pastries and breads, household supplies, fabrics, and the fragrant aromas of spices and scents of freshly baked Börek.[22] Shoppers from across the city, including tourists, stroll along the canal's banks past vegetable stands. Turkish German women pull shopping carts filled with vegetables behind them, while sellers shout out the newest sale prices in a mix of Turkish and German. On the canal, tourists float by in boats while microphone-amplified voices of tour guides emanate through the trees from the banks.

Covering about twenty square miles of cobblestone streets, Kreuzberg and Neukölln's buildings range from eighteenth-century preserved village structures to mid-twentieth-century-style apartment blocks—with a few green spaces and parks dotted in between. After the collapse of the Berlin Wall in 1989, the two districts were suddenly located adjacent to the new city center instead of in the shadow of the wall. The 1990s were marked by a period of nationalist euphoria and a construction boom for building a new global Berlin. After an abundance of failed large-scale construction projects and an overestimation of initial growth in the real estate market, which had failed to materialize, the city plunged into a fiscal crisis in the late 1990s. This period was marked by rising unemployment rates and poverty, especially among migrant communities and asylum seekers (Lanz 2007,

124).[23] With high unemployment rates in Kreuzberg and Neukölln, local politicians and national media increasingly labeled the districts as troubled immigrant neighborhoods.

As many refugees from the Middle East and Africa were not permitted to work in Berlin, they have had few options to find work beyond informal or criminalized economies. While national and local media center their attention on crime and drug dealers in local parks and green spaces, many Black people and Berliners of color who are racialized and labeled as migrants or refugees (independent of their actual status) have experienced racial profiling by local police in their everyday lives (see also El-Tayeb and Thompson 2019). After the turn of the millennium, conflicts and fights at several local high schools triggered nationwide debates about violence and an alleged resistance to integration among Turkish and Arab migrant youth.[24] Parts of Kreuzberg and Neukölln were increasingly stigmatized as hot spots and moved to the center of policing strategies and racial profiling. Since then, community organizations such as Reach Out Berlin, ISD (Initiative Schwarzer Menschen in Deutschland), and Black Lives Matter Berlin, as well as refugee activist groups such as Women in Exile and the VOICE Refugee Forum, have chronicled racist violence among local police and continue to demand institutional change.[25]

Education and derelict urban environments are code words in a political discourse that claims the failure of multicultural society and emphasizes the need for integration of migrants of color. While unemployment, poverty, and crime remain a reality in parts of Kreuzberg and Neukölln, this discourse tends to locate the source of social problems in migrants themselves. Some of the districts' neighborhoods have entered the national imagination as so-called ethnic enclaves, *Problembezirke* (problematic areas), or *soziale Brennpunkte* (hot spots or combustion points) that threaten to turn into closed-off "ghettos" and parallel societies (*Parallelgesellschaften*) outside the state's reach, posing a hazard to the social order.[26] Comparisons to ghettos in America and the French *banlieues* at the edges of Paris abound.[27]

This heightened national attention paid to Berlin's migrant hot spots has occurred in a broader European political context in which migration from the Middle East and Africa has become the focus of a new racism that centers on "cultural difference," especially of Muslim migrants, and the dereliction of urban neighborhoods (see also El-Tayeb 2012). In the aftermath of 9/11 and subsequent "refugee crises," nationalist, anti-Black, and Islamophobic agendas have framed many local and national political responses. Allusions to hot spots—a term used to describe migration hubs and arrival centers across the Mediterranean and Europe—stigmatize these spaces as dangerous sites of otherness and potential hazard. The physical environments that Muslims and other migrants of color inhabit thus become markers of immutable difference and are thus racialized.

In Germany, these racialized ecologies of migration involve not only the racialization of space and place (see also Brown 2005; Waquant 2008), but also the ways in which racial inequalities structure more than human relations. These ecologies are situated within a national discourse that approaches migration via a framework of integration to the extent that the terms have become synonymous (Ronneberger and Tsianos 2009, 143), at least symbolically. Since 2006, conferences such as the Islam Conference and Integrationsgipfel (Integration Summit) have been organized. These conferences are highly publicized events that gather political and social actors from unions, migrant organizations, political parties, and industry to discuss and solve "problems of immigrant integration" and develop a "national integration plan." Yet efforts like mandatory language instruction and integration classes do not apply uniformly to all migrants; instead, they specifically apply to migrants of color from the Middle East, Africa, and other regions in the global South.

Social accountability is thus placed on people to "catch up" to white liberal European standards and to prove themselves worthy of inclusion in the public arena, in policy, and in daily practice (Ronneberger and Tsianos 2009, 137, 149).[28] Migrants from the Middle East are especially imagined to be part of a homogeneous, non-Western, backward, and patriarchal Islamic culture that lags behind and stands in opposition to a secular Europe. Echoes of colonial efforts to "civilize" communities of color abound. As Kien Nghi Ha (2006, 16) has pointed out, integration, in this way, becomes a "dazzling and seductive fix point" across not only German but European political discourse, signaling "ideological innocence, inner stability, economic efficiency and cosmopolitan openness all at once"—leaving whiteness and Eurocentrism as central elements of liberal political discourse intact. Consequently, integration becomes "an official concept of political control of immigrants" (Ronneberger and Tsianos 2009, 143) that displaces a broader discussion of exclusions and racism as structural elements of the social fabric.

In this context, social projects such as the so-called Quartiersmanagement were created to combat racial segregation, poverty, and "urban decay" in "areas with special need for development" such as the Kottbusser Gate in Kreuzberg and North Neukölln (Marcuse 2006).[29] These initiatives seek to improve "quality of life" by funding neighborhood education and crime prevention projects, but also through environmental initiatives such as neighborhood cleanup days, urban gardening projects, street tree-planting activities, or school nature outings. After the Social City program was implemented, some neighborhoods transformed significantly, with mixed results: while unemployment rates went down (also due to the end of the fiscal crisis) and new educational opportunities were created, property and rent prices rose, displacing poorer residents, migrants, and people of color. With housing advertised to international professionals attracted to Berlin's "gritty" and cosmopolitan neighborhoods, gentrification has become a big concern in neighborhoods such as North Neukölln, and local activists have organized to fight displacement.

As the spatial politics of migration become matters of concern in the city (Mandel 2008; Ronneberger and Tsianos 2009, 142), policy-making and public discourse often take on an environmental bent and assume specific ecologies of "diversity" in the city. Representations of migrant neighborhoods as hot spots gloss over a history of state intervention into migration and its impact on urbanization processes and place-making (Mandel 2008, 89–91; Ronneberger and Tsianos 2009). Whereas the Nazis forced Jews to segregate and live in ghettos, post–World War II residence regulations have attempted to balance populations and distribute non-EU immigrants—especially those from Turkey—across Berlin neighborhoods (Mandel 2008, 89; Ronneberger and Tsianos 2009, 144). The underlying racist assumptions in these policies are that a large concentration of migrants of color has a potentially explosive quality and that what is assumed to be spatial segregation threatens to destroy society. As a consequence, non-German citizens often account for only 20 to 30 percent of the population in districts that are nevertheless perceived as predominantly Turkish, Arab, or migrant spaces.

The attempt to counter the danger of segregation by creating spatial balance and maintaining diversity also appears in urban greenery policies. A "Green Berlin" brochure published by the city follows this rationale:

> From an urban planning perspective, a city quarter that is supposed to function and attract permanent residents requires above all a balanced blend of living and commerce, of residential, transportation and green spaces and, not least, a heterogeneous population in which old and young and different nationalities can live together. The qualification and upgrading of public spaces is an essential objective of urban development, and it benefits the residents of all districts of the city. Green

spaces and recreational areas are of elementary importance especially in densely built-up inner-city areas. They reduce noise and pollution, thereby improving the quality of life. . . . Not least, green spaces also have a social function as meeting places insofar as they contribute to the integration of all segments of the population. (SenStadt 2009, 55)

The value of diversity, both human and nonhuman, is invoked by politicians, planners, and policy-makers and is captured in words such as *Abschottung* (walling off), *Toleranzschwellen* (threshold of tolerance), *Brennpunkt* (hot spot), and *Belastungsgrenzen* (impact limits)—terms that conjure images of fire, impact, and walls to suggest that immigrants constitute a force of nature and are walling themselves off from the rest of society, reaching thresholds and limits.

The 2010 publication of a book by Thilo Sarrazin, former center-left Social Democratic finance minister of Berlin, offers a view into the ecology of these racialized fears. *Deutschland schafft sich ab* (Germany does away with itself) triggered heated national debate and initiated a decidedly biopolitical, spatial, and racialized turn in political discourse. Although the book received strong opposition from some Social Democrats, it directed focus to Muslim migrants' alleged unwillingness to integrate into German society—a theme that continued to shape much public debate for years to come. Painting a gloomy picture of a mentality of state dependence in the crumbling capital, Sarrazin accused the city's Turkish and Arab communities of not being "economically productive," except for "selling fruit and vegetables,"[30] and thus of not participating "in the normal economic cycle" (*Lettre International* 2009) across multiple generations. Infused with biological and cultural essentialisms, Sarrazin's text fixated on migrant reproductive rates and an alleged lack of education among Muslims.[31]

Sarrazin's book also claimed that immigrants' lack of environmental consciousness left traces of dereliction on the city's built and natural environment—for example, by littering streets with old furniture or electronics, or by barbecuing in the city's parks and producing garbage and smoke. Comparing Neukölln and its "increasing atmosphere of despair" to the Harlem of the 1950s, the text portrayed an embattled Germany in which migrants "colonize" city space and bring "traditional cultural beliefs"— imagined to be patriarchal—from rural Anatolia without care for their local surroundings. Although Sarrazin's theses did not remain unchallenged, these images of physical decay and danger in Germany's migrant spaces have continued to infuse rhetoric across the political spectrum.[32] For example, the anti-immigration populist party AfD (Alternative für Deutschland) has drawn on this imagery to support its portrayal of refugees "flooding" into Germany like a natural force bringing ruination upon cities.[33]

These scenarios of urban environments as ruins invoke what Andrew Light (1999) has called the metaphoric transformation of urban space into a wilderness marked as alien or savage: the unknown at the edge of civilization that comes to haunt white imaginations of the city. With its emphasis on separation and "backwardness" pitched against European middle-class rationality, this imagery stands in the way of understanding the complexities of urban life (A. Light 1999, 140).[34] Moreover, as Indigenous feminist critic Erica Violet Lee points out about the racialized settler colonial politics of wastelands, the idea of wastelands has functioned as a common tool in the maintenance of racial inequality and colonial control: when the land and bodies of communities of color are equated with wastelands, they are rendered unworthy of collective care (Lee 2016). Yet wastelands can also become spaces of care and healing in which people refuse the existing and exclusive definitions of worthiness (Lee 2016).

While Light's and Lee's analyses refer to the North American context, many Berlin neighborhoods that are inhabited by communities of color are also framed as "urban wilderness," entangling the ecologies of urban space with racialization. Exceeding what some scholars have called the "new racism" in Europe—defining difference in cultural rather than biological terms—racialization here is mapped onto space and physical environments while rendering Berlin as a crumbling German capital and Europe as in ruins.[35] Such foci on decay and disconnection elide the actual forces that deprive people of sustainable futures and ignore the ways in which migrants and communities of color relate to and make urban ecologies otherwise (see also Myers 2017b). It is with this attention to remaking and imagining urban ecologies otherwise that I now turn to the gardens of today's Berlin.

A Garden between a Mosque, a Cemetery, and a Former Airport

At the western edge of Neukölln, there is a small plot of land called the Pyramid Garden. It is nestled in between the runway of Berlin's former Tempelhof Airport, the Hasenheide (Rabbit Heath) park, a Christian and a Muslim cemetery, and one of the city's biggest mosques—the Berlin Türk Şehitlik Camii.[36] Since its opening in spring 2007, the Pyramid Garden has been tended by local residents. The garden project's official purpose, according to its founders and a small brochure handed out to all newcomers, is to create a place of neighborliness, community, and cultural encounter in a neighborhood with many migrant residents and previously little public green space. Offering space for local organizations to meet and network, the garden project aspires to contribute to the integration of people across cultures and generations into Berlin society, and to help change the reputation of Neukölln as a problematic district. Like other local integration projects (such as the Quartiersmanagement), politicians and local media have promoted the Pyramid Garden as a paradigm of integration.

When I first began participating in the garden's activities, things were just getting started. Some of the beds had already been planted, and flowers and vegetables were starting to grow: beans, tomatoes, lettuce, cabbage, potatoes, peppers, basil, and tarragon. Sunflowers towered over a bed of squashes, radishes, and a few herbs that peeked through the ground. In one corner, one of the gardeners had decided to leave a few "weeds" that had grown while the land was still abandoned; these ruderals, giant goldenrod, reminded him of the rubble plants growing after the war when he was a child (fig. 2.1).

A few years earlier, the plot of land had been maintained by the city's Office for Green Spaces (Grünflächenamt) and was used by the adjacent cemetery as storage space for equipment. Due to budget cuts and layoffs, the space had been shut down and was left unused—until the garden was started in 2007. Surrounded by red brick walls on three sides and a little fence bordering the cemetery, the empty space comprised half an acre of land. Toward the cemetery, you could see a little grove of trees and shrubs, with old, crooked graveyard stones peeking through. The mosque's minarets towered high above the land.

Someone gave the space the name "pyramid garden" because of the shape of the roofs on the adjacent storage barracks. By the time I arrived, an artist had set up shop along the edge of the plot, with a little garden shack. With permission from the city, he collected the gravestones from graves with expired tenancy in the cemetery. The gravestones ranged from marble to simple rock. Stacked up on top of each other, they now awaited a second life as art sculptures.

Integration with a Fence?

Although the garden's official aim was to foster the integration of Berliners across cultures and generations, its participants shared disparate hopes and dreams. For some, the garden was full of secrecy, wonder, and a sense of

FIGURE 2.1 Giant goldenrod (*Solidago gigantea*) in the Pyramid Garden.
Photo by author.

magic. For others, it was a welcome opportunity to socialize, build com-munity, and prove that the neighborhood was much better than its reputa-tion. Some people voiced a sense of surprise: the garden was riddled with bureaucratic nightmares and too often became a site of enforcement of white German ideas on how to relate to urban nature. Finally, for others, the garden simply provided a space for growing their own vegetables, fruit, and flowers—some of them familiar from home.

Mario was in his midsixties and had lived in Neukölln his entire life. Recently unemployed, he was eager to get busy. The formerly unused space and adjacent cemetery had always been a mystery to him but was also full of memories. As a child, he loved to follow the paths along the graves in the Christian cemetery. Beyond the bushes and a big gate cordoning off the cemetery's edges, you could see a half-moon peeking through from the Muslim cemetery. Playing marbles on the sidewalk as a child, Mario recalled Neukölln's streets being full of public life. The adults would sit outside on sidewalks or lean out their windows to chat with neighbors; this was long before people turned inward, toward their living rooms, hiding behind their TVs. For Mario, a white German Berliner, the era after World War II was never a story of segregation but one of mutual exchange—for example, when Turkish migrants settled in the neighborhood and bakeries adopted both local and Turkish recipes. Meanwhile, German and Turkish youths taught each other games on the street.

Yet many migrant gardeners told quite different stories about their lives in Berlin. Cem, in his fifties, had lived in Neukölln since the 1970s when he migrated from Anatolia to Berlin. As he had already participated in several neighborhood projects of the Quartiersmanagement in a small Neukölln neighborhood nearby (Schillerpromenade), he was interested in building a multicultural garden to help foster integration and good neighborly relations in the area. Together with his wife, Emine, his son, Ali, and his mother, Ayşe, who was in her late seventies, he began to cultivate one of the first vegetable beds in the garden. Cem was eager to have regular meetings and was interested in ongoing discussions about how the garden plots could improve. He also dreamed of growing vegetables to sell or share with other (multicultural) gardens across the city. When Ayşe became ill and Cem and his family were too busy taking care of her, their neighbors Serife and Mehmet took over their plot.

By spring of the following year, Serife and Mehmet had planted seeds they had brought from relatives living at the Black Sea near the city of Samsun. Beans, peppers, and savoy cabbage soon grew on the plot. Mehmet would have liked to grow watermelons too, but they would always fare badly in Berlin's chilly climate. The cabbage, however, thrived. In addition to sharing it with others in the garden and with kin, Serife also used it to make *dolma* every week: she cooked the leaves until they were soft, then wrapped them around rice and a mix of minced meat, onions, parsley, and other herbs and spices. Soon, an adjacent plot in the garden became available and Mehmet and Serife grew even more beans and cabbage (fig. 2.2). Some gardeners started teasing them for their "mass industrial production site" that now was able to feed the entire garden community. Yet Mehmet and Serife wanted an even bigger plot of land. During their thirty years in Berlin, they had lived in a small apartment without a garden or balcony. Growing peppers and tomatoes in pots on their windowsills, they had always yearned for the big gardens that provided sustenance for their families back in Turkey and the Black Sea area.

Mehmet had previously worked on an assembly line at a local electronics manufacturing company. When many companies moved away from Berlin after unification, he had lost his job and remained unemployed for years. While he now had a part-time job, he still had plenty of time to spend in the

FIGURE 2.2 Beans and cabbage in the Pyramid Garden. Photo by author.

garden—unlike Serife, who worked cleaning offices and homes full time. So Mehmet tended the garden, watered the plants, and did the weeding, and Serife took care of the harvest.

Their garden plot neighbor Nadira, who had fled Iran after the revolution, lived in a small apartment a few blocks away. She had wanted a piece of land in Berlin for a long time. For her, the garden plot was a peaceful refuge in the middle of the city. Nadira's vegetable beds featured tall sunflowers, radishes, savory Persian basil, and tarragon that her sister had brought from Iran.

Thomas, a self-proclaimed native Berliner and one of the garden's founders, had also lived in Neukölln for many years. After years of struggle with the district government for access to the space, he was proud that the garden was finally coming to life. In his vegetable bed, tomatoes, squash, basil, and arugula were thriving. In addition to his volunteer work in the garden, Thomas ran a small environmental consulting company. Based in Neukölln, the company had initiated a series of projects to transform the local urban environment—ranging from a campaign for a "cleaner Neukölln" that encouraged residents to pick up dog feces on the street to building aviaries in courtyards or cultivating flower patches around street trees. Many of these projects were funded by the Social City program and were supported by several local Quartiersmanagement in Neukölln.

Thomas lamented a widespread carelessness among people in the neighborhood and what he called a negative attitude toward their environment (*Umwelt*). To him, as an entrepreneur, the multicultural garden represented a chance to demonstrate that people, as he put it, do not rely on the state to take care of their leftover objects on the street and clean up after them. In addition to improving the neighborhood's image, for Thomas, greening the city meant caring for one's social surroundings, connecting with neighbors, and getting past a fear of bureaucracies by working together with institutions to grow plants in public spaces.

On weekdays, Thomas, Serife, Mehmet, Cem, Nadira, and Mario showed up whenever they had time, to water plants and tend the garden. On the weekends, people socialized, worked on communal projects, and met to discuss things that needed to be done. The garden meetings were often animated by quarrels. One sunny Sunday morning, while a visiting newspaper photographer was taking pictures of the diverse plants in the garden, members met to discuss the garden's future. The main item on the agenda was the upcoming opening party. A heated debate unfolded about the size and publicity of the event: Should there be 200 guests and a big stage for musicians? Or would a big crowd trample the vegetable beds and grass and destroy everything? As the meeting went on, quarrels multiplied. Several gardeners on limited budgets criticized the high membership price for garden plots (200 euros per year) and lack of access to communal gardening. While communal activities so far had included helping to clean out the shed, watering plants, and deciding on major changes, some had neglected their duties. In addition, Susanne, a German student, and Nadira were upset at Thomas for cutting down a tree in a corner of the garden without consulting others. Other gardeners complained about a neglected vegetable bed, overgrown with weeds, and suggested giving the plot's caretakers an ultimatum to pull the weeds by a set deadline.

Another point of dispute was the relationship between the gardeners and the artist, Klaus, who used part of the space but who did not participate in any gardening activities. Someone had recently knocked down and broken one of Klaus's sculptures. He was now requesting reimbursement and that a fence be erected between the garden and the art space. Grudgingly, the gardeners decided to agree to his demands—in the interest of public relations and to avoid the perception of the gardeners as reckless.

The following Sunday, everyone gathered again in the afternoon to build the fence. Just as people had begun to lay the groundwork for the construction, Fred, a neighbor in his sixties who had an allotment garden in another part of Neukölln, came by, curious to inspect the new garden. When he saw the gardeners building the fence, he was infuriated. Familiar with elaborate fencing from his own allotment garden association, he was frustrated with what he considered to be a German tendency to build fences around everything. Just as Thomas was placing fence posts into a fresh cement base, Fred launched into a tirade: "Why do you need a fence here? People will jump over it anyway if they want to damage the sculptures." Thomas responded, joking, "We are building a fence between art and nature"; and Nadira said, "You only have a civilized garden if there is a fence!" Fred continued in a cynical tone: "Yes, that's right. Over there is the enemy! Watch out! Why do you need cement in the ground to hold up the stakes of the fence? Why does it need to be so sturdy? It's like a fortress! Who will lean against it so that it needs to be covered in cement? Wild boar? That's what you call preparing for the next war. I thought this was a multicultural garden. No, this is integration with a fence!"

With his rant at the fence, Fred was reacting to what he considered an all-too-familiar German adherence to rules, orderliness, and a tendency toward excessive fortification. Built into concrete, the fence was literally set in stone. Like Fred, others also voiced frustration at the constant bickering and proliferating divisions in the garden. People's hopes for a peaceful refuge in the middle of the city were crushed by endless fights over bureaucracy, rules, building fences, ripping out weeds, saving gardeners' reputations, cleanliness, and chopped down trees. In addition, with fairly high annual fees, many could not afford to pay for a garden plot. For some, the garden thus resembled a gated community, creating its own insular nature rather than a transformed urban ecology reaching across difference. Indeed, the gardeners' bickering revealed the slipperiness of "integration." The constant bickering also suggested that integration via care for plants did not work out in predictable ways: contrary to the ideal of a peaceful refuge that connected people, fences popped up, bureaucracies got in the way, trees were cut down, and frustrations were voiced. Worse yet, high fees excluded eager gardeners. But in spite of the conflict and with no other options for other land, the gardeners stuck around. And even beyond their garden's hedges, other, less well-funded and less publicized gardens emerged.

Maria Mama

The Hasenheide, or Rabbit Heath, is a park in Neukölln directly across from Pyramid Garden, the mosque, and the former Tempelhof Airport. Covering about 50 hectares of green meadows, traces of nationalism and the city's imperial history pervade the park's landscape. Dotted with oak and beech trees, elderberry shrubs, a rhododendron grove, a small pond with luscious vegetation, and winding paths throughout, the park features a small kiosk, an orientalist-themed "adventure playground," an open air theater and cinema, a basketball court, a skateboarding area and miniature golf course, a nature trail, a leash-free zone for dogs, and a small petting zoo with goats and sheep.

The park's name harkens back to its original use as a royal rabbit-hunting ground. In the seventeenth century, the local elector, who acquired the land and built a fence around it, incited the anger of local farmers who had used the meadows as pasture for their livestock. In the early nineteenth century, the first public gymnastics facility was opened here by Friedrich Ludwig Jahn, the nationalist founder of the eighteenth- and nineteenth-century German gymnastics movement.[37] An admirer of the Hasenheide, Alexander von Humboldt once wrote about the park while he was traveling through Russia: "Ganz Sibirien ist eine Fortsetzung unserer Hasenheide" (All of Siberia is a continuation of our Rabbit Heath).[38] In 1936, the Hasenheide was landscaped as a park in the tradition of the *Volkspark* or *Volksgärten* (people's parks/gardens) created at the turn of the nineteenth century in Germany with the intention of providing urban residents access to nature and recreation. After World War II, one of Berlin's many rubble hills was constructed at the edge of the park; today, it towers seventy meters above the park's landscape.

Since the early 2000s, the park also moved to the center of discourses on crime. Portrayed as dangerous in national and local media, images abound of escalating battles between "bands" of Arab and African drug dealers, many of them refugees. Framed by these images, police seem helpless in the face of escalating conflicts, and the park's pristine landscape appears to be "lost" to local crime. Meanwhile, media often proclaim the Hasenheide as something of a no-go area for "normal" (meaning white) German citizens, revealing the highly racialized public affects surrounding the park.[39] At the same time, "wild barbecuing" (*wildes Grillen*)—especially popular among Turkish German Berliners—was outlawed in the park a long time ago. A series of neighborhood groups initiated events to "take back the park" by caring for its nature—for example, by organizing a leaf-raking day or constructing a new nature trail.

Despite the media and public flurry, there is a small corner of the park invisible to local authorities, situated between bushes and adjacent to a meadow of sunbathing nudists. Cultivated by a group of friends and former coworkers, this secret garden features fruit trees, sunflowers, tomatoes, strawberries, cucumbers, mint, peppers, and a few nettles in between. Hidden in the shrubs, there is also barbecue. The gardeners, all men ranging from their late fifties to seventies, live nearby and come to the park every day, bringing food, plants, drinks, and card games. Most of the gardeners migrated from rural Anatolia to Berlin in the 1960s or 1970s, when Turkey signed contracts with West Germany to tackle unemployment by sending migrant workers to cities like Berlin to help rebuild the country and boost Germany's economy from the ruins of war. When Hakim arrived in Berlin in 1969, he was assigned a few square meters of living space in the city's migrant barracks.[40] In the following decades, the West German government asserted that Germany was not a country of immigration and introduced regulatory measures to limit guest workers' rights to stay permanently in Germany (Mandel 2008, 148). As a result, Hakim, like many other Turkish Berliners, continued to be perceived as a temporary guest worker.

Hakim felt that he had paid a big price in Germany, working jobs that required strenuous physical labor for so many years. Like Hakim, many of his friends and colleagues depended on walking aids or wheelchairs and suffered from physical impairments at a relatively young age. Indeed, due to hard physical labor and environmentally hazardous working conditions, rates of early retirement and disability among Turkish immigrants and Turkish Berliners have been disproportionately high. Studies show that close to 50 percent of former guest workers have faced serious illnesses during their time in Germany (Lüneburg 2006). Women have been especially affected. Despite some growing awareness about health and care inequities, city administrations, public health officials, and social service institutions have given these little attention in Berlin for a long time. Due to Germany's long-standing commitment to only temporary work and visa permits, and its fairly late affirmation as a country of immigration, no special arrangements have been made for the care of elderly migrants. In much public debate, frail health is often attributed to the actions of migrants themselves and seen as a consequence of their lack of integration. Here, language skills, an assumed lack of cultural networks, the "stress of migration," and migrants' focus on return are used as the rationales for the development of health issues, instead of the consideration of working conditions and labor rights (see, e.g., Lüneburg 2006).

Hakim had worked for an electronics company assembling adapters, but due to a chronic neck injury from years of repetitive manual labor, he, like Osman Kalın, who built the Berlin tree house featured in the story told at the beginning of this book, had to retire early. A widower, he had a dog—a Doberman—that he began taking to the park for walks and training sessions. Soon he and the dog participated in agility championships, winning prizes. Then one year, when Hakim went to Turkey for the summer and left the dog with his brother and cousin in Germany, the dog's leg was injured; it never recovered. The dog's health deteriorated and, when it died, Hakim started going to the park every day to play music and see his friends—like Kadir, who had lost his eyesight as the result of a workplace injury. According to Hakim, they began cultivating the garden because "we were here all the time anyway." It must have been Erol, another of their friends, they recalled. Bored, he started moving the earth back and forth one day as he sat on the bench chatting with them. In fact, Erol claimed that he had accidentally dropped some sunflower seeds and they eventually sprouted. Called *ayçekirdeği* in Turkish, they are a popular social snack of which you can see traces across Berlin's sidewalks.

Whereas for Hakim, Berlin was a pile of rubble and concrete, their garden was the antithesis of that. In the garden, he was able to breathe. His friends called it "Maria Mama" because someone had found a marble figure resembling Maria, the mother of Jesus, and placed it in the middle of the vegetable bed. Maria Mama was in constant flux: people kept adding tomato seedlings, brought seeds sent from Turkey, or ripped out dead plants. Most of all, the garden was a nursery for withering plants: everyone brought plants they didn't need or ones that were doing badly on apartment windowsills. Yet altogether, Maria Mama was a failure—at least according to its caretakers. One day, someone stole the apple tree. Then the figure of Maria Mama disappeared; a pink stuffed rabbit replaced it. Worse yet, with increasingly hot and dry summers, the soil was not fertile enough and water was scarce (fig. 2.3). Hakim had struck up a deal with the owner of a nearby kiosk to use the faucet, but carrying water across the park was a tedious business. Still, he was hopeful: he dreamed that strawberries would cover the entire meadow the following year.

∾ ∾ ∾

Not unlike Osman Kalın's gecekondu garden, Maria Mama constitutes a ruderal ecology: it fills a gap not only between the city's landscaped meadows and exclusionary environments of nation-making but also in Hakim's life. In

FIGURE 2.3 Maria Mama garden during a particularly dry summer, Hasenheide park. Photo by author.

both makeshift gardens, ruderal ecologies are not necessarily characterized by an absence of cultivation; people-plant relations are shaped by systems of control, and yet their interactions also create openings for new forms of cohabitation (see also Myers 2019) that do not adhere to the places assigned in official definitions of public space, private property, and multiculturalist schemes. It is in this sense that ruderal ecologies carry seeds for change.

At first glance, Maria Mama might look like an object of nostalgia, an ephemeral project of elderly men who have become superfluous—if it is visible at all. And yet, the men's relation to the park's landscape and their cultivation of this little garden sit squarely among contemporary celebrations of urban nature and multiculturalist efforts to integrate migrants racially cast as other via the care for plants. Instead of waiting to be granted a costly garden unit, the gardeners of Maria Mama took over a space and created a sociality of neighbors and coworkers in the absence of work and access to public resources.

Cobbled together from withering plants and discarded seeds, and with clandestine access to a public water supply, Maria Mama is far from authentic. In fact, when I asked the gardeners, they seemed rather indifferent to whether this was a Turkish or religious garden. After all, once it was stolen, the figure of Maria was quickly replaced by a pink rabbit. Providing a space of hospitality for plants, found objects, and chance encounters, they instead created a fragile garden ecology that, far from value-free nature or anesthetic greening, exposes histories of damage and makes viable what has been left behind. In our conversations, Kadir, Erol, and Hakim all recounted experiences of being marked as culturally and physically other in German society. They commented on how their life trajectories had been deeply shaped by layers of racialization and exclusion—including their exploitation as cheap "foreign" labor embedded in the logic of the so-called guest worker contracts, the health and body screenings they were subject to when recruited to Germany, and the racist discrimination they experienced in Berlin's labor and housing markets. Their everyday lives were full of reminders of their continued status as suspect strangers in a city and country that (although it was beginning to recognize them as part of a multicultural nation) continued to deny them full citizenship and for several decades had cast them as guests, soon to return "home."[41] Hakim's remark about Berlin being less a green city than a city of rubble best captures the sense of damage and exclusion they experienced both in their lives and in their relation to the city's ecologies.

As Frantz Fanon (1963, 250) observed, racial and imperial formations are forms of power that sow seeds of ruination in bodies and psyches as well as in landscapes, sensibilities, and things (see also Stoler 2013, 9–10). At a historic moment when not only are the bodies of Middle Eastern migrants coded as other, suspected of being unwilling to integrate, but their relation to the urban landscape is framed as unruly, under scrutiny for leaving traces of dereliction or posing a threat, Maria Mama's gardeners challenged their positioning as out of place. In their own words, they created a space to "breathe." A project of recuperation for both plants and people, Maria Mama, like the gecekondu garden, exposes the frailties of ruderal ecologies and projects that challenge urban nature as defined by private property and urban planners—projects in which people, plants, and seeds follow the traces of communication and injury, and in turn inspire action to forge new more-than-human socialities.

While some gardens are the matter of fragile dreams, others turn into a nightmare—at least for their neighbors. And although, as in the case of Maria Mama, they may appear to be a failure or annoyance one year, their seeds lie dormant in the ground, ready to remake alternative ecologies of belonging out of the ruins of Europe's ethnic divisions and racism.

Courtyard Gardens and the "Crazy Cat Lady"

"The rabbits! The RABBITS! They escaped again." Imran's voice sounded desperate on the phone. Nursen, Imran's neighbor, an avid gardener and owner of two cats and two rabbits, had just had surgery and now was in the hospital for ten days. Imran had volunteered to help Nursen out by taking care of her garden and animals. Yet after only two days, it was clear the enterprise was proving more difficult than she had imagined.

Imran and Nursen were tenants in a five-story apartment building beside the old ship canal (*Landwehrkanal*) in Neukölln. Imran, in her midthirties, lived with her husband and two children in a two-room apartment on the third floor. Nursen, in her early seventies, occupied a one-bedroom apartment on the ground floor, together with her cats and rabbits. Formerly public subsidized housing for low-income families, the building had recently been sold to a private investor after the city discontinued its public housing programs. Worries about raised rents were in the air.

I had met Nursen the year before, in 2008, at a neighborhood rally against cutting down hundreds of willow and cottonwood trees that grew along the canal—a popular local green space and hang-out. Drawing lots of neighbors, the protests focused on the increasing commercialization of the neighborhood. Private boat companies carrying crowds of tourists had sped up their boats to increase the number of tours they could accommodate in a day. As a consequence, waves were running high, and the side of the canal was quickly eroding. With trees unable to keep their roots in the soil, the city had decided to log all the trees that, in their view, posed a hazard to public safety. Yet the neighbors were unwavering and fought for different forms of care for the canal's ecology. Determined to keep the destructive profit-making strategies of the boat companies in check, the protests had already been going on for months. As we stood next to each other, forming a human chain alongside the canal one day together with hundreds of other people, Nursen's boisterous sense of humor and unruly attitude quickly captured my attention.

Soon, we met regularly for strolls through the neighborhood, or we sat on her balcony chatting and sipping çay (tea) while she rolled herself a cigarette. Intrigued by my interest in urban ecology, Nursen shared her views about more-than-human diversity in the city, and about neighborhood politics. Although she saw herself as an ally and caretaker of animals and plants, she liked to poke fun at German environmental attitudes, including my own, and local forms of multiculturalism. For her, both seemed to foster bounded cultural identities and domesticated nature—they required that everyone stay in their little niche, whether Turks, Arabs, white Germans, queers, local anarchists, or Nursen's own garden and animal companions. In her everyday life, equipped with a wheelchair due to a back injury, Nursen crossed all of those boundaries.

Nursen's apartment had a small back patio that looked out onto the inner courtyard of several nineteenth-century apartment buildings. The buildings' back walls, lacking windows, were dotted with holes from World War II artillery. Birds would nest in these holes in the spring, inhabiting the war-torn ecologies of buildings in the neighborhood. Right outside the patio, there were a few bushes, a small patch of grass, and a playground. Both inside her apartment and in the back courtyard, Nursen created space for the rabbits and cats. On the ground next to her balcony, she cultivated a small garden plot. Now carnations, roses, tulips, tomatoes, and a few pepper vines were thriving between the courtyard shrubs and the carefully mowed lawn. On the grass, she had put up a little hut for the rabbits, in which they could hop around protected from neighbors' dogs and cats. Fındık and Minoş, Nursen's own two cats, came in and out through the back door and roamed the neighborhood and along the canal across the cobblestone street. The rabbits, too, would sneak out the back window or patio, both at ground level, and would hop around the grass in the back courtyard or in Nursen's vegetable and flower garden.

While Nursen was in the hospital, Imran's task was to feed the animals and let them in and out of the apartment. While the cats were fairly easy to take care of according to Imran, the rabbits did not stick to the rules—they would constantly sneak out the back door, and Imran would have to chase after them, all over the courtyard and the adjacent playground. With two children and working half time, Imran was overwhelmed with it all, tired of running after the rabbits without end. But most of all, she was worried Nursen would run into trouble again—as she had many times before.

Indeed, because of her garden and unruly critters, Nursen was caught in a constant flurry of conflicts with neighbors and the housing association. Neighbors complained about her "illegal" tomatoes and peppers. They had called the police on her when the rabbits were loose, hanging out in the children's sandbox in the courtyard, and when the cats appeared on their balconies. The association argued that, by growing her own plants, Nursen was using common space in inappropriate ways. By letting her animals roam freely, she and they were taking over and disturbing the peace of the shared courtyard. Nursen's landlord was especially displeased to see the rabbits hop around in between the children playing in the playground right next to her garden. Yet Nursen would argue back, pointing out, for example, that the kids loved the rabbits, and stating that the housing association had a skewed sense of urban greenery and how one should inhabit it. In fact, the association had recently cut back all the ivy in the courtyard, displacing most of the birds nesting in the now exposed walls.

Worse yet, the quarrels with the housing association were not the only ones. Due to a back injury and spinal illness, Nursen was forced to retire early and now depended on a small pension, dwindling public assistance, and a wheelchair (which she jokingly called her Mercedes because it was fully automated and equipped with lights). Hoping to receive an allowance for a new coat rack and bed, she quarreled with the local social assistance office (*Sozialamt*). Yet the social worker there did not comply: Nursen was not frugal enough. She spent all her money on her needy animals and on cigarettes! So the story went. Having paid for her imprisoned son's attorney years before, her debts had piled up. Nursen thus gleaned and collected things wherever possible: with her automated wheelchair, she picked up food at a nearby soup kitchen, collected old furniture from the sidewalk on garbage pickup days, traded her garden vegetables with neighbors, or picked fruit in nearby vacant lots. Since she had the automated wheelchair, she felt mobile enough to do all these things and was also able to discover the city in new ways.

To both the housing association and the social office, Nursen was an annoyance, a "crazy cat lady," constantly bending the rules with her "illegal" garden and its four monster inhabitants. Nursen, in contrast, did not see any reason why anyone would be bothered by the animals or a few vegetables and flowers growing between ugly bushes. Plus, the cats and rabbits were family. After finding one of the cats, Minoş, on a street in Istanbul, she had smuggled her on the plane to Germany, along with the two rabbits. In Berlin, Minoş had gotten in trouble with other street cats and almost lost one of her eyes, which Nursen now called the 500-euro eye. Some might say that Nursen treated her animals like humans. Indeed, they were her closest kin. Her husband was dead, and her daughter had cut off ties when Nursen continued to support her incarcerated son. Other family members, like her granddaughter, came by to visit once in a while. Yet her granddaughter, too, thought Nursen was crazy, too opinionated, or a burden and "backward" because she wore a headscarf and talked to Allah too much. Nursen in turn accused her granddaughter of being brainwashed by all the talk about the lack of integration of Turkish families into German society and European culture, and for not taking her grandmother's beliefs seriously enough. The cats and rabbits gave Nursen an anchor and provided a form of support and care. But they did not always stick to her rules. As a neighbor pointed out, if Nursen ever left, the animals would surely stay and continue to keep the neighborhood on their toes!

As a single mother, Nursen had worked on an assembly line for a phone manufacturer and also as a cleaner for many years in Kreuzberg and Neukölln. Like many others of her generation, she felt like she had paid a big price for her time in Germany, working too hard. Having lost many in her family, her garden and animals provided a sense of community. She had worked herself "broken" ("wir haben uns alle kaputt gearbeitet")—a phrase I also heard the Maria Mama gardeners and other former migrant workers of Nursen's generation use many times. In addition, growing unemployment after unification disproportionately affected noncitizens and pushed many migrants into early retirement (Lanz 2007). "We were not careful enough," Nursen told a friend and me as we had tea one day. It was the day before the fortieth anniversary of her arrival in Germany. "We did not know our rights then and didn't defend ourselves. And now many of us are sick or in the wheelchair. Especially women who contracted for work on the assembly line. I let myself be bossed around and I constantly worked overtime—and I was a single mother with two children and even had a second job!"

In Turkey, Nursen had dreamed of Germany and a better life. "Home" was fragile for her—a site of transition and continuous renegotiation. She had grown up in a small village in southern Anatolia, where her father owned a bakery. In the late 1950s, like many other Anatolians, her family migrated to Istanbul in search of work. They lived in a gecekondu at the outskirts of Istanbul. When many of their neighbors signed up for short-term labor contracts in West Germany in the 1960s, both Nursen and her sister decided to give it a try as well. They joined in the circulation of new migration technologies—and dreams—that had developed to support the effort to rebuild Europe from the ruins of the war and to boost Turkey's economy at a time of economic instability and high unemployment. When she arrived in Berlin, Nursen, like Hakim and other "guest workers," was assigned a few square meters in one of the city's migrant barracks. In the succeeding years, a number of policies affected the urban residence of Turkish migrants in Berlin—including Nursen. In the 1970s, the country still limited migrants' ability to stay in West Germany permanently while also taking steps to increase "integration" for those who desired to stay. For example, the federal government made residence permits conditional on long-term work contracts, or required proof of children's school attendance and an "adequate dwelling" of at least twelve square meters per adult and eight square meters per child in order to avoid overcrowding (Mandel 2008, 148).

From the viewpoint of property owners, neighbors, and social workers, Nursen's community of vegetables, flowers, cats, and rabbits was a site of failed integration. Yet considering Germany's history of migration policy, as well as Nursen's own life story, her quarrels and the efforts and sleepless nights she went through to write letters, make phone calls, seek legal advice, and defend her courtyard garden and animals can be seen in a different light. Equipped with a wheelchair and with a community of critters in tow, Nursen crossed the neatly managed units of nature and culture that private property, the state, and neighborly relations allowed for. Unlike the multicultural Pyramid Garden, her garden was seen as a parallel society. And yet it transgressed people's efforts at domesticating what counted as desirable urban nature or migrant culture. While her garden posed a nightmare for some, for Nursen it was paradise.

But Nursen's garden story would take yet another turn. In the summer of 2012, after trying to reach her for days, I walked past her apartment and found several handwritten notes stuck to her windows, reading in German: "Gentrification is happening here!" (Hier wird gentrifiziert!) And, "I, retiree, and in a wheelchair, have to go. But I won't!" (Ich, Rentnerin und im Rollstuhl, muss gehen. Aber ich werde nicht!) After asking about her whereabouts in the neighborhood, I soon found myself next to her at a gathering, surrounded by neighbors who had cobbled together a protest camp consisting of two wooden shacks on a public square named Kotti in Kreuzberg. People in the neighborhood were gathered to protest recent rent hikes and the displacement of migrants. And, like Osman Kalın's tree house, the protest camp was called a gecekondu, in reference to the makeshift urban dwellings built at the outskirts of expanding Turkish cities. Happy to see Nursen, I asked how she was. She looked at me disapprovingly: "Don't you pay attention to the news? I am famous now!"

Indeed, as I quickly caught up, I realized Nursen was all over the local papers and TV. A national TV channel had just featured a five-minute interview with her, in which she talked at length about her cats and rabbits, stating it was only over her dead body that she would leave her garden. In the preceding months, her landlord had doubled the rent and threatened her with eviction both because she had failed to pay her rent and because she had an "illegal" garden. Nursen was not the only one facing eviction: all the other Turkish German residents in her apartment building had moved out—except for Imran, who had recently begun serving as a janitor for the housing association. As parts of the neighborhood had begun to gentrify, more than three thousand low-income individuals and families, many of them migrants living in formerly subsidized housing, received eviction notices and now faced displacement from their lifelong communities to Berlin's outskirts. Soon, a neighborhood initiative formed to support Nursen. A series of public protests around her and other neighbors' potential evictions followed. The news featured many images of Nursen, heading the protest marches.

Sometimes, a small garden community can spark a social movement.

Reprise

Gardens are contested terrain—they can be sites of both enclosure and unexpected care and companionship. Berlin's gardens are certainly not immune to capitalist urbanization or racializing practices that see becoming rooted in the land (*Bodenstaendigkeit*) as a prerequisite for belonging. Relating to plants and land can be haunted by white desires for wealth and a "civilized" urban life. Yet there is no single story to be told about gardens in Berlin today. Instead, gardening practices provide heterogeneous tools for creating connections and solidarities among people, plants, animals, seeds, and land (Hinchliffe et al. 2005; Hinchliffe and Whatmore 2006). The gardeners of Maria Mama, the Pyramid Garden, and the courtyard garden all expose the fallacies of (neo-)liberal forms of multiculturalism (Hale 2005) and practices of integration that govern, commodify, and essentialize difference by defining what counts as an appropriate garden or an appropriate relation to nature in the city. Instead of waiting to be assigned a garden plot, the gardeners in this chapter take over space. These takeovers are not immediately intelligible or recognizable as political within a multicultural or capitalist logic that sees gardening as an expression of national and cultural belonging or simply as a leisure activity that enables wage labor.

In the Pyramid Garden, gardening, framed as a form of integration, becomes a matter of bureaucratic negotiation, fence construction, and frequent conflict. Although people hope to wall culture in and keep history out of their gardens, both come flooding back in. While gardeners bicker about ingrained desires for designing gardens as enclosures and as sites of control over people and plants, the seeds and dreams that circulate in this garden inspire people to collaborate and cross social boundaries. In contrast, Maria Mama and Nursen's courtyard garden more explicitly challenge existing white German standards of how to inhabit urban nature. In these secret gardens, people, plants, and animals conspire with each other to build more livable worlds (Choy 2011; Myers 2019) in an urban environment that for decades has extracted migrant labor and has cast migrants as outsiders.

Nursen and the Maria Mama gardeners forge forms of care that rehabilitate bodies, biographies, and lands, reworking the fallout from past and present exclusion, exploitation, and neoliberal reform. Doing so, they challenge multiculturalist agendas that turn a blind eye to that very fallout. Even more importantly, as Berlin's gardeners conspire with plants and other living beings, they build worlds beyond the racialized and colonizing language of integration—a language that approaches what is conceived as the urban environment as though it contains seemingly separate cultures that bring ruin upon the city. These gardeners refuse a limited definition of worthiness that excludes them and the urban landscapes they inhabit.

The ecologies of Berlin's makeshift gardens help forge both connections and divisions. They are spaces of cosmopolitan dreams and embodied solidarities. Yet they are not immune to power dynamics or becoming tools of bureaucratic control. In them, Berliners make claims to land in a context of unemployment, a growing retreat of the welfare state that demands that people become resilient, and a political climate in which the unemployed become superfluous and in which migrants are seen as being unwilling to integrate. While they might be objects of nostalgia or subversion at one moment, these gardens can also become sites of policing and gentrification at another. Or they might fall prey to drought the next year. Attending to the heterogeneity and open-endedness of these gardens and their stories, we can begin to see how such fragile strategies of survival are never authentic or pure, but are instead situated within histories of disturbance and damage.

Following the persistent ruderal worlds cultivated in these gardens and in the city's inhospitable milieus can sharpen our understanding of the politics at stake in emerging urban ecologies. Socialities between plants and people in Berlin's gardens do not always adhere to those envisioned in the city's shiny brochures on multicultural gardening. Not unlike the Berlin gecekondu garden discussed in the introduction of *Ruderal City*, Maria Mama and the courtyard garden do not fit into official categories of politics, urban nature, or gardening for (national) integration. Instead, these gardens' socialities grow in the gaps—not only of private property, or the city's landscaped meadows, or other urban green-space infrastructure but also in people's lives. Rather than offering refuge from social ills or escape from the city as a space of nonnature (M. Caldwell 2010, 133), Berlin's makeshift gardens thus become sites of possible attentiveness, transformation, companionship, and more-than-human care—forms of care that mainstream multiculturalism continues to make invisible in urban centers across Europe.[42]

Parks

3

PROVISIONING AGAINST AUSTERITY

On a sunny Saturday, the park's central meadow bustles with people. Starting around noon, the vendors, most of them women, arrive at the park—on foot, by bus, by underground train, or by car. Setting up their stands, they spread blankets and mats and put out coolers, cooking utensils, and little plastic stools and tables. The women stick colorful sun umbrellas into the ground and stack up vegetables and fruit in front of the mats to sell. While they heat up small gas stoves for cooking, the aroma of spices, vegetables, and meats—an elaborate mixture of tangy and sweet scents—soon fills the air. Sounds of chatter and laughter echo across the park. Children chase each other through the rows of sellers and shout at each other in exhilaration. Many of the women sit on mats, stirring pots and pans, preparing soups and rice dishes or frying fish and meat while chatting with their neighbors. Meanwhile, the men carry cooking supplies, chop vegetables, or sit in lawn chairs set up on the fringe of the meadow. Most of the female vendors trade and sell their food with each other and to park visitors, who are lured by the aromas spreading across the meadow and who eagerly try out the different flavors. In the evenings people often sit together in small groups playing cards or gambling.

The Preußenpark (Prussian Park) is a small park dotted with meadows and lined with pathways and large beech trees; it is located in the district of *Wilmersdorf*, near what once was the center of West Berlin. Adjacent to middle-class nineteenth-century apartment buildings and several large high-rises today, the park was originally landscaped at the beginning of the

1900s—at the height of Germany's imperial history—as an "unprecedented modern meadow, offering space for local citizens to camp out and play" (Christoffel 1981, 164). Equipped with a refreshment hall and playground, the park offered bourgeois white Germans a leisure space for promenading, sitting on lawn chairs, sunbathing, or taking their children for a stroll.

Today, visitors to the Preußenpark affectionately call it the "Thai Park," the "Thai Wiese" (Thai Meadow), or the "Thai Picnic." A seasonal phenomenon, the park transforms from a sleepy meadow into a bustling community picnic starting in early April or May. Through September or October—on weekdays and weekends, rain or shine—people from the local Thai, Laotian, and Vietnamese communities gather on the park's central meadow to prepare, share, trade, and sell food. During the fall, women sell the mushrooms they have gathered in the forests on the outskirts of the city; they spread chanterelles, porcinis, and boletus mushrooms across their mats. On warm summer days, as many as three to four hundred people gather on the meadow. Other Berliners and sometimes a few tourists join. Yet even during colder months of spring and early fall, a persistent group of approximately sixty people—equipped with down jackets, wool hats, gloves, blankets, tarps, and hot tea—keeps the Thai Park alive.

While the Thai Park has existed since the mid-1990s (Ha 2012), it did not receive more widespread attention in local newspapers and a few tourist guidebooks until the mid-2000s. Images abounded of "wild" hordes taking over the park's meadow, illegally selling food, drugs, and sex. Some neighboring white German middle-class residents have refused to go to the park, expressing their disdain for the masses on the meadows, the noise, garbage, and strange smells. Yet these images also sit side-by-side with yearnings for exoticism and travel to Berlin's "small Thailand." Some of the occasional visitors emphasize the park's tranquility and praise its authenticity as they comment on its colorful market and vending culture. In contrast, the local municipality has eyed the park's community with suspicion for years and closely monitors vending activities, at times conducting controls by the city's so-called Office of Order (Ordnungsamt).[1] As preparing and selling food (without a license) is illegal in public space in Germany, the Thai Park has triggered citywide debates about illegal vending, the appropriate use of public green space, and practices of citizenship. In autumn 2017, the park came under scrutiny again when municipal authorities threatened to shut it down due to concerns over safety, "illegal" food production, and "hygiene" in the face of its unwieldy popularity, which seems to increase each year.

In Germany, the history of urban green spaces and public parks is closely intertwined with white German and European middle-class norms about public welfare and urban sociality as well as with the display of the nation and its imperial aspirations. As I have shown in previous chapters, green spaces have also served as material-semiotic resources to mediate social conflicts, redefine citizenship, and negotiate racial and class inequalities. Whereas gardens were a source of food for urban residents and today are framed as sites of multicultural encounter, public parks have provided bourgeois and working-class citizens a space for recreation from work and the stress of urban life, allowing them to "restore their health and exercise in connection with nature" (Jackisch 2009, 52). As Berlin quickly grew into a city of the working classes with rental barracks in the early twentieth century, urban planners increasingly sought to confront what they saw as a class crisis by developing green spaces throughout the city. As in other urban areas in Germany, nature and urban green space thus became tools for "making citizens" (Angelo 2021) and for governing populations considered to be prone to moral decay and deteriorating health (Rosol 2006). These tools of governance encouraged an enjoyment of urban nature seemingly devoid of any labor, and thus included activities such as "civilized walking," running, picnicking, or dwelling on the lawn (Wimmer 2001).[2] Via such activities, parks offered spaces in which to experience what it means to be a citizen and German—while also enforcing the idea of social integration—as strangers met in a single public space. Instead of hosting fancy restaurants or cafés, some people's parks in the *Volkspark* tradition specifically catered to the working classes, with small kiosks or taverns providing hot water for workers to brew their own tea or coffee. Yet this ability for people to tap into public resources for food and recreation disappeared by the mid-twentieth century.

While the creation of public green space and cultivated urban nature were tools for regulating class conflict, controlling the meeting of "strangers" in the city, and governing working bodies, they also catered to a moral panic about the collapse of a white bourgeois moral order that always also had its correlation in the colonies. As Noa Ha (2014) has shown in her work on the coloniality of European cities, the production and regulation of the very materialities of European metropoles, their wealth, architecture, streets, canals, cultivated lawns, and goods, is built upon the plundering of people and land in the colonies as well as the working classes in Europe. This protection of white European wealth also functioned via the disciplining of white European sexual, class, and racial moralities both in the colony and the metropole (Stoler 1989).

It is within this historical and colonial context that unregulated labor and the gendered intimacies of food production have largely been barred from public green spaces—except in a few designated areas. The Thai Park, together with other "barbecuing" practices in Berlin's parks (see chapter 4), challenges this history and exclusion of food production and racialized labor from public urban nature: cooking in public (and selling the products) exceeds the boundaries of recreation—narrowly defined as unpaid labor and associated with white European ideals of cleanliness, health, and hygiene—and it offends German cultural assumptions about how to inhabit urban nature. Indeed, in the Thai Park, female vendors do not simply recreate from work; instead, according to their own descriptions, they blur the very boundaries between leisure and work, production and consumption. Spending time in the park, they cook together, exchange food, and gossip, and thereby provision the community. For them, the park thus offers a space of solidarity amid experiences of gendered reproductive and racialized (affective) labor, especially also in their marriages with white German men (Ha 2012). Appropriating this urban green space as an economic and affective resource, the Thai Park vendors transform the cultural meanings of what counts as an urban park and as the affordances of nature in the city.

Although far from uniform, austerity policies have had an impact on many immigrants' lives in the past two decades. Since the collapse of socialism, many Berliners' life trajectories have been unmoored, and many, especially migrants and people of color, have lost their jobs and have had to explore new, often fragile strategies to sustain their livelihoods. Yet despite these developments and amid ongoing municipal controls, the Thai Park has persisted for many years.

In this chapter, I track the Thai Park's gendered and racialized intimate economies, its socialities, and sensory politics—and the ways in which these provide opportunities to transcend planned economies of green space, welfare, and white public affects of urban nature. As Catherine Fennell (2011) has shown in her work on public housing in Chicago, neoliberal reforms often tie demands for self-responsibility to a reconfiguration of sensibilities, senses of comfort, and embodiment among urban residents. In a similar vein, recent welfare reform in Germany has attempted to shape a sense of living and eating frugally. The vendors, customers, and visitors in Berlin's Thai Park unsettle these sensory politics envisioned by austerity measures and both reimagine and change the actual landscape of the park to nourish new solidarities. Through food production, vending, socializing, and gambling, and by performing place and creating a "Thai space," the vendors rearrange the economy and ecology of the park. Here, rather than follow the framework of integration that dominates public discussion of migration in Germany, I trace "instances of disarticulation" (Simone 2004)—practices that run alongside conventional workings of institutions, municipal governments, formal economies, households, and identities.

Utilizing a ruderal analytic for understanding this park in Berlin thus means tracing the intimate economies and sensibilities that come to life in the ruins of the welfare state and at the edges of the city's institutions and formal economies. These are alternative futures that might already exist in contemporary cities but that are overseen or undervalued in existing modes of experience or writing (see also de la Cadena 2019; Roy and Ong 2011; Tadiar 2009, 9). Seeking out such alternative futures is also a way of writing against the narrative foreclosures inherent in the subjectivities produced by global capitalism and the nation-state. In this spirit, I engage Neferti Tadiar's (2009) strategy to track the "things" that "fall away" and Anna Tsing's (2015) stories of a "contaminated diversity," which is not recognizable within familiar modes of production, experience, and subjectivity. As Tadiar (2009) points out, contemporary urban developments produce all kinds of "surplus people and populations" and disposable forms of life. To center attention on these unrecognized lives that "fall by the wayside of history" (15) is thus to highlight the hidden human costs of metropolitan achievement and to attend to the forms of living and eating together that happen despite of it. Eating well together here depends on the makeshift economies of the Thai Picnic as vendors provision and craft a life in the cracks of official economies, discourses of the neoliberal state, and planned use of public green space.

Origin Stories

The story about the origins of the Thai Park begins sometime in 1993 or 1994—just around the time when unemployment rose in Berlin. Some people say it all started with the woman with the purple hat. She still sells in the park today. The story goes like this: The purple hat lady used to live close by the park. One sunny weekend, she spent the afternoon picnicking with her family on the park's meadow. Having had the most pleasant afternoon that day, they returned the next weekend, and then again the next. Soon, more family members joined, and the word spread quickly. More and more people started coming to the park. Several women had the idea of preparing and cooking food. They brought pots and pans and stoves. And as others heard about the "Thai Picnic," even more people came—not only Thai, but also Vietnamese and Laotian families. Soon occupying the entire meadow, people started trading and selling food to each other. People were happy to be outside in the fresh air instead of sitting in their small apartments. For some, it seemed like the Thai Picnic had always been there.

In subsequent years, migrants from all over Southeast Asia have come to the Thai Park as vendors and buyers, or simply to visit family and catch up with friends. Many travel up to an hour by public transportation. Once in a while, people visit the park from across Germany, or tourists stop by. Most of the sellers are Thai, Vietnamese, or Laotian women. Some bring their relatives and children. Others come with their friends and partners, or alone. Many of the Thai women have white German husbands and partners, who tend to join early in the day, help carry food, set up the mats and cooking utensils, or chop vegetables. Then, for the rest of the day, the German men sit in small groups on lawn chairs at the edge of the bustle. In their fifties and sixties, most of these men are unemployed or have part-time jobs. In contrast, most of the Laotian and Vietnamese women in the park have partners of the same nationality who sit and work together with them on the mats. The park's community thus comprises a diverse array of migration histories and transnational trajectories.

Most of the Thai women (of all ages) are from rural provinces in northern Thailand such as Chiang Mai province. Some grew up in or near Bangkok and migrated to Germany as domestic laborers or through marriage. In the 2000s, many lost their jobs or had to leave their work because of health-related issues. For example, one woman whose chicken foot soup was particularly popular among vendors in the park had for years worked at a local chocolate factory. After she was laid off, she found new jobs packing batteries and as a cook. It was hard, repetitive work, and soon she started having arthritis and pain in her joints. So she retired and went to the park instead. For her, it was better to work at the park than to continue the repetitive labor or sit around at home.

The Thai women's biographies reflect the trajectories of Thai labor migration to West Germany since the 1970s, when many people came from the rural northeastern and northern regions of Thailand. From the 1990s onward, many women also migrated from the central and southern regions, where tourism is a key industry. Thai labor migration to Germany has been highly gendered, with women comprising about 85 percent of the

Thai community in Germany (Pataya 2009).[3] Many Thai women are married to German men, yet the specific trajectories of their migrations vary: some migrate as single mothers in search of economic security in order to support their children; others come as sex workers; some meet German men in Thai tourist areas and relocate to Germany as their fiancées; and still others seek German husbands with whom to build a family and a new life with economic stability. Some women already have kinship networks in Germany. Others facilitate their migration through friends and brokers working with individual German men, marriage agencies, or transnational syndicates (23). Because of German immigration policies, for many, marriage is the only means by which to legally immigrate to Germany and also receive a work permit.

In contrast to the Thai women, the stories of the Vietnamese migrants at the park often reflect the dual histories of Vietnamese migration to either East or West Germany during the Cold War.[4] Most Vietnamese and Laotian vendors came to West Berlin in the late 1970s as political refugees.[5] From 1978 onward, about 40,000 Vietnamese, Laotian, and Cambodian refugees who had fled the political turmoil and ethnic conflict during and after the Vietnam War by boat received political asylum in West Germany (Bui 2001, 16). For the first few years after their arrival, these migrants usually lived in asylum homes and then later moved to their own apartments; they often found employment in the metal industry (Hillman 2005, 86).[6] Others had spent part of their lives in East Berlin during socialism—they had migrated to East Germany as part of the GDR's training and study programs initiated with North Vietnam since the 1950s.[7] In the 1980s, the East German government signed a bilateral agreement with the reunified Socialist Republic of Vietnam to offer training to Vietnamese workers in enterprises in East Germany.[8] These industrial training programs were viewed both as a strategy to increase the labor supply to German industries and as efforts to develop aid and solidarity with countries in the global South (Hillman 2005, 86). With contracts lasting up to five or more years, many Vietnamese workers were able to find employment in the garment industry. A small portion of their income was allocated to the Vietnamese government, and some was paid in the form of consumer goods. By 1989, about sixty thousand Vietnamese migrant laborers lived in East Germany (Hillman 2005, 90). In the months before the Berlin Wall came down, thousands of Vietnamese migrants crossed the border from East to West Germany and applied for political asylum there (Bui 2001, 16).

After the collapse of socialism in 1989 and the unification of East and West Germany, Vietnamese migrant laborers were confronted with a completely new situation. Their future became a topic of heated debate within Germany as well as between the German and Vietnamese governments. A large number of East German enterprises laid off their Vietnamese employees or asked them to leave by offering bonus payments (Bui 2001, 17). While many Vietnamese faced deportation, some returned in the late 1990s or early 2000s as asylum seekers. In 1993, the unified German government introduced a policy that allowed migrants who had participated in the labor and training programs under the socialist government to extend their visas if they could show proof of regular earnings, housing, and a "clean" criminal record. Yet as unemployment was rampant in these years, many had difficulties finding new employment. It was at this moment that informal and shadow economies offered new opportunities for making a livelihood. Thus, many former contract workers began to work as street vendors and cigarette sellers, or they turned to self-employment and opened tailor shops, small restaurants, floral stands, grocery stores, and Asian snack bars. At the same time, images of cigarette smugglers and petty criminals dominated public discourse on Vietnamese immigrants in reunified Germany—especially in Berlin (Bui 2001). As anti-immigrant sentiments grew in the aftermath of unification, several asylum seekers' homes were attacked in former East Germany, and Vietnamese residents also became the target of this violence.[9]

These diverse histories of migration—and the different work and job opportunities that accompanied them—were all present in the park's social, material, and economic fabric during my fieldwork and visits to the park between 2007 and 2019. When I spoke with vendors, there often was a shared sense that things had been better before the Berlin Wall came down. Most Vietnamese families and Thai women, as well as their German partners, had fairly secure jobs before unification. Then everything changed. Many vendors lost their jobs in the city's crumbling manufacturing industry or had to close down their small businesses. Finding new jobs became unpredictable, so many soon received the so-called Hartz IV unemployment benefits and were thus compelled to live on tight budgets. Some Thai women found work in the hotel industry as maids. Others did seasonal labor and, like Manee, one of the Thai vendors who was in her early forties, worked in a local fish factory during the winter, not knowing whether they would get hired again the next year. Thus, the Thai Park offered not only a viable economic alternative in the summer but also additional social support in frequently precarious labor or domestic situations (see also Ha 2012).

Similarly, many Thai women's German husbands or partners had lost the basis of their livelihoods and now received Hartz IV social benefits. As the city's center shifted toward the formerly Eastern districts, such as Mitte, Manee's partner, Arne, for example, lost his thriving bratwurst stand, which had been located next to a popular beer garden in the former Ku'damm area of West Berlin. Arne's hot dog stand had been situated on a small lot that was sold to a private investor who wanted to build a hotel—so Arne lost his lease and was evicted. Then, in the 1990s, as some put it, everything "went down the creek" (alles ist den Bach runtergegangen), and what once was the thriving center of West Berlin became somewhat marginal. As economies and livelihoods shifted after the fall of the Wall, you never knew exactly where the new "center" was.

Cultures of Austerity

Preparing, selling, and swapping food all day long, the Thai Park community of vendors provided not only viable resources for sustaining livelihoods but also an antidote to the austerity of welfare and state formulas for how to live "frugally" on unemployment. In Germany and throughout Europe, tropes of austerity and indulgence have populated debates about the economy, the labor market, and the welfare state since the 2000s. In a period of recession, many European governments, including France, England, Ireland, Germany, Greece, and Spain, made significant changes in their social systems. This included cutting pensions and social benefits and reducing health and education services and state support for the unemployed to counter "deficits" and bolster "stability." In this state of "permanent economic emergency" (Žižek 2010), austerity policies flourished.

In Germany, austerity made a particularly strong appearance after the turn of the millennium. At the time, the Social Democratic and Green government introduced large-scale reforms to the labor market and welfare system—the most comprehensive reforms in postwar Germany since 1949 (see Heinrich 2004). Titled Agenda 2010, referring to the EU's Lisbon Strategy and its 2010 deadline, these reforms aimed at reducing unemployment, health, and pension benefits. They also sought to transform the social security system and introduced tax cuts to enable economic growth and strengthen Germany's position in the global economy.

The so-called Hartz measures were a key component of these reforms. Developed by the Committee for Modern Services in the Labor Market, the

"Hartz Committee" was led by Volkswagen's personnel director, Peter Hartz. The Hartz policies took effect between 2002 and 2005. Whereas the Hartz I–III reforms aimed at creating jobs and producing flexible labor, Hartz IV primarily affected welfare and unemployment benefits (*Sozial- und Arbeitslosenhilfe*): it reduced both welfare and unemployment rates and joined them into a single system.[10] Under this system, in order to receive unemployment benefits, Hartz IV (or ALG II, Arbeitslosengeld II) recipients have to provide proof of their efforts to seek employment. They can also be forced to accept a job offered to them through a state job center. In cases of noncompliance, Hartz IV claimants face the reduction or loss of their benefit payments.[11]

As Hartz IV primarily affects people who either have been unemployed or only have a very low income, the word entered the national imagination as a synonym for long-term unemployment benefits, and it has since been associated with a "culture" of poverty in public imaginaries. The Hartz monthly allowance (in 2022, it was 449 euros) is to be used for buying groceries and medications, for paying utilities and phone bills, and for transportation and clothes. After 2005, austerity measures particularly targeted Hartz IV recipients—with some politicians suggesting cutting parental support for recipients and further restricting coverage of rental support. While some have praised the Hartz measures for reducing unemployment rates and paving the way for Germany's more recent economic boom, the controversial reforms also triggered protest marches across the country, especially in former East Germany. Critics have argued that lower unemployment statistics remain unreliable, since many of the unemployed do part-time work and thus do not enter the Hartz IV statistics. Trade unions, several political parties, and community organizations have criticized the reforms for dismantling the welfare state, increasing economic inequalities, and pushing more people into precarious labor markets and low-paid work (Heinrich 2004).[12] Thus, for many, Hartz IV and the Agenda 2010 have become synonyms for neoliberal economic policies, à la Reaganomics and Thatcherism (Heinrich 2004).

In Berlin, austerity coincided with ongoing restructuring of the city's economy and built landscape after unification. As urban planners, politicians, and policy-makers sought to create a new German capital and a global city, Berlin turned into what many referred to as the world's biggest construction site; and for many years the local housing market boomed. In this transformation into a service city of global capital, urban planners and economic policy-makers pushed to deindustrialize large parts of the city.[13] Thus the Treuhand, the trust agency responsible for privatizing East

German enterprises and organizing economic unification between East and West, closed down most manufacturing companies in the eastern part of the city (Lanz 2007, 123). By the mid-1990s, the situation radically switched from boom to bust: planners had overestimated the willingness of global developers, banks, and insurance companies to take up residence in Berlin. Many publicly funded construction projects lost their funding (143), and much of the newly built urban infrastructure remained unoccupied in the city center for a long time. As a result, the inflated housing and real estate markets collapsed, and the city plunged into a debt crisis. Furthermore, with ongoing deindustrialization, unemployment rates rose high above average throughout the city—ranging from 15 percent to more than 20 or 30 percent in some districts (123–24). Although unemployment significantly decreased again in the course of the 2010s, Berlin's unemployment rates and numbers of Hartz IV recipients are often higher than the national urban average in Germany (with especially high rates in districts such as Neukölln).[14]

None of these developments has been uniform. As with other urban reform efforts, they constitute heterogeneous experiments that translate into diverse new experiences and subjectivities (Rofel 2007). Nevertheless, the restructuring of Berlin's economy and the rush to transform the city into a global metropole was deeply racialized and has had particularly negative impacts for migrants in former West Berlin, as discussed in chapter 2 (Lanz 2007, 124). The life trajectories of many migrant workers in the city's former East have been marked by increasing employment insecurity. As many Vietnamese in East Germany lost their jobs after unification, it was not until 1997 that former contract workers received the same legal status as West German migrant laborers, and thus the right to claim social and unemployment benefits. Many Vietnamese thus became entrepreneurs in shadow economies and developed trade networks with formerly socialist countries—for example, selling untaxed cigarettes and coffee from neighboring Poland. As these informal economies stretched across reunified Germany's new borders with Poland, discourses around "Vietnamese zones of crime" racialized and criminalized these communities, stereotyping them as using up state social support and participating in illegal trade of cigarettes and weapons (Bui 2001; Lanz 2007, 128–31).[15]

During this moment of financial crisis and emerging informal economies, cultures of austerity took center stage in Berlin. The Berlin Senate introduced cuts to its public care and housing expenditures. As anti-immigrant sentiments grew in the mid-1990s on the heels of postunification national euphoria, many blamed the economic crisis on rising racism. Whereas conservatives tended to explain xenophobia as a "logical" response to increasing numbers of immigrants in the country, Social Democrats and the Green Party often saw it as an outcome of social anxieties unleashed by economic restructuring and the loss of secure employment (Lanz 2007, 133). Since the turn of the millennium and especially on the heels of the so-called refugee crisis of 2015, national media have portrayed migrants as taking advantage of social benefits, and migration policies encourage "self-help" among migrants as a key means to integration.[16]

In the face of flailing local economies and a lack of public funds in the 2000s, both Berlin's urban landscape and images of it changed. Former mayor Klaus Wowereit made the famous statement that "Berlin is poor but sexy" (McGrane 2009), and in this context Berlin's "creative industries" became a selling point to pitch the city as a creative cultural capital, paving the way for intense gentrification processes that are still ongoing in the 2020s. As the city sold much of its public property in the center to private investors (Lanz 2007, 143), local municipal services were reduced to a minimum. This led to what some have called a "crisis of public green space" (Rosol 2006) that affected public services, such as garbage collection, street cleaning, and winter snow removal, and left parks and green spaces unmaintained for long periods.[17] Yet new social practices moved into the emerging cracks that opened up as the city's landscapes and economies transformed.

Enacting Austerity: The Hartz IV Menu

In 2008, a German politician, mentioned in the previous chapter, came up with a recipe to enact austerity by putting an end to immigrant wastefulness and the unemployed's indulgence in state benefits. Thilo Sarrazin, former board member of the Deutsche Bundesbank (German Federal Bank) and senator of finance in Berlin for several years, commissioned a three-day menu plan for the unemployed. According to his calculations, Hartz IV recipients should be able to "eat well" on a minimal budget—to be exact, on 3.76 euros per day. The menu allowed for bread rolls, muesli, or wholewheat toast for breakfast; spaghetti, sausages, or soup for lunch; and salad, bread, and cheese for dinner (fig. 3.1). With only 3.76 euros, his "Hartz IV menu plan" promised to provide a balanced and healthy diet to the poor.[18] To prove the Hartz IV menu and its thesis, a state employee at the Financial Office checked and calculated the prices in local discount supermarkets. The details of day one of the plan turned out as follows:

	TAG 1		TAG 2		TAG 3	
FRÜHSTÜCK	2 Brötchen	0,30	80 g Müsli		3 Scheiben Vollkornbrot	0,12
	25 g Marmelade	0,06	1 Banane	0,40	2 Scheiben Wurst	0,30
	20 g Butter	0,10	1/4 Liter Milch	0,25	1 Scheibe Käse	0,25
	1 Scheibe Käse	0,25	20 g Honig	0,35	2 Tassen Kaffee	0,10
	1 Apfel	0,24	2 Tassen Kaffee	0,08	1 Glas Saft	0,30
	1 Glas Saft, 200 ml	0,30		0,10	20 g Butter	0,10
	2 Tassen Tee	0,10			1 Mandarine	0,25
MITTAG	Spaghetti Bolognese		Gemüsesuppe mit Fleisch		Bratwurst mit Sauerkraut	
	100 g Hack	0,38	100 g Kartoffeln	0,05		
	125 g Spaghetti	0,15	1 Möhre	0,05	1 Bratwurst	0,38
	200 g Tomatensauce	0,40	1 Stange Porree	0,05	Kartoffelbrei	0,25
	div. Gewürze/Öl	0,10	1/2 Kohlrabi	0,30	150 g Sauerkraut	0,12
			Rindfleisch / Gewürze	0,30	Gewürze/Öl	0,20
				0,65		
SNACK	1 Kaffee + 1 Joghurt	0,40	1 Glas Tee		1 Kaffee + 1 Banane	0,30
				0,05		
DESSEN			2 Scheiben Brot			
			2 Scheiben Käse	0,12	2 Scheiben Brot	0,12
	1/2 Gurke	0,30	1 Scheibe Bierschinken	0,50	100 g Kräuterquark	0,30
	130 g Leberkäse	0,56	100 g Krautsalat	0,15	1 Scheibe Schinken	0,30
	200 g Kartoffelsalat	0,34	20 g Butter	0,20	2 Tomaten	0,27
		3,98 Euro	Summe	0,10	2 Glas Tee	0,10

FIGURE 3.1 The Hartz IV menu for a "one-person household." Image from Schomaker (2008).

Breakfast: 2 bread rolls, 25 grams jam, 20 grams butter, 1 slice of cheese, 1 apple, 1 glass of juice, 2 cups of tea.

Lunch: 100 grams ground beef, 125 grams spaghetti, 200 grams tomato sauce, spices/oil.

Snack: 1 cup of coffee and 1 yogurt.

Dinner: half a cucumber, 130 grams meat loaf, and 200 grams potato salad.

(Troesser 2008)

Each gram of food was carefully measured and was just enough to cover basic daily caloric needs. Above all, the main requirement for what many would later jokingly call the "Sarrazin diet" was rigorous abstinence and austerity—no cigarettes or alcohol, no fresh vegetables from local markets, and no fresh goods from bakeries were included in the recommended menu.

Soon after its publication, the "Sarrazin diet" stirred up a national debate and received both affirmation and criticism from across the political spectrum.[19] And it sparked a flood of publicly staged calculation, shopping, and cooking sessions. Journalists flocked to supermarkets to try out the "Hartz IV menu" and calculate its accurate pricing. Others came up with recipe books and brochures for Hartz IV recipients (Roth 2008). As one journalist at the conservative weekly magazine *Die Welt* wrote when she tried the "Hartz IV diet" for five days, in trying to provision oneself with 25 grams of jam, one slice of cheese, and 130 grams of meat loaf, one was confronted with the mathematical challenges of buying in bulk rather than individual serving sizes. If 130 grams of meat loaf is supposed to cost

56 cents, would it be appropriate to buy an available 400-gram package for 1.69 euros (Troesser 2008)? Confused, she had to get out the calculator on her cell. Would a Hartz IV recipient be able to afford a cell phone in the first place? And what to do with the rest of the 270 grams of meat loaf if you did not want to eat meat loaf four times a week? The same was true for the ground beef, the spaghetti, butter, and sauce. In the end, the journalist composed several modest meals combining the ground beef and meat loaf—and some of the food went bad.

Within the gaps in these meticulous calculations and their exuberant public mutations, a (cynical) world of austerity emerged. Actual measures of control over Hartz IV recipients' choice of foods were periodically implemented, including the introduction of so-called shopping certificates and demands for receipts, which permitted social assistance offices to surveil and stigmatize people's consumer choices. In Berlin, the food plan took on a special urgency as political discourse increasingly cast immigrants as having no qualms about "utilizing" the German welfare state and not displaying an appropriate (Protestant) work ethic. The publication of Sarrazin's (2010) book, *Deutschland schafft sich ab* (Germany does away with itself), as well as several interviews with him, contributed to a further proliferation of such images of Berlin's migrants—often equated with Hartz IV recipients—as wasteful and as not participating in formal economic cycles. In Sarrazin's narrative, images abound of Berlin's Hartz IV recipients wasting energy, living in cozy warm homes with the windows open to regulate the temperature. This discourse was thus rampant with racist and middle-class fantasies stigmatizing people on the basis of the neighborhoods in which they resided, while casting them as environmentally unaware.

Although not without controversy, the Hartz IV reforms and Sarrazin's statements paved the way for an ongoing national discourse that claims multiculturalism has failed while continuing to fire up anti-immigrant rhetoric on the political right, especially among parties such as the AfD (Alternative für Deutschland [Alternative for Germany], founded in 2013). The emergence of the AfD and the strengthening of right-wing populist movements across Germany set the stage for new demands for more restrictive immigration, economic, and welfare policies that "crack down" on supposedly "unproductive," "superfluous" migrants.

In her article on the Hartz IV menu, the journalist Julia Troesser describes how she dreamed of the sweet smell of freshly baked chocolate croissants—a luxury that would certainly be strictly prohibited under the Hartz IV diet. Yet one person's dreams and desires for indulgence in luxurious foods might be another person's nightmare. While the food and cooking in the Thai Park affronts the senses and sensibilities of some, to others it provides the possibility for communal gathering, exuberant trade, the sharing of memories, and indulgence in delicious foods from home—in addition to being a source of income for some, however insecure it might be.

Indulgence

The Thai Park community provides an antidote to the austerity of welfare discourses and state formulas on how to live frugally on unemployment. Cooking, preparing, and selling food, as well as gambling, are its key strategies. On any summer day, an abundance of fruit and vegetables is available for purchase—from mangoes, *longan, mangosteen*, papayas, and *rambutan*, to *pak choi*, cilantro, bamboo shoots, *kanah* (broccoli leaves), and Thai basil (fig. 3.2). Women prepare and indulge in a wide variety of dishes: fried mackerel, green papaya salad (*som tam*), spring rolls, fried shrimp, various rice dishes with chicken or tofu, pad thai with shrimp, crab cakes, different soups (with chicken feet, or regular chicken or beef), and skewered sour sausages (fig. 3.3). Others sell desserts: freshly cut mango or Thai apple (*poodza*) served with a mix of sugar, salt, and spices; rice cakes; golden threads (*foi thong*); sticky rice; and coconut desserts wrapped in (banana) leaves. Drinks range from Coca-Cola, beers, tea, and caipirinha to Thai iced tea, *air bandung* (a Malaysian sweet milk drink with rose syrup), *pandan*, or grass jelly drinks (fig. 3.4). Some vendors also offer children's toys like plastic bubbles, Hello Kitty colored pencils, and bubble gum. Several Thai women offer massages to other sellers and their friends.

The vendors cook for their families, eat together, chat, and sell and trade dishes with each other. (Visitors usually pay more for a dish than sellers do when they negotiate with one another—for example, a pad thai dish sells for three euros between sellers and for five euros for others.) There is never a shortage of available foods throughout the day. Each afternoon, a vendor from an Asian grocery store in the nearby underground train station comes by with a shopping cart full of produce. During a busy day, people run out of supplies and buy from him to stock up on *pak choi*, rice, sauces, or fresh coriander and basil. Other informal trade networks cross in the park: in the evening, right before dusk, a few Polish or Turkish vendors roam through the park offering cheap goods from Poland, just a fifty-mile

FIGURE 3.2 Mangoes, *longan*, and *mangosteen*. Photo by author.

FIGURE 3.3 Sour sausages and Thai apples. Photo by author.

FIGURE 3.4 *Pandan* and *air bandung*. Photo by author.

ride east of Berlin. Many Thai, Vietnamese, and Laotians buy cigarettes, alcohol, and coffee from them.

Hi-Lo

People at the Thai Park indulge not only in food, trade, and conversation but also in games of chance. On warm summer nights, the park is often crowded until midnight. As dusk approaches, the Thai Picnic slowly mutates into an open-air casino. Vendors set up small gas lamps, creating islands of light amid a gloomy meadow. Then, as the park grows dark, a couple of foxes, rabbits, or a flock of crows might appear to peruse the area for leftover food, carefully sneaking past clusters of people across the grounds.

This is the time of *hi-lo*—a dice game in which you can lose it all, wreck your life, or win big.[20] Illuminated by lamps, several playing fields pop up under the beech trees at the edges of the park.[21] The game works like this: a large tablecloth, divided into handwritten subfields, each with two or three numbers written on them (each number under ten), is spread out. The dealer throws three dice onto a little plate with a basket on top. Before the roll, everyone places their bets on the different combinations marked on the tablecloth. The goal is to predict the right number combinations of the dice. The choices on the cloth are single numbers, number combinations, or "high (hi)," or "low (lo)." The croupier's assistant makes sure everyone finishes placing their bets in time before the next round. The assistant also provides players with drinks. Once all the bets are set, the dealer throws the dice. All combinations ten and under count as low (lo), and all above eleven count as high (hi). "Hi-lo" is any combination that adds up to eleven. If you have placed your bets on a two-number combination that wins, you get three times your bet amount back. If you place it on lo, and the dice add up to less than eleven, you get twice the amount—the same is true for high. If you win a hi-lo combination, you get seven times the amount you placed as a bet. The dealer collects the bets and distributes gains to the winners. Then, the players place their bets once again, the dice are rolled, and the game continues until late in the night.[22]

Two families run the hi-lo games: several young brothers in their thirties from a Vietnamese family, and two Laotian sisters in their fifties. The two sisters run the games with mostly women who tend to place lower bets—usually between one- or two-euro coins—whereas the men usually place their bets at ten euros or more. While some people just come by for a quick game, others play all night.

In the dim light of the gas lamps, money moves back and forth between vendors, customers, and dealers. Some people use the money they made during the day selling soup, stir-fry, spring rolls, and salads. If they are lucky, they make even more. If not, they lose it all. People gather around the game, sitting on small plastic stools or on a mat or pillow. Some stand on the sidelines of the game, throwing in their bets once in a while. Still others just stand close by and watch. Chatter fills the air. Focusing on the quick staccato of tumbling dice and money bustling back and forth, it is easy to get hooked once you start playing. You will want to chase after that one exuberant moment when the dice tumble to eleven and you strike hi-lo. There are stories of people losing almost everything, wrecking their lives and marriages. Even some of the players themselves consider the gambling indecent or a waste.[23]

Hi-lo creates expenditure, the desire to make it big. And above all, as everyone gathers around the game, it creates sociality. Thus, the game follows a logic of indulgence in time, money, and community: you chat and have a beer with your neighbor while observing the tumbling dice in anticipation of the next strike of luck. This is not the logic of austerity or the efficiency of utilitarian economics. As Alan Klima writes, "Gambling does not pretend to asceticism" (Klima 2002, 249). Not unlike the funeral casinos in Klima's ethnography, hi-lo does not "contribute to a production of individuality that might be folded into a new economic order" (260). And although gambling can also be read as capitalism's fetish, creating a neoliberal subject, and as "everything that is wrong, unreal and 'fetishistic' in global economy," it also generates value, a "'commerce' in community itself" (260).[24] Similarly, by trading and selling foods, Thai picnickers create an abundance of everyday relations and intimacies that have become scarce in profit-driven, extractive, and large-scale economies. As fragile and risky as it may be, this "economy of abundance" "runs right alongside the market economy where the good that is served" (Kimmerer 2020) is not profit, but community and cooperation.

Amid the gambling, there is one man in the park who carefully calculates people's "expenditures of happiness and disappointment" (Klima 2002, 248). His name is Erhan, and he carries a small booklet with him and jots down combinations of numbers as he wins and loses. Convinced that there is a trick or a method behind the throwing of the dice, his booklet is filled with pages and pages of hastily scribbled numbers. Erhan is one of the few Turkish German men in the park, and he is married to Nuan, who identifies as Thai. Nuan and Erhan make their living keeping the park clean. Nuan is paid by the municipality to clean and monitor the restrooms adjacent to the park. Erhan clears the meadow every evening of leftover trash—and all the vendors pay him five euros every day. While he works on the meadow, he takes little breaks and plays hi-lo. Each time he plays, he takes notes on the dice combinations, trying to figure out the "method" behind the game and improve his predictions. People tease him. They say he is addicted to the game. Yet Erhan persists keeping track of people's chances—and calls his book of numbers his bible.

Signs and Solidarities in the Gaps of Austerity

Gambling and food vending without license are usually prohibited in Germany. Yet people at the park have skirted official rules and made use of ambivalence and gray zones. In response to their indulgence in gambling, cooking, and vending and the large gatherings during the summer, municipal authorities have made several attempts to regulate the Thai Park community. In 2006, the municipality of Wilmersdorf put up signs at four of the park's entryways. Written in Thai, English, and German, the signs list new rules of conduct (fig. 3.5). Tacitly citing German norms about what counts as appropriate recreation in a park, the rules prohibit the following:

FIGURE 3.5 Rules of conduct, Preußenpark (Thai Park). Photo by author.

- barbecuing, cooking, refining, and lighting or operating
  a fire
- putting up garden furniture (such as tables, stools, tents, and
  umbrellas) to avoid damaging the lawn
- using coolers to an extent that exceeds the usual quantities
  for a household
- selling goods and offering services
- keeping dogs or other pets off-leash and not removing dog
  droppings immediately
- bicycling
- producing noise with musical instruments or stereos
- using the meadow after 10 p.m.

Yet surprisingly, in addition to these regulations, a fenced cooking area of about two hundred square feet was built on the far side of the park at one point. A sign next to it read, "cooking and barbecuing area." Inside the fenced area, park users were allowed to prepare food on little cement circles. Yet if anybody wanted to use the space, they had to drag all their food and utensils for about a ten-minute walk across the park from the Thai meadow to the cooking area. In the end, hardly anyone ever bothered to go there. The official "cooking area" remained empty.

Instead of using the official cooking areas, people snuck around the rules—their actions ranged from setting up versatile small market stands that could easily be disassembled or moved to performing "being Thai." Many vendors actively trafficked in stereotypes about being Thai. For example, drawing on cultural stereotypes of the Thai as peaceful, the vendors regularly praised the Thai Park for being laid back and clean. Sometimes explicitly, sometimes implicitly, they would position themselves in opposition to "Arab and Turkish immigrants" frequenting other parks in Berlin. Many emphasized that the Thai Park was the best park in town, that things were more peaceful, clean, and multicultural than in other parks—especially the Tiergarten.[25] Yet after 2017, as the park became more popular and was praised in tourist guides, municipal authorities repeatedly threatened to regulate the park's community more strictly, or even shut it down completely.

During the summer, the local Office of Order (Ordnungsamt) regularly checked in to ensure that park-goers were sticking to the rules. When patrols approached, the first person to spot them would send a high-pitched whistle across the park. Within seconds, plastic stools were hidden in bags, sun umbrellas disappeared, and, if it was a rainy day, tarps were torn down and folded together in a flash. The dice games too would vanish swiftly. One time I sat on a little stool at the park chatting with several sellers, and when we heard the whistle, Nim, one of the sellers, quickly pulled the stool out from under me—much to my puzzlement. When the officers went through the park and inquired about everyone's activities, people said, "We are having a family picnic!"—marking a private space and presenting a familiar image of the Asian extended family. Then the officers asked about each individual's belongings; every adult is allowed to have two coolers. Most of the time, the sellers had more than two coolers. To help out, everyone who did not bring any food claimed one or two of the coolers. If a cooler was not claimed, the officers took it with them. If they found a sun umbrella or any plastic stools, they did the same, as it was against regulations to set up any private furniture. One weekend, Manee had two of her coolers and two plastic stools taken away. She went to the Office of Order the next Monday and had to pay a fine. They gave her back the coolers—but the food in it had spoiled.

The state entered the park not only via regular patrols. Rumors spread about city officials spying on vendors from a high-rise office building across from the park, or even from a helicopter flying overhead. Thus, although people were able to sneak around official attempts to create order and control activities in the park, a dreadful sense of the state's presence always lurked around the corner.

Interlude

My own "arrival" in the Thai Park was tightly linked with navigating official rules myself. I conducted fieldwork in the Thai Park during three consecutive summers between 2007 and 2010, and then again in the summers between 2013 and 2019. I spent time at the park speaking to vendors, their families, and visitors, and to residents who did not partake in the park's economy. I participated in everyday activities, such as buying food and drinks, occasionally helping set up stalls, picnicking, eating, sitting around, and chatting. Sitting with vendors on the meadow throughout the day and often until late at night, I participated in and observed daily interactions between families, customers, and local municipal authorities. I furthermore engaged with people's worries about their daily income, debts, and financial insecurities, and I listened to gossip about other vendors as well as frequent complaints about the rainy bad weather in Berlin.

Although white German women came to the park to buy food, it was unusual for them to spend any prolonged time talking to the vendors. Thus, when I first approached some of the vendors about my research interests, they eyed me with suspicion: Was I a spy for the local municipality, the Office of Order, or even worse, the police? As vendors were regular targets of control by the city, not surprisingly, their initial reaction was to keep me at a distance. The vendors' reactions highlighted the various layers of class, gender, and racialized power dynamics between a white German researcher based in the United States doing fieldwork with migrant communities in Europe.

As Heath Cabot (2019) has pointed out, US anthropology continues to make so-called migration crises in Europe into a business and career-building enterprise in which mobile scholars study precarious refugee and migrant communities and turn that very precarity into an object of study. This reinforces the logic of migration regimes in which migrants and border crossers become targets of policing, surveillance, and research (Cabot 2019). This logic ultimately also strengthens what Aisha M. Beliso-De Jesús and Jemima Pierre (2019, 71) have argued is the white supremacy of anthropological practice itself. Upheld in myriad ways, via citational, institutional, and research practices, whiteness continues to be a seemingly unmarked category of power, which is always also an integral element of state governance and security. It is this very link that the Thai Park vendors who kept their distance, or who suspected me of being a spy, were acutely aware of.

Furthermore, being based in the United States mattered and offered a fraught entry point into what anthropologists would call my field. In many conversations with vendors, unexpected and yet power-laden overlaps in my interlocutors' biographies and mine would catch our mutual attention: many of the vendors had traveled to the United States or had kin there and were fond of American popular culture; they were thus intrigued to talk to the "student," and later "the researcher from the US." Furthermore, being attached to multiple continents triggered many shared topics and concerns, including worrying about faraway kin who were aging or seriously ill. The park in this sense provided social support to its participants, myself included, as everyone shared worries and hopes about loved ones across distances and found consolation in mutual stories of illness, laughter, and healing.

Yet like in all power-laden research encounters, moments of solidarity, collaboration, and empathy do not erase hierarchies, privilege, mistranslations, or betrayal (Visweswaran 1994). Acknowledging this, even after I had spent more time at the park, some people remained at a distance, tolerating my presence but otherwise ignoring me. Others seemed to become more comfortable and began to speak more frankly with me. It was not until one particular incident, though, that I more fully realized how much the Thai Park community was built on coconspiring (Choy 2011; Myers 2019) against municipal authority and racialized urban governance. One day, the patrol went through the park and several municipal officers asked everyone present to claim their food. Nim, the vendor I was sitting next to, realized she had too many coolers. Following her prompt, I quickly claimed two of them so she could evade a citation or worse. After the rush, several people later approached me with a friendly nod and a smile on their face—much to my surprise. It struck me that only after conspiring to sneak around the controls exercised by the Office of Order did vendors acknowledge my existence. Although, as Clifford Geertz famously pointed out, complicity in evading officialdom is one way to make friends and create social bonds—even to build ethnographic "rapport" (Geertz 1973)—white anthropologists most often continue to be able to claim their white privilege (or that of their passport) when caught up in these very border zones of control. Thus, rather than indulge in these shared moments of evasion, my task was to be alert to and cognizant of the ways in which privilege becomes complicit with governance and policing, and to listen to the park members for when support or intervention was desired, or when more mundane tasks such as simply carrying or claiming coolers were needed.

The Park's Intimate Economies

Practices of exchange in the Thai Park were closely bound up in intimate relations among sellers, and thus they were shaped by kinship, region, race, class, and gender. Some of the vendors had become experts in preparing different specialties. For example, a woman from the Chiang Mai province specialized in spicy papaya salad, while another woman's chicken feet soup was especially popular. Then there were the so-called mushroom women who picked mushrooms in the forest and sold them in the park. Spatial divisions in the park usually followed lines of gender and nationality: most of the Thai, Laotian, and Vietnamese female vendors occupied the core of the meadow. Toward the entrance of the park were the Vietnamese and Laotian families who ran the hi-lo games. All the way on the meadow's edges, the German husbands sat on their lawn chairs, usually observing the hustle and bustle on the meadow, except in the mornings and evenings when they would help their wives and partners by hauling goods and utensils to and from the park or by chopping vegetables. They were mostly superfluous during the greater part of the day, while the women were clearly in charge of the trade and exchange—and the income. And some of the women even hired their own (mostly female) assistants to help them cook, mix drinks, cut fruit, or distribute money and watch over bets in the hi-lo games.

Aside from these gendered spaces of activity and expertise, divisions between public and private did not make much sense in the park. As Manee, one of the vendors, once put it, the park was both an extended living room and a public mini-market. Many of the female vendors felt that even if sometimes going to the park was not all that lucrative, it was still better than sitting around at home and being bored. Manee laughed and said, "I even bring my own blanket and pillow!" Yet for a living room, the space on the meadow was quite busy. People, goods, and money moved back and forth and circulated all over the park. Some vendors traded mushrooms for money, or rare items such as wild boar stir-fry. Others exchanged their lettuce or fresh fruit for someone else's soup or noodles. Money circulated freely. Oftentimes, one vendor would borrow money from another to purchase staple ingredients to prepare food to sell, or they might use it to play hi-lo for a while. Then, once they made some money, they would pay back their debts. Generally, food vendors made less money than the people who ran the hi-lo games, but their income was more constant—something around 50 euros per day, which, if sellers came to the park daily during the summer, could add up to 1,500 euros per month.

When he assisted his uncle with the hi-lo games, Kip, who was Viet-namese, carried bills and coins with him so he could provide people with change. Sometimes he played with the money himself. When he lost, it would go back into the hands of his uncle (which he called the "bank"). Every day, Kip received money from his uncle for helping out. He called it his pocket money. Similarly, Oma (the Laotian woman running the other hi-lo game) would sometimes start the day by borrowing money from her sister who also ran a game—maybe around 100 euros. On a bad day, Oma made somewhere between 10 and 50 euros. She hardly ever lost any money because she made sure that people distributed their money across the game, and not too many would put a large amount of money on hi-lo, which paid seven times the amount of the bet. The best days for her were when many people played, and she sometimes made up to 1,000 euros. I heard others complain that she was too wasteful: when she made good money, she would go to the casino and gamble it all away! But when she did win, she gave her sister the money back or would wait a while before going to the casino again. That is how money circulated.

All of this borrowing and lending seemed generally to go rather smoothly in the "conduit of fiscal liquidity" (Klima 2002, 261). Everyone was able to keep track of things. Yet, once in a while, frictions emerged. Work relation-ships were saturated with different kinds of affect—feelings of friendship, loyalty, affection, pity, and at times anger and disappointment. Sometimes people got into quarrels over their mutual expectations, broken bargains, growing debts, and payments that did not come through. A fight would emerge and resentments would persist until the person who was in default would finally pay back a debt. Oftentimes, people went so far as to cut off connections with each other after passionate disagreements. For example, Manee had worked for Duan, selling mushrooms, fresh fruit, and drinks. One day Manee told me she had stopped working for Duan. They had been quarreling a lot and Duan was complaining that Manee was not working fast enough. At the same time, Duan was not consistent with her payments to Manee, switching from paying her ten euros one day to thirty on another. It kept changing constantly and Manee was not happy about it. One day, Duan called her at home and yelled at her, telling her that she felt taken advantage of and was disappointed. Manee could not take it anymore. They talked and talked, and yelled and cried. As she described the phone conversation to me, Manee rolled her eyes in annoyance. She said to Duan: "OK, let's part in a friendly way then," and hung up. Otherwise, the conversation would have gone on and on. And although Manee kept rolling her eyes, she also seemed distraught about the disagreement. She first did not want to part ways with Duan. But what could she have done? Buy all the fresh fruit and other ingredients for making drinks herself? Although she initially was hesitant to part ways, she ultimately did. And it turned out OK, she concluded.

However, this also meant that Manee had to rely more on her partner, Arne. Whereas before Duan had organized transportation, it was now Arne who hauled all the goods to the park via public transportation. He often complained about it—the load seemed to be getting heavier and heavier! Each time they came to the park, Manee and he would have to put all the food onto several small carts and take them on the underground train.

Forms of exchange in the Thai Park were thus deeply entangled with relations of gender, kinship, ethnic ties, and affect. In particular, the transactions between female vendors forged intimate economic bonds among women. And as the "breakup" between Manee and Duan illustrates, when these economic bonds turned fragile, many female vendors had either to seek new entrepreneurial collaborations or to fall back on and become more dependent on the help of their spouse. In her ethnography of the intimate economies of Thai markets in Bangkok, Ara Wilson (2004) traces the key role of Thai market women in Thailand's entry into global economies in the past and present. Developing a notion of "intimate economies," she shows how capitalist systems of production and exchange are closely intertwined with cultural meanings and identities of everyday social life, such as gender, kinship, sexuality, and ethnic ties. She defines intimate economies as "the complex interplay between . . . intimate social dimensions and plural economic systems in a context shaped by transnational capital" (11). Because they blur the boundaries between public and private, capitalist and noncapitalist transactions, as well as profit and affect, intimate economies often trigger public anxieties (20). Similarly, the Thai Park's intimate economies reshuffled existing constellations of gender, public space, and formal/informal labor markets. And yet it is precisely the blurring and disarticulation of these boundaries by the park's intimate economies that confused Berlin's municipal authorities and, in fact, enabled the vendors to escape regulation by "pretending" to be having a family picnic while acting as sellers and participating in an extended face-to-face "economy of abundance" (Kimmerer 2020).

The Mushroom Lady

The intimate economy of a mushroom can have a strange scent, both sweet and bitter.

Like a few other vendors, Manee collected mushrooms in the late summer and sold them at the park (fig. 3.6). Manee grew up in a village near Bangkok, and when I initially met her, she was in her early fifties. Unlike the journalist's unmet desire for croissants mentioned earlier in this chapter, Manee indulged in the scent of mushrooms and dreamed about them.

Looking back at her life, Manee once said to me that she feels like everything has been a roller coaster ride—up and down—not unlike a hi-lo game. When she was younger, she was married to a Thai man, and they had a child. Then, a few years later, her husband started being abusive. Manee ran away. After some time, the opportunity arose to go visit a friend who had immigrated to Germany, so she came to Berlin. Only two years later did she return to Thailand to fetch her daughter, Tukata. Manee got married to a German man. It was an arranged marriage: she put an ad in the newspaper looking for a German husband and received hundreds of responses. She picked her new husband out of a final choice of three. Her son is from that marriage.

For several years, Manee worked all the time and only took care of the children. But then she met an American and fell in love. They snuck away together and went on several road trips. When her mother died suddenly, her lover bought her a plane ticket, and they flew to Thailand together. She took care of her mother's funeral and spent time with her family. And when everything was taken care of, she left with her lover to go to the United States for six weeks. They traveled to Colorado and Florida and took a boat tour in Tennessee—and gambled in casinos.

Like other women in the park, Manee had provided for her family back in Thailand for many years. From her earnings in Germany, she bought land for her parents and siblings and provided financial support for them to build a house. And although she returned to Bangkok regularly, she could not imagine going back for good. What would she do there? She probably would just have to fix the old broken house of her sister and nieces again and take care of everything. And now, even her father was gone. Two years earlier, Manee was on her way back from the forest where she had picked a lot of mushrooms. Suddenly her phone rang, and her sister from Thailand said: "You should come if you want to see Dad." One of his arteries had burst and he was in a coma. Manee cried. She had just picked all these mushrooms

FIGURE 3.6 Stein-
pilze (*Boletus
edulis*, or porcini).
Photo by author.

that would now go to waste. She flew to Thailand and her father was still
alive. She said to him: "Dad, if you can hear me, squeeze my hand." He
did not, but she still felt like he knew she was there. The next day he died.

In late summers and in fall, Manee and other Thai women regularly collected mushrooms in several forests at the city's western edge. The Spandauer
Forest, situated along the western border of the city, comprises one of the
city's large deciduous woodlands and hosts several nature reserves and many
different kinds of mushrooms—ranging from chanterelles (*Cantharellus
cibarius*) and porcinis (*Boletus edulis*) to Rotkappe (*Leccinum vulpinum*)
and puffball mushrooms (*Bovist*). Some areas of this and other forests
were closed to the public and the pickers had heard rumors about munitions from World War II being found in the forest. Another favorite
location for mushroom picking was a forest and heathland, the Döberitzer
Heide, located just outside the city limits, southwest of the Spandauer Forest. Because of its heavy military use during World War II and its use as
military training grounds during the Cold War, munitions were scattered

all over this area. As a consequence, much of the forest was closed off to the public, which made it an ideal place to sneak in and collect mushrooms. One day, the Heinz Sielmann Foundation—named for a famous wildlife filmmaker and photographer—bought part of the area in order to open an animal park. They were planning to bring in bison and wild horses and make it into something like a "wilderness area." Thus, those sections of the forest were even more strictly cordoned off. But neither the nature reserves nor the animals nor the munitions could keep the women away. They usually headed out there around four or five o'clock in the morning, sneaking through the fence to avoid the patrols. Sometimes, the women spent up to eight hours picking mushrooms. Then they would return to Thai Park and sell them for fifteen euros a kilo—about a third of the price in regular grocery stores.

Manee's daughter, Tukata, often teased her mother about the mushrooms. In her view, the mushroom picking did not really seem to be about money. She thought it was strange how the women kept going to the forest and would return, exhausted, without even having made much money. "It's like therapy to them! Everyone goes together and they enjoy it so much," she said. Indeed, for Manee, the mushrooms' lure was entangled with moments of rupture, displacement, and loss. Providing something like an anchor for healing amid turmoil, the mushrooms themselves were nonetheless situated in a risky landscape of unexploded ordnance, fragile (female) solidarities, volatile love affairs, and precarious labor.[26] Sometimes, Manee wondered whether she was, in fact, addicted to mushroom picking. In the peak season she would go five times a week, or even more. One year, she had not gone picking mushrooms for a while and was supposed to have surgery. A day before the surgery, she was nervous and talked to a friend who had been going to the forest. "Why don't you come with us? You can lie in bed for the rest of the week—do something now to distract you!" So, Manee went along. They found lots of mushrooms and were in the forest all day! She knelt down a lot and was very exhausted that evening. She could hardly sleep and kept thinking about the mushrooms all night. The next day, all her muscles ached—and she had to have the surgery! It was a mess! Then, after her surgery when she awoke from the anesthesia, her thoughts traveled immediately to the mushrooms. She saw them in front of her eyes. Again, the next night, she could not sleep. She kept hallucinating about the mushrooms. They were constantly there. She could even smell them. They just would not let her go! Their abundance in the forest was like a gift with which to remake the currencies of scarcity in her own life.

As Manee told me the story about the surgery and the mushrooms, she repeated a gesture with her hands, imitating the shape of a mushroom and holding it in front of her face very tightly. Closing her eyes, she slowly inhaled the mushroom's scent. She kept repeating the gesture several times, cherishing the mushrooms' gift, until I could almost sense the sweet smell of the chanterelles myself.

Refuge

Kip was in his midthirties when I first met him in the park. During the summers, he would be at the park almost every day, helping out his older brother and uncle who ran one of the hi-lo games. Also present were his younger brother and father, who was usually dressed in a gray suit and hat and who used a walking stick, as well as his aunt and nieces and nephews, who often ran after Kip, teasing him or demanding his attention with a new game. In the afternoon, he was responsible for setting up the game and keeping it running smoothly. While his uncle threw the dice, Kip kept track of the money and distributed the wins and collected the losses. He gave the players change if they needed any and got them something to drink when they were thirsty. Wearing jeans, a T-shirt, a jean jacket, and a baseball hat, Kip seemed never quite as well prepared as most park-goers who donned thick jackets to combat the cold in the fall or on chilly summer evenings.

Having been unemployed for a while, Kip depended on the extra money he was making at the park. Also, as he put it, being in the park was less boring than sitting around at home, or, as he often had to, dealing with confusing bureaucracies to receive his social benefits. Kip regularly found himself working through incomprehensible paperwork, which he tried to fill out with great care. But each time he sent it to the social office, there was something missing, and the officials complained. Then, after sending in more information and documents, he would receive a letter in the mail saying he had responded too late. It would take months for the money to come through—if it did at all. It was mind-boggling to him. Others shared similar stories. Many Thai women grumbled about having to depend on their husbands to translate the highly formalized language of German bureaucracy to them.

Kip was born in Vietnam in 1970. Tropes of repeated displacement populated the story of his own and his family's migration: a few years after his birth, his family fled the political turmoil and violence in Vietnam to live in Laos. Although his parents were able to tend a small piece of land and had a few chickens, they were not doing so well. Then one day, his mother said to Kip and his siblings that she would send them on an adventure that night. Kip had no idea what was about to happen, but it sounded intriguing. That same night, Kip and his siblings crossed the river to Thailand on a makeshift raft—many people joined them, but his parents stayed behind. He still remembered the leeches on his legs as they crossed the river. He could not recall when his parents followed. But at some point they did. They all lived in a refugee home in Thailand for two years. Things were not so easy in Thailand, either, and the Thai resented the Vietnamese. So his parents discussed whether to try to go to the United States. Kip was excited. He did not know what it would be like there, but he remembered hearing a song from a jukebox in Laos. He had no idea who it was. Later in Thailand he learned it was Elvis Presley. And because he liked the song, he liked America. Yet it turned out to be impossible for his family to go there. Instead, they received political asylum in Germany and lived in another refugee home on the edge of West Berlin for several years.[27] That was in 1979.

Kip fashioned himself as a solitary person and as what he described as an outside observer of what was going on in the park. He also expressed his cynicism and dismay vis-à-vis the gamblers—especially his father, who had gambled the family's money away. Although he came to the park almost every day, he hardly ever gambled himself—at least not with his own money. He knew a lot of people—in the park and at its fringes—but would not call them friends. Maybe it had to do with the fact that he had always been in the middle of everything, as he put it: four of his brothers were older, the other was younger, and so were his three sisters. Everyone approached him with their concerns. In the end, he often did not know whom to turn to if he needed advice himself. Sometimes he wondered whether he became this way that night when he crossed the river. Or when he came to Germany and did not speak a single word of the language and was reprimanded by his teachers for things he did not understand. His arrival in Berlin was a shock: Who were these people and what did they want from him? All the children at school were curious, but he had no interest in them. And the teacher never seemed happy with anything that Kip did: "What are you doing? You have to learn more! Why don't you understand? What kind of sweater are you wearing? That looks dirty!" Kip still remembered it all.

When I first met Kip, he had no formal job and was receiving Hartz IV benefits. He had started an apprenticeship with a carpenter a few years before and then was laid off, because his boss said he was not trying hard enough. The local job center had offered him the unpaid apprenticeship after a short period of unemployment. Kip would rather have studied art, but he had to take the offer, which was a prerequisite for qualifying for Hartz IV unemployment benefits. He did the job grudgingly. Now he felt that there was a big void in his life. He did not know what to do next. All he cared about was painting and graffiti. But how could he make money from that? In fact, he was working on a booklet on graffiti, art, and Confucianism. Maybe one day he would find someone to publish it.

Kip prided himself on having done a lot of graffiti all over Berlin—and especially for knowing the ins and outs of the underground train system. Once, he pointed to the bushes on the side of the meadow: between them was the emergency exit of the underground train station next to the park. With only a good screwdriver to lift up the door to the shaft, you could be inside the underground tunnel in no time. During the week, the last train runs by at 12:45 a.m. You wait until the last train passes, then you go in and are all by yourself. The possibilities are limitless. You do not need any light, because the lights are on anyway, which is not the case with all underground lines in Berlin. In the early 1990s, at a time when nobody was at the Thai Park yet, Kip would often venture down into the tunnel and spray-paint.

Not unlike the Thai picnickers, for Kip spray-painting the subways offered a way to rework the city's infrastructure and to remake his sensory relation to it in ways that diverged from official, intended uses. Yet in contrast to the Thai Park's sociality, spray-painting provided a space of solitude and refuge from the material-symbolic violence of municipal patrols, everyday racisms, confusing bureaucracies, and austerity measures in the labor market and welfare system. Moving underground opened a space of creativity for him in which it became possible to disrupt an otherwise seemingly inescapable neoliberal urban governmentality (Alexandrakis 2016). Though Kip became invisible, slipping through the cracks of police surveillance and the city's transport system below ground, above ground the Thai Park community was highly, even hyper, visible. Yet by performing its "tradition" as a family picnic, it too evaded officials' perception and created a world of reciprocity and refusal to stick to the rules.

Reprise

In this chapter, I have traced the emergence of new, informal economies and intimate socialities in a public green space amid the ruins of a racialized labor market and the dismantling of the welfare state. The Thai Park provides a respite from the structures of austerity that have privatized public resources and have led to state formulas for how to live frugally on unemployment benefits: seen within its own framework, the park community indulges and finds pleasure in abundance. Its vendors and actors seek to provide good food and eat well, which means more than just making profit or consuming a balanced, healthy diet; such provisioning also means, as Heather Paxson (2013, 5) suggests, participating in a shared sentiment and crafting of a life. Continually laying claim to this public green space—by putting up sun umbrellas, stools to sit on, and tents and tarps for rain protection, and by sitting in the center of the meadow throughout the summer—the vendors brave not only cold weather and rain but also municipal definitions of how to inhabit urban green space. In fact, the picnickers are remodeling the park's *oikos*—which in the Greek sense of the term signifies home, or house(hold) (see also Paxson 2013, 32)—by redistributing wealth and the relationships that sustain their own lives.

At the same time, the food, objects, and intimate economies circulating through the Thai Park defy racialized images of immigrant Hartz IV recipients being wasteful and illegitimately relying on social benefits. Participants in the park's economy—the vendors, gamblers, and customers—create their own food economy and sociality alongside more anonymous formal market economies that center on profit (see also Kimmerer 2020): the Thai Park is not a self-organized urban soup kitchen providing "charity," but a food swap and open-air casino that seeks to outwit governmentality and that responds to the reduction of "social welfare" by coming up with a formula on how to live and eat well in precarious times. Yet from the perspective of city officials, this does not count and is often seen as "cheating" the state.

In his analysis of street food economies in Mumbai, Jonathan Anjaria points out that street vendors have emerged as politically charged figures in contemporary studies of urban informal economies: the figure often holds the promise of collective resistance against the destructive forces of global capitalism and neoliberal policies (2011, 2016). Instead of celebrating street vendors as inherently subversive and as an informal proletariat (M. Davis 2004) that signals a new emancipatory politics, Anjaria highlights how vendors' strategies and desires are enmeshed with the state, neoliberal discourse, and modern sensibilities of urban order in often contradictory ways. Similarly, as I have shown, while Thai Park vendors create a sensory experience of consuming foods from their homelands, they also adhere to notions of order and cleanliness and perform racialized images of the Thai or Southeast Asian family picnic to evade municipal controls. Leveraging these performances, they distinguish themselves from the stereotypes of welfare recipients or supposedly more unruly barbecuers in other parks of the city. Furthermore, the park's intimate economies—including vendors' relationships to material objects, to food, and their use of public space—cannot easily be explained as a direct result of urban restructuring and austerity policies. To demonstrate this, I have attended to provisioning practices, subjectivities, and the things that "fall away" and are not recognized within familiar modes of production, political subjectivity, and discourses of austerity. For example, Erhan's hi-lo notebook, both a "bible" and an accounting book for calculating risk and insecurity as a way of life, meticulously traces expenditures and chance while figuring out the formula for a lucky strike. Deviating from existing categorizations of cultural difference and religion, Erhan's "bible" and the hi-lo gamblers do not follow the logic of state plans for a frugal life. Similarly, Kip's fragile efforts to make a living in Germany and his memories of displacement—attached to the leeches that accompanied him on his journey across the river to Thailand, and illuminated by bright lights as he sprays graffiti in the underground—are dulled by the boredom he feels as he monitors the constant circulation of money in the park. Together, these efforts and practices open up ambiguous spaces of sociality and subjectivity otherwise elided in political discourse about immigration and "immigrant wastefulness." And last but not least, the smell of Manee's mushrooms exceeds an economy of efficiency: picked in forests of unexploded ordnance and newly founded nature parks, the mushrooms' smell is both haunting and sweet. It provides a source of temporary healing and triggers gentle memories of loved ones far away or gone forever.

The Thai Park community comprises forms of sociality and exchange not clearly recognizable within the logic of formal economies and the welfare state. Perhaps this is the very reason it has been able to persist for so many years despite official controls. And yet, the community's future is uncertain: as of summer 2021, plans to regulate the Thai Park and transform it into an officially registered and monitored street food market have been underway. What this will mean for the park's embodied socialities and homemaking practices remains to be seen.[28] Within the Thai Park's socialities so far, we can trace the emergence and future possibility of intimate economies and social worlds of coconspiracy. In these worlds, the provisioning of food holds a promise to create a sense of belonging and solidarity for women in an everyday life shaped by gendered labor migration, austerity policies, and volatile intimate relations in their domestic spaces (see also Ha 2012).

The Thai Park's heterogeneous practices and unexpected neighbors took over the meadow at a historic moment in Berlin, when unemployment increased, local economies flailed, and precarious labor conditions prolifer-ated. Anna Tsing (2015, 2012) has similarly described off-the-grid economic strategies of survival in the disturbed landscapes of contemporary capital-ism. The unruly diversity of such alternative strategies at the peripheries of capitalist modernity resists being summed up by modern knowledge (Tsing 2015, 33)—instead these strategies form a "cacophony of troubled stories" and patchy practices that exceed the "rigors of domestication" (Tsing 2012, 96).[29] And although one might easily dismiss the Thai Park as yet another strategy of privatizing or individualizing a public safety net and creating resilience via commodified ethnoracial practices, it has been much more than that. With its intimate economies, the Thai Park forges solidarities across racial, ethnic, and gender divisions. Vendors draw on images of the Thai as peaceful, and they perform an "authentic tradition" of Thai markets run by market women to distinguish themselves from other unpopular park users in Berlin's public imaginaries—the theme of the next chapter. And while they cater to these existing stereotypes, the park-goers' material circuits exceed a commodification of ethnic or racial identities and formal capital flows. The park's cooks follow a recipe different from the austerity plans of the Hartz IV menu, or "Sarrazin diet," and other state schemes. Although this cooking practice might seem ephemeral and certainly is never really outside anything, it has sustained alternative urban livelihoods and infrastructures—and it has done so with persistence and creativity for a long time.

4

BARBECUE AREA

All barbarians must barbecue and all who barbecue must be barbaric.
—Andrew Warnes, *Savage Barbecue*

Berlin has a serious barbecue problem.
—*Berliner Morgenpost*

If Turkey joins the European Union, we will go to Paris and barbecue in front of the Eiffel Tower!
—barbecuer in Istanbul

Thin layers of smoke hover in the trees. A few rays of sun make their way through the gaps between leafy treetops, creating an ephemeral palimpsest of shadow and light that cuts through the forest in long lines (fig. 4.1). An effect of smoldering coal, roasting meat, and burning tobacco, the clouds form a meeting place of many aromas and particles. They are the product of communication, a weekend ritual to slow down time and add flavor to the day. Yet the layers of smoke are also a warning sign: they are the trace of fire. Amid the gray haze lurks fire's potential to destroy order and break down the boundary between wilderness and the city, nature and culture, and civilization and chaos.

This corner of Berlin has been the foggiest place in town each summer for many years. If you walk down the boulevard that stretches along the banks of the Spree River, you reach the edges of Berlin's largest green space, the Tiergarten (Animal Garden). Approaching the park's meadows, you smell the

FIGURE 4.1 Smoke wafting in between tree branches in the Tiergarten, Berlin. Photo by author.

fragrance of barbecued chicken, lamb, or beef, boiling tea, and sweet tobacco. On weekends, many Berliners, especially Turkish German families and other members of the local Middle Eastern communities, extend their lives and homes into Berlin's green spaces like the Tiergarten. In what local media often refer to as the summer's peak barbecue season, Turkish Berliners of all generations gather on meadows in the city's parks. Sometimes meeting in small groups of three, sometimes in large extended families of thirty or more, people spread out picnic blankets to sit, eat, and play games while the kids run around (fig. 4.2). The parks fill quickly each morning, so many families head out early. Some arrive with just a few things; others pack an elaborate setup for the day. Blankets, plastic folding chairs, wooden chairs, kitchen tables, hammocks, prayer rugs, and always, most importantly, a small grill are hauled to the park and set up as surrogate living rooms. Tennis rackets, soccer balls, card games, and chess and backgammon boards are brought along as well. As smoke emanates from the grills, *shishas* and teapots offer opportunities for additional socializing and add to a perfect meal.[1]

The mixture of fire, smoke, and aromas produced by local barbecuers has captured Berliners' attention for many years. And not unlike the Thai

FIGURE 4.2 Barbecuers in the Tiergarten. Photo by author.

Park, the Tiergarten has been at the center of that attention. For some, barbecuing is a site of pleasure—an afternoon spent eating, chatting, and relaxing with family and friends in the park. For others, it is an insult to the fresh air produced by Berlin's cherished "green lungs" and an annoying disturbance in an island of tranquility amid the fast-paced city. And whereas the cooks in the Thai Park perform an image of the peaceful Thai, the barbecuers of the Tiergarten (and other parks) offend German sensibilities and ideas about control over nature in different ways. In particular, the media describe "Turkish barbecuing" as a "savage practice" and use terms like wild barbecuing (*wildes Grillen*), framing Middle Eastern immigrants as urban Europe's ultimate other. Concerned with environmental pollution, the city's Office for Green Spaces (Grünflächenamt) has closely monitored wild barbecuing and its traces—large amounts of litter, smoke, and bad smells—since the 1990s. These measures to regulate use of the Tiergarten and other parks have especially targeted Turkish Germans, Middle Eastern migrants, and other communities of color. Today, barbecuing is outlawed in most of Berlin's parks—especially parks in neighborhoods with large migrant populations such as Neukölln. The city has designated specific areas for barbecuing in a few select parks. After repeated earlier attempts, the district administration of Berlin Mitte placed barbecuing in the Tiergarten on its political agenda in the fall of 2011, and a ban took effect in 2012. Although some persistent barbecuers refuse to stick to the rules, barbecuing slowly vanished from the Tiergarten in the following years. While a few new barbecue areas were added in other parks, such as the Tempelhofer Feld, some opponents have argued that barbecuing should be outlawed across the city (Pasch 2013). These efforts to control barbecuing have been met with resistance from Berlin's barbecuers while setting off national and transnational controversy over the limits of multiculturalism, appropriate uses of green space, and the protection of nature in the city of Berlin and beyond, even as far as Istanbul.

Why did barbecuing become such a charismatic object of controversy? And why has it captured people's imagination across Berlin, Germany, and Europe? To answer this question, I track barbecuing and its material traces—smoke, litter, and smells—as border practices in this chapter. Specifically, I argue that barbecuing is a border practice situated at the racialized boundary of the "civilized" European city and its others, marking the boundary of the human and nonhuman. Barbecuing is less an activity with deep cultural meanings than a ritual that functions as a "busy intersection" (Rosaldo 1993, 17): it marks territories and bodies, and it exposes competing notions of citizenship across a nature/culture divide (Stoetzer 2014c).[2]

Barbecuing is a method of cooking with the heat and smoke of burning wood or charcoal. This practice leaves traces—smoke and ashes—and thus changes the city's atmosphere. Creating a breathing space for some while polluting Berlin's green lungs for others, barbecuing transcends multiple divisions of everyday life. By attending to the affective worlds that surround barbecuing, we can get a glimpse of the imaginative and racialized geographies and ecologies at work in the remaking of citizenship and the nation. Yet even more importantly, like other ruderal worlds and encounters, barbecuing operates in the very categorical breakdown between divisions of urban life, including the city and the countryside, nature and culture, the human and nonhuman, as well as the boundaries of Europe and its racialized others. The improvised and ephemeral nature of barbecuing requires a method that reads between the lines of official histories and seemingly straightforward accounts of what barbecuing means. This calls for a slow process, letting the smoke unfold and allowing the meat of the matter to roast for a while.

Tracing local media and municipal responses to barbecuing in the Tiergarten, I will therefore start by showing how these responses utilize a deeply racialized language of seemingly natural and homogeneous categories such as Turks, Arabs, and (im)migrants. Furthermore, human-animal/land relations (including the eating of meat) framed as inappropriate serve to caricature people and associate them with invasion and a threat to civilization. By describing state and popular definitions of what constitutes appropriate ways of inhabiting urban green space, I illustrate how these definitions become entangled with ideas about nature, about bodies and practices that are seen as out of place, and thus with a broader politics of nationhood, racism, and urban space in Germany and beyond. Turkish Berliners' strategies of inhabiting and remaking green space in the Tiergarten grapple with and challenge these politics. Exploring their strategies, I ask: How does barbecuing create a sense of place and yearning for nature in the city? And how does this sensibility renegotiate everyday experiences of displacement and racism?

Looking beyond the Tiergarten and the nation reveals barbecuing to be not only a marker of difference but also an embodied practice that remakes citizenship and the urban fabric across Germany and Europe. Indeed, barbecuing incites debate across national borders. In the city of Istanbul, straddling the borders of Europe and Asia, barbecuing inflames public affects at Europe's fringes. The chapter thus concludes by examining how these affects surrounding barbecuing in Berlin, Istanbul, and beyond echo cosmopolitan anxieties about the presence of rural migrants in the city and shed light on larger questions of citizenship and the role of Turkish and Middle Eastern immigrants in contemporary cities across Europe. Yet before attending to these questions, we first turn to the Tiergarten. The history and ecology of this park is closely linked to the making of the German empire, the modern nation, and the more recent transformation of Berlin into a new European metropole. And for centuries, this green space has been a looking glass of the domestication of more-than-human relations and bodies in Berlin.

The Animal Garden

The wounds of war may be healed, but the scars are green.
—Merilyn Simonds, "Guns and Roses"

Located in the new center of the city near the Brandenburg Gate, the Tiergarten is Berlin's largest, oldest, and probably most famous park, often referred to as the green lungs of Berlin. As the city tends to be several degrees hotter than the surrounding countryside, the park provides a crucial source of cool, moist air. Covering 210 hectares, the Tiergarten is among Germany's largest inner-city parks. It comprises a variety of landscapes, ranging from meadows and high-diversity mixed forest—including sycamore, Norway maple, oak, hornbeam, European beech, birch, elm, and alder trees—to carefully landscaped lawns, from rose and beer gardens to a small creek and several ponds. The park provides a habitat for many species of birds, insects, and mammals such as foxes, rabbits, squirrels, martens, bats, rats, and mice (Schicks 1995, 14).

From the famous Victory Column at the park's center, several large boulevards stretch out in a star shape, dividing the park into six main parts. Along these boulevards, one can walk past tree-lined walkways and view many sculptures graphically depicting Prussian aristocrats enacting hunts of animals in the park, such as deer, buffalo, and wild boar. These scenes point to a long history that goes back to the year 1530, when the park stretched over a much larger area. But even more than that, they enact the domestication of land, forests, and meadows as well as the evocation of wild nature in the name of urban civilization—one of many competing imaginaries of the city, nature, and the nation that thread throughout the park's history.

In the sixteenth century, keeping wild and exotic animals was the province of electors and kings, demonstrating their power. At this time the park spread all the way to the Royal Palace, serving as a showcase and hunting territory for the elector of Brandenburg (Kaselow 1999, 32).[3] It was then a fenced park and was inhabited by many animals such as foxes, deer, and wild boar. As Berlin grew over the next few centuries, the hunting grounds were reduced in size. In the seventeenth and eighteenth centuries, the Tiergarten slowly grew into a carefully landscaped recreational forest. Following a baroque philosophy of nature's rationality, local electors created a geometrically ordered network of tree-lined pathways converging at the castle and thus pointing to the centrality of state power (Carmesin 1995, 30). During this time, the forest area also served as a refuge for people fleeing the Huguenot wars. Receiving favorable treatment among Prussian elites, French Protestants, often referred to as *Réfugiés*, were allowed to put up tents in the forest area in 1750 and to offer beverages to city dwellers. The tents thus served as so-called garden restaurants at the edge of the city. In addition, hoping to boost Prussia's exports, the elector of Brandenburg (who did not like hunting) offered small pieces of land to the Réfugiés—many of whom worked in the textile trade. On these lands, the Réfugiés were able to grow mulberries to feed and raise silkworms for silk production (Twardawa 2006). Yet after years of planting mulberry trees and bushes, these efforts failed miserably due to poor harvests on Berlin's part-sandy, part-swampy soils.

In the nineteenth century, the area was transformed into a Prussian national park with a new design by Peter Joseph Lenné, including a pleasure garden, several memorials, and a complex network of alleys and walking paths. Following the idea of a people's garden, Lenné also added less visible and clearly ordered areas (and thus highly controversial ones) that could serve as spaces of encounter and recreation for Berlin's residents—especially for the poor and working classes living in crammed rental barracks in the expanding metropole (Carmesin 1995, 34). After the turn of the twentieth century, during the Weimar Republic, public reformers and landscape architects envisioned more visible spaces of public encounter for collective exercise and gymnastics in the tradition of the people's parks (*Volksparke*) (Carmesin 1995, 37–38).

During the fascist era, the Tiergarten became part of Nazi plans to build "Germania." The Nazis planned to reconstruct Berlin into a world capital by ridding the city of what they considered provincial architecture in relation to other imperial centers such as London and Paris. Most of the buildings that the Nazis envisioned were never built, but in an effort to reorganize the city along a North–South axis, the main avenue through the park was widened and the so-called Victory Column was relocated to the park's center.[4]

During World War II, the Tiergarten was largely destroyed when Berlin was heavily bombed. Many trees were burned. In the immediate aftermath of the war, Berlin residents used the park as a place to grow vegetables and hunt for rabbits (fig. 4.3). Many trees were also cut down for firewood.

When Berliners confronted the question of how to dispose of the large piles of rubble throughout the city, one proposal was simply to pour a layer of rubble over the Tiergarten. Although some rubble was used to fill in bomb craters (Schicks 1995, 15), these plans were ultimately abandoned, and the new city government instead moved the rubble to dumping grounds near other parks and forests in the city and at its edges.

The Tiergarten did not remain a void for long. In the late 1940s, the city government called the destruction of the Tiergarten's forest "the biggest scar left behind by the war on the city landscape" and made its reconstruction a top priority (*Telegraf* 1949). In the following years, West German and other Western European cities donated thousands of trees to be planted in Berlin. This reforestation took place even during the Berlin blockade and the so-called Berlin airlift, when trees were flown from all over Germany and Europe into West Berlin. The first tree planted after the war was a linden tree.

FIGURE 4.3 Berliners planting potato seedlings near the ruins of the Reichstag, Tiergarten, Berlin, May 1946. Photo by Fred Ramage, reproduced courtesy of Getty Images.

During the division of the city and after the construction of the Berlin Wall, the Tiergarten transformed into a border zone. It acquired important meaning as a green space for West Berliners, who now found themselves surrounded by the wall and cut off from the surrounding countryside. In the shadow of the wall, various communities settled in different areas of the park: the gay community and nudists sought out secluded areas, German and immigrant families picnicked and barbecued in front of the Reichstag, and sex workers strolled along the main boulevard (Strasse des 17. Juni) of the park. This all happened at a time when Germany's so-called economic miracle set in and many residents retreated to private gardens and vacation homes in their search for green space, leisure, and a middle-class lifestyle (Staudinger 1995, 48).

After unification, several edges of the park, especially on its eastern side, were designated to be clear-cut to make space for the construction of new government buildings in the unified capital. Environmentalists organized protests against this planned transformation, with only partial success, saving a small patch of land. Today, the park is located adjacent to the unified capital's government district and train station, and it borders the Brandenburg Gate and the former course of the Berlin Wall, now marked only by a row of cobblestones in the pavement. From the 1990s onward, the Tiergarten became home to large-scale events like the Love Parade and public viewings during the World Cup and European soccer championships.

Changing imaginaries of power, the nation, and urban nature have deeply shaped the Tiergarten's landscape. The park's vegetation and use have changed repeatedly: originating as hunting grounds, it was transformed by baroque and modern landscaping ideals, by the city's rapid expansion during industrialization, by deforestation and bombing during the war, and by national reconstruction during the postwar period. For many Berliners today, the Tiergarten both symbolizes Berlin's unique location in modern German history and conjures up memories of war, persecution, and division. Now, the park is home to many unplanned more-than-human communities, which once again trigger anxieties about the boundaries of nature, the city, and the nation.

Barbecue Area

In the opening scene of the movie *Babakiueria*, a group of Australian Indigenous people arrives by boat on the shores of what appears to be unknown land (Featherstone 1986). Encountering a small crowd of white European Australians who hang out and picnic at the beach, the Indigenous group asks them: "What is the name of this place?" One of the white Australians pauses in confusion and, with a blank expression on his face, reads the sign right next to him: "Errr. Barbecue Area."

Tricked by their own imagination, the travelers are convinced they have set foot on the previously undiscovered territory of "Babakiueria." They colonize Babakiueria and take control over its inhabitants. Through this role reversal between white and Indigenous Australians, the film satirizes and critiques racial stereotypes and colonization. It shows white European Australians as an ethnic minority that becomes the target of anthropological research and paternalistic colonial policies designed to integrate them into Aboriginal society. With this role reversal *Babakiueria* exposes the myriad layers of the material-symbolic violence of white settler colonialism—and the ways in which colonial power, as Frantz Fanon has shown, turns both people and land into unruly primitive nature that requires taming and control. Meanwhile the complexities of people's political and economic existence are caricatured and ignored (Fanon 2004, 182).

Not unlike the racialized dynamics exposed in *Babakiueria*, the Tiergarten became the focal point of concerns about the practice of wild barbecuing and the role of racialized others unwilling to integrate into civilized society. Yet here we do not have a satiric role reversal; instead, we have the full colonial dynamic of contemporary European and German political discourse on migration, multiculturalism, and integration. For three decades, the park's meadows were a popular destination for Turkish Germans to picnic and barbecue during the summer, prompting ongoing controversies around pollution and the appropriate use of public space. In addition, similarly to *Babakiueria*, Berlin's debates turn barbecuing into a matter of culture, thus inventing barbecuing and picnicking in urban parks as cultural traditions with attached meanings of backward otherness (see also Özkan 2008, 127). In these debates, the "barbecue area" (*Grillgebiet*) is framed as a seemingly distinct cultural territory in which Turkish and Middle Eastern immigrants—imagined as homogeneous groups—have taken over German lands (fig. 4.4). From this perspective, barbecue area emerges as a tradition, a rural lifestyle that expresses lower class status and backwardness—everything that offends the urban civilized and bourgeois order. Local newspapers, politicians, and some white German Berliners see the park as a lost country beyond municipal help, and some literally name it a site of "mass migratory invasion" (*völkerwanderungsähnliche Invasion*) (see Flamm 2009). In these images, barbecuing is framed as a breach of civilization: it invades urban space with smoke and smells, while the barbecuers leave piles of trash behind. And yet despite these attempts to rein in the practice—including the smoke emanating from the barbecues and the lurking threat of fire breaking out—barbecuing, indeed, transgresses the social-material order of the city and challenges its racializations and colonial logic.

Barbecuing entered German national politics in the 1990s, although many people, including migrants, had been barbecuing in parks already for more than a decade. Just a few years after the unification of East and West Berlin, city officials began to worry about the appropriate uses of green space and the representative function of the Tiergarten, which was no longer situated in the shadow of the Wall but right in the new city center. Arguing that groups of "Turkish barbecuers" were taking over the park and displacing German citizens (Flamm 2009), conservative politicians and public officials lobbied for the close monitoring and curbing of wild barbecuing and its traces: litter, smoke, and bad smells. After ongoing controversy in the Berlin Senate, the city's Office for Green Spaces (Grünflächenamt) set

FIGURE 4.4 *G* as in *Grillgebiet* = "BBQ area." Park map at one of the entrances to the Tiergarten. Photo by author.

out new regulations in 1997 that outlawed barbecuing in public parks except in designated barbecue areas (Flamm 2009). As a consequence, many public parks—especially those located in migrant neighborhoods, such as Neukölln and Wedding—were now completely off-limits for barbecuing.[5] Accordingly, the city published a brochure with rules and several "barbecue maps" charting those urban territories in which barbecuing was still allowed (SenStadt 2004) (fig. 4.5).[6] Among barbecuers, these regulations triggered various migrations, especially between some migrant neighborhoods in former West Berlin and the city's eastern districts, where barbecuing was permitted in several parks.[7]

In the Tiergarten, a few meadows between the Spree River, Bellevue Castle (the German presidential residence), and the Strasse des 17. Juni became one of sixteen remaining barbecue areas in Berlin, attracting barbecuers from across the city. Yet these new restrictions did little to settle the controversy, which has continued smoldering for years. At the end of the 1990s, Berlin's conservative mayor Eberhard Diepgen donated a birthday gift to Volker Liepelt, one of his party friends and an opponent of barbecuing in public parks: an electric grill. On the birthday card he wrote: "Volker

Grillen in Berlin
Having a Barbecue in Berlin
Berlin'de Mangal Yakma Kuralları
الشـوى فى برلين
Жарить на гриле в Берлине

FIGURE 4.5 "Grillen in Berlin / Having a Barbecue in Berlin," brochure cover page. Courtesy of SenStadt (2004).

Liepelt's resistance agitates open-air mass barbecuing—hence, vote for the home barbecue by and with the Christian Democrats!" (Richter 1999). In the early 2000s, suggestions increased for a new barbecue police to prevent any wild barbecuing beyond the designated areas (Hasselmann 2005). The city's Senate Department for Urban Development published an elaborate rule book in five languages (German, English, Turkish, Arabic, and Russian) on how to barbecue in the city. Its detailed recommendations included: use only special designated areas; do not collect branches in the park; do not grill anything that does not fit on your grate (i.e., don't grill a whole animal); do not ignite a fire on the ground; do not put trash into open containers because it will attract crows, foxes, and rats (SenStadt 2004).

In 2009 members of the conservative party suggested introducing a general five-euro barbecuing fee, igniting protest among other political parties and large parts of the local population (Flamm 2009). In April of that year, after a series of sunny spring days and media reports about excessive barbecuing in the Tiergarten, the barbecue debate once again resurfaced on local municipalities' agendas. The city's Office of Order reported that it had registered ninety-nine offenses against park rules in the first few months—almost as many as during the entire previous year. In addition, local authorities conveyed that municipal services were understaffed and their financial resources dwindling. They suggested that private security services or local prisoners should thus be responsible for the cleanup. "What if the state just left the garbage in the parks?" a local politician asked in a news interview (Schmiemann and Schoelkopf 2009). Cracking down on garbage, the city's Office of Municipal Sanitation also came up with the idea for a special hotline for concerned citizens to report littered areas all over Berlin, especially in parks. Other local residents proposed a "sweeping force" of concerned citizens, equipped with brooms and dustpans and ready to set out and go through the parks and neighborhoods for cleanup. Their cleaning status would be available online.

As conservatives introduced various measures to regulate barbecuing, many of these rules remained heavily contested. Members of the Social Democratic (SPD) and Green Parties debated the possibilities and limits of local restrictions on barbecuing. In 2003, German president Johannes Rau defended barbecuing in Berlin's parks and said this practice should be considered a cultural right of all Turks living in Germany. In response to his statement, conservative politicians and media lobbied a campaign against barbecuing. Germany's (and Europe's) best-selling tabloid newspaper, the *BILD*, circulated a petition asking Berliners whether barbecuing should be outlawed in their city (Özkan 2008, 127). In everyday conversations, I often heard Berliners poking fun at the endless debate and the rather helpless "barbecuing police" trying to control masses of people hanging out on park meadows in the summer. At the same time, community organizations such as the Turkish Union (Türkische Bund) and members of the SPD, the Green and Left Parties, and several tourist organizations continued to voice strong opposition to the city's barbecuing rules, celebrating barbecuing as a symbol of multicultural Berlin. The Social Democratic Party member Ephraim Gothe called barbecuing a symbol of "lived integration" (Flamm 2009). Similarly, the Green Party repeatedly argued against outlawing barbecuing, advocating instead for the installation of advisory signs about environmentally conscious barbecuing (*umweltbewusstes Grillen*) in parks. Party members emphasized the multicultural and socially integrative dimensions of barbecuing, arguing that it obviously corresponded to a broad need in the population in a dense city where, for many, there are no other possibilities for collective barbecuing (Gülfirat 2005; see, e.g., Lange 2011).

The Green Party has also used images of the Turkish German community barbecuing in Berlin's parks in their campaign leaflets. In the summer of 2002, in response to efforts to restrict barbecuing, two Green Party members, Wolfgang Wieland (Berlin's mayor at the time) and Özcan Mutlu, organized a multicultural barbecue in the Tiergarten to illustrate solidarity across cultures. Local media reported on the event, showing Wieland cooking meat and offering beef and chicken to his guests. Wieland was also quoted as saying that Berlin knows about barbecuing because of Turkish migrants living in the city. Since barbecuing is the favorite leisure activity of many Middle Eastern migrants, he saw it as a testimony to the encounter of different cultures in Berlin. Hence, conservative attempts to get rid of it in the Tiergarten should be stopped. Further, Wieland stated, "Immigrants are part of our society. Everybody is welcome to barbecue and picnic here." Yet he made one request: "They must make sure to take care of the environment" (*Hürriyet* 2002). In Wieland's words, barbecuing becomes not only a matter of cultural otherness but also a threat to the environment. A crucial element of an imagined integration of immigrants thus turns out to be environmental consciousness and public responsibility.

In response to these debates, the Turkish-language media officially declared barbecuing in Berlin to be an important element of the "Turkish cultural tradition" (*Hürriyet* 2002). Many Turkish newspapers with German editions, like *Hürriyet*, reported on clouds of smoke in Berlin's urban parks (see Gülfirat 2005; *Hürriyet* 2002), and closely followed plans to outlaw barbecuing throughout the city. For example, referring to a city decree that banned barbecuing throughout Berlin during the World Cup, a Turkish newspaper headline read: "Ban on Barbecuing for Turkish People during the World Cup" (Ismet 2006).

These Turkish-language reports made their way into German newspapers. Emphasizing that Berlin's parks were crowded with Turkish barbecuers every summer, the local butchers quoted in *Hürriyet* also found a voice in the Berlin newspaper *Tagesspiegel*: "Turkish people love meat. . . . Among all the people in the world, the Turkish are the barbecuing world champions" (Gülfirat 2005). Furthermore, several Turkish butchers reported difficulties in supplying the large demand for meat during summer months. Drawing on *Hürriyet*'s portrayals, the *Tagesspiegel* article was framed by photographs of barbecuers in the Tiergarten, surrounded by smoke and piles of trash (Gülfirat 2005). Yet the *Tagesspiegel* also criticized the *Hürriyet* (and other Turkish newspapers) for celebrating barbecuing as a Turkish cultural tradition and for affirming meat consumption as a sign of wealth without considering its environmental impact on Berlin's green lungs. Indeed, the *Tagesspiegel* article claimed that when Turkish newspapers say, "Don't touch our barbecue" (Gülfirat 2005), they overlook the piles of trash or the trees suffering from smoke and heat in the park.

Turkish organizations like the Turkish Association Berlin-Brandenburg (Türkischer Bund Berlin-Brandenburg, TBB) also reacted to complaints about trash left behind by barbecuers and made strengthening environmental consciousness in the Turkish community one of their major goals. Eren Ünsal, a member of the organization, stated, "Environmental consciousness is closely tied to the question of integration."[8] During one trash-pickup event, according to the association's report, about "fifty young—most of them Muslim—people from ten different countries gave a good example of environmentalism by taking away the garbage left in the 'Tiergarten' park with forceps and bags. The campaign should strengthen the environmental awareness of immigrants, as stated by the organizers. Some members of the Bundestag were also present at the campaign." In addition to trash being picked up, flyers were put up on trees in cooperation with Berlin's Foundation for Nature Conservation and the antiracist organization INSSAN that monitors Islamophobia (fig. 4.6). The flyers had been painted by children from local kindergartens and they featured nature drawings with Muslim, Christian, and other religious and philosophical proverbs about the environment. Yet curiously, on all sides of the debate, barbecuing became a matter of culture associated with a particular group—Turkish and Middle Eastern migrants (see also Özkan 2008, 127)—and barbecue area emerged as a distinct cultural territory in which migrants had taken over German lands.

After a long controversy, the district government of Berlin Mitte decided to ban meat grilling in the Tiergarten from 2012 onward. When picnickers did not adhere to the new rule in the first few months of the ban, the district introduced a special task force to patrol wild barbecuing in the park and, if necessary, charge high fines (Pasch 2013). As a result, the aromatic traces of barbecuing increasingly disappeared from the Tiergarten's landscape. As many picnickers moved on to other parks, they once again triggered concerns about smoke, smells, and overcrowding. This caused new voices to emerge to ban barbecuing in other parks as well (Pasch 2013). Temporary bans of barbecuing during summer months due to overcrowding, heat waves, and fires have occurred on a regular basis ever since.

FIGURE 4.6 Flyers on trees, Tiergarten. Photo by author.

Fire, Smoke, Meat, and Garbage

In these efforts at containment, barbecuing turns out to be a site of intense contestation over the boundaries of multiculturalism and the protection of nature in Berlin. A matter of culture, barbecuing becomes a racialized practice of occupying and shaping urban nature. In both public debate and media images, as well as in everyday life, the material-symbolic traces of barbecuing trigger anxieties around cleanliness, pollution, and transgression. Barbecue areas are utilized as proof of a failed integration of Turkish immigrants into German society as well as the lack of state control. Covered with blue garbage bags and endless smoke clouds, the Tiergarten and other parks generate stories of excess, unrefined consumption, and bad environmentalism. These material traces evoke fears of transgression and feelings of disgust—and they become signifiers of a racialized otherness.

Many news articles have described how smoke threatens to pollute the green lungs of Berlin: "Hundreds of people have crowded the area; black or white smoke is rising everywhere" (Fülling 2011). Reports of an invasion of smells have proliferated: of burned chicken wings, lamb thighs, meatballs, and garlic. Charred patches of grass and burning trash cans have evoked a sense of the park being burned down. Images of Turkish immigrants sitting on the lawn, their faces covered in smoke, have abounded in the media.

The Tiergarten and other parks have been declared at risk for smog pollution from excessive barbecuing. Although the Tiergarten should belong to everyone, a local news report cited a Berlin politician saying that "if the Tiergarten continues to be so carelessly ravaged, then people in nearby districts will soon suffocate from smog" (Rittner 2005). In these urban doom scenarios, smoke infuses the city and its neatly landscaped spaces of nature. A harbinger of fire, it threatens to break down the boundaries between order and chaos, civilization and wilderness, and nature and society. Fire is always both a social and a natural reality (Bachelard 1964, 10), and as Andrew Mathews has shown, "fire is a powerful symbol of chaos, often marking the destruction of order in both the social and natural worlds" (Mathews 2003, 78). As fire and smoke became the targets of state control in Berlin's parks, the city's migrants and communities of color were held responsible for them.

In addition to smoke and fire, images of garbage populated media reports. "The barbecue problem in the Tiergarten is a garbage problem," one article stated. "On a nice weekend, more than twenty tons of rubbish are collected in the Tiergarten alone" (*Berliner Morgenpost* 2009). According to local politicians, the Tiergarten had been in need of "rescue" for a long time. Others "gave up" on this area of Berlin a long time ago, claiming that barbecuers are dangerous (Schmiemann and Schoelkopf 2009).[9] This framed the "barbecuing problem" as a battle of the city against "wild migrant hordes," who produce trash, as was also captured in yet another report: "Every Monday, the Barbecue Meadow in the Tiergarten looks like a battlefield. The city clears away the garbage of the migrants. Yet the conflict keeps smoldering" (Flamm 2009).

Garbage and waste often carry racial meanings and are a potent "polysemous symbol of disorder and threat to community" in debates about urban development (Gregory 1998, 125). In Berlin, the garbage left behind by migrants and cleared away by municipal services signified a turf violation and a threat to the coherence of an assumed natural national community. Furthermore, for many, it symbolized what national media have increasingly claimed: that Middle Eastern migrants have failed to integrate, are wasteful, and take advantage of the state.

Tales of bloody and inappropriate meat-related practices added a final touch to this sense of a state of emergency in Berlin's parks. The opening scene in a featured article in the national weekly newspaper *Die Zeit* narrated a panorama of savagery: on a humid Monday morning, as the park slowly awakened and dew sparkled on the leaves, two big men with tattoos dragged a bloody leg of lamb out of the bushes—together with a great deal of trash, the last remnant of a normal barbecue weekend (Flamm 2009). Another article in the local newspaper *Der Tagesspiegel* reported on Turkish barbecuers hanging out on the Spree River shore, grilling a lamb, and camping right next to signs prohibiting barbecuing. Their transgression was interpreted as signaling provinciality, disconnection, and illiteracy vis-à-vis the written rules of urban public order, food consumption, and German environmental standards (Hasselmann 2005).[10]

Like the smoke and garbage, the excessive barbecuing of meat in public—and not in the safely bounded domestic realm of the home—functions in these reports as a sign of Muslim immigrant difference. This attention to meat echoes a longer history of casting certain meat consumption practices as signs of racial difference in Germany and beyond.[11] Thus, migrants' relations to animals (as meat), as well as their alleged tendency to pollute pristine urban nature with smoke and garbage, underscore their status as others whose behavior needs to be managed and contained. But even more than this, the meat-eaters themselves are made to appear almost animal-like, as out-of-control predators. This focus on disconnection and unruliness constructs the Tiergarten as a place of lawlessness and wilderness—a space beyond civitas—which also puts an ironic twist on the original purpose of the Tiergarten as a zoo inhabited by wild animals and as a showcase hunting ground. Imagined as wilderness amid the city, barbecue areas become an extension of urban hot spots, problematic districts, or the ghetto—images that, as discussed in chapter 2, have dominated much public debate about immigration in German cities, especially Berlin, since the turn of the millennium. Not unlike the racially coded language of crime in urban neighborhoods, the barbecue area figures as a wild or savage space amid a tranquil urban nature, and thus as a sign of Middle Eastern and Muslim immigrants' alleged urban *and* environmental illiteracy.

Tropes of urban wilderness have often been used "to justify the treatment of minority inhabitants of the inner city as 'savages' to be contained by the forces of civilization" (M. Bennett and Teague 1999, 6; Ross 1999). In Berlin, images of wilderness and violated urban nature symbolize the cultural otherness of migrants' bodies—and their racialization. As I have shown in previous chapters, there is a long genealogy of racial ideologies in Germany that inscribe difference not only onto bodies but also onto landscapes. In fact, the placement of different bodies in particular natural and urban landscapes has played a key role in the construction of whiteness and national identity throughout German history, particularly in Nazi imaginaries that linked nature and the nation with white bodies, discourses of blood, and public space (Linke 1999b, 1999c).

The charisma of barbecuing needs to be read within these legacies and the boundaries they draw between nature and culture, and the city and countryside. For example, as Uli Linke (1999c) has shown, a Green Party leaflet featuring a 1989 photograph of a public park in former West Berlin (perhaps the Tiergarten?) gives us a glimpse of "paradise" and racialized imaginaries of urban nature: next to a big sign spray-painted with black-lettered graffiti reading P-A-R-A-D-I-S-E, two white German nudists enjoy a tranquil afternoon in a carefully landscaped setting (fig. 4.7). Sitting in armchairs surrounded by trees and bushes, the man and woman are reading. In the picture's foreground, two men and one woman, who is wearing a small headscarf, are having a picnic.

Linke (1999c) provides an analysis of this picture's racial aesthetics and the construction of nature and white public space. For Linke, the clothing of the people who are marked as Turkish migrants here, their cooking on a grill, and their positioning on the ground accentuate this group's difference vis-à-vis the German nudists in their armchairs who are positioned as over-lords of nature. The clothed body of the Middle Eastern Other, according to Linke's analysis, signifies a lack of refinement, a commitment to traditional values, and a simplistic rural lifestyle, whereas the unclothed white bodies signify modernity, a cosmopolitan urban lifestyle, and the expertise of refined consumption. Rendered highly visible in the foreground, the migrants are nevertheless positioned at the margins of the nation while the naked German bodies, partially hidden by the shade of trees and bushes, are positioned within the natural domain at the top and at the center of the nation (Linke 1999c, 61–62).

Linke's analysis gestures at an important link between notions of race, place, nature, and the body in postunification Germany: in the paradise photograph, the placement and leisure activities of different bodies in a landscaped urban park come to signify racial difference. Linke argues that after the unification of East and West Germany, these symbols of bodies and wilderness in the city took on a distinctly nationalist agenda: an ideology of difference reemerged at this moment, and it celebrated the naked white body placed in natural settings. Echoing a longer genealogy of racial ideologies, body space and urban public space intersect in debates about

FIGURE 4.7 "Paradies," West Berlin, 1989. Image from Wahlprogramm 1989, Bündnis 90/Die Grünen, photo by Ralph Rieth, printed in Linke (1999c, 61).

barbecuing. In contemporary Berlin, their demarcations serve to redefine the borders of the European "civilized" city and the nation. People's relations to nature and more-than-human beings thus become a central site for the racialization of Middle Eastern or Arab bodies, particularly by constructing them as culturally other and "out of place"—and, in fact, as less-than-human.

Rather than assume a stable underlying racial unconscious that reifies established orders (the Nazi past in particular), we therefore see here how the categories of race and nature shift. While both are central products of modern political culture and government (Moore, Kosek, and Pandian 2003), they are mobilized in historically contingent ways (Dominguez 1986) and in relation to social struggle. Although notions of nature and the body can have both liberating and dangerous effects (Moore, Kosek, and Pandian 2003, 3), it is important, as Paul Gilroy reminds us, to connect past scenes of racial violence and colonial domination with the present *without assuming the same logic* (Gilroy 2004, 33).

Scholarship in geography and related disciplines has illustrated how stories about the cruel treatment of animals—such as illegal hunting, killing animals for religious rituals, or eating animals that in the global North are often kept as pets, such as dogs or cats—are used to characterize people as beastly and to mark inferiority (Elder, Wolch, and Emel 1998; Wolch 2002).[12] From this perspective, conflicts over human-animal practices—including eating meat—fuel ongoing efforts to racialize, dehumanize, and devalue migrants and people of color. However, with their focus on the figure of the wild and ungovernable Muslim or Arab, Berlin's barbecuing debates reveal the specificity and changing nature of Islamophobic public imaginaries—both in their colonial trajectories and in the post-9/11 era. As Ghassan Hage (2017, 32) has argued, the mind-body duality has nourished colonial and anti-Semitic classifications in different ways: unlike anti-Semitic and anti-Black racism, Europeans framed the Arab/Muslim as a source of pollution that was nevertheless unexploitable in the colonial era. By contrast, in the aftermath of the 9/11 attacks, the ungovernable Arab/Muslim body has become a dominant theme of (neo)colonial imaginaries in both North America and Europe. Here, the figure of the Arab/Muslim has increasingly been associated with a threatening undomesticated other of nature—represented in the figure of the "Muslim lone wolf," imagined in Western political discourse (2017, 33) to be prone to terrorism. This theme of ungovernability and the undomesticated speaks to two sets of policies that, as Hage points out, are at the center of contemporary neocolonial (and liberal) global government: an international order that seeks to contain mobility across national borders (in which Arabs/Muslims become a source of invasion), and national policies that aim to integrate racialized Muslim bodies (assumed to be unable to integrate themselves) into national space (37). Situated within this context, the requirement for racialized migrant communities to care for the environment according to white Western norms, as it is expressed in Berlin's barbecuing disputes, becomes a tool of secular urban governance (see also El-Tayeb 2012; Fernando 2013) integral to the maintenance of Europe's internal and external borders.

Curiously, barbecuing is also widely considered a German leisure activity—many people love to barbecue sausages (usually pork) and steak in the confined spaces of their homes, either in the kitchen, on the balcony, or in their gardens.[13] The resulting sparks, smoke, and smells are usually held at bay by vents, walls, or bushes separating one home garden from another. Yet with just a little bit of wind, sparks from the grill can float anywhere and ignite a forest fire. And there is more than the threat of fire. As the barbecue fire smolders, the sparks—which here are traces of not only friction but also sociality across boundaries of race and private property—reignite a sense of threat. While for some, smoke pollutes the green lungs of the city, for others, it provides a space to breathe.

Breathing Spaces

In the park you can breathe. The air is good—not like at home when you sit around and watch TV all day. And in the park, things taste different. The aroma is so much better. Even if you barbecue on your balcony, it's not the same as it is in the park. The air in the park makes for a better aroma. And the grease of the meat drips off the grill.
—Cemal, barbecuer in Berlin

Köfte recipe for a "city full of herbs":
½ kg minced beef
bulgur
two onions
several slices of dry white bread
parsley
cumin
sumac
black pepper
tomatoes
and a few other secret ingredients

On a chilly Sunday, Cemal called me early in the morning. Usually calm, his voice sounded excited and full of enthusiasm. Although the temperatures were a bit lower than usual for summer, the sun was out and it looked like it would not rain—ideal for an afternoon in the park with family, friends, a grill, and a curious researcher who was spending much of her time in the park anyway.

We met at the Tiergarten in front of Bellevue Castle. Cemal arrived with his sister, Yasmin, who was visiting from Istanbul, his cousin Ülkay, and his daughter; they were all on bicycles. We searched out their familial spot near the castle, under a large chestnut tree. Others had already gathered on the meadow, with grills, lawn chairs, blankets, carpets, and fold-out tables spread out on the grass. Smoke emanated from grills and spread in thin layers across the park. A savory smell was in the air. As we settled on the ground, spreading out blankets, Cemal unpacked his grill—a small, three-legged one. Ülkay brought cake, Yasmin made a salad, and Cemal unwrapped a huge container of *köfte* (Turkish meatballs). "It is a special mix, and it contains a whole city full of herbs!" he explained, pointing to the diversity of tastes and smells he brought with him in the form of herbs and other ingredients—parsley, cumin, sumac, black pepper, and tomatoes. Yet as I inquired about the full recipe, he remained secretive and would not reveal it to me.

The last time he had been in the Tiergarten, Ülkay had collected tree branches and hidden them in the bushes. Yet in the meantime someone had discovered them, and they were now gone. Ülkay and Cemal were not bothered since they had found a whole grill hidden in the bush the other day and took it with them. Everybody brought something to the park and took something with them as well. Cemal lit the fire and waved a small piece of cardboard to keep it alight. Watching the flames, we heard the sounds of mice rummaging in the undergrowth in the bushes next to us. Finally, as the fire calmed down and the coals began to smolder, Cemal took out the *köfte* mix, formed small meatballs, and put them on the grill.

As he fiddled with the utensils, rotating the *köfte* sizzling on the grill, Cemal reminisced about days spent barbecuing on the beach in Turkey. Cemal, whose family migrated to Istanbul from a small village in Anatolia in the 1960s, had moved to Berlin with his sister in the mid-1970s. He worked as a forklift driver for a local company for many years. In the 1990s, after unification, he lost his job. After a period of unemployment, he began working odd jobs and struggled to make ends meet. In contrast to his precarious job situation in Germany, he spoke excitedly about his memories of living with or visiting his family in Turkey. Barbecuing took on an almost nostalgic role in these memories.

"Instead of cooking at home, you go barbecue outside, on the beach and in the countryside," he told me. In Istanbul during the summer, his and many other families he knew would keep a grill in the trunks of their cars and would not miss any chance to leave the city to go picnic. This, he explained, is why barbecuing is a "Turkish tradition" and an expression of hospitality: if people join your picnic, even if they are strangers, you offer them food. From this perspective, cooking meat in the open and sitting on the ground all day were what recreation was all about—and it was healthier too. While Cemal emphasized the health benefits of barbecuing, he also expressed yearning for a simpler life, a desire to venture outdoors and escape the city. For him, barbecuing rekindled memories of picnicking with friends and family in the Turkish countryside.

Yet for Cemal, as for many other picnickers I spoke with, barbecuing conjured up feelings beyond nostalgia. Cemal explained that barbecuing neither was tied to the past nor polluted the city. Instead, it created a breathing space in the present—a space to take a break from everyday life. As Ülkay put it, the air in Berlin tended to be stifling. Berlin sometimes felt like a modern prison, an invisible border, because your everyday life is divided and you get slotted into categories: during work, you have to pretend to be a German, but at home you are a Turk. And when you are on the streets, you get ignored by Germans or simply treated as a foreigner, as the Muslim other. In contrast, Cemal pointed out: "In the park, you can breathe deeply. You feel freedom."

The park's public space and its fresh air contributed to a better flavor and aroma, such that barbecuing created a taste of freedom, a breathing space. As Cemal conveyed, by barbecuing in public parks, he and other picknickers refused to domesticate the grilling of meat. Instead, grilling meat in the middle of the city transgressed not only normative notions of urbanity and mass consumption but also a division of everyday life into two worlds: home and work, or the "native" German environment (*Umwelt*) and the space of immigrants.[14] Furthermore, in contrast to media portrayal of migrants' alleged ignorance vis-à-vis the urban environment, the Tiergarten and other parks served as key reference points in many of my interviewees' knowledge of the city.

As Cemal moved from one short-term job to another, he got to know the city in new ways. Over the years, he had worked all over the city—in a chocolate factory near the center; as a forklift truck driver in Kreuzberg; at the Office for Green Spaces on the edge of Berlin, in Spandau; and at a forestry station in the Grunewald, pruning trees and bushes all day long. Having spent a lot of time in the forest, he explained that he knew the city's forests like the palm of his hand, a statement that implicitly challenged public discourse about Turkish or Muslim immigrants' lack of knowledge about or connection with the city. In this regard, for Cemal, barbecuing was also about claiming knowledge and a sense of connection with the urban landscape—and thus a right to the city (Lefebvre 1996; D. Mitchell 2003). When he first came to Berlin, Cemal joked, he did not notice any Germans barbecuing in parks; then, as he put it, Germans saw all the Turks in the parks and some thus started to barbecue too.

In *Dancing with the Devil*, José Limón (1994) engages with a transnational discourse shared by upper-class Anglo-Americans and Mexican Americans that casts working-class Mexican men in the idiom of "human rubbish, animality, aggressiveness and abnormality—in the Christian realm of the devil, if you will" (124). Limón illustrates that the ritualistic production and consumption of barbecued meat (an event called *carne asada*), and the humor and language play that go with it, constitute a strategy for resisting dominant images of Mexican masculinity, and a form of class and ethnic distinction among Mexican American men in South Texas. From this perspective, the humorous enactment of body play and mutual sexualized taunting around meat consumption is not a matter of anxiety or cultural ambivalence but rather an expression of "carnivalesque critical difference, though never without its own [gendered] contradiction" (125–26). This form of play involves a parody-like exploration of alternative possibilities and the creation of a sense of freedom from everyday experiences of injustice and degradation (135).

When I went to the park with them, Cemal and Ülkay similarly engaged in a form of masculine play—for them, it was a "man's job" to put up the grill, prepare the meat, and barbecue it. Familiar with the lay of the land in the park, they knew where to find the right branches with which to help build a fire. But by performing expertise in food preparation and displaying their familiarity with informal park etiquette, they also distinguished and performed class and ethnic status. Similar to Limón's description, Cemal's insistence on minimalist consumption—sitting on the ground instead of lawn chairs, using wood coal, and not bringing too many fancy utensils—can be understood as a means of distinguishing himself from white German middle-class norms of appropriate behavior in public space and nature. On a basic level, of course, barbecuing is also about saving money, as one does not go to a restaurant or café for food. This is true even if eating meat remains a sign of wealth (however moderate), as not everyone can afford meat on a regular basis.

For the Tiergarten picnickers, barbecue areas were not constricted spaces of pollution and chaos but rather spaces where they were able to breathe and transcend a national discourse that marked them as foreigners. Barbecuing thus did more than draw lines of difference between civilized Europeans and Muslim others. It created a space in which questions about the future, about belonging to the city, and the seemingly immobile divisions of everyday life were opened up—albeit in gendered ways. In this respect, barbecuing can be read as a response to growing social divisions and to the constraining metaphors of troubled migrant urban spaces and the figure of a Muslim as threat. These metaphors have infused public discourse for decades, stigmatizing and devaluing the lives of Middle Eastern migrants in relation to the urban environments they inhabit in Germany. The barbecue picnic, by contrast, provides a makeshift material-semiotic practice that challenges existing divisions and normative notions of urbanity and allows people to "conspire" and breathe together (Choy 2011; Myers 2019) amid ongoing exclusion (fig. 4.8). Not unlike

FIGURE 4.8 Tiergarten. Photo by author.

Berliners' encounters with ruderal plants, these practices operate at the seams of the city's domesticated relations between people and land and other beings.

Barbecue City Istanbul

Despite all the barbecue cross- and back-talk, it was not until I took a trip to Istanbul to visit Cemal's and others' families that I realized that barbecuing incites debate across national borders. In fact, Istanbul, a hometown or intermediate stop for many migrants from Anatolia (including Cemal), has had its own barbecuing debate. In Istanbul, barbecuing in public parks and on beaches became a contested site where nationalist, secular, and urban subjectivities collided with rural, religious, and racialized ones in the 2000s. Istanbul's barbecuing debates provide glimpses of the larger political contexts at stake: rural-urban migrations, the role of Islam in Europe, the reshuffling of Europe's borders, and long-standing efforts to integrate Turkey into the EU.

In Istanbul, public parks and beaches along the Bosporus, the geographic boundary between Asia and Europe, have become the subject of controversy over class divisions and what it means to be European and modern. As you enter the Bosporus Strait, traveling from Bakırköy along the Marmara Sea toward the Golden Horn, you pass long stretches of green space. Constructed in the 1990s as part of rehabilitation projects to clean up and green the Golden Horn, these spaces offer patches of lawn squeezed between the water and busy roads. While trees and bushes provide precious cool shade in the summer, the parks also offer the only public access to the water.[15] Many families who picnic or barbecue on the grass are former migrants from Anatolia, and some of them might have relatives in Berlin. When they first arrived in Istanbul, many migrant families lived in the so-called *gecekondular*—housing structures that entered the Turkish national imagination as the migrant villages, makeshift shelters, ghettos, or slums of Istanbul.[16] Not unlike in Berlin, families bring their hammocks, blankets, carpets, lawn chairs, strollers, bikes, and—most importantly—grills to Istanbul's parks. Sitting on the grass or lying in the shade, local residents of all generations eat, chat, play backgammon, and drink tea. The menus range from tomato and cucumber salad, bread, *köfte*, *kebab*, fried eggplant, and peppers, to watermelon or simply a snack of sunflower seeds. When it gets crowded, people huddle around grills on small strips of grass right next to the road or even in the parking lots. During the summer, as temperatures rise, the heat mixes with the hot smoke of the barbecues, and the waterfront offers a slight breeze.

Due to concerns about environmental pollution, smoke, fire hazards, and cleanliness, barbecuing has been prohibited in most parts of Istanbul, including green spaces (Özkan 2008, 128). Nevertheless, you can see picnickers and barbecuers all over the city, which has triggered heated and ongoing controversy over the years. One debate was set off by an article published in the newspaper *Radikal* in July 2005. In it, the author, Mine Kırıkkanat, reports on growing cultural divisions in Istanbul's public spaces. She begins a tour of the city with the Istanbul International Airport, which she describes as the frontier of Europe, a beacon of modern Istanbul lighting up Turkey's non-Arab, modern side. In contrast, the ride from the airport to the historic city center reveals what she frames as the barbarian, dark Istanbul—an expression of urban backwardness, a scene of invasion by shantytown people and a giant barbecue:

> As men stretch out on the grass in their underwear, ruminating, women who wear black chadors or headscarves and are covered without exception, fan the barbecue, brew tea, and rock their babies. . . . This view is repeated every square meter: our dark people cook meat by the sea

toward which they turn their backs. It is impossible here to encounter one single family grilling fish. Perhaps, if they enjoyed eating fish and if they knew how to cook it properly, they would not just be lying there in their dirty white flannel; they would not be chewing and burping on the grass, scratching themselves; and perhaps they would not even be this chubby, long-armed and hairy! (Kırıkkanat 2005)

Dubbing this scene "Carnivore Islamistan," Kırıkkanat frames Istanbul's divisions of class, ethnicity, and region in the language of meat, consumption, dress, and the appropriate use of public space. Complaining about the urban poor taking over Istanbul's parks and beaches with grills, white underwear (*don*), and headscarves, the author draws on several controversial cultural images. Meat consumption—especially *kebab*, associated with Anatolian food—stands here in contrast to the Istanbul natives' preference for fish. Not unlike in Berlin's barbecuing debate, Kırıkkanat describes public meat consumption as an antiurban, uncivilized practice by first- or second-generation migrants from rural Anatolia—perceived as Istanbul's black Arabs—casting them as incompetent citizens. In addition, Kırıkkanat zooms in on the cultural politics of beachwear and the headscarf, accusing working-class men wearing the don and women wearing long cloaks of offending urban cosmopolitan sensibilities. The class and ethnic connotations of both meat and beachwear can hardly be overlooked. Kırıkkanat (2005) concludes: "On Sundays in the summer, it is not even Arabia that one encounters along the Bosporus. It is Ethiopia overfed with meat" (see also Vick 2005, 21; Zeybek 2006).

Kırıkkanat's article triggered an avalanche of responses. Some newspapers published stories about what they saw as the misuse of parks and beaches by the urban poor, while others critiqued Kırıkkanat's dismay as elitist, as an unacceptable denial of authentic (rural) traditions, and as discriminatory against working-class migrants from Anatolia.[17] In contrast to Kırıkkanat, these accounts defended what they framed as the tradition and authenticity of certain kinds of beachwear and barbecuing. Writers like Timur Danış spoke in favor of wearing the don, pointing out that it was a symbol of class status and poverty and thus should be worn with pride; Danış's satirical magazine *Leman* lobbied for a beach rally titled "Hold On to Your Underwear." Eventually, the municipal government responded to the debate by regulating barbecue use and the wearing of the don and headscarves on public beaches. Affirming middle-class European standards of civic enjoyment and mass consumption, guards soon patrolled beaches to make sure people adhered to the modern dress code of bathing suits (Vick 2005).[18]

As in Berlin, different parties attached different meanings to barbecuing (and beachwear) and thus engaged competing definitions of urban citizenship. In portrayals of public parks along the Bosporus, barbecuing was seen as an authentic cultural expression of the urban poor—an expression of a culture that conflicted with a Western, European, and capitalist style of urban living and refined consumption. Imaginaries surrounding picnicking and grilling meat thus illustrate the cultural disjunctures of class and regionality created by migration from the countryside to the city, in Turkey and beyond.

As Stephan Lanz (2005) has pointed out, a fissure between two symbolic communities and political movements lies at the heart of these disjunctures. Since the 1990s, the duality between the figure of the civilized cosmopolitan citizen and the uncivilized rural migrant, between "white" and "black" (and Arab) Turks, or what Lanz calls urbanites and anti-urbanites, has had a strong hold in both public and academic realms.[19] These figures appear in discourses about public green space in both Istanbul and Berlin: whereas the anti-urbanite stands for the provincial, uncivilized community led by affect and ignorant of how to act in public space, the civilized cosmopolitan urbanite is economically independent, barbecues on private property, and is both commercially oriented and environmentally conscious.[20] In Turkey these dual figures have emerged in the context of urbanization shaped by commercial interests and neoliberal development since the 1980s. In this respect, the barbecuing disputes also echo conflicts over the increasing privatization of public space that, for example, triggered extensive protests in Istanbul's Gezi Park at Taksim Square in 2013.

Reprise

Following barbecue's key ingredients (fire and meat) as well as its traces (garbage and smoke), we can see how barbecuing animates anxieties and creates pleasure, community, and a space to breathe in Berlin and beyond. Rather than a closed entity or practice, confined to a clear barbecue area, barbecuing is a makeshift practice that resists regulation and transgresses boundaries and national borders. As smoke, fire, and scents capture people's attention and are entangled with notions of otherness, wild barbecuing emerges as a border practice in which urban and rural, city and nature, and Europe and its racialized others are reshuffled in unexpected ways.

For some, barbecue's blend of fire, smoke, and smells creates a taste of freedom and a sense of connection to urban land that allows them to breathe and to take a break from everyday life and social exclusion. For others, barbecuing pollutes and disturbs the environmental and social order of the city. From this perspective, barbecuing is a barbarian practice that illustrates a lack of civilized knowledge and conduct on the part of Muslim immigrants in Europe. Both in Berlin and Istanbul, barbecuers become racialized—they figure as savage others threatening the civilized order of the city, the nation, and Europe. The barbecue areas in both these cities thus need to be seen in the context of what Kien Nghi Ha describes as Europe's increasingly strict demarcation of its inner and outer borders (Nghi Ha 2006, 16).

The figure of barbecuing and savage practices of cooking meat have long captured European cultural imaginations and are deeply entangled with the history of (settler) colonial expansion. In his book *Savage Barbecue*, Andrew Warnes explores the powerful racial connotations bound up in both the name and history of barbecue. Conventional etymology and history have claimed that Europeans encountered the Taino word *barabicoa* in the Caribbean, where it signified a wooden rack supported by four stakes that was used to slowly cook meat over an open fire (W. Caldwell 2005, 6). Challenging this origin story, Warnes shows that barbecue's story is a transatlantic one—and that its distinctive mythology of freedom, savagery, and masculinity has existed since the onset of European colonialism. Drawing on Eric Hobsbawm, Warnes argues that barbecue emerged as an "invented tradition" (2008, 4) in the European colonial gaze that represented the Indigenous practice of smoking foods as a sign of savagery and the wild. Barbecue mythology thus arose from "fraught colonial representations that sought to represent [non-Western] cultures as the barbaric antithesis of European achievement" (Warnes 2008, 6–7). The journals of Christopher Columbus and his crew reveal a long-standing European hunger for barbecue: repeated encounters with native culinary scenes are saturated with the same material-semiotic violence.[21] For example, Columbus's crew expressed marvel at the slow cooking process and the sweet fragrance of roasted fish on the beach, as well as bewilderment in the face of beastly serpents and other critters surrounding the scene. Across time, barbecue has stood in contrast to European sensibilities of meat cooking as a practice of controlling nature (Warnes 2008, 8) that occurs in the confines of the home. For Warnes, reports of encounters with barbecue engage a colonial discourse that claims to recognize the humanity of Indigenous communities while subjecting them to cultural assimilation (2008, 16). The similarity of the word *barbecue* to *barbarism* is thus not coincidental and arises from the stereotype that "all barbarians must barbecue and all who barbecue must be barbaric" (7).

In Columbus's narrative, cooking serpents' meat is what casts non-Europeans as uncivilized, barbaric others. In contrast, in today's barbecue encounters in Europe, it is the roasting of an entire animal that is deemed too close to undomesticated nature. Meanwhile the alleged lack of environmental literacy among migrant communities also offends European sensibilities. The consumption of animal meat as a symbol of otherness thus reappears in current discussions of multiculturalism and, together with barbecue's traces of garbage and smoke, serves to juxtapose "Turkish cultural practices" against a presumed German environmental consciousness. Yet, not unlike in early colonial encounters, Berlin's barbecue debates engage the full spectrum of the ambivalence of racialized sentiments vis-à-vis cooking meat in public: On one hand, there is fascination with the sweet fragrance of spices and slowly cooked meat, and with an imagined colonial frontier associated with barbecuing. On the other hand, barbecue arouses a sense of revulsion against what colonial European narratives cast as a primitive practice beyond the pale of civilization.

Considering this logic, the demand to care for the environment as a prerequisite for integration into German society and Europe becomes a neocolonial strategy of urban governance. It engages the image of the undomesticated colonial other—represented here by the figure of the Muslim/Arab—and is an integral tool to the maintenance of Europe's internal and external borders. As Kien Nghi Ha (2006, 16) points out, discourses and policies of integration enact a form of neocolonial violence that, while on the surface aiming at inclusion, ultimately places the demand for change onto the racialized communities themselves. Constituting a central element of contemporary European political culture, this integration framework claims ideological innocence, environmental and economic rationality, and cosmopolitan openness, thereby setting white Europe as the unquestioned and unquestionable norm.

Challenging these imaginaries and practices, the Tiergarten picnickers reinvent barbecuing as a practice that creates connections both to their everyday lives and migratory histories, and to their desires for freedom and a breathing space from their marginalization in a European city. In both Berlin and Istanbul, barbecuing is therefore less an activity with deep cultural meanings than a ritual that functions as a busy intersection, "where a number of distinct social processes intersect" (Rosaldo 1993, 17). The practice

FIGURE 4.9 End of barbecue area. Photo by author.

and social space of barbecuing can be read as a "crossroads" that "provides a space for distinct trajectories to traverse, rather than containing them in complete encapsulated form" (17). Rosaldo's notion of a busy intersection or crossroads can help conceptualize cultural practices as the crisscrossing of multiple and porous forces of power instead of static, self-contained, and homogeneous units. This perspective shifts away from identifying distinct patterns and broad generalizations and toward identifying heterogeneous processes, dialogue, and questions of social change (21). While utilizing such a notion of intersections for my inquiry in this chapter, I have traced barbecuing from the perspective of a ruderal analytic. In contrast to Rosaldo's cultural inquiry, following a ruderal analytic means highlighting embodied practices and meanings that emerge in the interstices of patterned structures of power and in the erosions of Europe's bordered landscapes that have been shaped by colonial and racial violence. These embodied practices always involve more-than-human worlds.

Indeed, the threat of fire in the city—lurking between the lines of barbecue debates—is a reminder of competing and muddled borders. Not unlike plants flowering amid a city's rubble, fire points to how cultural practices in the city are not separate from nature; neither are humans ever fully in control of the urban landscapes they build. Fire usually emerges at the city's fringes, but in Berlin and Istanbul's barbecue disputes it erupts as a central specter. Traveling via "air's substantiations" (Choy 2011, 139), the smoke that fire produces inhabits the borderlands between the city, the human, domesticated nature, and wilderness. And like air, smoke "disrespects borders, yet at the same time is constituted through difference" (Choy 2011, 165). Thus, the smoke emanating from Berlin's barbecues takes on a palimpsest of meanings that blend into each other in unexpected ways, and yet are linked to ongoing struggles against persistent structures of domination.

Barbecue's appeal is not only that it breaks down the violence of categorical distinctions between the European civilized self and the non-European or Muslim other. As barbecuing transcends claims to authenticity and continues to assert its presence in Berlin, it reopens a central question for Berlin picnickers, like Cemal and so many other urban residents: Who inhabits and can claim a sense of connection to urban lands? Which bodies and lives matter in the city? And who and what can connect and conspire with each other? Through the practice of barbecuing, the city becomes a habitat where this question is mapped anew.

Forests

5

LIVING IN THE
UNHEIMLICH

In the stirrings of the unhomely, another world becomes visible.
—Homi Bhabha, "The World and the Home"

The traces of the past years could be seen and felt everywhere. The paint on the walls of many buildings had crumbled. The fence, walling off the camp from the surrounding forest, had started to rust. Dandelions grew through cracks in the cement around the buildings. With the collapse of the socialist regime, the base was deserted, and its buildings had stood empty for years. Not only had nature returned but its boundaries had been redrawn: right during unification between East and West Germany, the surrounding landscape was transformed into one of the first nature parks in the March Oder region of Brandenburg. Then, in 2007, the half-ruined barracks found a new use. The local administration in Zarin[1] leased them to two parties: the so-called Sozialpark Märkisch-Oderland, a subcontractor who provided housing for refugees, and an individual contractor who fixed up the remaining facilities. Asylum seekers from Kenya and many other countries (including Nigeria, Sudan, Iraq, Cameroon, and Vietnam) now found themselves living in isolated shelters in the ruins of the former military barracks—just thirty-five kilometers east of the city of Berlin. Tucked away in the forest, this refugee home, which everyone called the *Heim* (home), was invisible to many local residents (fig. 5.1).[2]

Looking out the window from Virginia's room, all you could see was trees. In her midthirties, Virginia had recently arrived from Kenya. Her

FIGURE 5.1 Screenshot from the movie *Forst* (2005).

room, shared with another Kenyan woman, was located on the second floor of the former barracks. In it, the furniture was carefully arranged: a wardrobe, a few bookshelves, two beds, three chairs, and a table. On the bookshelves, there were several photographs of other women who had lived in the room in the past. Virginia did not know their names, but she had heard that they now lived in Berlin.

Until just a few months ago, Virginia had lived in a village in the Rift Valley in Kenya. She was growing maize there with her family on a small piece of land. In late 2007, shortly after the national election, Mwai Kibaki, a member of her ethnic group, the Kikuyu, announced victory over Raila Odinga, a Luo. Soon, tensions arose in her village. Many people disputed the election results and were upset at what they perceived to be election fraud. For them, Kibaki's claim was another expression of the long-standing, unquestioned advantaged social status of the Kikuyu.[3] In her village, different ethnic groups had coexisted with each other in the past. Virginia herself was Kikuyu and was married to a Luo man. And yet, after Kibaki's announcement, neighbors and relatives became enemies overnight. Supported by opposition party leaders, local Kalenjin and Luo youths began to chase after and attack Kikuyu people. Some were stabbed, others' houses were burned down. Then, Virginia's neighbor's house was set on fire. Virginia was forced to leave her husband and her children in a rush. Together with other villagers, she fled to the forest. There was no return for her. After hiding for two weeks in "the bush" and then staying in a refugee camp outside the Rift Valley, she managed to leave the country with the help of the Red Cross.

Suddenly, a loud noise interrupted Virginia's story and jolted us back into the present. BAM, BAM, BAM! The sounds emanated from the forest and cut through the air. Then there was a short pause. And then again: BAM, BAM, BAM! For just a moment, we took the sounds for those of gunshots. It was as if the military base had come to life again. Had the soldiers returned for their drill exercises? Startled, we peered out the window into the forest. Silence enveloped the trees. A cold breeze entered the room.

This chapter is about an unhomely dynamic at work in the remaking of Europe's borders at the periphery of Berlin. It is also about stories of mysterious sounds, corroded landscapes, and a mercurial forest in the middle of Europe. The sounds of gunshots cutting through Virginia's story in my opening to this chapter are my guide for navigating through this landscape—a landscape that is the result of many reborderings: between Europe and its others, between nature and culture, between socialism and capitalism, between East and West Germany. In an uncanny way, these sounds echoed the very violence Virginia had fled. Their unclear origin suggests that to understand what is going on in this place, we have to let go for a moment of what we think we may know about Germany's forests or about migration (this field of social life and knowledge production that is so deeply fraught with bureaucratic and [neo-]colonial power dynamics). Instead, I track a sense of dis-place-ment—a feeling of the *un-heimlich*. In German, *unheimlich* means both unhomely and uncanny. In the most literal sense, unheimlich refers to the state of not having a home. But it also describes a sense of uncertainty—a displaced perception in which something seems familiar and yet remains strange—a state of not being able to trust your senses. Freud ([1919] 1955) has theorized this cognitive dissonance as the psychic dimensions of the uncanny.[4] This cognitive dissonance involves a stirring that provokes fear—a situation in which something once known and familiar has become unfamiliar and yet is resurfacing and becoming familiar again (becoming *heimlich*, homely). In the face of the unheimlich, the boundaries between reality and fiction, animate and inanimate, and material and psychic reality become blurred: a symbol, desire, or psychic force assumed to be irrelevant or dead exerts its force. A sense of the unheimlich is thus characterized by a subtlety of feeling—usually associated with unease and confusion. Its analysis requires a method of making oneself vulnerable to a sense of disorientation (124).

Drawing on Freud, postcolonial theorists such as Homi Bhabha have employed the notion of the unhomely to describe the postcolonial condition of displacement and to refer to the psychological ambivalence of living in between worlds and yet being expected to be authentic (Bhabha 1992, 142). Deliberately using the estranging word *unhomely* in English, Bhabha points to the displacements and ambiguities of that which cannot be easily accommodated: like the word *unheimlich*, the unhomely blurs the borders between home and the world, in which the domestic and the home "become sites for history's most intricate invasions" (142). Being "unhomed," as Bhabha points out, is not the same as being homeless but refers instead to moments in which "the border between home and the world becomes confused" (141).

While utilizing this conceptual spectrum of the term, I track the unheimlich ethnographically—as a sense of dislocation and anxiety that is produced by inhabiting a toxic and potentially violent environment. In this environment, fear of invisible forces takes over space (Masco 2006). Via a series of vignettes, I describe the unheimlich as it comes into being in the sensory stirrings of everyday racisms—the experience of being in limbo at the forest on the edges of a European metropole—and as it emerges in a social/material landscape in which the value of objects, personal histories, and imagined futures has shifted.[5] Unlike in Freud's account, which, relying on a colonial logic, relegates the animate to the realm of the primitive, the unheimlich, I argue, offers a window into hazardous ecologies of the nation and racialized exclusions at the edges of European cities today. And even more importantly, it gives us glimpses of the social worlds that fall by the wayside of these exclusions. In the following vignettes, refugees, activists, and other local residents recount their stories of cognitive dissonance, dispossession, and the unmaking of home in Zarin. These stories shed light on what it means to inhabit the ruins of socialism and live amid the persistent colonial dynamics that continue to shape European border politics and migration (see also Davies and Isakjee 2019; Gutiérrez Rodríguez 2018).

As news about the so-called refugee crisis proliferated in the summer of 2015, Germany was at the center of much of the debate: close to one million people sought asylum in the country, many fleeing war, political conflict, and persecution in the Middle East and Africa. Yet, beyond the media and scholarly focus on this and other sudden crises, there are other stories to be told.[6] In Germany, one of these other stories leads into the woods.

Attending to people's affective relations to the local landscape at Berlin's peripheries reveals the often less-visible unhomely dynamics of a crisis that has been long in the making—a dynamic that cannot be fully captured by the contemporary moral economy inherent in Europe's migration policies that oscillate between compassion and repression (Fassin 2011; Ticktin 2011) or between indifference, xenophilia, and xenophobia (Borneman and Ghassem-Fachandi 2017), or by a public debate that increasingly demarcates between "deserving refugees" and "undeserving migrants" and then criminalizes the latter (Holmes and Castañeda 2016). In addition, much of the migration debate in Europe has focused on cities. Yet it is crucial also to consider the city's peripheries. Here, at the forest edges of Berlin, we have the flip side, if you will, of the previous chapters: displaced communities and people, who are racialized as migrants, are locked out in nature (instead of being framed as polluting or being disconnected from nature). In these forests near Berlin, the fraught colonial and racialized dynamics of Europe's asylum infrastructures come into full view.

Exploring affective states and forms of ruination at Berlin's forest edges, this chapter shows ethnographically how Europe's changing geopolitical formations and the displacements, economic precarities, and histories of violence that go hand-in-hand with them not only shape people's sense of self but also reside in and leave traces in their bodies, in environments, sensibilities, and things (see also Stoler 2013).[7] These formations affect not only the people seeking refuge from political conflict, economic precarity, and war but also East Germans who have lived through the upheavals of the postsocialist transition. Following the unequal resonances of the unheimlich across different communities aims at thinking between the "posts" (Chari and Verdery 2009) and asks about the ways in which postsocialist transformations have reworked national, colonial, and racialized ecologies in Europe.[8]

Yet before tracking the unheimlich, I first look at the ways in which different histories—of the modern German nation and the socialist state, of migration and shifting borders throughout Europe—have materialized in the March Oder region. I will then turn toward the refugee home, the Heim, and its surrounding landscape in Zarin. Listening to refugee and East German stories, I hope to make people's respective experiences of exile, postcolonial displacement, and postsocialist transition tangible. These experiences intertwine with multiple perceptions of the local landscape as unheimlich: a landscape populated with secrets and strange encounters— and yearnings for a different future.

FIGURE 5.2 Swampy ground with a drainage canal, March Oder region. Photo by author.

"Somewhere between Berlin and Poland"

As you leave Berlin by train, the city drops off abruptly like the edge of a cliff. The skyline of communist-era apartment buildings dwindles in the distance. The train speeds past a flat landscape dotted with meadows, pine forests, agricultural fields, and a few derelict buildings perched alongside weedy train tracks. Tucked between Berlin and Germany's eastern border with Poland, the March Oder region of Brandenburg is one of the most sparsely populated areas in Germany—it is a borderland of marshes and shifting sands (fig. 5.2).[9] In the eighteenth and nineteenth centuries, Prussian armies and engineers drained the region's wetlands to cultivate the land and build the foundation of the modern German nation and its economic power (Blackbourn 2006). In the first half of the twentieth century, fascism and two world wars left trails of death across the landscape; at the end of World War II, thousands of Polish, Russian, and German soldiers died here during one of the last battles that brought the Nazi regime to an end. After the war, the nearby Oder River, together with the Neisse River, was designated as the new border between Poland and Germany, and people were expelled from lands on both sides. Soon the March Oder region became part of East Germany and the "frontline of the Cold War" (Nelson 2005, 99)—a landscape reshaped by socialist land reform and strewn with military camps guarding the borders to the capitalist West.

After the Berlin Wall fell, part of the March Oder region was transformed into a nature park, called the Naturpark Märkische Schweiz (with Schweiz/Switzerland referring to the park's landscape of rolling hills). Together with Western environmentalists, the crumbling socialist East German state set forth a national park program to create several conservation areas in Brandenburg—many of them on former military territory. For some, the aim of the national park program was to take advantage of the moment of ongoing national transition and shift attention toward nature conservation and promote a mixed forest paradigm (*Mischwald*) instead of monocultures, especially given the prevalence of pine trees in the area.[10] Others considered the nature parks a gift for national unity and a building block for a new Europe. Thus bounded nature moved into the gaps opening up after socialism, and it aided in naturalizing the nation.[11]

With Poland's integration into the EU, the March Oder region is now no longer situated at Europe's periphery but has moved to its center. Today, tourist brochures praise the park's idyllic landscape: its deciduous forests, lakes, moors, meadows, and rich diversity of birds—a jewel amid the rather barren and sandy landscape of Brandenburg. Bicycle paths wind through the area, attracting ecotourists and weekend travelers from Berlin. Many of them follow the traces of famous German writers such as Theodor Fontane, who chronicled the rapidly changing countryside around nineteenth-century Berlin in his *Rambles through the Mark Brandenburg*. At the same time, several local tour guides offer so-called jeep safaris to explore the beauty of endless forests and "untouched" landscapes in this "undiscovered" land "somewhere between Berlin and Poland."[12]

"I Feel Brandenburg"

While political borders and the boundaries of nature have been redrawn in the region, new economic and cultural geographies have emerged as well. As elsewhere in Eastern Europe, the transition from socialism to a capitalist system was accompanied by rapid and often traumatic transformations.[13] While a unified Berlin turned into a new European metropole, on the eastern peripheries of the city, this transition took a different turn. In the two decades after unification, unemployment rates were especially high in the region—at times more than 25 percent—due to economic restructuring and the closure of local industries and military bases after unification. Many young people moved away, in search of work in the West. Although many local economies slowly recovered and unemployment rates decreased significantly in the second decade of the new millennium, the March Oder region, like other regions of Brandenburg, is still perceived as an abandoned place in the backwaters of Berlin.[14] Set apart as the West's other, it is seen as lagging behind the West (Berdahl 1999). A 2006 song by songwriter Rainald Grebe titled "Brandenburg" references this image of Brandenburg as an empty and boring place where nothing ever happens—a place you only pass on the way to somewhere else. While Berlin has become a global metropole where life is flourishing, Brandenburg is an empty and boring place where nothing ever happens. "I feel Brandenburg," he sings:

> There are countries where something is happening. And then there is
> Brandenburg. Brandenburg. . . .
> I feel so empty today. I feel Brandenburg.
> In Berlin, I am one of three million.
> In Brandenburg, I can soon live alone.
> Brandenburg
> I feel so empty today. I feel Brandenburg. . . .
> In Berlin, you can experience so much.
> In Brandenburg, the wolves are back. (Grebe 2006)

These images of Brandenburg not only respond to the region's economic situation but also echo a much older motif of the eastern frontier—a spatial imaginary that has a long history and has played a key role in Nazi ideas of the wild, backward East in need of colonization.[15]

No-Go Zones

Not only have national, economic, and natural geographies shifted in Brandenburg; since the mid-2000s the region has also become a site of debate over immigration policies and racial exclusion. Like other rural areas in the former East, Brandenburg is often perceived as what the media refer to as a no-go area.[16] The term *no-go area* has been applied to urban neighborhoods with high crime rates and to rural parts of the former East in the context of racist attacks on refugee accommodations. Originally the term emerged in the weeks before the World Cup in 2006, when in response to a series of violent attacks against immigrants, refugees, and citizens of color in several East German towns, former government spokesman Uwe-Karsten Heye warned people of color who were planning to attend the World Cup to avoid certain areas of East Germany. His mapping of the East, and especially rural regions, as no-go zones ignited a heated debate and had powerful effects on popular imaginaries of the East as an unhomely and inhospitable place for migrants and people of color—somewhat off the map from the rest of Germany.

Ironically, many asylum seekers—particularly from Africa—have found themselves living in these no-go zones for years. This is the outcome of changing national, regional, and EU asylum and immigration policies since the 1980s. While the outer border of the EU has been reinforced through tighter immigration and asylum laws, as well as by stricter monitoring of border crossings throughout the Mediterranean (Proglio et al. 2021; Tazzioli 2019), the centers of Europe have strengthened their strategies of isolating asylum seekers within their borders. In a climate that increasingly mistrusts political refugees and delegitimizes asylum as a political institution, these developments can be observed across Europe (Fassin 2011, 220). In this context, Germany's asylum law underwent several major revisions—ranging from the 1982 Asylverfahrensgesetz (Asylum Process Law) mandating that all asylum seekers be accommodated in so-called asylum homes, to changes in the constitution in 1990 that further narrowed the legal possibilities for seeking asylum, to more recent policy divisions between "deserving" refugees and "undeserving" or illegal/economic migrants amid public anxiety about the influx of refugees into Germany in the wake of the summer of migration of 2015 (Holmes and Castañeda 2016).[17]

In Brandenburg, the spatial isolation of asylum seekers is also a consequence of postunification asylum policies that created new urban shelters in former East German cities in order to equally redistribute asylum seekers between the East and West. After a heated nationwide asylum debate in the wake of rising numbers of asylum seekers fleeing the war in former Yugoslavia, and following numerous xenophobic attacks against urban refugee shelters in the 1990s, many counties relocated refugees to new "homes" in rural East Germany—often to the ruins of former military barracks in the forest. In this process, local social welfare organizations slowly retreated. Instead, private contractors and security services from the West took advantage of the resulting gap and signed long-term contracts with municipalities to accommodate asylum seekers (Flüchtlingsrat Brandenburg 2005; Pieper 2008).[18] When I began my fieldwork in the region in the late 2000s, four to six thousand asylum seekers lived in thirty refugee homes in different locations across Brandenburg (Mallwitz 2013). Their numbers rose to almost thirty thousand in 2015—when several new accommodations had to be opened—and then significantly decreased again by 2019 to closer to four thousand (BAMF 2019). Official legislation often does not allow refugees to work, and the so-called residential law restricts any travel beyond the county limits—which makes it illegal for many asylum seekers to take the train to Berlin, just a thirty-five-kilometer ride away.[19] In addition, with asylum infrastructures having been scaled down, many asylum seekers have remained in legal limbo for eight or more years. As Germany has responded rapidly to the 2015 influx of refugees from Syria via a series of new asylum policies, many asylum seekers who arrived in Germany before 2015 and had been in legal limbo for a long time faced faster and yet less careful processing of their asylum cases—and hence deportation.

As a response to these out-of-the-way camps as well as to several suicides in them, refugees and advocates have organized protests against spatial isolation and the residency law. Some have argued that the residential law echoes German colonial strategies of surveillance throughout West and East Africa. Introduced during German imperial rule, which lasted from 1884 to the end of World War I in many parts of East and West Africa (including Cameroon, Togo, Ghana, Namibia, Burundi, Tanzania, and the southern coastal region in Kenya), these colonial regulations segregated Indigenous from European populations and required Indigenous populations to claim residence in a particular region. The regulations then prohibited the movement of Indigenous peoples outside of their regions of residence—officially, as is common in colonial practice, not in the name of domination, but to "secure their protection" and "health."[20]

In the Märkische Schweiz Nature Park, a series of scandals surrounded the location and relocation of several refugee camps onto former military sites. When I first visited the region in the early 2000s, the latest scandal had involved a private subcontractor who ran the camp near the town of Ronersdorf and who had illegally hired refugees living in the Heim to build an adjacent ostrich farm (at the rate of one euro per hour). The ostrich farm soon became a popular stop for tourists, a place where they could buy exotic bird meat. Following protests, the refugee camp was moved in 2004 to an even more remote location on a former military base in the forest. The new "home" was envisioned as a temporary accommodation until a more "appropriate" location could be found. In the end, it took more than two years until the home was moved to its next location, where Virginia, the woman mentioned at the beginning of this chapter, would later live: an abandoned military base tucked away in the forest about two kilometers from the village of Zarin near the edge of the park.[21]

These developments illustrate that while the EU border no longer is close to the March Oder region, less-visible borders have instead moved into the region's forests. And whereas, like in many other European contexts, German rural landscapes—and its forests in particular—have constituted key sites through which to imagine the nation (Schama 1995), the question of who belongs and who or what is seen as "out of place" is once again reshuffled.

Unheimlich Part I: The Heim

"When I first came here, I thought this was a farm and we were just making a stop on the way to our final destination," Virginia recalled of her arrival in Zarin. Indeed, arriving at an old train station (fig. 5.3) and walking toward the refugee home, you encountered a landscape that clashed with the image of an urban, modern, and cosmopolitan Europe—the image familiar to Virginia and other asylum seekers from popular media culture.

Imagine, then, walking on cobblestone streets, past long stretches of forest. You pass several ruins—an old factory, an abandoned train station, telephone poles with their wires cut, and a few farm buildings (fig. 5.4), deserted and for sale, alongside a new discount supermarket. When you exit the village and enter the park, you pass a sign for the Märkische Schweiz Nature Park advertising its natural diversity. Walking along the road through a dense forest, you then see a bus stop, overgrown with grasses, and a rusty sign with the schedule for a bus running once a month—on the first Wednesday (fig. 5.5). Asylum seekers use the bus to travel to the local social assistance office (*Sozialamt*) where they report their presence on a monthly basis.

Not unlike the gaps in the bus schedule, the grasses and rust do their own work, asserting their presence in this space and unfolding with time. Across the street, a high rusty fence encloses a paved area that includes the barracks and the Heim. Entering through the main gate—open most of the time—you pass a sign that reads: "Use at your own risk. No winter service provided." Someone has cut a hole into the rusty wire of the gate; it is just big enough for a person to fit through (fig. 5.6).

FIGURE 5.3 Train station near Zarin, between Berlin and the Polish border. Photo by author.

FIGURE 5.4 Abandoned house in the March Oder region. Photo by author.

FIGURE 5.5 Bus stop, with service once a month. Photo by author.

FIGURE 5.6 Entrance to the Heim, with hole in the fence, and sign reading, "Use at your own risk. No winter service provided." Photo by author.

Right behind the entrance are the barracks, a few abandoned storage buildings, and a large U-shaped facility; a few Trabants with flat tires are rusting in front of the buildings.[22]

෮ ෮ ෮

The Heim was in one of the barracks. Usually pretty empty, it extended over three stories and had long, windowless hallways. Although, officially, around three hundred asylum seekers had been registered to live at the Heim, only between forty to seventy people lived here on a regular basis. People had come to Germany for a variety of reasons. Like Virginia, some fled ethnic violence in Kenya. Others, like Ari from Sudan, fled torture. And others simply sought a better life—like John, who was a celebrity in Kenya and had hoped to spend a few years making money that could finance his career back home, or like Duc, who had lived in East Germany during the socialist period but had returned home to Hanoi after German unification, and then came back again to Germany to seek medical treatment for an illness and to earn money to support his family in Vietnam.

Although one social worker was present on a regular basis, no one controlled who came in and out of the Heim during the day—except at night and on weekends.[23] Nearly all residents tried to live in the city. After years of waiting and enduring complicated bureaucratic procedures, some had managed to receive permits to live in apartments. Those who stayed were families still waiting for their permits; newly arrived asylum seekers like Virginia; older people like Ari and Duc; or people who were physically or mentally ill, had gotten stuck for legal reasons, or who lacked the social networks and energy to make a life for themselves in the city. Thus, many lived and worked "illegally" in Berlin (usually in temporary jobs as cleaning personnel, kitchen help, construction workers, and hotel maids). Many then only traveled once a month out to Zarin to claim their presence at the Heim and receive the few social benefits for which they were eligible. No one really knew who lived at the Heim on a regular basis or who stayed for a few days on their way to somewhere else. Yet for those who stayed, living in the Heim constituted a contested practice. Indeed, after staying in the Heim for months or even years, it was easy to lose your mind: people became miserable with boredom, madness, and illness—and some started to see ghosts. The Heim itself appeared to them to be afflicted with ghostly presences.

Heim means both home and asylum in German, and there are several meanings and ironies attached to this term. In Zarin, the term was somewhat ironic since nobody considered this a home but rather saw themselves as living in nowhere land. By contrast, the term *asylum* took on a double meaning: over the course of my fieldwork, several people told me they felt like they had been seeking asylum but ultimately found themselves living in an insane asylum in the forest. A Kenyan woman, who only irregularly stayed at the Heim, said: "People are crazy here! It's a madhouse!" And Jamal, who had lived in Zarin for years, described his own situation: "Sometimes I go into the kitchen and forget what I wanted there. I have forgotten what I wanted in this place. Why am I here?"

A sense of living nowhere in the forest and of things being off the mark haunted people's lives and their stories about this place. The Heim and the forest were anything but heimlich, and in a strange twist, were rather un-heimlich (unhomely/uncanny). In fact, for many, the feeling of this place in the forest was something to ponder over and over again.

Both living in the Heim and trying to leave it involved a series of risks. For many, the possibility of being checked up on by the police was always present no matter where they went. One had to learn to live with the con-stant risk of being ticketed for transgressing county boundaries and, after several incidents, the possibility of being deported: "You simply pretend everything is normal. You just go your own way. But the truth is that the controls make you feel haunted. No matter where you go, you feel like you have done something wrong, like riding the train for free. You feel like someone is following you," Virginia explained. Usually, these forms of racial monitoring and random security checks were conducted in trains and train stations on the way to or from Berlin. But they also occurred in the countryside—as I witnessed myself one day when walking with Mike, a Kenyan asylum seeker in Zarin. As we walked along the road near the Heim, a police officer drove by and stopped us to ask for our papers. Mike had a legal permit, so the officer had to let us go. To local white residents, as well as to tourists, these borders, harassments, and security checks were most often invisible—they were never asked for their papers. They (like me, the white anthropologist) could just walk right past the police. To Mike and other refugees, these border controls in the middle of the forest were part of everyday life. And they haunted his and others' perceptions of the place.

A less threatening sense of the unheimlich was also shared by others, including myself. Before my own first arrival at the Heim, Mike had ad-vised me not to go and talk to people immediately, but rather to pause for a minute, sit on a rock and simply look at the forest, the buildings, the fence, and the surroundings. He was convinced that just sitting down and SEEING and SENSING the place would tell me more than talking to anyone.

When I visited the Heim for the first time, I followed Mike's advice. I put my bike to the side and looked for a small tree stump to sit on. Yet, instead of having a quiet moment of observation, I suddenly heard heavy stomps in the distance. I was startled when I recognized the contours of two huge animals approaching the gate, running toward me, grunting viciously. "Wild boar!" I thought. I had heard stories of a growing boar population overrunning the Berlin countryside. In a hurry, I hopped on my bike and rode off as fast as I could.

Indeed, although my attempt at a moment of reflection had failed miserably, I did get a first glimpse of the unheimlich that day: riding off on my bike and with a racing heart, it turned out I had mistaken the watch dogs for wild boar, unsettling my own assumptions about what and who was at home in this place.

This sense of the unheimlich was also shared by the refugee activists and advocates in the region. Many activists I spoke with had organized against the isolated refugee homes for years and told stories about the controversies that surrounded them. But most had never spent much time in this particular Heim—for them it was gloomy and a madhouse. "Why would you want to do fieldwork in THAT place? People are crazy there and they seem to have lost their minds. Plus, most of them don't do anything all day and just sit and watch TV. There is nothing going on there," a Berlin refugee advocate said when I told him about my intention to speak to people in Zarin. His response also echoed the idea that Brandenburg is a boring place where nothing significant happens—especially in relation to cosmopolitan Berlin. Furthermore, several advocacy groups had also taken up images of the unheimlich, chronicling the psychological, social, and health consequences of living in Brandenburg's refugee homes, by publishing brochures titled *UnHEIMliches Brandenburg* (Unhomely Brandenburg) (fig. 5.7). Similarly, the movie *Forst* (Breuer, Hansbauer, and Konrad 2005)—a documentary film produced by Indonesian German filmmaker Ascan Breuer in cooperation with the African refugee activist groups the VOICE, Women in Exile, and Caravan for the Rights of Refugees and Migrants—captures a sense of cognitive dissonance as it is experienced by many asylum seekers living at the forest edges of German cities (Stoetzer 2014b). Here, the forest is both a space of rationality (as a site of management) and mystery, a site of isolation and violence, and also a space of subversion in which the banished tell their own story and make plans for their escape.

Even local authorities did not consider the Heim a home. When the county relocated the refugee home from its previous location to Zarin in

FIGURE 5.7 *Un-HEIMliches Brandenburg* (Unhomely Brandenburg) brochure. Courtesy of Flüchtlingsrat Brandenburg 2005.

2006, the village council debated the definition of the new institution and how it fit into existing zoning regulations. The current owner had registered the buildings of the former military barracks as a business in a commercial zone. And yet council members argued that the opening of a *Wohnheim für Zuwanderer und Asylbewerber* (residential home for immigrants and asylum seekers) in the same facility would not be in conflict with the existing zoning, since such a home (Heim) does not provide a permanent home and thus does not constitute "independent living" (*selbstbestimmtes Wohnen*), but rather a provisional accommodation (*Unterbringung*).[24] Hence the Heim was not categorized as a residential zone (*Wohngebiet*), and its existence did not conflict with the commercial zoning classification.[25] In the end, the council agreed they would not be liable for any accidents on the site. No extra lights were installed. Clearly, the Heim was not intended to be a home or homely.

Unheimlich Part II: Bush Stories

To exorcise not in order to chase away the ghosts, but this time to grant them the right
[to] . . . a hospitable memory . . . out of a concern for justice.
—Jacques Derrida, *Specters of Marx*

Although many people commented on the unheimlich in Zarin, they did so from very different perspectives. Whereas local advocates referenced the unheimlich in order to distance themselves from the refugee home's out-of-placeness (without being directly affected by it), the local administration referred to the literal un-heimlich—the nonresidential nature of the Heim—in order to institutionalize it as an inhospitable place. In contrast, a sense of the un-heimlich materialized in the everyday lives of those who lived in the Heim in very real and embodied ways. Many asylum seekers exclusively used the German term *Heim* when they referred to the refugee home in daily life, or when they spoke about the ironies of feeling displaced in what was supposed to be a home (Heim) and a space of refuge. Together with references to the unhomeliness of this place and its buildings, the residents' anecdotes and jokes about what they referred to as "the bush" provided a commentary on the affective state of endless waiting, as well as the ways in which racialized geographies and ecologies came into being in the March Oder region.

To Kenyan asylum seekers, being regulated by invisible, colonizing forces and being associated with the bush was all too familiar. It was as if the symbolism of colonial discourse had come true: local authorities had not only associated them with unruly, wild spaces in need of civilizing efforts, but literally placed them in these spaces. While the forest was a site of national pride and unification for local Germans, living in the forest, in the middle of Europe, at the edges of one of its metropoles, remained both familiar and strange to the asylum seekers. Indeed, living in the bush was crowded with the specters of colonial violence and power. In addition, many of the Kenyans living in Zarin came from urban areas and so being in a forest was unfamiliar for them. Europe had not turned out to be what they expected—a space of civilization, progress, and mobility. Overgrown with weeds, with a crumbling local economy, this place did not live up to its promises and instead in an ironic twist seemed strangely familiar to aspects of the urban life they knew. "Is this another Kenya?" Virginia sometimes wondered in the face of all the obstacles she encountered in her everyday life and the dispossession she had experienced in coming to Europe. "I expected everything to work smoothly and fast in Europe. You see it on TV in Kenya all the time. People are busy in Europe, and everything is in order—especially people's lives. Yet, in Germany, nobody seems to work hard—if they do work at all. People take it slow. They say: *Langsam, langsam!* When you go to the local village pub here, you see men drinking beer in the middle of the afternoon! And nobody bothers to clear out the weeds on the train tracks."

But people also experienced the unheimlich in embodied ways (and in their relations to each other). When Mike told me about his experience of living in the midst of the forest for years, he spoke of constantly having head-aches and of being made sick by the fact that he was not able to do anything: "We were there in the bush doing nothing, not really able to interact with anyone except the trees and wild animals." Fighting feelings of depression, he often would go running through the forest. One time he even chased after an antelope. When I questioned him, he insisted: "Believe me, it was an antelope! It had horns that go straight up. I can tell an antelope from a deer!"

Others, like Nangila, also from Kenya, who was currently living in the Heim yet hoping to live in the city soon, also referred to the forest as the bush. For him, the bush signified a place in the middle of nowhere, a place where a lot of refugees find themselves caught and feeling out of place—a place marked by danger and a struggle for survival. Others wondered: Were there venomous snakes in the forest? Did they convey traces of witchcraft? You never quite knew what risks were lurking in the forest. For that reason, Virginia and other women would not leave the Heim after dusk. They had heard stories of people running into wild boar on the street, on their way to the village at night. Even walking in the streets of the nearby village—deserted most of the time—a sense of the unhomely would follow you: "Everyone hides in their houses, behind a large fence. And when you say hello to someone on the street they look away. It makes you feel paranoid, as if you did something wrong," Virginia said.

This was a different bush than the untouched nature of exotic exploration advertised in Brandenburg tourist brochures, and yet it was oddly similar. One time when I went for a walk with Nangila and returned to the Heim in the bush, he poked fun at the odd conjunctures of different racialized constructions of place: "Wait and see. Tomorrow the headlines in the news-paper will be: 'Bushman gets lost in the forest and is attacked by a lion.'"

But the specters of wild animals were not the only ones in people's jokes. For many, the forest was inhabited by all kinds of creatures: lions, snakes, antelopes, and who knew what else. These specters were not strange, made-up tales; they pointed instead to something significant: this was less a story about the distant colonial past coming to haunt the European metropole and more a story of the persistence of a colonial dynamic in which Europeans (not only metaphorically) have placed African communities in "the bush" and other spaces in need of domestication. Only this time, it was the twenty-first century and the bush was in the center of Europe. These stories about unhomely encounters and being stuck in the bush thus not only echoed the long-standing legacies of restricting African mobilities in the context of European colonial administration—a strategy that Germans perpetuated throughout East and West Africa until the end of German colonial rule toward the conclusion of World War I.[26] The stories about the unheimlich also revealed that the continuing forces of colonial violence and racialization—and their ruinous effects—can be traced and sensed both in people's lives and in the very material environments that Europe's migration regimes create today.

In Zarin, Nangila's, Virginia's, and others' dreams and desires for a Europe full of possibilities clashed with the dire realities of being isolated in the forest. In this sense, the anecdotes about uncanny encounters can be seen as "power-laden cultural negotiations" (Tsing 1993, 90) and commentaries on the continuation and unhomeliness of colonial legacies—and their historical erasure. And they give us a glimpse of a lurking threat of violence and the risk of vulnerability while living in the forest.[27]

Considering these stories about unhomely encounters in the bush, a different sense of the uncanny/unhomely (unheimlich) emerges: unlike Freud's ([1919] 1955) theorization, people's accounts of the uncanny here did not rely on a colonial logic that defines uncanny situations and motifs as signaling the reemergence of "repressed infantile desires" or remnants of "animistic beliefs," considered to be irrelevant (such as instant wish fulfillment, the belief in secret harmful sources, or the return of the dead) (155). Rather than relegate experiences of animism to the realm of what Freud considers "primitive thinking," the Kenyan refugees' encounters with unhomely figures highlight that colonialism and racism—forces that cosmopolitan Europe and Germany claims to have surpassed—continue to exert themselves.[28] By emphasizing the strangeness and cognitive dissonance they experienced while being forced to inhabit Berlin's forest peripheries, the residents of the Heim exposed what it means to live in the unheimlich (uncanny) produced by Europe's asylum regimes and colonial amnesia. They illustrated that the colonial has never left Europe in the first place. The residents' discursive and physical placement in the German bush appeared "in the wake" (Sharpe 2016) of the past and present violence of slavery and racism. And it underscored the enduring colonial dynamics of segregation and racialization at work in European border politics (see also Davies and Isakjee 2019;

Gutiérrez Rodríguez 2018). Thus, it was not repressed "animistic beliefs" or animate worlds that came back to haunt people in Zarin but the spirit of colonialism itself. What Encarnación Gutiérrez Rodríguez (2018) has called a "coloniality of migration" expresses itself in the affective, cognitive, and physical states of disturbance and violence that contemporary asylum worlds have created. Therefore, we see that it is not animism but Europe itself and the everyday experience of racism that is unhomely.

For some, the threat of violence was anything but metaphorical. Many residents of the Heim had had encounters with neo-Nazis in the region.[29] In order to survive the German bush, you needed to be strong, both physically and mentally, Mike told me. Once, Mike had been harassed on the street by two local men. After the incident, he began to feel like someone was following him: "You start seeing them everywhere you go. It's like seeing ghosts." Indeed, soon after coming to Zarin, Mike, like other Kenyan men, began to exercise diligently: he ran every day and lifted weights that someone who had moved to Berlin had left at the Heim.

Seen in the light of these experiences, the stories about ghosts in the bush are commentaries on the racialized violence of living in the forest as well as on the wildness of racism itself—including the presence of neo-Nazis in the area. While pointing to the hidden voices of past and current racism and the colonial roots of Africans being placed within the wild, these references to the bush combined with refugees' efforts to shape their bodies against the surrounding racist wilderness articulated a critique of what Paul Silverstein has called the "savage slot" that immigrants and refugees have come to occupy in public and scholarly debate in Europe today (see Silverstein 2004). Refugees are often represented as a generic figure of the uprooted, as people out of and alienated from place and thus pathologized as "native gone amok" (Malkki 1992, 34). As Liisa Malkki (1995) has shown, the very figure of the refugee and its symbolic and political production are deeply entangled with a colonial dynamic: refugees emerged as an object of disciplinary power and as a category of social scientific knowledge production in the aftermath of World War II and decolonization (498). Whereas the refugee became the global legal and administrative category to manage and approach displacement, refugee camps, often modeled after military barracks, provided the spatial technology to contain refugee movements from the global South to the global North.[30] The political category of the refugee and the refugee camp as a modern political institution were thus built in the rubble of World War II and the struggle for decolonization. Yet while displacement from war, poverty, persecution, and political conflict across many regions in Africa and the Middle East is intimately tied to the continuing legacies of colonial rule, these entanglements have been largely ignored in twentieth- and twenty-first-century political discourse about migration and asylum in Europe (De Genova 2017; Gutiérrez Rodríguez 2018).

The stories about ghostly figures in the German bush thus shed critical light not only on colonial amnesia but also on the disciplinary power of the administrative and scholarly gaze on displacement that remains prevalent in much scholarship on migration and asylum (Cabot 2019). Indeed, many of my interlocutors had had their fair share of encounters with what they experienced as journalistic or academic tourism and extractive knowledge-making, and some initially responded to my questions about their experiences with annoyance: "Oh no, not another person who wants to study refugees and who comes here and asks us questions and then makes a career from OUR stories. They never return. They are all *jambazi* [thieves, bandits, or cheaters in Swahili]. Nobody cares a damn about us in the end." While pointing to dubious journalistic, scholarly, and other kinds of expert desires to create an image of the "real life" of refugees, these responses also resist the notion of refugees as uprooted, alienated from place, and without agency. Many Kenyan residents in the Heim insisted you could never trust any experts visiting Zarin—no matter whether they were anthropologists, journalists, social workers, government officials, or the police. After all, were academics not unlike thieves or, rather, spies for the local immigration office and thus in alliance with the state?

My interlocutors' refusal thus exposed existing scholarly, humanitarian, and journalistic desires to represent the "real lives" of refugees and to extract data from their experiences of pain, displacement, and loss. In fact, it rendered these desires and representations as exploitative and strange. Their refusal joins voices with recent writings on (ethnographic) refusal (Shange 2019a; Simpson 2007; Tuck and Yang 2014a, 2014b; Tuhiwai Smith 1999), the colonial dynamics of documentary accumulation surrounding refugee and migrant lives (Bhambra 2017; Dahinden 2016; De Genova 2017; Gutiérrez Rodríguez 2018; Malkki 1995), and anthropology's attachments to liberal humanism and its settler colonial legacies (Jobson 2020). Scholars working in Europe have drawn attention to the complicities of social scientific knowledge production and humanitarian practices with the neocolonial logics of border control and management (Bhambra 2017; Carastathis and Tsilimpounidi 2018; Dahinden 2016; Gutiérrez Rodríguez 2018; Ticktin 2011). Work on ethnographic refusal, in particular, has critically interrogated the colonial aspects of data collection and ethnographic writing.

In this context, refusal can become generative for developing decolonial methodologies and for empowering Indigenous, Black, and other racialized communities to control the ways in which they are represented. Honoring refusal can reshape scholarship from research design to data collection to analysis and ethnographic writing—for example, by deciding what not to write about, and by decentering harmful narratives that focus on suffering and thick description, instead of creating solidarity (Shange 2019a) and interrogating white settler societies (Simpson 2007).

In Brandenburg and throughout Germany, experts—including anthropologists—have benefited from displaced people's labor to tell their stories. Yet asylum seekers and other vulnerable communities are often forced to continue living precarious lives and remain empty-handed from their interactions with interviewers or humanitarian actors. Their refusal demands accountability. In my own research, while never being able to fully resolve the troubled power dynamics of research, the refusal of my interlocutors challenged me to ensure that they benefited from our interactions—for example, by sharing my knowledge of German bureaucratic processes with residents in the Heim who had to navigate the administrative labyrinths of their asylum cases, or by accompanying them in their travels through the March Oder region and (being a white woman with a German passport) operating as a buffer vis-à-vis police during random passport controls.[31] Furthermore, these moments of refusal redirected my own ethnographic analysis in the years that followed: rather than inquire about people's biographical "data" and their often-painful journeys to Europe or focus on narratives of suffering and psychological pain in ways that obscured the slow violence of everyday life under "asylum," it became important to redirect my analytical gaze onto Europe's and Germany's inhospitable environments—and their uncanny character. To do so also meant attempting to capture the critical description and analysis—and at times humor—with which my interlocutors commented upon these environments, and upon European society, racism, and white privilege. Focusing on the uncanny qualities of the landscapes the refugees had to inhabit in Zarin thus became a way of incorporating their refusal—and perhaps even refusing in solidarity (Simpson 2007)—in my analysis without pretending ever to be able to completely erase the power dynamics in the field (see also Stoetzer 2014a). Although the unheimlich may involve a loss of distinction, tracking it ethnographically and making my analysis vulnerable to it, I hope, offers a strategy to resist an objectifying mode of analysis—without chasing the ghosts away (see also Biehl 2013; Derrida 2006; Stewart 2007).

Unheimlich Part III: A Sleeping Giant

The refugee stories about unexpected creatures in Zarin would ring true in yet another respect. Later, on the same afternoon that Virginia had told me about her escape to Europe, I had a surprising encounter. As I entered the main gate to the refugee camp, a big silver car stopped next to me and a man with sunglasses rolled down the window, leaned toward me, and asked: "Do you know where the bunker is? I am scheduled to be there at four o'clock!" Puzzled, I shrugged my shoulders.

It was only then that I discovered the origin of the mysterious sounds that had punctuated Virginia's story earlier: hidden underground, beneath the U-shaped building across from the Heim, there was a "sleeping giant": a nuclear bunker built by the German socialist government in the 1970s, at the height of Cold War tensions. After being closed to the public for years after unification, the bunker had been purchased by a man who fixed it up, ran a paintball facility that was built on top of it, and rented out the military barracks to the Sozialpark. Thus, the sounds of gunshots had not come from combat exercises, but from a paintball station, hidden in the forest. Young men from the nearby village and tourists came here to wear army clothes and shoot at each other with paintballs. Walking on the road, you had to watch your step: paintball rounds were scattered all over the ground, and if you stepped on them, paint exploded on your clothes.

The bunker had now also been reopened—for Sunday tours offered to tourists and curious locals alike to go explore it and sense the atmosphere of the socialist past once again. Together with the people renovating it, the bunker seemed to inhabit a different universe that oddly sat right next to the refugee camp—an underground Cold War world, filled with nuclear fantasies and nostalgia. A month later, I took a tour of that world myself.

∾ ∾ ∾

Wearing our "original GDR" blue coats provided to visitors at the entrance of the bunker, we were well prepared for not only a big drop in temperature but also a chilling trip into the past. After descending seventeen meters below the earth, down several levels of steep stairs, we entered an underground world through a thick metal door. The temperature plunged down to eight degrees Celsius, and the air was filled with the sharp odor of mold. What followed was a maze of narrow tunnels and hallways (fig. 5.8), security steel doors and walls—up to three meters thick—air filters, pressure valves, water

FIGURE 5.8 Bunker tunnel. Photo by author.

gates, cooling systems, and diesel engines. The sounds of our footsteps and voices became more muffled the farther we descended.

Passing several equipment units stored on suspension platforms to absorb shock in the case of a bomb or nuclear attack, our first stop was the dining hall. In it, cups and plates were carefully arranged on tables—creating the impression that people had just walked out for a break and would be returning to have a meal at any moment (fig. 5.9). A newspaper was spread out on one of the tables. It was dated October 1987.

Then we proceeded to the "dispatcher room": a room crowded with computers and a big console in the middle with a red handle—the closing mechanism in case of emergency. Our tour guide praised the flashing displays of the control panel that made it appear as if it were only necessary to turn the operating handle to bring this underground sleeping giant back to life. A picture of Erich Honecker, head of the East German Socialist Party until 1989, hung on the wall. In case of a nuclear strike, this secret world

FIGURE 5.9 Coffee-table scene, re-created in the decommissioned nuclear bunker. Photo by author.

FIGURE 5.10 Doomsday clock in the former nuclear bunker. Photo by author.

of security technology would have enabled two hundred people to survive for three weeks without contact with the outside world. Yet, as our tour guide explained, the aim was not to enable sustainable survival on earth, but rather to gain just enough time to launch a nuclear revenge. This is what you call "mutual assured destruction," preparing for a world in ruins.

The clock in the computer room had stopped running. It was five minutes to midnight (fig. 5.10).

∿ ∿ ∿

Built by the East German Ministry of National Defense, the Zarin bunker served as an organizational and data processing center for the National People's Army (NVA) of the German Democratic Republic: it transferred data to the ministry of national defense and enabled communication between other units of the armed forces (Bergner 2008, 84). Originally, the builders had taken advantage of the location's natural conditions: the layers of gravel of the glacial Barnim plateau provided a dry and stable ground. The bunker itself lies hidden beneath a small hill in the forest. Until 1989, this was a top-secret location. Then, after the Berlin Wall tumbled and the East German military was dissolved, it was briefly used by the (West German) Federal Armed Forces. In 1993, the facility was closed and remained so until 2003.

After the tour, I met Heinrich, a man in his early seventies, who sat in the sun with two other men on folding chairs and on cargo boxes scattered at the bunker's entrance. They were fiddling with tools and cleaning the rust off metal scraps. Heinrich lived in a small room, with a fold-out couch, next to the former dining hall above the bunker. He described himself as the bunker's janitor. As we struck up a conversation, I learned that he had been a spy and an engineer in the GDR; he had traveled to different parts of the world to gather information on recent developments in Western military technology. Drawn into his narrative of secrecy, expertise, and Cold War masculinity, I followed him on a second tour, this time above ground.

Heinrich was transforming the bunker's front entry and dining hall into a museum. He collected objects, like flags, postcards, clothing, or tools for tapping telephones. Military coats and hats dangled from an old coatrack. Pictures of old Soviet fighter planes and the flags of several East German towns hung from the ceiling. A rug on the wall had Karl Marx's and Friedrich Engels's faces woven into it. Other socialist military gadgets were stacked on top of each other, with jackets and hats spread out between them. In the tiny room where he slept, there were more objects—piles of old military books, postcards, uniforms—spread out all over the floor. With these objects, he was cobbling together a museum of the Cold War era. His voice was full of pride. On my way out he gave me two East German fifty-mark bills, along with information about the bunker and his museum. In a low voice, with a sense of secrecy, he said: "Right here at the entrance, no one was allowed to go any farther. But this was also spy territory. Spies from the West were here, right here, where we are sitting."

By restoring the bunker and reassembling leftover military gadgets, Heinrich and his friends were preserving the material history of Cold War preparations for end-of-the-world destruction. They were not alone. Across the region, many so-called "bunker friend" networks had emerged aiming to restore former socialist bunkers.[32] Many local residents talked about them with a mix of curiosity and repulsion. A woman from Zarin once told me about having to leave a bunker tour early because she started to panic and had trouble breathing. For many, the East German state and military still incited both magic and horror.

At first sight, Heinrich's recycling practice and his museum catered to a yearning for the East and a nostalgia for socialist objects that has been popular across Europe. Attending to such nostalgic expressions in popular and material culture, anthropologists have directed attention to the connections between nostalgic yearning and nationalism (Boyer 2006; Boym 2001). From this perspective, nostalgia expresses a sentiment of loss and displacement, a longing for a time and a home that no longer exist or that never have existed. This longing can appear as a defense mechanism in times of historical upheaval (Boym 2001, xiv).[33] Yet Heinrich's and other bunker junkies' preservation of the material history of GDR visions of Cold War (in)security is not simply backward looking, but seeks to intervene in a world that has become unhomely and aspires to a shift in the value of objects, matter, and lives that have lost their value. In this sense, their preservation practices are oriented not toward the past but toward the future.[34]

As Heinrich pointed out to me, he, like others, had lost his job and had to invent his life all over again after the *Wende*.[35] His life simply did not fit anymore. In contrast, during socialism, things seemed to fit and were reliable—for example, the quality of roofs was much better than today. But even more than that: all objects were standardized! The battery for a car would also fit into a drilling machine or a flashlight. You needed only an intimate knowledge of these objects, their multiple functions and operations, and you had the power to make the state's standardization magic come alive.

Fiddling with rusty tools and military gadgets, recycling, and putting together anew can be read as a practice of creating value, of making the rubble and the things one is left with fit again—and thus repossessing a ruptured life to inhabit an alternative future. Recycling materials from the barracks was also a way of reassembling a space from which previous borders had disappeared and had created a gap, a zone in which the former coordinates of social life had crumbled, and in which the material life of an entire world was left to decay.

Not unlike the refugees, Heinrich remade a life from things left behind. Like the objects in the bunker, his life did not easily fit into the "familiar division of social and cultural life" (Bhabha 1992). And yet, by preserving the material history of imminent global destruction, Heinrich and his bunker friends yearned for a form of nuclear nationalism (Masco 2014) that anticipated the future in ruins and sidelined attention to antidemocratic forces in the name of an abstract sense of security (see also Shoshan 2016). Their sense of suspicion and Cold War conspiracy theory made them an unhomely and disconnected neighbor, right next to the community of refugees whose lives, in a different way, had been put on hold amid ruins.

Reprise

While the boundaries of nature and the nation have been drawn anew in the March Oder region since unification, the question of who and what is naturalized in this place has been reopened. The ethnographic vignettes in this chapter illustrate the unhomely politics of this process.

When the Märkische Schweiz Nature Park was founded during German unification, nature aided in naturalizing the nation. In this regard, it helped create a sense of *Heimat* (home) and *Heimlichkeit* (feeling at home). At the same time, in the midst of crumbling local economies and racial tensions, images of the March Oder region as an empty, boring, or dangerous no-go zone have marked the region as a place apart from the rest of the nation. Yet this popular notion of Brandenburg as unheimlich (unhomely) becomes more ambiguous when viewed from the perspective of those who inhabit the region. Tracing a sense of the unheimlich across multiple communities, I have attended to moments in which the experience of the built and natural landscape—the Heim, the forest, and the military ruins—ruptures and perception becomes vulnerable to the uncertainty of unhomely figures (Masco 2006).

These moments of rupture and cognitive dissonance point not so much to a region as to a place apart, and to the exclusionary forces at work in the remaking of the nation and Europe's new border regimes. In Zarin, these forces materialize in a landscape of rusty fences, weedy bus stops, and crumbling barracks; in bureaucratic infrastructures of surveillance, confusion, and boredom; and in people's sense of place. While Heinrich and his bunker friends tried to piece their lives back together and rebuild a sense of nuclear nationalism amid the rubble of the Cold War, Virginia's and other Kenyans' encounters with unhomely figures in Zarin told a different and yet strangely similar story. Like the bunker enthusiasts, their encounters attested to displacement and the loss of home amid Europe's rebordered political landscape and capitalism's promises. Yet in contrast to the bunker enthusiasts' yearning for national security and walled states, the asylum seekers' stories attested to the material, social, and psychological displacements at work in Europe's post–Cold War border regimes. They thus conveyed a sense of living in the unheimlich and uncanny amid the rubble of European colonialism and racism.

In *The Wretched of the Earth*, Frantz Fanon (2004) paints a portrait of colonial ruination. He writes that colonization and racism are forms of power that leave traces of decay and ruination in psyches, bodies, and landscapes: "A hostile, ungovernable and fundamentally rebellious nature is in fact synonymous in the colonies with the bush, the mosquitoes, the natives and disease. Colonization has succeeded once this untamed Nature has been brought under control. Cutting railroads through the bush, draining swamps, and ignoring the political and economic existence of the native population are in fact one and the same thing" (182). Thus, for Fanon, "imperialism, which today is waging war against a genuine struggle for human liberation, sows seeds of decay here and there that must be mercilessly rooted out from our land and from our minds" (181). As people in Zarin recounted stories of cognitive dissonance, they unveiled these very seeds of decay: in a strange twist of Fanon's description, national unification policies had both symbolically and materially converted former militarized zones into nature spaces in the formerly socialist East. Meanwhile, EU and national asylum policies separated refugees in camps in the forest and contained their political and economic existence in a labyrinth of bureaucratic regulations. As recent scholarship has shown, key components of (European) border regimes— such as the creation of refugee camps, hot spots and dismal makeshift shelters, or the abandonment of refugees to the risks of crossing the Mediterranean Sea—have been utilized to deter migration from the global South

(Davies and Isakjee 2019; Maestri 2017; Picker, Greenfields, and Smith 2015). They are deeply racialized and neocolonial devices because they specifically target Black and brown bodies while dehumanizing and exposing them to the harmful materialities of overcrowded detention centers, makeshift shelters, police violence, health risks, the heat of deserts, and the unpredictability of the Mediterranean Sea (Davies and Isakjee 2019; de Leon 2015; Joinda 2019). It is perhaps no coincidence, then, that other makeshift shelters for refugees across Europe have also been given nicknames such as the "jungle" (as was the case of the so-called Jungle in Calais, as well as the Moria camp in Lesvos) (Davies and Isakjee 2015).

As matters of ruination have received considerable attention in recent anthropological inquiry, ruination can be understood as a material and social process that creates affective and physical states of disturbance (Navaro-Yashin 2012).[36] Drawing on Fanon's account, Ann Stoler (2013) suggests an analytic of ruination to account for an ongoing social-material process that inflicts impairment and brings ruin upon people and livelihoods. Considering ecologies of ruination thus involves going beyond the singular focus on ruins as metaphor that is so central to Europe's introspective obsession with its own ruins *as monuments*, and pointing instead to wider social topographies and the physical and "social life of ruins" (Dawdy 2010): the lives and afterlives of racial violence, economic collapse, and interrupted futures that can be tracked in landscapes, bodies, and affects (Stoler 2013, 9–10). Yet, as noted earlier, it is important to remember that the term *ecology*, in its broad sense, refers to the study of the relations and interactions between organisms and their environments. With *oikos* (the prefix eco-) being the Greek term for house or home, ecology can also be understood as the study of house- or homemaking strategies (see also Paxson 2013, 32). Following what it means to live in the unheimlich and its ecologies of ruination then also involves tracking the affective, cognitive, and physical states of disturbance and impossible futures created amid the ruins of European strategies of homemaking. Indeed, the Heim in Zarin, itself a ruin, became an impossible, unhomely home for those who had to inhabit it.[37] Migrant experiences and accounts of the unheimlich (unhomely) asylum spaces throughout Europe thus reveal how colonial violence remains an integral element in the remaking of contemporary Europe (see also Gilroy 2004). Tracing such violence means accounting for social worlds that do not easily fit into familiar categories: among derelict public institutions, corroding infrastructures, and toxic landscapes, people remake their lives with the scraps of what has been left behind. The ruderal analytic that I have promoted in this book thus tunes into affective and physical states of disturbance and points to the limits of social inquiry that does not take disturbance and ruination, including its unhomely effects, into account. In an effort to portray the "true lives" (Fassin 2014) of migrants and refugees, life is too often ordered along bounded bureaucratic or scholarly categories (such as biopolitics and bare life, or other forms of structural violence).

In contrast, in the unhomely stirrings in Zarin's landscapes, overgrown with weeds, many objects and creatures acquire a strange new life: the sounds of paintball guns cutting through Virginia's memories; the sleeping giant of the nuclear bunker hidden under the hill; Heinrich's scrap metal, polished for display; the ghosts of neo-Nazis or random passport controls; antelope and other unexpected creatures in the bush; and a doomsday clock hidden belowground. It is in these stirrings that a rearticulation of past and present alternative social formations might become tangible. Thus, if we want to chronicle how old and new ecologies of exclusion and racial violence erupt across Europe and Germany today, it is important to account for their affective and material traces—and ask what it means to "feel Brandenburg."

6

STORIES OF THE "WILD EAST"

On a warm summer day, I sat with Sabine in her garden, drinking coffee and catching up. Wild boar and deer had recently taken over her yard: at night they snuck in, stomped all over the vegetables, and even ate some of them. While Sabine complained about the thieves, we could hear the engines of a Cessna circling above us. All of a sudden, there was a short pause. Moments later we heard screams. Looking up into the sky, I saw a big, colorful umbrella opening softly in the air—a parachute floating in the sky like a jellyfish. "Welcome to Brandenburg," Sabine said.

After the collapse of socialism, "wilderness" made a comeback in much of the Brandenburg countryside around Berlin. Like other rural areas in former East Germany, Brandenburg has been "shrinking" in the aftermath of unification—which means the region has been characterized by deindustrialization, high rates of unemployment (especially among the small migrant communities living in the region), and depopulation.[1] As noted in chapter 5, Brandenburg is often seen as a place apart, lagging behind the West. Located in East Brandenburg, between Berlin and Germany's border with Poland, the Naturpark Märkische Schweiz is similarly imagined as an abandoned place in the backwater of Berlin. Popular imaginaries cast the region as wild or empty space, associated with both its prevalent dry, sandy soil, which is poor in nutrients, and the swampy wetlands of the Oder River and its notorious floods. For many people living in former West

Germany, the March Oder region is a place one passes through on the way to somewhere else. Industries and people moved away after unification, many buildings were abandoned, and factories turned into ruins. Tropes of doom and decay abound.

At the same time, the specific ecology of the region has become both a conservation strategy and part of a marketing strategy. Tourist brochures praise the March Oder region as a natural paradise, and adventure tourism of all sorts has been thriving: parachuting and canoeing have become popular outdoor activities, and so-called Jeep safaris explore the beauty of its "untouched nature" and "endless forests."[2] Berlin newspapers and weekly magazines advertise the region, like much of the city's surrounding countryside in Brandenburg, as a land of discovery, populated with secret histories, underground bunkers, and ghost towns (TIP Redaktion 2017). With the conversion of close to 30 percent of Brandenburg's territory into nature parks and biosphere reserves—a network of protected "national natural landscapes"[3]—much wildlife that had previously disappeared from the region has returned. Wolves and great bustards have found protected habitats. And the populations of other rare animals, such as wild geese and beavers, have increased again. But unwanted wildlife has also appeared, and large wild boar populations roam the countryside, including Sabine's garden.[4]

In the course of the postsocialist transition, Western environmentalists introduced concepts such as close-to-nature forestry to replace the former singular focus on industrial production in the area. Consequently, many pine and beech forests, as well as the many lakes, moors, river valleys, floodplains, and riverside meadows in the region, became part of protected areas. Thus, nature and wilderness have been produced and remade through assemblages of environmental and economic policies, transportation routes, changing forms of land use, scientific discourse, and mapping practices.

Yet this is only part of the story. Although engaging a language of wilding or rewilding (Lorimer and Driessen 2016) amid postsocialist ruin, rewilding always also involves practices of curating nature, local habitats, and infrastructure. As Brandenburg's landscapes are redefined, its ecologies and built environments have been remade across the region. New streets, bicycle paths, town squares, and renovated buildings are seen as preparing the region for a more modern future. Since the 2000s, competitions such as *Unser Dorf hat Zukunft* (Our village has a future) have been popular in many towns in Brandenburg (MLUK 2021). While there have been numerous efforts to revitalize the region, many streets and houses have been renovated.

During my fieldwork in the area, ruins often stood right next to newly painted houses and new supermarkets. In addition, although the March Oder region and other parts of East Brandenburg have had some of the highest unemployment rates in Germany since unification, unemployment decreased in the course of the 2010s—especially in the western areas close to Berlin and its growing suburbs, known as the "bacon belt" (*Speckgürtel*).[5] At the same time, many of the region's landscapes have been "modernized"; for example, with increasing investment in alternative energy, wind farms have begun to dot the region.

Thus, while the region has often been referred to as "the end of the world," this end looks different depending on where you stand (Rada 2004). Indeed, the region's political topographies and disparate voting patterns reflect diverging visions of the future: while there has been widespread popular support for social democratic, progressive, green, and conservative political parties, Brandenburg has also witnessed a stark rise in support for white nationalist, right-wing, and anti-EU political parties such as the AfD (Alternative für Deutschland) that began to form a substantial part of state and county governments since elections in 2019.[6] There has also been a broad spectrum of right-wing and neo-Nazi organizing in the region—including AfD or NPD (Nationaldemokratische Partei Deutschlands) events, youth group meetings, and small-scale underground music festivals (Horte 2019).

Furthermore, far from being untouched nature, the region, like the rest of former East Germany, experienced a speculative boom in the 1990s, in which property regimes were reshuffled and formerly state-owned forest and agricultural land, as well as enterprises, public housing, and military property, were privatized.[7] Throughout this privatization process, thousands of people lost their jobs in the area. In the context of land reform, Brandenburg also became one of the regions with the highest percentage of GMO agriculture in Germany. For several years, the region thus became a battleground in conflicts over genetically modified plants, and calls for a GMO-free March Oder region abounded, especially among environmentalists and some local small-scale farmers.[8] So-called close-to-nature forests stood side-by-side with genetically modified fields. While pristine nature returned, mutating organisms flourished.

In this chapter, I explore the politics of nationhood and nature at work in postsocialist transformations of the "Wild East." More specifically, I ask how the nation is remade through nature and the wild in the March Oder region: which bodies—people, plants, animals, landscapes, and things—are marked as wild, or are seen as being out of place, and outside of the national body. Following this question, I engage several ethnographic vignettes and track narrative and material practices of making "wild country" (Rose 2004). In Zarin, practices of making wild country operate across different registers: they encompass economic strategies, enactments of space, and processes of racialization that engage unruly bodies, landscapes, affects, and economies. Tracking a series of practices of making the "East" into "wild country," I shed light on how attempts to transform ecological habitats and make nature and the wild matter in times of economic collapse articulate with racialization (Heatherington 2010)—and also with efforts to challenge existing exclusions.

Wildness (*Wildheit*), wilderness (*Wildnis*), and the *wild* are ambiguous terms. The wild has a long, violent trajectory in the history of (settler) colonialism and has been an integral element in the making of Europe. As discussed in chapter 5, marking both land and people as wild has been a key tool of colonization and its civilizing mission (Fanon 2004). In her book *Reports from a Wild Country*, Deborah Bird Rose (2004, 5) reflects on an ethics of decolonization that offers modes of historical reflection that are not based on the erasure of past and present violence but instead rely on responsive attentiveness. Turning colonialism's logic and terminology against itself, she defines the wild as the process of colonization and the specter of racism itself: "Wild people (colonizers) make wild country (degrading, failing). Colonization and the wild form a matrix: settler societies and their violence" (Rose 2004, 4). In Zarin, the wild emerges from the cracks of frail economies and the ruins of socialist ecologies. Pursuing the question of what and who is understood to be wild (or unruly, feral, or in ruin) (Lorimer and Driessen 2016) and who does the speaking with what effect, I also ask: In what ways do these instantiations of wildness overlap with, or depart from, notions of home (*Heimat*), the domesticated, or the alien? And what glimpses of ruderal worlds that are neither wild nor domesticated might we see in them?

The following ethnographic vignettes offer a view of a region that has been in transition and is often transformed into an imagined frontier space "somewhere between Berlin and Poland"—an in-between space where postsocialist and postcolonial (or rather neocolonial) worlds meet. While some remake their livelihoods in the gaps of crumbling postsocialist economies, others embark on a new life within the regulatory systems of Europe's changing border politics. In the process, landscapes and lives do not turn out to be as anticipated: a forest stops making sense, a refugee home becomes an ostrich farm, train trips go nowhere, a nature park turns into "the bush" in the middle of Europe, and a region to the east of Berlin becomes the

"Wild East"—an odd "safari wilderness," where adventure entrepreneurs, tourists, unemployed locals, migrants, and refugees meet. In the face of these practices of unmaking, remaking, and in fact, making up place, some people are puzzled, some find adventure and joy falling out of the skies, others explore entrepreneurial opportunities in funeral speeches and safari tours, and still others traverse the entire country only to bring their dreams all the way back home again.

Addressing these ethnographic vignettes, I first turn to the romance of landscape and the production of (neo)colonial imagery in local performances of the Wild East. Following the routes of one entrepreneur, a local safari guide who searches out wilderness (and retraces the rambles of nineteenth-century German novelist Theodor Fontane), I read the production of wild spaces both in its longer historical context and in the postsocialist moment. While this first part of the chapter addresses imperial and (post)colonial melancholia (Gilroy 2006; Rosaldo 1989) and its commodification, the second part is about rupture: as local forests and farms have been restructured and the local built environment has been transformed, people's biographies have been interrupted. Through the eyes of a forester who worked in the socialist forestry industry, I trace conflicting ideologies of what constitutes a "good forest" and what constitutes an appropriate strategy to deal with the postsocialist transition. In the last section of the chapter, we will return to the refugee camps in the region that were also at the center of the previous chapter: here, I track the post–Cold War transformation of the forest from a militarized space to a place that accommodates displaced people. Again, lives and places have been transformed and interrupted, yet in very different ways: Kenyan migrants express their dreams about Europe and experiences of displacement via accounts of the "wildness" of racism. For them, the violence of asylum policies and the disturbing materialities of refugee homes in the region's forests produce a life without traction. Following these different accounts of the wild and wild(er)ness, I examine the material-symbolic politics of race, nation, and nature—and the social life of displacement—at work in the remaking of postsocialist and (neo)colonial landscapes.

Part I: The "Wild East" Safari Tour

Our guide greets us with a big smile at the train station. Wearing khaki cargo pants and a beige straw hat, and equipped with binoculars and Ray-Ban sunglasses, Lars Reichelt is well prepared to guide today's group of visitors, three Berliners and me, through the Brandenburg wilderness—and so is his car. At first glance, the sturdy dark green Land Rover seems oddly out of place in the empty parking lot next to the train station. Yet, as we climb in and settle on the sideways benches in the back, the world slowly begins to shift. The terrain technologies of our tour guide and the Land Rover are set into motion.

We head out of town, stopping at a traffic light at a small intersection. "The last traffic light we will see for the rest of the day," Lars conveys to us with a sense of promise and mystery. Just a few moments later, the Land Rover veers off the road onto an unpaved forest path. Winding our way through the woods, we follow this bumpy path. "Welcome to the March Oder region!" Lars proclaims to his guests. "We are in one of the least populated regions in Germany here. We are all on our own—except a few bicyclists." Ready to search out hidden places at the borders of "civilization" and "wilderness," we learn that we "will soon begin to see things from a different perspective" as the tour makes its way along meandering paths, known only by a select local few.

As the trees clear for a moment, we pass the Zarin train station. Near the train crossing, a small gravestone on the side of the road stands as a reminder of the train raid of Zarin. The raid happened at a time when the Eastern train line (Ostbahn) of the Prussian Empire connected Berlin to the March Oder region and all the way to East Prussia and the Russian border. One day, someone stole pieces of the train tracks. The train derailed. Fire erupted and was extinguished by the village men; many people died. Standing beside the tracks, looking at the gravestone, we begin to sense the aura of a different time—a time when trains stretched across empires, a time of sneaky sabotage, tragic derailings, and what our tour guide describes as "honorable men."

As we continue through the town of Zarin, we pass a deteriorating castle—the former residence of Duke Friedrich Wilhelm Carl von Schmettau (1743–1806). Paint is coming off the building's walls. The majestic front stairs have begun to crumble. The roof is partially torn off. A few plastic tarps barely cover the gaping holes, exposing the interior to the elements. After the Berlin Wall tumbled, someone bought the castle and began to renovate it; on one wall, you can still see samples of different paint colors. The owner received money from Berlin at the time—as did many others who renovated dilapidated houses in East Germany. Then, out of the blue, he disappeared—with all the money—and no one ever saw him again. The castle fell into ruins.

Next, we hit the road again, passing colorful, freshly painted buildings and ramshackle barns as we drive down a winding path through a large meadow. What once was the duke's carefully landscaped English garden has turned into a large field, overgrown with lush vegetation. Behind a few large oak trees, on a small hill, we see the outlines of a building: a pyramid towers over the hill and peeks through the trees. A Prussian general, cartographer, and landscape architect, Duke von Schmettau had imagined that the pyramid would become his grave, our guide explains. Yet the duke died in the war against the French army and his vision never materialized. The pyramid was left to decay and was reconstructed in 2001. At a small clearing a few steps from the pyramid, we park on the side of the road. Lars pulls a huge eighteenth-century map out of a hidden box and clips it on the side of the car (fig. 6.1). On the map, Berlin is a tiny, village-like settlement. The Tiergarten park (now in the city center) is situated at the edge and leads straight into the countryside. A small dot, Zarin is marked farther east on the map. Sending soldiers to all corners of Prussia, measuring and using large so-called border oaks as orientation points, the duke of Zarin authored this first map of the region. With his maps, von Schmettau assisted Frederick William II, King of Prussia, in draining the Oder marshes and "taming" the unpredictable meandering of the Oder River.[9] As we stand here today on the meadow, surrounded by trees and in the presence of the hidden pyramid, gazing at the map, the landscape begins to look different: with the eyes of the cartographer, we chart what appears as half-known. The region becomes once again swamps and wetlands, a wild territory in need of ordering and mapping. And in it, the pyramid appears as hidden treasure we stumbled upon by chance.

This arrival scene in the woods sets the stage for the tour's hodgepodge way of seeing, navigating, and performing the region's wilderness and otherness. The tour participants find themselves in the middle of a make-believe excursion: mapping and exploring hidden traces of history, we begin to see the landscape with different eyes. The map, the Land Rover, and the pyramid transport us into a time and place when the March Oder region was an unpredictable landscape of river valleys, fens, moors, swamps, and wetlands in need of domestication—a conquest over water that would enable the development of large-scale agriculture and transportation infrastructure and thus the making of the modern German nation and its economic power (Blackbourn 2006). Having served as border markers in cartography, oak trees carry the aura of surveillance and suggest the geopolitical power of

FIGURE 6.1 "Off-road adventure tour." Photo by author.

empire. Via the tour's own mapping practice, a different world emerges: a world of travel, exploration, and colonial aspiration—but also a world crowded with accidents, exile, and sudden deaths.

As we continue, driving down a bumpy dirt road through the woods, we listen to the tunes of American country music. Then, Lars turns up the volume for the song "Brandenburg" by German singer-songwriter Rainald Grebe, evoking a sense of settler colonial travel amid the Brandenburg wild. Driving through the forest, we pass an eerie landscape of war; the ground is dotted with the former foxholes dug by Russian and German soldiers during the last battles of World War II. From the size of the trees and dips in the ground, our tour guide explains, you can tell where soldiers hid in ditches and where tanks had once stood. A landscape crowded with the memory of dead bodies and fascism's unexploded ordnance unfolds before us. Once in a while, a deer peeks through the grass from a nearby game reserve.

Then, farther east, tobacco fields.[10] The drained wetlands of the Oder stand as reminders of imperial conquest over nature in the eighteenth and nineteenth centuries: when the Prussian engineers and armies built canals and drained swamps to pave the way for agriculture in the era of Frederick the Great, they introduced new crops such as the potato. The tour continues along a route that is cobbled together with stories of doom and failure: a former socialist collectivized farm stands empty after having been reclaimed by its prewar owner. The fruit trees at the front of the farm are abundant with apples, their branches crooked from the weight. Gleaners roam between the trees, having a feast with sparkling smiles on their faces. Finally, the tour ends with a visit to another castle that has fallen into ruin. Its now-musty rooms have become the storage unit and makeshift art gallery of an elderly couple. In the front entry hall, which is crowded with paintings, wooden sleds, a treasure chest, and other odd antiques, we pick sweet, dark-purple plums out of a big basket on the table.

Lars is in his early fifties and grew up in Dresden, in East Germany. Before unification, he lived in East Berlin and worked as a car mechanic. When the Berlin Wall came down, he soon lost his job and then worked odd jobs for a while. Then, a few years later, he came up with the idea of offering tourists "safaris" in the countryside around Berlin, and he started his own business. Being in "nature" and seeking out "adventure" and hidden places seemed like the perfect thing to do and a great way to make money. And although he now makes only half the amount he used to, he says it is the best job he could hope for. Aside from his "safari" tours, he also offers an array of other adventure-themed tours: he takes tourists through the Naturpark Märkische Schweiz; he takes weekend travelers and locals on bunker tours and arranges paintball matches; or he organizes trips in which people can drive former Soviet tanks (which a friend has specialized in fixing up).

Lars's tour is a hodgepodge of various time frames that stage different forms of wilderness in Brandenburg—an imagined frontier space between the wildness of land and people, and their domestication. Cobbling together disparate motifs of the "African safari" and "Wild West" frontier with settings of postindustrial ruin, the tour has no unifying narrative. It is a make-believe (and highly selective) "safari" of abandoned villages in which "nothing happens," featuring hotels that went bankrupt, stores that closed down, deserted cobblestone farm buildings, and houses with wooden planks covering their windows. It is a landscape of ghost towns set amid "wild" and "empty" land in an ancient basin with hills that originated during the last ice age. Authenticity is certainly not the point in this tour. As we drive, we learn to navigate the terrain via maps, cars, canoes, songs, binoculars, and a camera. With his Land Rover, Lars develops a deeply gendered and racialized terrain technology of mastering and domesticating nature: equipped with four-wheel drive, the Land Rover overcomes any environment, from the Saharan steppe to rapidly flowing rivers, jungles, and deserts—all the way to "wild Brandenburg."[11]

The kind of wilderness knowledge Lars seeks to convey is all about masculine colonial appropriation of land and the lure of the wild: driving through a sand pit near an abandoned quarry, canoeing up a small river, and shooting bows and arrows at bales of hay on the far side of a field. We are made to feel as though we could overcome any obstacle. And yet, at least according to his narrative, it is the seeming absence of local infrastructure and large-scale tourism in the region that creates that special "safari feeling." Using stereotypes of place that draw on the image of the "Wild West" of North America and the "wilderness" of the "African bush"—stereotypes that have a long history in German popular culture—Lars creates the German "Wild East" and makes it into a marketable asset.

But not only do the parameters of place shift in the course of his tour: traveling back in time, we move on cobblestone and unpaved roads. By invoking a history of undrained wetlands and swamps, our safari tour conjures up the conquest of nature and the consolidation of the nation in a region that is currently situated at the periphery. A Wild West romanticism of outlaws, derailed trains, and stolen tracks mixes with an imperialist nostalgia for a time when trains stretched across empires, connecting Berlin with the eastern territories of Prussia—and when "treasures of nature and wilderness" could be found in "faraway lands" during Germany's colonial rule and the colonization of Africa and the Americas. And Lars's practice of creating an imaginary space of wildness is not unique or an exception in the March Oder region. Other wild space performances abound: ostrich farms, close-to-nature forests, or a nearby "Western town" that, among other performances, stages Native American powwows while drawing on a large subculture of so-called Indian reenactments that has existed across Germany and eastern Europe for many years (Berger 1974; Red Haircrow 2018; Sieg 2002; Stoetzer 2019). Indeed, some people claim that the Wild West, or perhaps more appropriately the Wild East, begins right at the edge of Berlin.[12]

Interlude: Frontiers and the Wild in European and German Cultural Imaginations

The images of the "East" as "wild space" that are created in Lars's safari tour and other local reenactments echo a variety of other—much older—motifs of the frontier between civilization and wilderness. These motifs have played an important role in the intellectual and political formation of Europe (Berger 1974; Wolff 1994), and their spatial imaginaries have had multiple lives throughout European history. Racialized assumptions about place and people inherent in notions of wildness and wilderness provided a key rationale for settler colonial domination and violence (Fanon 2004; Taussig 1987) and continue to do so today (H. Davis and Todd 2017; Rose 2004; Simpson 2007; TallBear 2011).

Engaging Western imaginaries about wilderness and the wild as a spectacle, the idea of the African safari emerged in the context of European colonization and scientific exploration of the African continent. The word *safari* means journey in Swahili, and it originated from the Arabic word *safar*, to travel, tour, or voyage. The word first appeared in the nineteenth century in the English- and German-speaking world, and it was used to describe travels throughout Africa, usually by wealthy white European colonists and scientists who sought to observe wildlife, or by those involved in the colonial slave trade. A gendered metaphor for colonial, white, and masculine notions of travel (Eeden 2006, 352), the African safari is thus closely entangled with European efforts to extract resources and labor by controlling and domesticating land, people, animals, and plants on a continent imagined as wild.[13] In the nineteenth and twentieth centuries, the African safari became associated with expeditions and big game hunting—as a display of white prestige and Western technology—and then with wildlife tourism (354). The safari also inspired literature, film, and fashion throughout the global North—ranging from writers like Ernest Hemingway; to photographers like Leni Riefenstahl (Meiu 2008); to fashion styles such as khaki pants, safari jackets, and pith helmets (which all originated as colonial military uniforms); to car culture, as with the Land Rover (Eeden 2006).[14]

In Germany, so-called safari-themed tours and parks are a common genre today—often with a postsocialist or urban twist. For example, alluding to Western stereotypes about the socialist East as other, guides offer "urban safaris" in Berlin in which tourists can explore the city in former

East German cars such as the Trabant. There are also safari-themed wildlife parks such as the Serengeti Park in Lower Saxony and several reality TV shows based in East Africa (such as *Reality Queens auf Safari*).[15]

Contemporary wilderness motifs also echo long-standing German fascination with the American frontier and the Wild West, which deepened during European emigration to the Americas in the nineteenth and twentieth centuries.[16] For example, one of the best-selling authors in early twentieth-century Europe was Karl May, who wrote a fictional series of Wild West adventures. Although most of the stories are written as a first-person narrative from the perspective of Old Shatterhand (a white German settler, as whom May would occasionally dress up), May did not visit the United States until late in his life, when he had already written a large part of his work.[17]

These yearnings for the American frontier and "wilderness" corresponded with nationalist and imperial desires for expansion throughout German history.[18] With wilderness areas slowly disappearing in the course of urbanization and industrialization, many Germans ironically began to identify with Native Americans as victims of environmental destruction and community fragmentation.[19] This kind of colonial mimicry and appropriation is an integral element of exploitation, dispossession, and violence—and, as critical race scholars based in Germany, such as Peggy Piesche, have pointed out, it is also an expression of a form of whiteness that does not need to position itself (Piesche 2017) vis-à-vis the harm inflicted on racialized and Indigenous communities.

In the twentieth century, May's stories and other images of the American West inspired Nazi ideas of a wild, backward East in need of colonization. Nostalgia for the wild and the idea of a "noble savage" played a key role in Nazi racial discourse: wilderness was simultaneously yearned for and in need of taming and control.[20] After the war, May continued to have a strong influence on German popular culture, as evidenced in the so-called Winnetou movies of the mid-1960s in West Germany and the anticapitalist Westerns in East Germany, where May's work was outlawed.[21] Inspired by these movies, a large subculture of "Indian" and "Wild West" hobbyists emerged.[22] Performances of May's stories became increasingly popular well beyond the Cold War, and they continue to capture large audiences today.[23] There are still several Wild West towns and so-called Indian villages in Berlin and Brandenburg. As Indigenous activists and critics such as the Berlin-based filmmaker and writer Red Haircrow (2018) in their film *Forget Winnetou* have shown, these German fascinations with Indians are a microcosm of the continuing violences of racism and colonialism in Europe and the urgent need for more paths toward repair.[24]

Cultural imaginaries of "the East" as untamed land also have a more local trajectory in Brandenburg. David Blackbourn traces the mystique of the frontier between wilderness, civilization, and the Wild East in his analysis of the "conquest over nature" in nineteenth- and twentieth-century Prussia, including Brandenburg. As Prussia expanded, frontier images abounded, including notions of an "Amazonian landscape" of rivers and marshes (and sand). For example, Frederick the Great compared the marshes of Polish Prussia to Canada. When Slav fishermen were displaced by German farmers, the new settlements adopted names such as Florida or Philadelphia (Blackbourn 2006, 303). Images of American expansion also played a role in Brandenburg-Prussian efforts to colonize West Africa (Guettel 2010). In addition, the idea of the frontier made an appearance in nineteenth-century romanticist writings, such as Theodor Fontane's *Rambles through the Mark Brandenburg*. Here Fontane wrote that, after "a rain-drenched boat journey across the Wurstrauer Marshes," he and his companions felt "as if we had traveled over the Kansas River or a Prairie far in the West" (quoted in Blackbourn 2006, 293).

Thus, as Blackbourn (2006, 295) writes, "The German frontier was in the East." During World War II, this "urge to move East" (*Drang nach Osten*) engaged a racial discourse of place that carved out an ideology of blood, soil, and "living space" (*Lebensraum*): drawing on the figure of the "hardy settler," as well as the figure of the "Indian," fascist Germans framed themselves as a people without sufficient land and in need of expansion. The goal was to occupy the space in the east and to bring the "green of German culture to the Polish 'wilderness'" (Blackbourn 2006, 293). In this imperial imaginary, German settlers would tame the "endless primeval" forests and the "alien wilderness" of Poland and create a "paradise," a "European California" (Blackbourn 2006, 301). At the same time, notions of the wild and rewilding the landscape, as well as a persistent disavowal of domestication combined with antiurban sentiments, were central to a sense of national belonging and Nazi conservationists' and zoologists' attempts to expand German Lebensraum into the "Wild East" (Lorimer and Driessen 2016).[25]

Beyond these echoes of German and European fascination with frontiers, safaris, and the American West, what does it mean to invoke wilderness and wild space in postsocialist Germany today? I suggest that recent practices of creating the Wild East as a space of otherness (such as experienced on Lars's safari tour) respond to experiences of regional economic marginalization by engaging changing constellations of race, nation, and place.

Lars and other Wild East entrepreneurs participate in a narrative practice, a genre of "wilding"—a practice of creating wild space that I encountered throughout the countryside around Berlin and that can be traced in other deindustrialized regions in former East but also West Germany (see, for example, Hagemann 2006). In this practice, the countryside around Berlin is staged as untamed land and as a frontier—both a physical place and an affective space that white, mostly German or European, tourists can "discover" and travel through. With his mix of cowboy and colonial safari drag, Lars leads his tours through open, seemingly lonesome spaces of white European unlimited possibility. Wilderness becomes an entrepreneurial strategy: making an asset out of regional economic plight and social struggle, Lars taps into national stereotypes about the March Oder region and rebrands the region as exotic and wild. In the process, his and other local reenactments create a sense of national belonging and regional white identity that specifically addresses an urban audience visiting the countryside.[26]

This sense of belonging depends on the (symbolic) erasure of Black, Indigenous, and people of color. While creating that special safari feeling, Lars shifts and mixes perspectives of both local insider and colonial traveler through the postsocialist countryside. He thus caters to nostalgic (Western) conceptions of the socialist past and mingles them with colonial nostalgia and an ambivalent desire for and consumption of racialized otherness (Sieg 2002) that is key to articulations of whiteness (hooks 1992; Piesche 2017).[27] Mixing bodily enactments of the safari and the American frontier, Lars invokes a time of empire that precedes Germany's release of some of its eastern territory, as well as the loss of its colonies after World War I. Thus, performing wilderness and making wild country indulges in settler colonial modes of historical reflection that are indifferent to, and in fact erase, the dispossession, violence, and genocide that the making of frontiers and the "new World" unleashed (Rose 2004, 5).

This erasure echoes a persistent and common myth in Germany that because of its relatively short duration of thirty years, German colonial violence was contained and minimal compared to that of other colonial empires such as those of the French and the British. This belief ignores the longer history of German involvement in slavery (Yildiz 2020) and colonialism.

And it stands in the way of a more comprehensive understanding of the role of colonialism in shaping contemporary Germany and Europe. Moreover, this erasure needs to be situated within the larger political context of contemporary Europe, in which both mainstream and right-wing political movements indeed whitewash the violent histories of their respective nations while lamenting the loss of power of the nation-state and its imperial aspirations (Bhambra 2017).[28] In Germany, this trend has gone hand in hand with a long resistance against the demand for reparations for colonial genocide (such as the genocide against people from Ovaherero, Nama, and San groups in Namibia),[29] as well as attacks on efforts to decolonize the education system or to initiate the return of stolen cultural artifacts from former German colonies (Biallas 2018).

It is important to remember that such silencing of colonial violence is not new: as Michel-Rolph Trouillot (1995) has argued, it is part of a wider story of global domination, in which Europe and the West are not forced to consider the perspective of the world (see also Bhambra 2009, 2; Hall 1991). As Fatima El-Tayeb (2020) has shown, this colonial amnesia continues to shape the ways in which futures are being imagined across European public discourse, especially in regard to migration. Yet German unification offered an opportunity of rupture in which existing historical narratives collapsed and memory had to be remade.[30]

It is precisely that moment of rupture and collapse in which Lars's tour and his retelling of local history operates. Yet by objectifying "unruly nature" and commoditizing the ruins of socialism, Lars caters to broader European fascinations with the imperial ruins of Western capitalism (Stoler 2013) without considering the perspective of the world and the formerly colonized. As Ghassan Hage (2016) has pointed out, at a time of proliferation of crises—from climate change to the so-called migration crisis—ruins, unruly nature, and images of regional plight in the global North are common themes in public perception and in discussions of migration and environmental change. This kind of "ruin porn" also expresses fantasies of colonial reversal at a time when governability itself—such as different nations' abilities to shore up their borders and domesticate "others," as well as capitalism's extraction of natural resources—is crumbling (Hage 2016). In both cases, human and nonhuman "barbarians" threaten to wreak havoc upon previous forms of governability. Mimicking colonial traditions of "exploration" and transferring them onto the East German landscape thus also enacts a desire for white mobility and a social status that evades the histories of appropriation and violence (Piesche 2017) that are at the center of the making of colonial frontiers and European history.

Part II: Rewilding the Forest

In the 1990s, in the years immediately after unification and as formerly state-run local industries disappeared, hopes were high that tourism would flourish in the Brandenburg region. To prepare for this future, the county offered seminars to train local unemployed villagers as tour guides. Excited about the opportunity, many people signed up, including my friend Sabine (mentioned at the beginning of this chapter), who had lost her job with the former Forestry Institute in Eberswalde after the collapse of the socialist regime. However, tourism never really picked up and things turned out differently. A decade later, when I met her, Sabine thus occasionally worked as a nature guide in the Naturpark Märkische Schweiz. Once in a while, she offered walking or bicycle tours through the marshlands, but it was impossible to make a living this way. Sabine thus joined a local organic farm, run by Berliners, as a seasonal worker. And soon she started to specialize in yet another profession: funeral speeches. Learning the craft of giving funeral speeches and homages to the dead, she was hired to attend funerals in churches throughout the region—a region with an increasingly aging population.

Sabine once said to me: "Socialism disappeared and left a big gap. And what came in its place? Capitalism, yes. But what ACTUALLY happened? Nothing!" In the face of growing unemployment and dwindling local economic opportunities, people had to be inventive about how to make a living. And indeed, like she did, people came up with unconventional entrepreneurial strategies. Yet for Sabine, this was arduous. And some fared better than others in this transformation. "Some people just did not go through or understand the changes since 1989! They had a hard time," she explained to me ("Einige Menschen haben den Wandel seit 1989 nicht so richtig mitgemacht oder verstanden"). This is when she told me about Mr. Jasinski. Mr. Jasinski was a forester in the March Oder region from the 1960s until shortly after unification in 1990, when he had to retire early. According to Sabine, he "didn't go through the changes," and he definitely had a different perspective. Her comment caught my attention and curiosity. What was the right way to look at the changes? And what did things look like when you did not understand them? And what did the forest, the park, and the region look like from the wrong perspective? Equipped with these questions, I reached out to Mr. Jasinski.

∾ ∾ ∾

In late July, Mr. Jasinski was busy harvesting. Together with his wife and a small number of animals, he lived on a small piece of land at the edge of the forest near the town of Müggelsdorf, on the southwestern border of the park. When I visited him one Thursday afternoon, I rode my bike from Zarin, across the train tracks, over a long cobblestone alley lined with beech trees. I passed several grass meadows interspersed with small canals used to drain water off the meadows. On the side of the path, a small park map was posted to guide the way, and a sign prohibited garbage disposal in the meadows. I continued through the forest, where I briefly chatted with a family picking mushrooms. Leaving the forest, I rode along a narrow paved road dotted with speed bumps intended to protect migrating frogs from cars. Mr. Jasinski's house appeared on the left, next to a large, harvested field. A pile of firewood towered at the gate to the property. The house, probably built sometime in the 1950s, had a tiled roof. Gray paint was coming off the side. I rang the bell.

Mr. Jasinski and his wife, who used to be a chemist at the former local agricultural research institute, greeted me, and after a short chat we went to the lush garden behind the house, bursting with fruit trees, flowers, and a little vegetable bed. Thirty cats (as he told me), many of them kittens, and some chickens roamed around. A donkey, several sheep, and a horse stood in an open stable next to the garden. We sat down at a big wooden table at the center of the garden and began to chat about the socialist land reform and privatization. Many lots, hitherto in collective hands, were returned to their original owners from before the division. Today, many of the lots in the area had undeclared ownership and many houses remained empty.

Mr. Jasinski was not native to this area. He had spent his childhood years in East Prussia. During World War II, he, like many others, fled across the Oder River with his family and friends from their village to Bad Frankenhausen in Thuringen, farther south. Like he and his family, many German refugees from East Prussia also settled in the March Oder region after the war, when Germany ceded the territory east of the Oder River to Poland. Much later, he studied forest science in Eberswalde and received his degree there.[31] He then was transferred to become the local forester for part of the March Oder region in Klausberg, taking on responsibility for five districts.

Aside from him, three women and five men worked there. The women were responsible for "forest care"—mainly ripping out those plants that were considered weeds and clearing out unnecessary undergrowth—while the men were loggers. Then, in 1989, the Berlin Wall came down and everything changed. He soon lost his job and had to go on unemployment until his retirement benefits kicked in.

As we talked, bees buzzed around us (and were, in fact, so loud that they obscured parts of the recording of our conversation). A few tractors rattled by, slowing down for the frog-protection speed bumps on the road. Describing his life, work, and the changing forest, Mr. Jasinski traced the transformation of the landscape—and the history of the nation—through his own biography. In his stories, the March Oder region emerged as a landscape of constant change and hardship: after German refugees from East Prussia crossed the Oder River into this region during World War II, thousands of people died in the forest during one of the last battles between Russian, Polish, and German soldiers. Today, you can visit a memorial and museum in a small town close by.

After the war, when Germany was divided into the Allied zones and Brandenburg became part of the Soviet zone, much of the local pine forest was cut down in order to pay reparations to Russia. In addition, since there were no coal reserves in the area and many people were starving and freezing during the cold winters of 1946 and 1947, many local residents as well as people from Berlin plundered the forest and cut down trees for firewood. It took years for the huge forest clearings to regrow. With the ongoing division of Germany, the East German state aimed at self-sufficiency in agricultural and forest production. As a result, the socialist government introduced a wide-scale land reform, collectivizing farms and forests—thus further transforming the rural landscape.

A local research institute was reopened in the immediate aftermath of the war to research the agricultural possibilities under the "extreme conditions" in the March Oder region. The soil in the area is sandy, and there is very little rain. Because of this sandiness, it has often been referred to as "the sandbox" of the former Roman Empire, and it has faced new obstacles since German unification, including an increase in heat waves and forest fires due to climate change. In fact, from Mr. Jasinski's perspective, the region is desolate because of its very proximity to the "unnatural" city of Berlin. As he put it: "Berlin takes all the rain away!" Located to the west, the direction from which the rain comes, all the rain tends to pour down over Berlin's densely built environment, he explained. But, as before the war, pine trees

FIGURE 6.2 Industrial pine forest, Brandenburg. Photo by author.

have thrived under these dry, barren conditions. Alongside collectivization and large-scale land reform, the East German government created an industrial forest that depended on clear-cutting and tight control of "weeds"—a forest that was highly productive (fig. 6.2). The region was called the "bread tree" of the March. After unification of East and West Germany, things fell apart. In fact, "everything went down the creek" (German expression for things going downhill). Mr. Jasinski lost his job. Since everything in East and West existed twice ("es gab ja alles doppelt!"), many local institutions were closed down. In addition, Western environmentalists and foresters came to Brandenburg, fundamentally restructuring forestry. They laid off most of the people who were working in the forest at the time. And they wanted to do things just as they had in the West: they wanted a mixed forest and planted lots of oak trees.

This radical shift in forestry policy and environmental discourse was an outcome of changing ideas of what constitutes good forest management. Tracing the effects of the unification on former East German forestry, Arvid Nelson (2005, 175) has shown that in the wake of unification, politicians such as East Germany's last president, Lothar de Maizière, already aimed at developing a new "concept of the forest," assigning ecological and cultural values precedence over wood production. Thus, competing ecological and economic ideas about the ideal forest became an important element of unification and the redefinition of German national identity. Whereas an industrial forest had previously been a good forest, after unification, ecological approaches emphasized abundance and complexity while "restoring economic and social diversity to the farm and forest landscape" (175). As a result, postunification land reforms prohibited large-scale clear cuts and introduced "close-to-nature forestry" (*naturnahe Waldwirtschaft*), modeled after Western concepts, to replace the former singular focus on industrial production. While hardwoods increased up to 40 percent, implementation of these reforms was slow due to lack of funds.

Western environmentalists critiqued the devastating pollution in many East German cities as well as the monocultural forests in the countryside (Nelson 2005), and projects of remaking nature played key roles in national unification efforts.[32] In Brandenburg, the 1990 creation of several nature reserves, including the Naturpark Märkische Schweiz, sought to protect the "national natural landscapes" covering 30 percent of the state's territory. Seen as a "gift" to unification, the creation of these nature parks helped naturalize the nation.[33] As formerly eradicated or rare wildlife has been reintroduced into the region, renaturing parts of the lower Havel River in Brandenburg has also become one of the biggest river relandscaping projects in Europe. In the course of these initiatives, imaginaries of nature and wilderness have become central to the construction of national subjects and to definitions of what constitutes good citizens.[34]

At the same time, with population decline and dwindling economies, "wilderness" has also become an important imaginary for urban as well as rural restructuring. In urban areas, this has often meant that planners move away from classic greening policies by preserving gaps in the urban fabric and enabling spontaneous nature to emerge in abandoned lots or former industrial areas. In rural areas, wilderness, seen as the almost inevitable outcome of population decline and dwindling economies, has become not only a marketing strategy to foster tourism (as in Lars's safari tours) but also a concept associated with uncontrollable natural and social processes. Thus, especially in the context of deindustrialization and population decline in former East Germany, new paradigms of land use have emerged: strategies of renaturing often run alongside or conflict with modernist schemes of land use and intensifying agriculture (such as using GMOs), or ideas about sustainable tourism (Rink 2009, 276).

In Germany, then, postunification reforms have engaged changing ideas about how to order nature and society. As Cordula Kropp (2005) has shown in her work on river landscaping in the 1990s, not only did forest management schemes change, but so did concepts of how to shape rivers and entire ecosystems. While trying to reestablish a coexistence of humans and nature, approaches that favored the "liberating experience of wild natural rivers" often replaced, or at least sat side-by-side with, an understanding of rivers as "engineered canals" (Kropp 2005, 489)—thus opening up possibilities for undoing modernist schemes and creating alternative conservation and landscaping practices.

Yet for Mr. Jasinski, local initiatives for a close-to-nature forest "did not make any sense"; in fact, for him, they were unsuccessful and irrational. Thus, when seen with the eyes of the former socialist state and considering local ecologies, the postunification forest—and much of the landscape in the region—had stopped making sense: "Nobody could see through this anymore. This was not explicable for a normal thinking person!" he said to me.[35] A lot was ruined. And in the process, not much remained of what had been. Even the newly planted oak trees all ended up dying.

Everybody who knew anything about local conditions said it would be crazy to plant oak trees in the first place, Mr. Jasinski continued. Despite their institutional anchoring, Westerners lacked local knowledge and did not take into consideration that the weather is extremely dry, which is why oak trees stood no chance. Oaks—a mythical symbol of Germanness, just like the forest itself—fared badly in this process.[36] But not only were Western environmentalists unfamiliar with the dry climate, they were also blind to local tree diversity: "If you walk around here with open eyes, you actually see that the forest is mixed: there is the pine, but also oak and beech and other types of trees in the undergrowth. And of course, lots of weeds (like the annoying *Traubenkirsche*)!"

Tracking how the industrial forest changed to a forest in need of preservation and diversification, Mr. Jasinski challenged Western environmentalists and their lack of local knowledge and history. He thus also formulated a critique of national narratives about the forest and its diversity—that is, the desire for oaks and the creation of a "German forest." Like many others who have experienced the changes since 1989, he expressed a longing not only for standardization and trust but also for a way of seeing the forest with the eyes of the socialist state and, in this case, acknowledging the industrial forest's ability to produce trees and its validation of local expertise. Not only did he echo the conflicting visions of nature conservationists and local residents, he also challenged a common environmentalist story about East and West Germany: a story that traces the failure of socialism *within* the forest and claims that the downfall of the regime could be discerned in the country's dismal monocultural forestry (Nelson 2005).

Following Sabine and theorists of nostalgia such as Svetlana Boym, one could argue that these sentiments of loss and displacement, a longing for a time, a home, and a forest that no longer exists, is a form of nostalgia that "inevitably reappears as a defense mechanism in a time of accelerated rhythms of life and historical upheavals" (Boym 2001, xiv). And surely, the forest in Mr. Jasinski's narrative becomes part of an injured regional identity and once again plays a key role in the national imagination: recounting both the war and unification, Mr. Jasinski tells a story of regional loss of power. But even more, his story critiques national environmental narratives under market capitalism and conservation efforts that ignore local ecologies and communities.

From Mr. Jasinski's perspective, renaturing or rewilding the forest did not make much sense. First, in his opinion, the industrial forest was not monocultural after all, and second, the newly introduced trees did not fare well in the dry and sandy soil. Thus, while the oak is seen as a national symbol, for Jasinski it became a symbol of what went wrong with national unification and its unitary logic of wiping out local knowledge, expertise, and infrastructures. While nature had returned in the gaps that opened up after the collapse of socialism, people's biographies, like Mr. Jasinski's, did anything but fall into place. In fact, many people's life trajectories were severely disrupted. Mr. Jasinski described these disruptions with a sense of bewilderment amid a wild, irrational, new social and physical landscape. Moreover, with his critique of efforts to make the region more wild and less domesticated ecologically, Mr. Jasinski also lamented the long-standing history of German conservation paradigms that utilized the wild or rewilding as tools for asserting political power, domination, and colonization of the East (Lorimer and Driessen 2016). His critical comments about the wild thus resonate with what Krista Harper (2006) has traced as two meanings of the wild: in her ethnography, Hungarian environmental actors critically invoke the wild to refer to the ways in which ecological problems and the market were restructured in postsocialist Hungary. The term appears in two senses: First, it describes the wildness of capitalism (*vadkapitalizmus*), and thus serves as a critique of postsocialist renderings of the market as a natural force and as the inevitable triumph of capitalism, in which political elites present the new social order as a natural order while legitimizing major dislocations in people's everyday lives (Harper 2006). Second, the notion of wild conveys a sense of being out of control. Not unlike in Hungary, in East Germany this corresponds to many people's views that privatization enriched the lives of a select few while the large majority found themselves in a precarious situation amid increasing social inequalities.

Yet curiously, Mr. Jasinski's sense of bewilderment also resonated with many refugees' stories in the region. "I feel like I live in a confused world. Everything is *ver-rückt* [dis-placed, de-ranged, crazy]," Amanda, a Kenyan asylum seeker, told me in a conversation, pointing to the odd contradictions of her own situation of being stuck in legal limbo in the countryside without work, without a more permanent permit to stay in sight, and without money to get her out of untenable circumstances. Thus, it is crucial to turn to yet a different sense of the wild that I encountered in the March Oder region, within a set of different and yet connected displacements.

Part III: The "German Bush"

Nowhere

"It's different when you come here as a tourist," Nangila told me. "You have something to do. It's nice and green and you like it, coming from the city. But if you stay in the forest for a long time, you get used to it. You don't see these things anymore. There is nothing for me to do in this forest. It's like living nowhere. Yes, maybe you can see this place on the map. It's in Germany. You can point to it when you look at a map. But it is nowhere. Boredom sets in and it takes over. You don't know where you are. You are away from everything. You are in the forest. And maybe you go to these places in the *Landkreis* (county). But after a while you know all of them and you don't know where to go. You are not allowed to work; you are not allowed to go to Berlin. You have no aim. There is nothing. It's like living nowhere."

While forests were significantly redefined in the years after the fall of the Wall, the creation of nature parks and infrastructure for tourism was an important means of producing new economic possibilities, especially in the unemployment-ridden rural areas of former East Germany. As many asylum seekers were relocated from West to East Germany as part of postunification immigration policies, abandoned military barracks in Brandenburg's forests offered easy—and cheap—locations at which to accommodate them. In the immediate years after unification, many formerly East German counties, although often not explicit about their goals, scrambled to receive funding for accommodating refugees in their vicinity (Pieper 2008).[37] Thus, refugees also became entangled in aiding the economic recovery of rural regions. Seen from this perspective, strategies of making nature matter in this time of economic transformation not only articulated *images of otherness* (Heatherington 2001), but also literally became *means of racialized exclusion* as people found themselves living in remote locations in the forest.

Nangila's and other asylum seekers' stories about their experience in the forest, dreams of Europe, and encounters with Brandenburg as a wild space in the middle of nowhere put yet another twist on the idea of the Wild East frontier. And not unlike Mr. Jasinski's story, theirs is not a romance of landscape but a dream of a land gone awry.

The Ostrich Farm

In 2004, local news of corruption in the *Heim* near Ronersdorf, situated in the forest close to the Naturpark Märkische Schweiz, had spread: the manager and subcontractor of the home had illegally hired refugees living there to build an ostrich farm right next to the camp, and paid them at the rate of one euro per hour.[38] When the story made it into the newspapers, the Heim was closed down and a new location was opened later. Generally, the county allowed asylum seekers to work for so-called one-euro jobs at the Heim for a certain number of hours per month. Yet the owner of the camp found a way around both these regulations: allegedly hiring several asylum seekers to work in the Heim (and not on the adjacent facilities), he simply signed up the same people under different names. Thus, one person could work up to eighty hours per month and make only eighty euros. The money to pay them came from the county, which did not bother to check up on him.

Nangila, Eli, and many other asylum seekers had worked on the farm. Of course, as Nangila explained, they knew perfectly well that they were being exploited. Still, they thought it was better than doing nothing. They built the stables and the fences and cleaned the entire farm once the animals had moved in. One time they even did advertising for the farm by performing an African dance. "And what did we get for it?" Nangila asked. "An ostrich egg and some ostrich meat!" This was not a unique incident, but it resonated with other situations in which refugees were asked to perform. One time, a few people from town and the local "integration network" had initiated "an

African evening" at the Heim. Other Africans from nearby refugee homes in Brandenburg took the train (illegally) to join the event. All they got for their efforts were flowers, as Nangila pointed out. And they did not even have enough money for the train ride back.

After the scandal, the Heim then moved to a different location near the village of Friedwalde, and the Sozialpark took over management in 2004. Many asylum seekers protested because the new Heim was so far removed from the city and once again located on former military facilities. The new management promised them that this would be a temporary accommodation for a few weeks. In the end, people lived there for almost three years, during which Maria would walk an hour through the forest both ways, every morning and night, to reach the nearest bus stop and take the train to Berlin for her language classes. Meanwhile Eli gave rides to the kids on his bicycle, so they could go to kindergarten in the village. (Petra, the German girlfriend of one of the asylum seekers, remembers driving behind the others in her grandmother's car, helping with the move to the Heim, and being horrified about going deeper and deeper into the forest.)

Today, the ostrich farm is a popular stop at which tourists try "exotic" bird meat. Other ostrich farms in Brandenburg even advertise their businesses as the perfect spot for a weekend outing in an environment with "African flair." Right next to the farm, you can now view another former nuclear bunker that was once part of a secret network of facilities of national defense. Like in Zarin, it is being fixed up and is open to occasional tours.

For many asylum seekers, Europe was an imaginary space of progress. And yet their experience in the March Oder region departed in so many ways from that imaginary. Many people joked about their everyday life in the "German bush," mocking what they experienced as a space of physical and symbolic wilderness.

And there were survival stories.

Arrival Stories and Trips to Nowhere, or Three Chickens in Frankfurt

For many, life in the Heim was often without traction. This was a source of frustration and disorientation for those who had lived in the forest for years. Yet it was also a subject of much storytelling and humor. Survival and odd arrival stories, trips to nowhere, and ordinary absurdities abounded. In these stories, German words like *ver-rückt* (dis-placed/de-ranged, crazy), *Dorf* (village), *Heim* (home), *Krankenstadt* (sick city), and *Busch* (bush) stood on their own amid English phrases in which the jokes were told. Repeating these words, people pointed to a sense of displacement, interrupted mobilities, and a landscape of wilderness and dereliction.

One time, Nangila recalled, he and other Kenyans got on the wrong train in the wrong direction and traveled to Poland by accident (and thus put themselves in jeopardy, especially as Poland was not part of the EU at the time). "This place is so flat here," Nangila explained. "You never know where you are and which direction you are going. All you see is trees." Another time, coming from Berlin to Zarin, Eli fell asleep on the train and missed his stop. Thirty minutes later he found himself in Kostrzyn, Poland. He got stuck there because a tree had fallen on the train tracks and no trains could return west to Berlin and the March Oder region.

Yet this was nothing compared with what happened to him when he and Maria were still living next to the ostrich farm in Ronersdorf. They had been in Germany for just a few months. Everything was new to them. Maria was pregnant with Sasha; Neema, their first daughter, was three years old. All they were doing was sitting around in the Heim and waiting for things to change. One day, an opportunity came along. Snoop, a twenty-three-year-old Kenyan (nicknamed after Snoop Dogg, the American rapper), who also lived at the Heim most of the time, told Eli that he would go to Frankfurt. He had a friend with a house there, and Eli could come stay with him on the weekend. Eli was excited and thought this might be a good opportunity to go and try to find a place for himself and Maria and the children.

But things turned out to be quite a bit more complicated.

As Eli was getting ready to go to Frankfurt, he walked to the local store, about five miles from the Heim, to purchase presents to bring with him. At that time, all asylum seekers received chipcards instead of cash for their monthly supplies.[39] Eli and his family (the three of them) received one chipcard for 400 euros per month. The card allowed them to buy food—and only food—at the local supermarket and at a few other grocery stores in the region. They were not able to buy clothes, beer, or anything else using the card. "Who needs so much money for food? What do you eat? A chicken every day? Also, in those days, we always cooked together with other Kenyans in the Heim and so things were cheaper because we shared," Maria commented.

But on the day Eli decided to go to Frankfurt, he bought A LOT OF FOOD. He bought several chickens, rice, drinks, and many other things. And he carried all of it with him. Four plastic bags! He could not buy anything with the chipcard in Frankfurt because the card was not valid there. So he took all the bags with him. (As he told us this, he waddled from one side to the other, to illustrate the heavy weight and bulkiness of his luggage.

Maria and I chuckled.) Eli walked through the forest to the bus stop and then took the train to Berlin. From there, he took the "Wochenend-Ticket" to Frankfurt by slow train. It cost only twenty-five euros, but it took forever to get to Frankfurt. More than thirteen hours, clear across the country. When he finally arrived in Frankfurt, he called Snoop. Snoop acted weird right away and said: "Ah, hi, Eli. Naaaa, it's not a good day today. Call me again in two days!" And then he hung up. Puzzled, Eli tried again. While he desperately let the phone keep ringing, several Kenyan men whom he had met on the train earlier passed by and, seeing he was upset, asked him what was going on. Eli explained the situation to them. One said he could not take him with him because he was staying with his German girlfriend, and she would not appreciate it if he were to bring more of his countrymen home. The other three men were also staying with a friend. One of them, called Adam, tried to convince the others to take Eli with them. They had stepped away from Eli and he could hear them talk in Kikuyu. They started arguing. "What do you mean? I can't just bring random people that I don't know with me to the house!"

After a few moments of going back and forth, they decided Eli could stay with them and invited him to come along. He could not have taken the train back that same day anyway on his ticket. But they told him he could not bring all the chickens and the food with him—their friends wouldn't know where to put all that food because they had a small refrigerator. So Eli put all the groceries, including the chicken, in a locker at the train station. And he stayed the night with his new friends.

The next day, Snoop was still not available. And so, Eli went back to the train station and took the food out of the locker. He gave Adam one of the chickens to thank him. With the rest of the bags of food and the other two chickens, he took the train back to Berlin. Maria was so surprised when she saw him come back with all those bags the next day!

Months later, Eli found out that Adam, one of the Kenyan men who had taken him to their friend's house that day in Frankfurt, was sick and in the hospital in Frankfurt an der Oder. Eli decided to visit him, and Adam was touched to see him, since hardly anyone had come to visit. They have been friends since. As for Snoop, after a few months of not speaking they traveled together to Frankfurt, and Eli let Snoop pay for the trip. "You owe me! This whole trip the other day was for nothing, and it cost me eighty euros!" So he got him back for it.

As Eli told us the story, he pulled us into a world of absurdity, disappointment, humor, and unexpected friendship. Poking fun at his own unpreparedness vis-à-vis the challenges of living in the German bush, as well as his own naïveté about Snoop's unreliability, he narrated the story as a tragic comedy. Not unlike in *Waiting for Godot*, he was caught in an eternal cycle of waiting. But most of all, his mocking storytelling provided a critical commentary on the absurdities of asylum regulations, fragile social networks, the sad ironies of the chipcard system and the residential law—and, most of all, the difficulties of trying to get a life on track in this place. In the end, Eli had traversed the country, equipped with a bunch of dead chickens, to invest in his dream of settling down somewhere and starting a life, only to bring his chicken—and dreams—all the way back ("home") again.

Eli was unable to stay in Frankfurt, not only because the residency law did not allow him to be there in the first place, but also because he lacked financial and social resources. The trip also turned into an ordeal because his preparation and means of travel were complicated by the isolated location of the Heim in the forest, the chipcard system, and a resulting lack of social and material resources. Taken together, the affective geography that he was forced to navigate helped maintain a sense of separation between Germany and migrants, between rational and irrational, between civilization and wilderness—and it placed his own life in the latter set of categories.

A Spy at the Table

In early September 2009, some people at the Heim took a trip to Seelow, a town where many soldiers had died during World War II. I had been staying at the Heim the day before, when news spread that everyone at the Heim was invited to attend a conference in Seelow that dealt with topics of integration and immigration in the March Oder region. The refugees were invited to attend and to take part in a performance. Most people had only a vague idea of what this event was going to be about. Nevertheless, many Heim residents decided to attend, and I accompanied them. A long trip by bus, train, and then bus again, took us through the park to Seelow. The early morning performance involved a role reversal: some of the attending refugees were asked to enact European border officers checking the papers of the mostly German conference attendees, and giving them permission—or not—to enter Germany. While the organizers had imagined that this role reversal of refugees playing border officers would be critical of racist border controls, many of the asylum seekers felt quite differently.

During lunch break at the event, everyone gathered in the upstairs hall, where soup was being served. Steven, Nangila, Eli, Maria, a few other people from the Heim, and I sat around one of the tables, while others who attended the conference had already settled elsewhere in the room. After exchanging stories about the day so far, a dispute between Steven and Nangila broke out. Steven had had enough of the event. He wanted to go back to the Heim and tried to get others to come with him. "OK, we have done our performance this morning. That's why we came here. We're done. Let's go now," he said impatiently. Nangila disagreed and urged him to stay.

"Why would we want to stay?" Steven responded. "What is this whole event about anyway? Does anyone understand what this is about? What in the world are they talking about? What is this? I have a name tag, but they didn't even print my name on it! It's all handwritten and the S in my name, Steven, looks like a dollar sign! What is this? But look, Nangila's name IS printed on HIS tag!" Yet Nangila defended himself, explaining he had gotten a printed tag because he signed up for the conference the day before, unlike Steven, who just signed up on the day of the event. Steven, unimpressed by Nangila's defense, got out the conference brochure that had been handed out to everyone at the beginning of the day. Flipping through the pages, he became more agitated.

"Look, people's faces are in here. It's the same people who organized this today. This is the 8th Integration Summit in Seelow. They have done this already seven times? And things are still as bad as they are!! Explain to me, what are we doing here? We did this performance. We even came yesterday and rehearsed it. And who gives us anything? We didn't even get ANY money for this. I have had enough. I am going. I have other things to worry about than doing silly performances."

"You go and ask them," Nangila said, trying to calm him down. "And they will be able to explain. What else would you do right now? And you did get SOMETHING: you got some coffee and food all day. You got a good lunch."

Steven, obviously unsatisfied with Nangila's response, looked at him with suspicion: "Ah, now I know. They are paying YOU for this. This is what it is. They are paying you, so you get us motivated to go. That's why you are so eager about us going. You are their spy. Tell me, how much are they paying you? What else do they want you to get us to do?"

Although Steven's accusations against the organizers of having hired Nangila in order to plot against everyone else were only half-serious, and although they had a joking undertone to them, they nevertheless did get to the heart of a more serious matter. Expressing his feelings of distrust, Steven conveyed a sense of conspiracy that was not only evident at this particular event, but which also infused everyday life in Zarin in many ways. The day after the summit in Seelow, I learned that several people at the Heim also accused Nangila of plotting with the organizers of the conference because he had not told them about the event ahead of time. Thus, accusations and suspicions circulated among the refugees, creating a whirlwind of resentments not only against each other but, most of all, against the institutions, bureaucratic processes, integration industries, and racialized exclusions surrounding them. From the perspective of living in the forest for years, while facing uncertainty, isolation, and struggling to find traction, the odd language of "integration," with its staging of community events, looked like a conspiracy, a bad joke. Everyone was being interpellated and hence a possible suspect.

Rumors of corruption circulated in other contexts as well. The Sozialpark was obviously profiting from many residents being officially registered in the Heim yet staying in Berlin. It received money from the county for each resident, no matter whether they were actually present at the Heim. Moreover, a sense of suspicion became palpable in the face of the seemingly arbitrary bureaucracies as well as the specter of state power and racism—a sense of suspicion and the *unheimlich* that people experienced in their everyday lives at the Heim. But this sense also went far beyond the Heim and seeped into other moments and places.

These stories illustrate that racism created permission for rampant double-talk, corruption, and exploitation. This in turn elicited in many refugees a sense of the wild, a blurring of boundaries—a wildness and arbitrariness that might lurk just around the corner at any moment. Deborah Bird Rose (2004, 4) has defined the wild as the process of (settler) colonization and the specter of racism itself. Settler societies with their inherent violence utilize the wild to legitimize extraction, domination, and dispossession in the name of civilization—yet it is the very colonial order that wreaks havoc on the land and on lives of the colonized. In a similar sense, the wild as seen from the perspective of East Africans living in the March Oder region was the result of a process of making wild country—a landscape that, in Amanda's words, was *ver-rückt* (dis-placed, crazy) because it was based on racial exclusions, displacements, and the violence of the asylum system. The wild, from this perspective, illustrates the ongoing coloniality of migration (Gutiérrez Rodríguez 2018) and asylum in Europe: it captures affective and embodied states of disturbance, dehumanization, and violent abandonment that contemporary asylum worlds create (see also Mbembe 2003). In light of this, it is, as mentioned earlier, no coincidence that many European refugee encampments—such as the notorious Jungle, located on a former landfill in Calais, France, or the shantytown sections of the Moria camp in Lesvos, Greece—have been named "the jungle" or the "bush" by their inhabitants.

For many Kenyans living in the region, the odd mixture and convergence of disparate practices, affects, and places created a sense of the absurd and the untamed—all of which emerged in the face of everyday racisms, murky bureaucratic procedures, the restrictions and arbitrariness of the residency laws and other regulations, ongoing legal limbo and boredom, a daily struggle to find traction, the remoteness of the Heim, the unhomeliness of the camp's surroundings and the military barracks themselves, as well as long routes of travel in the forest, and the circulation of mutual suspicions. This sense of the absurd exposes a widespread public concern, utilized in both mainstream and right-wing political discourse, that claims refugees benefit from bureaucratic inefficiencies as nonsensical itself.[40] For many in Zarin, joking about bureaucratic and everyday absurdity and a sense of bewilderment became a means for keeping one's sanity. As Donna Goldstein (2013) has shown, this sense of humor and laughter in the face of injustice and everyday violence may at first glance seem "out of place." Yet absurdist storytelling can become an affective coping strategy and social commentary that unveils the slow violence that racialized and economic inequalities create in everyday life (Goldstein 2013; see also Mbembe 2001).

As Eli once put it, sometimes, when you do a lot of comedy, the line between reality and joke becomes muddled. And, similarly, the line between belief and disbelief, between humor and outrage, blurs in the face of rampant and "wild" inequality.

Reprise

In the March Oder region, frail and crumbling economies have left gaps in people's biographies and in the local landscape itself. As Sabine gestured at, socialism collapsed and capitalism moved into its place, creating role reversals, displacements, and shifting borders. Conservation policies introduced new forest diversity paradigms. Refugees moved into former military spaces and built an ostrich farm, while others in the region reenacted war or went on safari. Foresters became funeral speech experts, Kenyan asylum seekers performed as border guards, and letters easily were mistaken for dollar signs. From Lars's safari tour to the Integration Summit, there is no unifying, simple story to tell.

And yet, in the juxtaposition of these stories, we see that images and practices of staging the wild interrupt each other. As the Kenyan refugee voices expose the dispossessions created in contemporary migration regimes, they also shed new light on white German enactments of postsocialist and colonial frontiers. Indeed, these enactments are turned not only toward a seemingly distant past but toward the present of Europe and the world. As Ghassan Hage has shown, images of unruly nature have high currency in the contemporary political context in Europe (Hage 2017). Specifically, fascination with ruins and wilderness caters to a postcolonial and imperial melancholia that sees "civilization" being undermined by both neoliberal policies and the influx of migrants from the Middle East and Africa (Hage 2017).[41] The ethnographic vignettes in this chapter trace the very disparate effects of this melancholia in different actors who inhabit the March Oder region. And in their juxtaposition, we see the violence of white silences as well as their normalization.

Both Mr. Jasinski and Lars mobilize and stage the wild in the postsocialist landscape. Mr. Jasinski references the wild to express his skepticism of national unification and to express his outrage at the ways in which capitalism has affected people's lives and local ecologies. For him, the wild refers to the undoing of "rational" socialist forestry practices, the erasure of local ecological knowledge, and the experiences of dislocation in the face of capitalism's seemingly natural force. Lars, rather than critiquing capitalism, stages the wild as an entrepreneurial strategy. Lars's safari cobbles together a tour of imperial ruin that celebrates "wilderness" amid the remnants of former empires, amid the rubble of a once-divided nation, and amid the wreckage of socialist infrastructure. While he mocks Western stereotypes about the area, he uses and commodifies these stereotypes to create a marketable new local identity.

In both of these white men's enactments of wild Brandenburg, the violence of past and present bordering practices (between Europe and racialized others, between civilization and wilderness) are rendered invisible. Lars's lack of engagement with the violent histories that underlie colonial "exploration" and frontiers is striking and echoes a wider public sentiment across Europe. Similarly, Mr. Jasinski's yearning for a Cold War model of global authority and national order risks fueling a nationalist narrative of decline, one that not only remains silent about the violent dynamics of nationhood but actually reinforces it. For these two men, wilderness once again silences—and in fact becomes a refuge from—history (Cronon 1996).

As postcolonial and critical race scholars have shown, this silencing and amnesia is an integral element of contemporary political discourse in Europe that nevertheless claims to be cosmopolitan and humanitarian (Bhambra 2017; Gilroy 2006; Gutiérrez Rodríguez 2018). In *Postcolonial Melancholia*, Paul Gilroy (2006) shows that colonial histories remain largely unacknowl edged across Europe today and most often only surface as nostalgia. This feeds into the belief that Europe need not be accountable for the violence of the past—a belief increasingly expressed in narratives across the European political landscape, and especially articulated by the political right, including those of right-wing German parties like the AfD, which have widespread support in the March Oder region. These narratives also negate current global disparities and Europe's role in conflicts in the global South, all of which cannot be disentangled from migrations to Europe in the first place. As such, contemporary political discourse about asylum and migration frames refugees as historically disconnected from Europe, depicting their presence as a rupture in Europe's social order (Gutiérrez Rodríguez 2018, 18). As Fanon (2004) argues, this silencing of the histories, bodies, psyches, and experiences of racialized communities lies at the center of colonial violence and, one might add, continues to do so in Europe today.

Refugee stories break these silences open. As the "wild" appears not only in white German residents' enactments of postsocialist transformation but also in Kenyan narratives, former schemes of a "natural" and social order are undone or are converted into something that no longer fits previous categories. In the face of growing anti-immigrant rhetoric and the resurgence of white nationalist movements across Europe and Germany, might these mobilizations of the wild offer other possibilities of historical reflection that can build much-needed solidarities instead of deepening divisions and silences? Christina Sharpe (2016) analyzes how the specter of colonial violence and slavery continues to haunt Black lives in the diaspora while producing conditions of containment and regulation. And yet there is also an insistence on exceeding these effects. Entanglements of space, time, and injustice in the wake of white supremacist and capitalist violation are ongoing (2016, 5). "In the wake," Sharpe writes, "the past that is not past reappears, always, to rupture the present" (9). While her analysis focuses on conjoined metaphors and realities (such as the wake, the ship, the hold, and the weather), in Zarin, it is in the trope and mobilization of the wild that we see the specter of colonial violence as it takes hold of people's lives, bodies, and worlds in the European asylum system.

Rather than silencing violent histories, Eli, Amanda, and others' experiences in "wild Brandenburg" and the "German bush" point to the continuities of colonial dynamics and the racialization of Black and African migrants in Europe. Their stories of mutual suspicion and attempts to get their lives on track reveal the corrosive effects of the European asylum system. In the stories of the ostrich farm, the trip to nowhere, and the Integration Summit, the narrators reveal how the very institutions that claim to provide asylum and refuge are fraught with containment, exploitation, and dispossession. When they are asked to mimic Europe's border control practices or African cultural traditions, Eli and Nangila expose and refuse that mimicry, as well as the extraction of their labor and social workers' disregard for the actual structural conditions of their lives. In the face of their isolation in the forest, the common rhetoric of integration rings hollow and is in fact, as Eli points out, a form of violence.

From these perspectives, the wild signals the specter of the colonial, the site of historical reflection and embodiment, and the struggle to develop modes of knowing and inhabiting history that are not based on the erasure of violence and racism. Yet Eli's, Nangila's, and Amanda's insistence on surviving the wild, in the "German bush," claims a presence that exceeds this violence. As East African asylum seekers speak of living in wild country, they engage the wild against the grain of its European meanings. Turning the metaphor back onto white Europeans, they mobilize it to expose continuing colonial legacies and harm despite Germany's and Europe's pretense of embodying civilized, democratic society and humanitarian values. In this narrative turn, the category of the wild breaks apart, and its racialized divisions of civilized versus wild, guest versus native, and that which constitutes the domestic and the home come undone. Articulating their sense of estrangement vis-à-vis "living in wild country," the refugees reflect on the afterlives of colonial violence and the ways in which these take hold of their lives in the present. And it is with the sharpness of humor and critical storytelling that they insist on pushing back and interrupting that hold.

EPILOGUE
SEEDING LIVABLE FUTURES

In the first couple of decades of the second millennium, nationalist and anti-immigrant voices have surged and echoed across Europe and the world. While European governments have solidified austerity policies on a long-term basis, a renewed sentiment of Europe being under siege and needing to protect its national borders is spreading across the continent. Given recent political conflicts and the profound social transformations taking place across the Middle East, (North) Africa, and Europe, fears of an uncontrolled influx of refugees have led EU nations to differentiate between deserving and undeserving refugees—and embark on a radical revision of border controls within Europe and along its outer edges. The rise of right-wing social movements and increasing support for white nationalist and anti-immigrant political parties such as the AfD (Alternative für Deutschland) in Germany, the Front National in France, or the Lega in Italy signal a deepening of social divisions and a racialized crisis of hospitality that is not limited to Europe but affects the political fabric across the globe.

As disputes over Europe's borders and its "home affairs" resume, public policy and political discourse about European cities continues to focus on urban disconnection and division. This has only intensified in the wake of the ongoing wars in Syria and Ukraine, where refugees have witnessed deeply unequal welcoming to Europe. Throughout the EU's efforts to reshape its border regimes, Germany has often been at the center of the debate. In cities across the country, national and local bureaucracies improvise again and again to accommodate asylum seekers. Debates about the distribution and management of refugees invoke racialized metaphors of natural disaster, destruction, and the wild. Such references bolster a sense of embattlement in cities that, supported by right-wing mobilizations, call for efforts to curb migration. At the same time, political discourse locates the "problem" of migration in migrants themselves—and especially in their supposed lack of productivity and belonging to the urban landscape that is assumed to bring ruination upon German cities. As I have shown in this book, we can trace the echoes of ideas about what it means to be German and the notion of *Heimat* in debates over the supposedly parallel worlds that migrant communities create, where urban hot spots threaten to disrupt the order of the civilized city. Such contestations over the porosity of Europe's outer and inner borders in the urban fabric play out, in part, as a struggle over how to define life and the very boundaries of the human: efforts to fortify national and European borders are always also decisions about who lives and who dies, and about whose lives are exposed to risk or deemed valuable at the edges of the continent and within.

There has been a surge in ethnographic analyses of migration in Europe arriving on the heels of the summer of migration in 2015 (Cabot 2017). As the climate emergency intensifies and the nostalgia for empire justifies war and militarization in many parts of the globe, displacements of humans and nonhumans are likely to increase in this century. The future will thus hold many more "refugee crises." But the very terminology of a crisis is misleading because it limits political imaginations and seeks to contain the issue, obstructing a view of the *longue durée* of migration, colonial violence, racism, war, and displacement in Europe and the world (see also Masco 2017). Beyond a media and scholarly focus on a sudden crisis, there is another story to be told. In Germany, this story leads into the thicket of the country's forests and ecologies of urban life. Here we see how migratory movements, environmental change, and racial formations have been shaping the social-material fabric of German and European cities for a long time—long before they erupted into mainstream political arenas and punctured Europe's pretense of having transcended racism and its colonial past.

In telling this alternate story, *Ruderal City* has argued that the notion of separate cultures and a celebration—or condemnation—of nature and wilderness in the city are inadequate tools with which to capture the heterogeneity of urban life. Instead, the ruderal analytic I have promoted foregrounds unruly, more-than-human alliances amid displacement and inhospitable environments. Following different travelers and dwellers in Berlin and at its peripheries—including plants, animals, and people—the preceding chapters shed light on the ways in which various actors remake urban worlds.

Beginning with the story of sticky goosefoot and other ruderal plants, I have shown how the experience of urban breakdown during and after World War II inspired new "arts of noticing" (Tsing 2015) among Berlin botanists that diverged from postwar urban imaginaries about nature thriving in the ruins of nationalism. Sticky goosefoot's ruderal ecologies offered a guide for the chapters that followed: pointing to the unexpected lives in the ruins of capitalist extraction and to nationalism's obsession with ethnic and racial purity, they remind us that urban nature is always the outcome of histories of migration, labor, displacement, and environmental destruction. Neither domesticated, bounded nature and culture nor the untouched purity of wilderness—the stuff nationalist and imperial dreams are made of—ruderal ecologies provide an alternative mode of attention with which to approach the heterogeneities and vulnerabilities of urban life. In this way, the ruderal analytic encourages thinking across registers and telling multiple stories at once. This method of juxtaposing and gleaning reveals that multiple interpretations and histories are present in a landscape. In them, we see glimpses of life in collapsed and yet violent structures of inequality that nevertheless might create openings for reaching across difference, forging new alliances, and building the world otherwise.

As different neighbors inhabit the same landscape, unlikely junctures and openings develop: courtyard gardens offer a place of multispecies kin and neighborly resistance against gentrification; barbecuing in the park becomes a practice of both making a mess and creating a space to breathe and eat together; and a pine forest turns out to be a socialist ruin and a site of nuclear nostalgia, in which people grapple with the specters of colonial power. Populated with this motley crew of actors and sites, the book's narrative arc began with plants growing out of the war's rubble, and it ended with the unhomeliness of life in the wake of colonial and racial violence in the forests of Berlin's peripheries.

Ending with unhomely encounters and ghostly figures serves as a reminder that conspiring across differences and cultivating more democratic futures entails accounting for the ghosts of past and present violence that are embedded in the fabric of life. While ruderal ecologies point toward unrealized potentials that lie dormant in a city's material-social fabric, they remain deeply ambiguous figures: they are also a warning sign of the possibly nightmarish and deadly outcomes of capitalist extraction, nationalism, militarization, and racism. This becomes an ever more urgent issue as climate change, habitat destruction, and decreasing biodiversity reorder planetary life.

Throughout the research and writing for this book, multiple wars, police violence, pandemics, toxic spills, and extreme weather events have erupted onto urban landscapes across the globe. The lifeworlds of many Indigenous communities have faced end-times for several centuries. The experience of having one's world turned upside down from one day to the next is now the reality for an increasing number of people, albeit to unequal degrees. These ruptures expose and further deepen long-standing racialized, gendered, and classed inequalities that shape not only urban but also planetary vulnerabilities. In the initial weeks of the COVID-19 pandemic, social media and news networks were awash with images of wildlife taking over cities under lockdown. In Berlin, for just a moment, there was once again an eerie sense of calm. Those who could sheltered in place. As many urban infrastructures slowed down or stood still for several weeks, wildlife, including hawks, foxes, and wild boar, ventured out into the streets during unusual hours.

Yet the "weedy" lives reemerging in these ruins of a pandemic and other global emergencies must be cautionary tales: while we do not know what the future holds in the wake of these emergencies, it is clear that the slow violences (Nixon 2011) of land extraction, industrial agriculture, factory farming, and the increasing encroachment on wildlife habitat via urbanization, to name just a few factors, have contributed not only to the temporary "rewilding" of cities but also to the displacement and extinction of many species and to a rise in zoonotic diseases. Amplified by the corroding forces of racial, gender, and class inequalities, they pose a hazard for planetary health and survival. While some wildlife returns and the air above many cities may be clearing momentarily, other cities are ravaged by war, or wildfires, floods, or storms that are a consequence of climate change. Meanwhile, many people are struggling to breathe, whether due to exposure to pollution or new viral diseases or to police brutality. And yet, amid these inequalities, struggles for social and environmental justice rise to challenge these destructive legacies of relating to and inhabiting the world, and seek instead to create alternatives.

The stories and unexpected alliances chronicled in this book bear witness to the ways in which slow violence, displacements, and social exclusions are embedded in and work through multispecies relations and urban ecologies—in often unhomely ways. But they also attest to creativity at the margins of the city—and the possibilities of seizing moments of rupture. At a time of increased loss of hospitable habitats, critical anthropological engagements with urban ecologies face the challenge of more explicitly mapping the mechanisms that shape which lives flourish amid disturbed environments—and which do not. By attending to how different neighbors inhabit the ruins of nation-making, economies of dispossession, and domestication, the perspective of ruderal cities, I hope, can help cultivate unruly forms of critique and practice that combine a concern for more-than human livelihoods with a commitment to building more livable cities in the rubble of the twenty-first century.

NOTES

Introduction

1 Many Berliners, especially people living in Kreuzberg, love to tell Osman Kalın's story. Both local news and Turkish newspapers have reported on his garden frequently in the past (e.g., *FAZ* 2007; *Miliyet* 2000; Niendorf 2008; Reuters 2009). Osman Kalın passed away in May 2018, and his family's tree house (*Baumhaus*) was again featured in international news. My version of the story draws on conversations with Kalın's son, daughter, and neighbors, as well as on local narratives and news reports.

2 *Gecekondu* (or *gecekondular*, pl.) is a combination of the Turkish words *gece* (night) and *kondu* (placed). In contrast to a Turkish gecekondu, the Berlin version did not serve as the main residence for Osman's family. For a survey of the literature on gecekondular and changing representations of rural migrants as other in Turkey, see Erman (2001).

3 Forms of "disturbance" include vegetation removal through herbicide use or mowing, drought, fire, and soil erosion (Grime 1977).

4 Edge effects occur at the boundary between different habitats. While they usually imply changes in community structure and can increase biodiversity, the nature of these changes can be highly variable (e.g., Laurance et al. 2007).

5 See Gandy (2022) and Light (2009) for an analysis of different strands of urban ecological thought in the twentieth and twenty-first centuries.

6 In Germany, the term *Migration* is often used interchangeably with *Einwanderung* (immigration). Both are often racialized and become deeply fraught categories of governance. With this in mind, I use the term *migration* to refer to movements that include both people with formal visa status and

those without. I reserve the term *immigration* for those instances in which the intent of immigrating has been formalized or when referencing public discourse on immigration. Similarly, I use the terms *Turkish German* or *Turkish Berliner* to refer to both migrants and descendants of migrants from Turkey who use these categories as self-identification.

7 Although a ruderal analytic troubles the notion, I continue to use the terms *nature* and *urban nature* throughout the book to refer to categories of urban planning and management, as well as to capture the ways in which my interlocutors invoke, challenge, and otherwise make these categories meaningful in their lives.

8 As part of this moment, the human ceases to be a singular, self-creating actor. Yet amid pronouncements of overcoming anthropocentrism, humans often continue to appear as key agents in scholarship on new materialisms and the Anthropocene. In many instances, it is still *anthropos* at the center, as "man" contemplates his own ruins (Haraway 2016). Until very recently, some of this scholarship has contained remarkably little reference to earlier forms of reflexivity, specifically those marking the cultural critique and writing culture moments in anthropology, or to feminist and postcolonial critiques that highlight language, power, and embodiment (see Fortun 2012; Helmreich 2014). Even more importantly, the long legacy of contributions of Black and Indigenous critics and scholars of color for grasping the colonial, racialized, and gendered dynamics at the core of environmental destruction continues to get sidelined (H. Davis and Todd 2017; Jegathesan 2021).

9 Under scholarly consideration for several decades, the term *Anthropocene* seeks to account for a new geological era that marks the ways in which humans have fundamentally altered the earth's geological development and shaped its atmosphere—not unlike the forces of glaciers or volcanoes. Debates about the term and when to place the beginning of this era—such as the advent of global trade, colonization, industrialization, the emergence of agriculture, or nuclear proliferation—abound (see, e.g., Hannah and Krajewski 2015; Haraway 2015). H. Davis and Todd (2017), Yusoff (2018), and Ferdinand (2022) point to the centrality of settler colonialism and slavery in shaping the destructive modes of inhabiting the world that have led to the Anthropocene. For an overview of emerging feminist and critical race ethnographies that intervene in universalist storytelling about the Anthropocene, see Ebron and Tsing (2017).

10 This work also challenges social theory's confidence about who counts as a social actor, opening up a sense of agency in which "the world kicks back" (Barad 1998) and interferes with human schemes (Latour 2004; T. Mitchell 2002).

11 While humanities scholars have explored the emergence of European modernity in relation to literary, architectural, and cultural representations of ruins (Boym 2001; Hell and Schoenle 2010), many ethnographies trace the cultural and material lives of ruins. For example, Masco (2008) high-

lights how ruins emerge as a central element of nuclear nationalism, while Schwenkel (2013) delineates the material and affective attachments of Cold War urban restructuring and (post)socialist citizenship. Walter Benjamin's (2006) work has shed light on the ruins of capitalist modernity and, like the writings of W. G. Sebald, explores the legacies of nationalism and fascism in European urban landscapes (Buck-Morss 1991). The image of the ruin also exposes the limits of modern conceptions of linear time and space as planned by humans.

12 For a discussion of ruination that captures the paradoxical nature of infrastructure as productive and destructive, see Howe et al. (2016).

13 For exceptions, see Tsing (2015) and Weston (2017).

14 In his nuanced discussion of her work, Mark Anderson (2013) shows that the radical potential of Ruth Benedict's antiracist analysis stood in contradiction to the fact that she modeled solutions to racism in relation to the problem of integration of European immigrants, without questioning that very framework or addressing the specificity of racial distinctions and their origins in settler colonialism and slavery.

15 While some scholars have cautioned against taking the category of postsocialism for granted because of its heterogeneous historical trajectories (Humphrey 2002), ethnographers have shown that postsocialism continues to be useful for analysis because it serves as an allegory to shape people's subjectivities, memory, and cultural practices, and because its cultural forms provide a foil from which to evaluate global capitalism (Berdahl 2010; Rofel 1999, 2007; Verdery 1996). By showing that concepts such as the market, liberal democracy, and the economy are ideological vehicles rather than material realities, anthropologists of Eastern Europe have deconstructed central categories of European experience (M. Caldwell 2004a, 2004b; Lampland 1995; Verdery 1997, 2003). Europe, as the fraught reference point of much anthropological theory (Asad 1997), continues to serve as a looking glass in this scholarship to reflect back upon anthropology (Herzfeld 2010).

16 With growing and contested EU expansion, most EU members have become part of the Schengen Area and are required to adhere to its regulations. For discussion of the complexities of EU regulation of migratory movements, see Feldman (2011); Hess, Tsianos, and Karakayali (2009); and Tazzioli (2017).

17 For a genealogy of changing EU border regimes before and after 2015, see, for example, Hess and Kasparek (2019) and Kasparek (2021).

18 Since 2015, this passage has increasingly become dangerous due to stricter controls and asylum policies, as well as criminalization of nongovernmental sea rescue efforts. Between January 2014 and October 2019, 18,892 people died attempting to cross the Mediterranean Sea (PRO ASYL 2020). This number excludes deaths due to police brutality and racist attacks, deaths in detention centers and asylum units, or suicides.

19 The term *summer of migration* has been suggested as an alternative to the crisis language that is usually applied to the events of the summer of 2015 when more than a million people applied for asylum in Europe fleeing the war in Syria and the Middle East.

20 While a rich tradition of scholarship has highlighted the historical contingencies of the social construction of race (Dominguez 1986; Hartigan 1999; Visweswaran 1998), as well as the negotiation of racial, ethnic, and gender formations in diverse global contexts (M. Anderson 2009; Clarke and Thomas 2006), the study of race in continental Europe has remained marginal for a long time (Brown 2005; Gilroy 1987, 2004, 2006; Hall 1992; Harrison 1995). Earlier research highlighted the relationship between racism and nationalism (Balibar and Wallerstein 1991; Gilman 1982; Mosse 1985). Another concern has been whether contemporary migration discourses that assume an unassimilable cultural other can appropriately be labeled racism (Balibar 2004; Glick-Schiller 2005; Silverstein 2005; Stolcke 1995). Some scholars argue that Islamophobic and anti-immigrant sentiments should not be labeled as racism because they move beyond the nation-state and do not construct biological difference (Bunzl 2005). Others have criticized this position, emphasizing that shifting ideas of racial difference and the nation, often couched within a language of culture, shape not only national but supranational European practices (Glick-Schiller 2005). In this view, nation-building projects remain dependent on attacking the fundamental rights of migrants and on implementing and enforcing new forms of state control that target Muslim bodies as potential threats to "national security" in the so-called War against Terror.

21 For an analysis of the racialization of the very figure of the migrant in public debate and migration studies, see Silverstein (2005).

22 See also, for example, Decolonize Berlin—an association of different activist and civil rights groups that critically address German colonialism and its continuities in German society with the aim to implement strategies of decolonization in education, science, business, and urban planning (https://decolonize-berlin.de/en/organization, accessed December 30, 2020).

   Struggles for decolonization in Berlin have especially also focused on the erasure of the violence of colonialism within Berlin's built environment. See, for example, Sandrine Micosse-Aikins's (2017) analysis of the Humboldtforum.

23 Recent ethnographies have offered crucial tools to examine the spatial dimensions of nationalism and racism (Shoshan 2016), tracing how migrants and communities of color challenge notions of citizenship and reshape European cities via claims to urban space (Brown 2005; Çağlar 2001; Glick-Schiller, Çağlar, and Guldbrandsen, 2006; Kleinman 2019; Kosnick 2007; Mandel 2008; Pred 2000; Sawyer 2006; Silverstein 2004). Work that has destabilized the Euro-American centeredness of much urban theory

crucially adds to these conversations. See Baviskar (2007), Mbembe (2003), and Simone (2010).

24 In a commitment to "thinking between the posts" (Chari and Verdery 2009), my research shares the premises of work in the anthropology of postsocialism, postcolonial studies (Gilroy 2004; Stoler 1995), and subaltern urbanism to develop comparative and transnational frameworks for analyzing contemporary urban life under globalization and liberalization (Roy and Al Sayyad 2004).

25 Ethnographies of Berlin have tracked Cold War divisions in the pre- and postunification city through analysis of intellectuals and media markets (Boyer 2001, 2005), the police (Glaeser 2002), or changing notions of kinship, the state, and nation (Borneman 1991). Moreover, research on the "New Berlin" has examined the metaphorical construction of history and memory in built landscapes (Till 2005; Jordan 2006; Huyssen 1997; Ward 2011), the symbolic reconstruction of Berlin as capital (Binder 2001, 2009), or the historical relationship between national identity and architecture (Ladd 1997). Only rarely is this scholarship in conversation with ethnographies of identity formation in migrant and refugee communities or poor neighborhoods or ethnographies of labor migrants and race (Amrute 2016; Bendixsen 2005; Çağlar 1995; Knecht 1999; Mandel 1996, 2008; Pecoud 2002; Soysal 2001).

26 See also the essays on Germany and Berlin in Brantz and Dümpelmann (2011).

27 The name Berlin is often associated with the animal on the city's coat of arms, the Berlin bear, and the German diminutive *Bärlein* (little bear). Yet Berlin's etymology more likely derives from the city's natural history and Slavic origins. From the sixth century onward, Slavic fishermen established settlements in the region that later became Berlin. One origin story of the name is that it stems from the Slavic term *Brl*, which means marsh, swamp, or damp place (MacDonogh 1997, 4). Another version refers to Rhenish and Dutch colonists in the twelfth century: they called their settlement *to dem Berlin*, which means "a bend in the river" (Pundt 1972, 5).

28 The sewer network in particular became a source of ongoing conflict between the East and West German governments throughout the city's division. For a comprehensive history of Berlin's twentieth-century urban infrastructure, see Moss (2020).

29 Like Yanagisako and Delaney (1995), my argument here accounts for the ways in which categories such as race, nation, and gender operate to make social inequalities appear as part of a natural order. At the same time, as they argue, it is important to not abandon an analysis of the meanings and relations that used to define these domains (11).

30 Berlin has a long history of preservation policies. For example, before Berlin officially became integrated into one city in 1920, the "enduring forest policy" (*Dauerwaldvertrag*) of 1915 preserved forest areas in and around the

city on a large scale. Forests provided both water resources for the city and a space of recreation for urban residents. Featuring public "restaurants" that offered water and spaces for Berliners to bring their own food, the goal was to prevent social conflict and unrest (Weisspflug 1999). Berlin's forests are also shaped by a history of militarism. From the mid-eighteenth century on, the Prussian state financed almost half of its military and war actions through forestry in Berlin-Brandenburg.

31 This also includes water and agriculture (SenUVK 2022c). The German term *Brache* can be translated to "wasteland" or "fallow," signifying a piece of land that is not utilized for profit. For discussion of the term and its significance in Berlin, see the film *Natura Urbana: The Brachen of Berlin* (2017), directed by Matthew Gandy; and Lawton et al. (2019).

32 For a detailed discussion of Africans living in Germany during the colonial period, as well as a history of colonial fairs and anti-Black racism focusing on "uncivilized nature people" as part of colonial anthropological science and eugenic movements in Germany and beyond, see Oguntoye (2004, 1997), El-Tayeb (2001), and van der Heyden and Zeller (2002).

33 Demographic categories are a contested terrain because the census and most statistical data in Germany (and in France) do not include racial or ethnic categories. This colorblind lens stems from historical concerns about cementing ethnic or racial identity and targeting communities of color, as was done during fascism. National statistical data and the Statistisches Bundesamt (Federal Statistical Agency) therefore rely on categories of citizenship (e.g., German vs. foreigner, or German vs. Turkish) on the one hand and "migratory background" (*Migrationshintergrund*) on the other. The latter identifies a "person with a migratory background" as someone who was born without German citizenship or who has at least one noncitizen parent who migrated to Germany after the 1950s (an extended definition also includes grandparents) (www.destatis.de/DE/Themen /Gesellschaft-Umwelt/Bevoelkerung/Migration-Integration/Glossar /migrationshintergrund.html, accessed June 3, 2022). Following these statistical categories, as of July 2019, close to 106,925 Berliners had Turkish citizenship and around 130,000 had citizenship from countries in the Middle East (Statistisches Bundesamt 2022). However, these data exclude people who have German citizenship and those who identify as Turkish, Middle Eastern, or Arab. Similarly, it is unclear how many Black people reside in Germany. Initiatives such as the AFROZENSUS, launched in spring 2020, estimate that there are one million Black, African, or Afro-diasporic people living in Germany. See also my discussion of additional statistical data on Southeast Asian migrants in Berlin in chapter 3.

34 See, for example, Thilo Sarrazin's (2010) controversial book, *Deutschland schafft sich ab* (Germany does away with itself), discussed in chapters 2 and 3.

35 Since the mid-2000s, the term *Heimat* has made a comeback throughout the political landscape in Germany. During the Nazi period, the idea of Heimat

was expressed as hatred against anything foreign (including Jews, who were seen as having scorned the natural world). Ultimately, this involved efforts to relocate human and nonhuman populations in order to restore national belonging, and it culminated in extermination. Yet as Lekan (2004, 6) points out, discourses of Heimat have been heterogeneous throughout German history and have included democratic understandings in addition to racist and nationalist ones.

36 The urban jungle is yet another colonial trope in which immigrants are cast in dehumanizing ways. Examples include media coverage of male Middle Eastern refugees as sexual predators during Cologne New Year's Eve 2015–16, or portrayals of migrant sports celebrities (such as the German Ghanaian soccer star Boateng brothers). In other contexts, perpetuating the violent history of colonial exhibitions, people of color are naturalized as inhabitants of nature spaces: in 2005, the Augsburg Zoo hosted an "African village," a performance and market of African crafts, setting off antiracist protest (Glick-Schiller, Dea, and Hoehne 2005).

37 According to immigration law, courses aiming to teach German language and culture to immigrants can be required for non-European immigrants, but they are not mandatory for Westerners like US nationals (Nghi Ha 2010, 164).

38 By the end of 2015, close to a million people had sought asylum in Germany. In Berlin, more than 55,000 people applied for asylum that year. Between 2017 and early 2022, these numbers decreased. In 2019, as of October, only 5,299 individuals had applied for asylum in Berlin (Landesamt für Flüchtlinsangelegenheiten, "Zahlen und Fakten: Zugangslage Flüchteter, 2019," accessed July 20, 2020, https://www.berlin.de/laf/ankommen/aktuelle -ankunftszahlen/artikel.625503.php). The major countries of origin were Syria, Iraq, Iran, Nigeria, Turkey, Afghanistan, Eritrea, and Somalia (PRO ASYL, "Fakten, Zahlen und Argumente," accessed July 20, 2020, https:// www.proasyl.de/thema/fakten-zahlen-argumente/). Not all applications for asylum are processed, and in many cases, applications are turned down and people deported.

39 According to the UNHCR, the term *asylum seeker* refers to an individual seeking international protection whose status has not yet been determined, irrespective of location. *Refugee*, in contrast, refers to an individual "recognised under the 1951 Convention relating to the Status of Refugees." Since 2007, the latter term is increasingly used to refer to people in a "refugee-like" situation and hence often conflated with *asylum seeker*. (See UNHCR, "Refugee Data Finder," accessed March 31, 2022, http://popstats.unhcr .org/en/overview#_ga=2.211964628.1711905925.1574189046-2028994220 .1537303912). For ethnographic analyses of the problematic language of crisis and the portrayal of refugees as victims versus illegitimate economic refugees or potential terrorists, see Holmes and Castañeda (2016) and the Hot Spots series in *Cultural Anthropology* in 2016 (e.g., Ticktin 2016).

40 For a broader analysis of wave metaphors, see Helmreich (2019).

41 In a well-known example, in the days following the 2016 New Year's cele-brations, Cologne residents submitted 500 complaints about sexual assault by, as municipal authorities phrased it, "North African and Arab-looking men." In subsequent weeks, the image of refugees shifted from stories of innocence to stories of sexual aggression, greatly impacting public debate about asylum policy. The German Federal Center for Health Education also launched a campaign to educate refugees on matters of sexuality (Yildiz 2017).

42 Berlin's relation to the surrounding countryside in Brandenburg changed dramatically after the fall of the Berlin Wall. During the Cold War, the wall cut off connections between West Berlin and the countryside. While networks for electricity were separated, financial and practical reasons pre-vented a full separation of the sewer network (Book 1995, 184). West Berlin thus used the Eastern hinterland for waste disposal and wastewater man-agement, causing conflict between the East and West German governments. As West Berliners' travels to the countryside were highly regulated, outings to the area became especially popular after 1989 (184). Furthermore, the GDR's legacy of large farms and fields continues to shape the agricultural landscape in eastern Germany, including Brandenburg.

43 In Germany, until very recently, the word *Rasse* (which translates to "race" but also "breed") has been defined in biological terms, with little discussion of the social construction of race. In the spring of 2020, following nationwide Black Lives Matter protests against racism and police violence in Germany and Europe, this led to debates about whether the word should be deleted from the constitution.

44 See also Ruth Wilson Gilmore's (2007, 28) definition of racism as "the state-sanctioned or extra-legal production and exploitation of group-differentiated vulnerability to premature death."

45 In contrast to ruins, rubble is considered formless material without value (Puff 2010; Simmel 1983), and hence not memorialized. Analysts such as Gordillo (2014) promote rubble as an analytic that highlights forms of de-struction that, although invisible, are constitutive of the production of space.

46 See Cherkaev (2020) for a discussion of the ethnographic practice of glean-ing chance encounters in the field.

47 See also my discussion in chapter 5. For a wonderful manifesto of patch-work ethnography that includes a consideration of the patchy process of fieldwork and the fieldworker's personal, social, and labor conditions, see Günel, Varma, and Watanabe (2020).

48 Similarly, AbdouMaliq Simone (2004, 12) tracks the disparate social worlds that emerge alongside urban institutions—the "emotional fields" that people build to create a sense of physical connection to place. In this sense, changing the materialities of cities also reshapes who gets to flourish, live, and die, altering the meaning of urban life itself (Simone 2016). Simone draws on Mbembe's account of mobile forms of sovereignty to examine

urban practices as "a patchwork of overlapping and incomplete rights to rule" that attest to intertwined agendas, infrastructures, enclaves, and individual ways of making a livelihood by inhabitants of African and Southeast Asian cities (Simone 2010, 306).

49 For other ethnographic accounts of the *unheimlich*, see, for example, Ivy (1995) and Stewart (1996), as well as Lepselter (2005) and Masco (2006) on the uncanny in the ruins of Cold War American militarism.

1. Botanical Encounters

1 Sticky goosefoot is also commonly called Jerusalem oak, feathered geranium, or ambrosia, the last not to be confused with *Ambrosia artemisiifolia L.*, a ragweed that causes hay fever.

2 See also Reidl (2005) on ruderal spaces comprising heterogeneous locations including rubble fields, abandoned land, and the edges of streets, train tracks, or canals.

3 Sticky goosefoot has pharmacologically active elements. It is anti-asthmatic, anti-catarrhal, and has been used to treat headaches in homeopathic medicine (Sukopp 1971, 7). A cultivar called "Green Magic" was developed in the Netherlands and has a delicious nutty flavor. For its uses in Greek mythology and South America, see Small (2006, 300).

4 In fact, sticky goosefoot turns out to be a bioindicator of the city's history and trade and the ecological effects of the war's vast destruction, including changes in soil, temperature, and urban climate. Similarly, lichen on tree bark has been studied in urban ecology, as its growth differs in response to air pollution. A lichen-free zone in city centers is usually surrounded by zones of increasing lichen growth toward urban peripheries. In Berlin and Leipzig, lichen growth has served as a way to map and document changes in air quality across time (Sukopp 1998, 10).

5 Much scholarship on postwar urban Germany, and on Berlin in particular, has focused on the role of architecture and city planning for reimagining the postfascist nation. At the same time, there is a rich body of literature in environmental history that tracks continuities and changes in landscape planning and environmental policy and their significance for reconstructing the nation after the war (e.g., Brüggemeier, Cioc, and Zeller 2005; Lekan 2004; Zeller 2005). An emerging literature unsettles this divide between urban and environmental scholarship (Brantz and Dümpelmann 2011; Dümpelmann 2019; Gandy 2013, 2022; Lachmund 2013).

6 Urban aerial bombing did not originate in this moment but drew on techniques tried out by the British and German militaries in World War I (Diefendorf 1993, 4; Lindqvist 2001). In the 1920s, airpower theorists and military strategists, such as Billy Mitchell in the United States and Giulio Douhet in Italy, promoted bombing as a technique of the future with which to destroy the "nerve centers" of their enemies' urban industrial societies

(Diefendorf 1993, 5). In 1939, after Japan had staged such attacks on Chinese cities two years earlier, Germany began the aerial bombings of Warsaw, and then London, Rotterdam, and Coventry in 1940 (Dower 1986, 39). As part of Hitler's plan for the "Germanization" of the East, a large proportion of the Jewish population in Warsaw and many other European cities was murdered and deported to concentration camps; large parts of Warsaw were razed to the ground by German troops.

7   As Sebald (2004, 15) points out, the origins for the Allies' decision to area bomb also lay in their interest in regaining imperial power in Europe, Africa, and Asia.

8   Like the zoo, the Berlin Botanical Garden and Museum were also largely destroyed—and with it, large collections of Germany's colonial botany (Lack 2002; Zepernick 2002).

9   It is estimated that there were 75 million cubic meters of rubble in Berlin (Diefendorf 1993; Till 2005).

10 See also Susan Buck-Morss (1992) on anesthesia, and the inuring and numbing of human senses in the context of capitalism, war, and modernity.

11 Before the bombings, Albert Speer and other architects also created elaborate plans for rebuilding Berlin into what they imagined would be the world capital of "Germania," ridding it of its "foreign," Jewish, and communist elements. Architects and engineers planned to use stones and the tiles manufactured in concentration camps such as Sachsenhausen, northeast of Berlin, to rebuild the city (Till 2005, 40).

12 See Wolschke-Bulmahn (2005) on the central role of landscaping and gardening in Nazi "Germanization" efforts and the expulsion and extermination of Jews and Poles. For a discussion of divergences in blood and soil ideology, see Bassin (2005).

13 From this perspective, industrialization and urbanization led to deterioration of the countryside and disfigurement and erosion of Germany's national identity (Lekan 2004, 4). Landscape preservationist movements, which emerged at the end of the nineteenth century, articulated a cultural politics in which the nation was imagined through natural landscapes. This legacy continued over time, as Germans repeatedly reinvented the border of their national political community as natural: in the contexts of authoritarian constitutional monarchy (during the "Second Empire"), parliamentary democracy (the Weimar Republic), and racist dictatorship (Nazism) (Lekan 2004, 5). Yet, as mentioned previously, this ethnoracialist discourse of an embattled homeland (*Heimat*) always existed side-by-side with democratic and pluralist understandings (Lekan 2004, 6).

14 The notion of *Bodenständigkeit* assumed an innate connection of Germans to the soil and land. Throughout the nineteenth century, it inspired colonial imaginations of rural settlements as colonies and the "Germanization" of the Prussian countryside—and it was also used as justification for dispossession in the colonies (Cupers 2016, 1245).

15 American and British officials thought this would create planned chaos, disrupting the international economic system and the economic power of the West (Orlow 1999, 208). In particular, US officials argued that if put into practice, the Morgenthau Plan would have given Russia "continental hegemony" (208).

16 In this sense, postwar urban planners were in line with urban imaginaries during and before the war: they regarded Berlin's densely populated workers' housing and tenement barracks as responsible for social tensions and left-wing politics (Schildt 2002, 143–44). In addition, many planners who had been practicing during the war continued their jobs afterward, and postwar urban reconstruction drew on their experiences from planning "Germanized" cities in Poland (Schildt 2002, 143). See also Reichow (1948).

17 This approach was supported by the Western Allies, the United States in particular.

18 Local media in East Berlin favored recycling rubble for construction instead of landscaping it into hills and complained that most of the rubble was not reused. For example, in 1952 the *Berliner Zeitung* featured a headline: "Rubble Stones Are Floating on the Spree River," expressing outrage that much of the rubble heading to the dump piles was being wasted and could still be used for building (see Keiderling 1999a, 41).

19 These natural landscapes were imagined as lifting the city above the wreckage and healing what some considered the "rubble psychosis" (*Trümmerpsychose*) of people after the war (Lachmund 2003, 238). Lachmund quotes a visitor to Berlin in 1952: "The public gardens, green lawns, the trees and bushes that exist here everywhere in front of and between [the rubble] give the impression of a miracle, as they cover the rubble like a green veil" (2003, 238).

20 Some former sites of Nazi crimes were also bulldozed and abandoned, such as the former Gestapo headquarters in the city center (Till 2005)—today they are the site of the Topography of Terror, an outdoor and indoor museum chronicling the history of Nazi terror.

21 Teufelsberg is estimated to contain the rubble of thousands of buildings, including a former Nazi military technology college. After debris disposal came to an end in 1972, the rubble heap was covered with soil and thousands of trees were planted on it. During the Cold War, the US National Security Agency built a listening station on top of the hill, now Berlin's highest elevation, to spy on East German military conversations. Rumors about the hill and station abound. During the Cold War, I was told, people believed that a Ferris wheel set up each year near Teufelsberg during the German-American fair increased the military base's technological capacity to spy on its socialist neighbors, resulting in a longer set up of the wheel each year. To make things even more bizarre, David Lynch considered buying part of the former military territory in 2008.

22 Despite fascist praise for the German forest, large parts of the country's forest reserves were cut down during the Nazi regime in order to make

autarky possible. After the war, forests continued to be logged heavily for firewood as well as for reparation payments to the occupying powers (especially in East Germany). In addition, extremely dry summers after the war led to increases in the bark beetle population (*Borkenkäfer*), ultimately destroying more forests. Many officials spoke of a national catastrophe of diminishing forests in 1947 (Schleich 2011).

23 "Die Linde am Grossen Stern," *Telegraf*, March 18, 1949.

24 The interview and conversation were conducted in German and Sukopp said: "Da ganz Berlin eine Trümmerflache war—zumindest, die Innenstadt, ist die Frage eigentlich wichtiger, warum ich nichts anderes gemacht habe." Sukopp furthermore pointed out that he began studying urban spaces "from the outside to the inside": his dissertation, finished in 1958, focused on the effects of waterworks and groundwater reduction on the marshes at Berlin's edges. Thereafter he turned his attention to the river and lakeshores near the city. By this point, he had also begun studying rubble spaces closer to the city center.

25 A few years earlier, botanists had also studied "alien" ruderal vegetation and unexpected bird life in bombed sites in Britain. They noticed new so-called fireflowers that emerged after the bombings and adapted to burned landscapes, rubble, and the gravelly spaces of railway embankments: the Sicilian Oxford ragwort, rosebay willowherb, Canadian fleabane, and escaped cultivars such as the Peruvian *Galinsoga parviflora* (M. Davis 2002, 382). For a longer history of scientific research on urban plant life, see Sukopp (1998, 2008).

26 The Botanical Association Berlin-Brandenburg (Botanischer Verein von Berlin und Brandenburg, BVBB) was founded in 1859, indicating a long history of hobbyist natural historians and civic natural historical societies in Germany. In the early nineteenth century, many urban societies—both scientific and hobbyist—ventured out to the countryside to research nature. The pursuit of natural history as a recreational activity was often tightly linked with patriotic ideas about the "nature of the fatherland." Yet, as Denise Phillips (2003) and Thomas Lekan (2004) show, the cultural dynamics of popular natural history ventures were far from fixed. In fact, leading naturalists' ties to political dissent in the 1840s added another layer to popular pursuits of natural history (Phillips 2003). Similarly, both racial nationalist as well as democratic and pluralist understandings can be discerned in late nineteenth-century landscape preservationists' efforts to popularize nature protection through outdoor activities and school reform (Lekan 2004, 6).

Scholz (1956) wrote his dissertation on West Berlin's rubble vegetation. In East Berlin, Ruprecht Düll and Herbert Werner (1955) provided important analyses. For a detailed discussion of East and West Berlin botanical networks, as well as botanical research on ruderal vegetation in other German cities, see Lachmund (2003, 240–41).

27 The emerging view of such ecology of anthropogenic blasted landscapes also echoed the almost simultaneous proliferation of ecological research ex-

ploring bombed atolls after World War II. The latter research and its blasted ecological systems theory was funded by the US Atomic Commission. For detailed discussion of the connections of ecological and ecosystems theory to Cold War politics, see Golley (1993), Hagen (1992), and Mitman (1992).

28 Native to northeast and central China and Taiwan, tree-of-heaven was featured in the 1943 novel *A Tree Grows in Brooklyn* by Betty Smith. Tree-of-heaven grows in abandoned lots and ruderal spaces across Europe and North and South America today. For a more comprehensive history of the tree, see Battles (2017), Del Tredici (2010), Hu (1979), Kowarik and Säumel (2007), McNeur (2018), and Stoetzer (2020a).

29 *Robinia pseudoacacia* was first introduced to Europe through the gardener robin in the Botanical Gardens in Paris. In Germany, it is called *Robinie, Akazie,* or *falsche Akazie.* As Sukopp explained to me, these trees adapted easily to Berlin's sandy soil. They were planted in the gardens of Britz and along railroads as a protective strip to prevent sparks from trains (running on coal) igniting forest fires in the larger pine forests.

30 Mugwort is a tall plant in the wormwood family that, in Europe, has been used for healing and as a magical herb to chase away evil spirits. In Chinese medicine, it has been used in acupuncture practices. In her book about wartime Warsaw, Diane Ackerman (2007) tells of Polish farmers using branches of the herb to keep witches from milking their cows, as well as Warsawians wearing mugwort garlands and tying sprigs of mugwort to doorways to keep away evil.

31 The term *dead eye* was introduced in 1967 by a geographer to refer to the area of forty square kilometers in the city center in which much of the built landscape had been destroyed (Sukopp 2007, 62).

32 While some plants flourished, others did not. The botanists thus not only tracked species diversity in the city but also the degradation of urban environments—especially involving lakes, rivers, bogs, and wetlands at the city's periphery. For example, in his dissertation on the Berlin fens, Sukopp (1958) noted a retreat of many species. Studies of Berlin's nature reserves in the 1960s showed similar developments—a result of lower groundwater levels, air pollution, and human land-use. At the same time, the Havel River vegetation, especially reeds, were retreating due to heavy boat traffic (Sukopp and Markstein 1989).

33 For a discussion of twentieth-century US urban professionals and their use of ecological metaphors to understand and manage urban human life, see J. Light (2009) and Mitman (1992).

34 Early research on rubble spaces made use of a spectrum of different theoretical frameworks, ranging from ecosystems theory to adventive floristics to phytosociology (*Pflanzensoziologie*). Botanists working with Sukopp, such as Scholz, tried to organize their floristic inventories of rubble spaces according to the classificatory practices of adventive floristics (the study of nonnative plants). Phytosociology, for its part, was based on the idea that

"plants settle according to the environmental conditions given at a specific site and will associate with each other in the form of stable vegetation units, or so-called plant associations" (Lachmund 2003, 246). These tenets of phytosociology and other plant association taxonomies also played a role in vegetation engineering and highway planning during Nazism as well as in the construction of parklands and rubble hills after the war (Lachmund 2007; Zeller 1996). For an ethnographic account of the complex politics of classificatory practices around "alien species," see Helmreich (2005).

35 While Sukopp and his colleagues tracked succession patterns of ruderal plants and their associations—and thus the temporal development of the rubble vegetation—by visiting them over a long period of years, the plants often remained unpredictable in their succession schemes (Lachmund 2007, 248).

36 While urban ecology developed methodologically out of landscape ecology, the idea of landscape took on a different meaning from the perspective of ruderal ecologies and became a tool for the "investigation of several adjacent ecosystems" (Sukopp 2008, 87).

37 Within Nazi ideology, the difference between southern and northern populations (both human and nonhuman) was seen as one between wildness and domestication. In this sense, nature became the "realm of absolute order, as opposed to the anarchy brought on by civilization" (Sax 1997, 6). On the history of the Nazi cult of wildness and the creation of wildness through eugenic controls, see Sax (1997).

38 For example, the flowering phases of *Tilia euchlora*, or linden, were eight days earlier in the inner city than at the city's edge. Between 1808 and 1880, the leafing of *Aesculus hippocastanum*, or horse chestnut, began an entire month earlier in Geneva (Sukopp and Wurzel 2003, 70).

39 Between 1800 and 1910, Berlin's population expanded from 170,000 inhabitants to 3.7 million. Median urban temperatures rose by 0.7 degrees Celsius vis-à-vis the countryside in the 1830s, by 1.4 degrees in the 1890s, and by 2 degrees between 1961 and 1980 (Sukopp and Wurzel 2003, 72). Over this time, frost days in the city decreased significantly below 64 days per year (vis-à-vis the 102 days or more in the countryside).

40 Ingo Kowarik, a student of Sukopp's and his successor as Berlin's Nature Conservation Commissioner, later distinguished between four forms of nature in the city, specifically promoting the most common form of "fourth nature," such as spontaneous vegetation in vacant lots, to be included in urban planning and conservation (Kowarik 1992). The other three forms are remnants of prehistoric landscapes, remains of agricultural landscapes, and artificially created green spaces (Kowarik 1992). The landscape protection policies passed in 2011 by the Berlin Senate Department for Urban Development also incorporated this distinction.

41 In 1968, Sukopp published a graphic depicting different urban habitats ranging from rubble heaps, railways, gardens, forests, and dump sites to

so-called filter beds and different types of built-up areas (Sukopp 2003b, 19–20). Displaying cross sections of the city, the illustration and subsequent maps produced an image of the city as ecologically heterogeneous space (Lachmund 2007, 80).

42 "Landschaftsplan, Arten-, und Biotopschutzprogramm" (Kowarik 1995). Provincial and federal German law seeks to protect urban wildlife via biotope conservation in urban planning (e.g., via the Bundesnaturschutzgesetz from 1976). This coincides with the idea that civic life is enhanced by a rich diversity of species in urban habitats.

43 As Gandy points out, many Nazi-era botanists who had followed nativist agendas continued to work in German academic institutions in the postwar era. Yet the urban ecological perspectives created by Sukopp and his colleagues' generation clearly departed from the "ideological tentacles of Nazi-era *Pflanzensoziologie*" (Gandy 2022, 130) and paved the way for ecology to enter progressive environmental politics in the 1970s and 1980s.

44 I am inspired here by Hustak and Myers's (2012) analysis of the ecology of plant-insect relations and their feminist and queer rereading of Darwinian models. For a similar strategy of "athwart theory," of reading sidewise and not taking for granted the contexts in which events or texts operate, but instead creating new ones, see Helmreich (2009).

45 Mary Douglas (2002) describes stickiness and viscosity as concepts that alert us to the properties of matter and the embodied interrelations between self and world. Drawing on Sartre, Douglas characterizes the relation between the experience of self and the world as one of viscosity. Viscosity suggests a state "half way between solid and liquid. It is like a cross-section in a process of change. . . . Its stickiness is a trap, it clings like a leech; it attacks the boundary between myself and it" (Douglas 2002, 47).

46 For a more in-depth discussion of unhomeliness and the uncanny, see chapter 5.

47 For a similar argument regarding the challenges of climate change to thinking across scales, see Chakrabarty (2012).

48 See AbdouMaliq Simone's (2004) focus on "cities yet to come" and the social worlds that emerge alongside urban institutions, economies, households, and identities, as well as Ananya Roy and Aihwa Ong's work on "worlding cities" (Roy and Ong 2011).

49 As Till (2005) points out, looking for traces and digging for material leftovers of fascism became central practices of memory work after the war— landscapes grew to be "central characters in stories that symbolize the past as well as the future" (67).

50 See Till (2005) and Jordan (2006) for detailed discussions of cultures of memorialization around the Nazi past and the Holocaust in both East and West Berlin. Till, in particular, discusses the trajectories of the Topography of Terror as well as the Holocaust Memorial and smaller memorials such as the so-called stumbling stones set on cobblestone sidewalks, which

mark former residences of Jews and other residents who were deported to camps.

51 See also diverse social media sites that focus on urban wastelands and ruderal spaces, marked by the hashtags #ruderal, #urbannature, and others.

2. Gardening the Ruins

1 First used as decorative figures in royal gardens, then in bourgeois front gardens (*Vorgärten*), and finally in the allotment gardens, the "garden gnome" (*Gartenzwerg*) is an icon of German national identity today.

2 Allotment gardens are often called *Schrebergärten* in Germany, referring to nineteenth-century German physician Daniel Gottlob Moritz Schreber. Schreber, concerned about the negative impact of urbanization on residents' health, promoted access to land for urban populations and especially for youths to exercise. Allotment gardens originally served as a food source, accommodation, and a space of recuperation for the urban working classes in the nineteenth century (Lorbek and Martinsen 2015). See also my discussion in the next section of this chapter.

3 Altogether, allotment garden lots cover more than 3 percent of city space in Berlin. And 75 percent of the gardens are property of the state of Berlin and administered by local district authorities. Some are owned by the Deutsche Bahn. Most residents apply for a garden plot with the local district authority. Via a lease, gardeners commit to obeying the rules of the Federal Allotment Garden Laws (*Bundeskleingartengesetz*) and individual garden associations (SenStadt 2012, 10).

4 In 2006, the Federation of German Garden Friends, an association with traditionally mostly German members, published a brochure and guide on integration in allotment gardens (Bundesverband deutscher Gartenfreunde e.V. 2006). A. C. Wolf states: "Integration takes place not only in the much attended 'intercultural gardens' but also in the one million 'normal allotment gardens' in Germany, where about four million people pursue their hobbies" (2008, 6).

5 The position of Representative for Integration and Migration (Beauftragte für Integration und Migration) has existed in Germany since 1978—formerly under the name Representative for Foreigners (Ausländerbeauftragter)—at city, state, and federal levels. Representatives for Integration and Migration usually work for the Ministry for Social Affairs and aim to represent the interests of immigrants in Germany and promote their integration into German society.

6 The original reads: "Im Garten ist mehr als frische Luft. Hier findet Austausch statt, hier wird Eigenverantwortung und Gestaltung praktiziert und man kann Initiative, Identifikation und Integration wachsen sehen."

7 Originally, women who had fled the war in Bosnia in the 1990s helped initiate the movement to create intercultural gardens—as well as the Intercul-

tural Foundation (Stiftung Interkultur) later on—in the city of Göttingen. As enthusiasm for the gardens grew, they sprouted in other cities across Germany, and the Stiftung Interkultur was created in subsequent years.

8 The foundation and some of its founders have won many awards, including the Award for Integration from the German federal president, the Award for Innovative Environmental Education from the Federal Environmental Ministry, and the Award for Civic Engagement from the Alliance for Democracy and Tolerance (see Urbane Gemeinschafts Gärten, "Netzwerk für Gemeinschaftsgärtner*innen," accessed February 7, 2022, https://urbane -gaerten.de/).

9 Beyond urban contexts, the coding of nature and the outdoors as a white space is global in its reach. Tracing the ways in which racial violence and slavery have shaped cultural understandings of nature in the United States, Carolyn Finney (2014) analyzes the racialization of the outdoors while also exposing how African Americans have opened up (new) possibilities for conservation and environmental politics.

10 Emphasizing the importance of nonhuman communities in living webs of care, Maria Puig de la Bellacasa's work highlights the ambivalent terrains of care. Engaging different dimensions of labor/work, affect/affections, and ethics/politics, her writing holds in tension the different meanings of care (Puig de la Bellacasa 2017, 5). From this perspective, care can be seen as "concrete work of maintenance, with ethical and affective implications, and as a vital politics in interdependent worlds" (5).

11 For example, British landscaping and gardening practices took shape at the very moment when England became a center of imperial power. The term *imperial landscapes* refers to material and aesthetic landscaping practices as tools for the fortification of cultural, economic, and political expansion— practices that are neither stable nor homogeneous across historical and geographic contexts (see W. J. T. Mitchell 1994, 9).

12 As part of the so-called *Pflanzerbewegung*, urban residents claimed and cultivated land to create alternatives to other more commercial approaches (see SenUVK 2022a).

13 Since the mid-2000s, activists have organized decolonial walking tours through Berlin that often include visits to the garden "colonies" of the "African quarter" in northern Berlin (the quarter had been named as such at the height of German colonial expansion). During these tours, activists speak about the colonial history of individual street names in Berlin, colonial euphoria during Nazism, and the current political situation in African countries such as Togo (after which one garden was named until 2014; see Schilp 2014), as well as the situation of African refugees in Berlin and Brandenburg.

14 As Hilbrandt (2021, 36) and Stein (2000) point out, the term *colony* thus also pointed to center-periphery relations within the European civilized city itself, and the urban garden became a site in which the boundaries between city, nature, and civilization were redrawn.

15 See also the introduction for a discussion of Heimat in German national discourse.

16 For a detailed discussion of the obsession with native plants during the Nazi era, see Gröning and Wolschke-Bulmahn (1992). For an intricate history of organic farming and other "more natural" ways of eating and growing food throughout modern Germany, including organic herb gardens in concentration camps, see Treitel (2017).

17 Moore, Kosek, and Pandian (2003) point out, for example, that throughout twentieth-century German history, Nazis and radical environmentalists shared a passion for organic bread, or that both Hitler and Black nationalists like LeRoi Jones used the notion of Lebensraum to make claims to territory with radically different political visions and implications.

18 While M. Bennett and Teague (1999) describe US middle-class white suburban families' desires for the insularity of suburban life, this also rings true for European contexts.

19 The long history of squatting in Kreuzberg bestows the district with fame across the world.

20 For a cultural history of the Döner sandwich, see Seidel-Pielen (2007).

21 The canal was built between 1845 and 1850. Its name means "defensive dike," referring to the former fortification area in front of the wall at the city's edges. Created to ease boat traffic and help transport goods and building materials to Berlin's Spree River, it also served as an overflow channel to the adjacent meadows south of the city.

22 *Börek* is a Middle Eastern phyllo dough pastry dish, filled with ground meat, feta, or vegetables.

23 On the 1990s construction boom, see also chapter 3, this volume, and Rada (1997).

24 In 2006, German teachers at the Rütli school wrote a letter to the Berlin Senate demanding security assistance and threatening to close down the school because they were unable to deal with student troublemakers. For months, national news was packed with reports about and responses to the letter. In the midst of this so-called school scandal, another scandal surfaced when it was revealed that several journalists reporting on the incident had paid teenagers to act like gangsters in front of their cameras.

25 See Reach Out Berlin, https://www.reachoutberlin.de/de/Unsere%20 Arbeit/Beratung/#en; the VOICE Refugee Forum Germany, http://www .thevoiceforum.org/; Women in Exile and Friends, https://www.women -in-exile.net; ISD (Initiative Schwarze Menschen in Deutschland Bund e.V.), http://isdonline.de; and Black Lives Matter Berlin, https://www .blacklivesmatterberlin.de.

26 The term *hot spot* is loosely defined by the Association of German Cities and Towns, an administrative association, as a residential district in which a conglomeration of social and environmental factors "negatively impacts" inhabitants' opportunities and living conditions (Deutscher Städtetag

1979). On the proliferation of the term across different realms including migration, pandemics, and biodiversity, as well as its military, biological, ecological, and cultural dimensions, see the 2019 Akademie der Künste der Welt conference proceedings featuring talks by Ayesha Hameed, Manuela Bojadziyev, Stefan Helmreich, and others (Akademie der Künste der Welt 2019).

27 Germany's history of Jewish ghettos during the Holocaust remains largely unmentioned; yet it lingers as a specter. For analyses of the racialization and iconic images of dispossession inherent in the notion of the ghetto, see Linke (2014, 2015) and Ronneberger and Tsianos (2009). Wacquant (2008) tracks "territorial stigmatization" and the moral panic about the *banlieues* of Paris as "ghettos" in France in the context of neoliberal capitalism, as does Silverstein (2004).

28 For a more detailed discussion of integration's entanglement with post–World War II migration and technocratic models of the welfare state, see Ronneberger and Tsianos (2009) and Lanz (2007). Until 1965, Germany did not have an immigration law and only relied on the 1938 "Ausländerpolizeiverordnung" (AVPO) of the Nazi state (Ronneberger and Tsianos 2009, 139).

29 The administrative term *area with special need for development* (*Gebiet mit besonderem Entwicklungsbedarf*) refers to neighborhoods marked by social segregation, poverty, high unemployment, and derelict urban environments.

30 Translation in *Spiegel International* (2009).

31 For a discussion of continuing biological essentialisms and genomic aspects of contemporary racism in Germany, see also Amrute (2016).

32 Politicians across the political spectrum criticized Sarrazin for promoting racism and he was sued for sedition. In December 2009, prosecutors dropped the lawsuit.

33 In this context, images of decay and vermin abound. In 2008, a member of the business-friendly Free Democratic Party (FDP) was quoted suggesting "new job opportunities" for Berlin's unemployed. Addressing the city's growing displaced rat population (after years of construction), he suggested that instead of collecting bottles, the unemployed could receive one euro for every dead rat (*Spiegel International* 2008).

34 On antiurbanism, see also M. Bennett (1999, 176).

35 See also Thomas Sugrue's analysis of "racial geography" in postwar America, where "many racist distinctions between black and white citizens were displaced onto supposedly more neutral observations of the differences between black and white neighborhoods" (M. Bennett 1999, 174).

36 Tempelhof Airport, built during the 1920s, was once the center of the Berlin Airlift. After its closure in 2008, part of the airport buildings were temporarily used for refugee housing in the wake of the war in Syria. The former runway that borders the garden was converted into a public park. The mosque, Şehitlik Camii, was built in 1985 and got its name from the

adjacent Muslim cemetery, which was built in 1863 for Ottoman diplomats, rulers, and soldiers (*şehit* means martyr, or soldier cemetery, in Turkish). The building thus references a history of Muslim sojourning in Berlin and Prussia that stretches back to the Ottoman Empire and its intimate connections to Europe. However, it is no longer possible to bury the dead in the adjacent cemetery. If buried in Berlin, the deceased must be placed in one of the city's few cemeteries that allow Muslim burials. Before 2012, when this practice became more widely allowed in Berlin, close to 90 percent of Muslim families in Berlin chose to send their deceased "back home." See Senatsverwaltung für Umwelt, Mobilität, Verbraucher- und Klimaschutz, "Stadtgrün, Friedhöfe, Begräbnisstätten," accessed July 20, 2020, https://www.berlin.de/senuvk/umwelt/stadtgruen/friedhoefe_begraebnisstaetten/de/islamische_bestattungen/index.shtml.

Today, many Muslims living in Kreuzberg and Neukölln use the mosque for daily prayers, socializing, and funeral ceremonies. Like many other mosques in Europe, Şehitlik Camii has become the target of public controversy. Monitoring the building's height shortly after additional construction in 2003, the Berlin building department argued that the minarets and dome were several meters above allowance. After a heated debate, the mosque's architect was asked to pay an 80,000-euro fee or else have the minarets demolished (Dölfs 2003). After 2010, Şehitlik Camii was also the repeated target of arson attacks, reflecting growing anti-Muslim sentiments in Berlin and across Germany and Europe.

37 A statue of Jahn commemorates the gymnastics site at one of the park's entrances.

38 Engaging a technique of "cross-fading" (Ette 2009) or the power-laden dynamics of "transculturation" (Pratt 1992), Humboldt's writings often blended different landscapes and places into one description. Humboldt's reports on his travels in Russia were thus rich in references and mirrored his experiences in the Americas and at "home" (Bisky 2009; Ette 2009).

39 The term *no-go area* signifies a space of immigrant crime, marking it as off-limits for white Germans. This use departs from the version of a no-go area as a space of racism, as discussed in chapter 5.

40 Turkish migrant workers comprised West Berlin's largest immigrant community. After World War II, Germany's agricultural and industrial interests, as well as high unemployment and economic instability in Turkey, triggered the development of a set of technologies of circulation—ranging from recruitment centers to medical exams to trains to short-term work permits—to bring migrant laborers from Turkey to Europe (Berger 1974). For further discussion of these East-West developments, as well as housing policies, see Çağlar and Soysal (2003), Lanz (2007), and Mandel (2008).

41 See also Partridge's (2012) analysis of the simultaneity of exclusion and inclusion, and the racialization of citizenship in Germany.

42   See also Gilroy's (2004) argument on forms of everyday conviviality being overlooked in mainstream multiculturalism in Europe.

3. Provisioning against Austerity

1   The so-called Ordnungsamt (Office of Order) is a municipal institution in the city and state of Berlin and other German states that is responsible for the maintenance of "security and order" in public space. In Berlin, each district has its own Ordnungsamt. Officers of the Ordnungsamt monitor traffic and other public space violations, such as selling food without license, excessive noise, or illegal garbage disposal, and they hand out citations throughout the city of Berlin. Although unlike police (officers are not armed), they can nonetheless perform identity checks in cases of a "suspected crime." Community groups have thus criticized racial profiling not only by police but also by the officers of the Ordnungsamt.

2   Continuing to the present day, Berlin's Green Space and Garden Offices are part of municipal administration. Yet historically, the creation of public parks and green space did not emerge on the political agenda on a large scale until the late nineteenth century. Whereas previous parks followed certain rules for clothing and conduct, the relandscaped parks of the nineteenth century expanded their scope of activities: no longer were they designed simply for "civilized walking"; instead, with larger meadows and fields, they allowed for more activities such as running, picnicking, and dwelling on grass areas (Wimmer 2001). Planners and urban reformers praised the environmental, social, and health benefits of green spaces to counter the toxic environmental effects of the city and its "social ills." Some public officials even suggested an ideal ratio of green space to each citizen—twenty square meters (Jackisch 2009, 54). Urban green spaces, or "people's gardens" (*Volksgärten* or *Volksparke*), provided spaces of exercise, recuperation, sociability, and the enjoyment of nature, as well as "refinement of manners" (SenUVK 2022d).

3   The Thai community in Germany has also steadily grown: whereas in 1975 there were about 2,000 people of Thai nationality living in Germany (with almost an equal number of men and women), by 2007 the community had grown to 53,952 (Pataya 2003; 2009, 22), and by 2021 it was around 59,200 in Germany overall and 4,750 in Berlin (Statistisches Bundesamt 2022).

4   As Hillman points out, this dual history, and the resulting unequal legal status as well as the history of the political situation in Vietnam, still impacts divisions within the Vietnamese community in Germany today (Hillman 2005, 95)—divisions that were certainly present in the Thai Park community. See also Malter (2014).

5   Since the Vietnam War, and especially after worldwide student protests against it, West German public discourse closely followed the political situation in Vietnam.

6   By 1984, the numbers of Vietnamese refugees accepted to West Germany decreased steadily (Hillman 2005).

7   During the Vietnam War, the East German socialist government also signaled solidarity with North Vietnam by encouraging unions, schools, and employers to provide material support for the population in North Vietnam (Bui 2001, 16).

8   East Germany had similar agreements with other socialist countries such as Mozambique, Angola, and Cuba (Bui 2001, 16).

9   Since the mid-2000s, the number of Vietnamese asylum seekers has increased in Germany, and there was also a wave of deportation of Vietnamese undocumented migrants in Berlin in the late 2000s (see *Deutsche Welle* 2009b). Overall, as of 2022, there were 110,515 people with Vietnamese nationality living in Germany, and 24,635 in Berlin (Statistisches Bundesamt 2022). These numbers do not include undocumented migrants, nor people who have received German citizenship.

10   Hartz I–III restructured and expanded so-called job centers (state-funded job agencies), creating possibilities for advanced training and offering new types of employment such as "mini jobs," with lower tax and insurance payments, and grants for individual entrepreneurs called the *Ich AG* ("Me Inc.").

11   Although these regulations are limited by constitutional rights, such as the freedom of movement, Hartz IV recipients have also been required to regularly report to state job agencies and provide proof of legal presence in the county in which they are registered.

12   These criticisms made it all the way to Germany's Federal Constitutional Court, which in early 2010 ruled Hartz IV benefit rates to be unconstitutional.

13   In the process of reconstructing Berlin's urban landscape, new forms of exclusion and displacement emerged. Whereas many considered West Berlin during the Cold War to be the capital of house squatters and conscientious objectors, planners and public officials set out to transform Berlin into the new German capital. Many formerly low-rent-housing neighborhoods, especially in the city center, quickly gentrified and turned into expensive residential and shopping areas in subsequent years (see Lanz 2007, 141; Rada 1997).

14   See, for example, the monthly unemployment and labor market statistics by the German Union Federation (DGB) at DGB Bezirk Berlin-Brandenburg, http://www.berlin-brandenburg.dgb.de.

15   Before their equal treatment with other (formerly West German) labor migrants was legislated in 1997, this racialized image of Vietnamese migrants as potential criminals also had effects on policy-making and the municipal government's willingness to grant these migrants legal status in Berlin (Lanz 2007, 131).

16   See also *Abgeordnetenhaus* cited in Lanz (2007, 135).

17 See McGrane (2009) on the reduction of municipal services in Berlin.

18 In 2008, 320,000 households received Hartz IV benefits (Onken 2008), whereas in 2021, with a growing overall population and in the midst of the pandemic, there were around 557,000 Hartz IV recipients. For more detailed statistics in individual Berlin districts, see Portal Sozialpolitik, http://www.portal-sozialpolitik.de/index.php?page=grundsicherungsdichte_berlin.

19 In fact, conservatives, leftist groups, and welfare organizations all raised concerns about the feasibility of the plan and its long-term health effects, possibly leading to malnutrition. In addition, a main target of criticism was that the plan omitted the fact that children were allocated only 2.28 euros per day for food according to Hartz IV (Geissler 2008). Others argued the plan's scrupulous and painstaking calculations ultimately scorned the unemployed and poor.

20 Hi-lo is often played in the Philippines, Thailand, and throughout Southeast Asia. It is similar to the game of *Sic Bo* (or *Tai Sai*, or *Dai Siu*) that also was brought to casinos in the United States via Chinese immigrants in the twentieth century.

21 Sometimes, a couple of small poker tables are perched right next to them.

22 At times, the "conduit of fiscal liquidity" (Klima 2002, 261) in the hi-lo game can be pushed even a step further: if someone places a bet, another player who ran out of money is allowed to move his neighbor's money onto a different combination, and thus place a bet himself. If he loses, he has to pay back the money to his coplayer. If he wins, he takes the gain.

23 As in Thailand, gambling is prohibited in public spaces in Germany, except in official casinos.

24 In his analysis of funeral casinos in Thailand, Klima (2002) draws on Georges Bataille's notion of expenditure to imagine an alternative political economy—an economy that is not based on a culture of utilitarian assumptions but on surplus, excess, and "accursed share." Thus, the key trope here is not efficiency, but expenditure: "*depense*: to use up, to consume, to spend, expend, to exchange value in an economy of the broadest, most expansive, expensive and wasteful wealth of the term" (242).

25 See chapter 4. As one vendor put it: "The Tiergarten is pure chaos! Even the police are scared and avoid that place, because they get in trouble there. And then the immigrants leave all the trash behind! In the Thai Park, all the garbage is cleared away in the evening. The park is clean!" And this praise for laidback "Thai culture" also was contrasted to "German culture": several vendors and visitors to the park stressed that in Germany everybody was always rushed and stressed, and nobody could ever relax. In contrast, the Thai Park was seen as much more peaceful by many.

26 This both resonates with and deviates from Anna Tsing's (2015) account of mushroom pickers and their cosmopolitan networks in the American Northwest. Tsing highlights moments of collaboration and coordina-

tion around "freedom" and shared memories of war rather than cultural identity. Similarly, the Thai Park mushroom pickers collaborate to evade efforts to domesticate immigrant economic strategies. And yet here, the chanterelles and porcinis become intense objects of desire in an intimate economy in which pickers perform "being Thai" and try to reassemble fragile socialities and a sense of autonomy within gendered forms of labor and kinship ties.

27 Kip's arrival occurred on the heels of the 1975 Indochina refugee crisis and the 1979 so-called Indochina Refugee Conference Agreement by the UNHCR, in which West Germany committed to granting asylum to refugees from Vietnam. They lived in a refugee home in Marienfelde, which at the time also accommodated refugees from East Germany to the West and was thus situated at the seam between the competing systems of Western capitalism and socialism—often called the "gate to freedom."

28 Due to ongoing criticism of low rates, the federal government also plans to overhaul the Hartz IV system and transform the Arbeitslosengeld II into a so-called *Bürgergeld* (citizen money) by late 2022 or 2023. While this will most likely simplify the application process and somewhat raise monthly allowances, many observers have pointed out that the overall system such as eligibility requirements will remain similar.

29 Tracking matsutake worlds in Oregon's forests, Tsing identifies a shift in cultural identifications among Asian American immigrants: while in the immediate post–World War II period many engaged a framework of assimilation, contemporary cultural practices are often routed through heterogeneous memories of war or narratives of freedom (Tsing 2015, 97).

4. Barbecue Area

Epigraph: The *Berliner Morgenpost* quote is from Schmiemann and Schoel-kopf (2009).

1 Shishas, or *hookahs*, are often also called *nargile* in Turkish. Introduced to Germany decades ago by Turkish and Middle Eastern immigrants, smoking shishas is a social event—usually undertaken with guests at home or in a café. Shisha bars are popular among people of all generations in Germany, and yet they continue to be marked as "ethnic" spaces. Aside from cafés, parks like the Tiergarten are one of the few public places where people smoke shishas. On February 19, 2020, two shisha bars in the city of Hanau became the site of a racist terror attack, in which nine people were killed and five were wounded. The victims were all people of color, including Turkish and Kurdish Germans and Sinti, as well as Afghan, Cameroonian, Bosnian, Bulgarian, and Romanian nationals. The attack triggered nationwide protests against right-wing racist violence.

2 Throughout this chapter and book, I use the term *citizenship* to refer to processes of self-making and being made within webs of power and the

nation-state (Ong 1996) that, as Hannah Arendt (1973) reminds us, also tend to define the parameters of the human.

3   Kaselow (1999) points out that it was common for eighteenth- and nineteenth-century European aristocrats to keep wild and "exotic" animals in parks (see also K. Anderson 1998). These included deer, foxes, wild boar, peacocks, and even lions, bears, and wolves. It was not until the mid-nineteenth century that some of these animals moved to zoos for display to a wider, bourgeois public.

4   The Victory Column dates back to the nineteenth century and commemorates several Prussian war victories. It remains a contested historical site with multiple meanings. Due to its glorification of military power, the Green Party and PDS at one point proposed to the municipal parliament that the statue be demolished—without success (Ladd 1997, 199). Aside from being seen as a symbol of Nazi violence, the column has for many years also served as the center for the Love Parade and provides the title of the city's major gay magazine. It was also featured in Wim Wenders's movie *Wings of Desire* as a place where angels meet.

5   Görlitzer Park in Kreuzberg is one of the few parks in a neighborhood with a large migrant community where barbecuing is allowed, but this is not without controversy.

6   For an updated list of permitted barbecue areas, see the city's official website, "Grillen in Berlin," accessed April 2, 2022, https://www.berlin.de/kultur-und-tickets/tipps/2431087-1678259-grillen-in-berlin.html.

7   On summer weekends, many barbecuers have to travel from Wedding, a formerly West Berlin district where barbecuing is completely prohibited, to barbecue areas in the East, such as in the postunification-era Mauerpark. In the immediate years after the prohibition, this change was especially significant because the spatial practices of many first- or second-generation migrants continued to adhere to preunification divisions between East and West Berlin, and people often felt at greater risk of racist encounters in the East.

8   For a discussion of the barbecuing debate by TBB, see "Ist Grillverbot in Tiergarten ein Kulturverbot?," TBB, accessed June 8, 2022, https://tbb-berlin.de///archiv/show/185/1.

9   The mayor of Neukölln claimed that municipal authorities were powerless against the barbecuing masses: "Even in Neukölln, where the problem is not quite as stark, it's *impossible* to handle it in a different fashion. Don't even bother sending patrols from the district Office of Order to a meadow with thousands of barbecuers. They'll get punched in the head" (Schmiemann and Schoelkopf 2009).

10 This notion of migrants as ignorant of and disconnected from the urban environment emerges in many media stories about barbecuing. Flamm's article in *Die Zeit* goes into great depth in claiming the urban incompetence of a Turkish woman who allegedly did not know how to read the Berlin

map and was familiar with only two specific places in Berlin: her own home and the Tiergarten (Flamm 2009).

11 In Nazi discourse, practices related to animal treatment and meat consumption were utilized to claim an asocial mentality of Jews and to support the idea that "non-Aryans" disrespected the natural world (Sax 2000). This was based on the assumption that the "human race" had become impure through both racial mixing and meat consumption—a major reason why many Nazi leaders favored vegetarianism (Arluke and Sax 1995, 230–37). In addition, colonial fantasies about savage meat practices, including the grilling of meat and cannibalism, were utilized to claim the primitiveness of the colonized, thereby justifying colonial and racist domination. See Warnes (2008).

12 Elder, Wolch, and Emel (1998) focus on specific human-animal relations that depart from a white Anglo-American norm and are considered out of place, such as dog fighting or treating dogs as food. These are interpreted as transgressions of species boundaries and serve as the basis for racialization. Griffith, Wolch, and Lassiter (2002) also examine how practices relating to animals function both as signs of racial otherness and as sites of resistance to racialization and marginalization among Filipinas in Los Angeles. For further discussion of the connections between urban nature, race, and colonialism (particularly zoos), see K. Anderson (1998), and Suzuki (2016).

13 On stereotypes about German fascinations with barbecuing, see Wilkens (2009).

14 As Ruth Mandel (1996) has pointed out, halal dietary rules—especially around meat consumption—have become an important concern for many people in order to avoid what is seen as moral contamination in Germany. Eating habits and meat consumption in public spaces can become not only a symbol of resistance and ethnic pride in Berlin but also a strategy to overcome pollution (147–66).

15 See Göktürk, Soysal, and Tureli (2010, 16). As real estate values are very high along the waterfront, upper-class residents or public authorities have had privileged access to seaside properties. See also Özkan (2008, 128).

16 See my earlier discussion of the gecekondular in the introduction. See also Esen (2005) and Lanz (2005).

17 Compare Koçal (2005) with, for example, Hakan (2005) and Özkök (2005).

18 It is important here to remember that modern Turkey, though largely Muslim, was founded as a republic in 1923 by Mustafa Kemal Atatürk, who envisioned his modern nation-state emerging from the remnants of the Ottoman Empire based on a French definition of secularism.

19 Stephan Lanz (2005) argues that the dual categories of urbanite and antiurbanite gained renewed currency in the 1990s, as images of doom began to dominate debates about city development in both Turkey and Germany. Yet, as he demonstrates for Istanbul, this duality fails to grasp the complexi-

ties of everyday urban life. Instead, it engages fears of blocked moderniza-tion and secularization that played a role in 1920s Turkish nation-building under Kemal Atatürk as well as in modernization efforts related to Turkey's entry into the European Union (Lanz 2005, 55–68).

20　In her study of public space in Istanbul, Özkan (2008) points out that many barbecuers challenged these conceptions. She quotes one park user: "None of us are legitimate in this country. . . . The owner of that expensive house is no more legitimate than I am. They launder money; we barbecue" (134).

21　As the journal of the fleet's physician, Diego Álvarez Chanca, reveals, Columbus's crew eagerly listened to Taino references to a mythical island called *Babeque*—abundant with pearls, gold, precious stones, and the sweet aroma of spices (Warnes 2008, 14). On their second journey across the Atlantic, when supplies were poorer and the crew's hunger even bigger, instead of finding gold, the men encountered a barbecue scene upon their landing at Guantánamo Bay—a feast of fish, rabbits, and serpents slowly cooked above a small fire.

5. Living in the *Unheimlich*

1　Throughout this chapter, I have used pseudonyms for villages and people to protect my interlocutors' privacy and anonymity.

2　While local residents, including refugees, social workers, and advocates, used the term *Heim* (home) some also referred to it as the even more charged word *Lager* (camp), thus pointing to the highly contested meanings and social lives of these locations.

3　In 2007, the erupting violence between the Kikuyu and Luo was, at least to some degree, unexpected by many. And yet it needs to be seen in the historical context of both the British colonial regime's policies and the specifics of the colonial liberation struggle in Kenya. Both had exacerbated tensions between the country's two main ethnic groups (see July 1997).

4　In his essay "The Uncanny," Freud ([1919] 1955) points out that the closest semantic equivalents to the word *unheimlich* in English are *uncanny* and *eerie*. But etymologically the term refers to *unhomely*—in German, the formal antonym to *heimlich*, which means familiar, homely, and domestic/ated (the opposite of wild), but also native, comfortable, or secretive (124). According to Freud, a sense of the uncanny arises not simply from intel-lectual uncertainty vis-à-vis the unfamiliar or strange, as Jentsch claimed, but rather in the encounter with something that is familiar and unfamiliar at the same time. The effect is cognitive dissonance and a vague sense of threat of secretive forces (155).

5　For other ethnographic accounts of the uncanny, see Ivy (1995) and Stewart (1996). Lepselter (2005) and Masco (2006) trace the uncanny in the ruins of Cold War American militarism.

6   As Cabot (2017) points out, there is an urgent need for ethnographic analyses of the histories and long-term effects of displacement in Europe since the field has recently been "oversaturated with research (and researchers) arriving on the heels of crisis" (144).

7   Attending to a sense of displacement, I draw on recent anthropological scholarship that traces the socialities and materialities of affective states (Stewart 2007; Stoler 2004) and geographies (Thrift 2004), emphasizing the relations between affect and material culture from postsocialist perspectives (Berdahl 1999; Boym 2001; Schwenkel 2013). I am also inspired here by a growing literature on the central role of both animate and inanimate beings in social life (J. Bennett 2010; Descola 2013; Haraway 2008; Ingold 2011; Raffles 2012) and scholarship that highlights how national and racial formations not only mark human bodies but also animate territories, ecologies, and nonhumans (Chen 2012; Moore, Kosek, and Pandian 2003; Stoler 2013).

8   My use of the term *racialized ecologies* is also inspired here by Jacqueline Brown's (2005) term *racial geographies* and expands it to attest to the ways in which not only perceptions of place but also their very materiality and ecology are structured by racial and imperial power.

9   In medieval Europe, a march (in German, *Mark*) was a borderland between different territories with different laws.

10 See Schama (1995) on the history of mixed forest ideologies in German forestry and environmental discourse.

11 As of 2016, more than 30 percent of Brandenburg's territory was protected nature and landscape area (*Landschafts- und Naturschutzgebiet*); see Land Brandenburg (2022).

12 Brandenburg Tours: Natur- und Erlebnisfahrten (home page), accessed July 3, 2019, http://www.brandenburg-tours.de.

13 Since the 1990s, anthropologists have developed nuanced ethnographic accounts of the cultural, economic, and political dimensions of the postsocialist transition (e.g., Blavascunas 2020; M. Caldwell 2004b; Dunn 2004; Lampland 1995; Verdery 2003). In Germany, scholars such as Berdahl (1999), Borneman (1998), and Boyer (2005) have traced various dimensions of this transition through analyses of kinship, intellectual life, environmentalism, media markets, the state, national identity, memory, and the intricacies of village life.

14 Unemployment rates in the March Oder region reached their height, above 20 percent, in the 1990s and then again in 2005; they slowly decreased after 2009 (from 14.5 percent in 2009 to 12 percent in 2012, with rates decreasing further to 5.7 percent in 2021 [LASV 2011, 2021]). Yet there are strong differences within the county of the March Oder region alone: in areas with denser populations, close to Berlin, rates were usually lower, whereas in other, less populated areas farther east, unemployment remained close to 15 percent until 2015 and then between 10 and 13 percent till 2021 (Landratsamt Märkisch Oderland 2022). Low-wage labor employment also re-

mained fairly high in the region until 2021. Overall, unemployment rates in the formerly East German states of Brandenburg, Sachsen, Sachsen-Anhalt, Thüringen, and Mecklenburg-Vorpommern have been significantly above national average since unification and continued to be so as of the end of 2021 (Brandenburger Sozialindikatoren 2011).

15 The figure of the frontier has occupied German cultural imaginaries since the nineteenth century (Blackbourn 2006, 293; Wolff 1994); it also inspired Nazi rhetoric to justify the expansion of space for the "German race" and the internal colonization of the East (Blackbourn 2006).

16 For a detailed discussion of imaginations of East Germany as a neo-Nazi space, see Shoshan (2016, especially ch. 2).

17 Before the so-called asylum compromise of 1992, Germany's post–World War II asylum law was considered to be fairly liberal compared with those of many other European countries. For example, West Germany's constitution granted asylum as a constitutional right, acknowledging the history of displacement of millions of refugees across Europe during fascism. After a heated nationwide asylum debate following German unification, changes to the asylum law and the constitution in 1992 narrowed the right to political asylum via a series of policies, such as the third state rule (mandating that people arriving in Germany via a third state that was recognized as politically safe would not be granted asylum). As a result, the numbers of asylum seekers and proportion of applicants receiving asylum status dropped dramatically between the mid-1990s and 2011 (Pieper 2008; PRO ASYL 2011; *Tagesschau* 2013). Those who applied for asylum often got stuck in legal limbo for years. While there was a publicly debated increase in asylum seekers, especially in 2015 and 2016 (due to increasing political conflict in the Middle East), both applications and the proportion of those granted refugee status continued to mostly decline again between 2017 and the beginning of 2022 (BAMF 2022).

18 After staying in a so-called first-arrival facility (*Erstaufnahmeeinrichtung*), people are "distributed" to homes in different counties according to quotas and in a process independent of their individual preferences.

19 Due to protests by refugee and human rights organizations, residency regulations (unique in Europe) have been loosened in some German states since 2015. As a result, in Brandenburg, asylum seekers with a residence permit (*Aufenthaltsberechtigte*) were allowed to travel within the state and to Berlin. In contrast, applicants with a temporary stay permit (*Geduldete*), or a record of violating regulations, such as violating the requirement not to work or the requirement that they reside in the refugee camp, were not allowed to leave the county unless they applied for a permit in advance.

20 See the VOICE Refugee Forum Germany, http://thevoiceforum.org/node /308; LabourNet Germany ARCHIV! (n.d.). On Germany's colonial policies in Cameroon, see Njoh (1997).

21 The population of Zarin was about two hundred people at the time.

22 Trabants are former East German vehicles that today have become relics of the Eastern bloc and socialism celebrated in popular culture across Europe.

23 The facilities were run by the private organization Sozialpark, originally a local consulting center for Russian German immigrants (repatriates). As Pieper (2008), chronicling the wider trend of privatizing of asylum homes in Germany, points out, although not an integral element of their services, it is likely that the accommodation of asylum seekers was added because of its profitability (195). Each month, the county paid the organization for accommodating each asylum seeker. Ironically, the Sozialpark profited from providing an inhospitable space as many, although officially registered at the Heim, did not stay there.

24 The site of the Heim was later renamed the Begegnungsstätte der Kulturen (Site of Cultural Encounters). In a labyrinth of slippery definitions, the council differentiated between *Wohnort* (dwelling or place of residence) and *Unterbringung* (accommodation) as different forms of habitation, thus defining the *Wohnheim für Asylbewerber* (residential home for asylum seekers) not as a home but as an accommodation.

25 Council members pointed out that refugee accommodations are not allowed in residential areas for exactly that reason.

26 German colonial rule throughout different parts of Africa (especially Cameroon, Togo, Ghana, Namibia, Burundi, Tanzania, and the southern coastal region in Kenya) was in some cases shorter than that of many other European countries—a fact that is often cited in order to minimize the effects and violence of German colonialism in political and scholarly discourse, as well as in everyday life. This tendency to downplay Germany's colonial past has also been evident in the ways in which history is taught in schools: while the history of the Holocaust and fascism are widely taught in schools in Germany, German colonial history continues to be only erratically and rather uncritically addressed (see Doughan 2022; Grindel 2015). Yet throughout its history, German colonial rule utilized genocide as a method of control, which had a lasting impact on social topographies throughout Africa and also profoundly shaped social life and political discourse in Germany throughout the nineteenth and twentieth centuries (see, for example, Bauche 2017; Naranch and Eley 2014).

27 Not unlike in Joseph Masco's analysis of the nuclear uncanny, a lurking threat is produced by inhabiting a risky environment—an environment in which fear of invisible forces colonizes space (Masco 2006).

28 This resonates with Ernst Jentsch's (1996) early rendering of the uncanny, in which the unheimlich refers to doubts whether an inanimate object might in fact be dead or alive.

29 There have been numerous reports of neo-Nazi and racist violence in the region since unification. For example, in 2018, there were right-wing protests in a nearby town against the construction of a new refugee home, and the food stand of a Syrian refugee was set on fire by local right-wing

youth that same year. In addition, right-wing, anti-immigration political parties have also had significant electoral support: in the 2019 state election, the anti-immigrant and right-wing political party AfD (Alternative für Deutschland) gained over 20 percent of the vote and thus became a strong force in the region. All other political parties who won significant votes refused to build a coalition with them in the state government, thus resulting in a coalition between the conservative Christian Democrats (CDU), the Green Party, and the Social Democrats (SPD). Ongoing police violence against refugees has also been criticized by refugee activist and advocacy groups in the region; see, for example, Flüchtlingsrat Brandenburg (2019).

30 International refugee law thus emerged in relation to the Allied forces' attempts to deal with the "refugee problem" in post–World War II Europe, especially in Germany. Moreover, as Malkki points out, in a horrible twist of history, former concentration camps were often converted into "Assembly Centers" for refugees (1995, 499).

31 To protect their anonymity and not subject my interlocutors to its disciplinary procedures, I also never conducted recorded interviews in the Heim in Zarin, and I made sure to always ask about permission to share certain information in my ethnographic writing.

32 Examples are the Verein Berliner Bunker Netzwerk and the Bunker Alliance Network Berlin-Brandenburg.

33 Boyer argues that rather than being called "Ostalgie," this trend should actually be called "Westalgie" (2006, 379) since in it, West Germans narrate the East as temporal displacement, as though "entering an East German space meant stepping backward in time" (373) while longing for a "normal" future that does not carry the burdens of the Holocaust.

34 For a similar argument about nostalgic yearnings shaping both national subjects *and* oppositional practices in postsocialist contexts, see Berdahl (1999) and Rofel (1994).

35 *Die Wende* in English means "the turn" or "turning point," and in Germany it is used to describe the social and political transformations of the unification process between East and West following the fall of the Berlin Wall.

36 For anthropological analyses of the social life of ruins and ruination, see, for example, Dawdy (2010), Gordillo (2014), Harms (2013), Navaro-Yashin (2012), Stoler (2013), and Tsing (2015).

37 See also Davies and Isakjee (2019) for an analysis of migrant camps as "ruins of empire."

6. Stories of the "Wild East"

1 For an introduction to the early literature on shrinking regions and deindustrialization in Germany, see, for example, Oswalt (2006a, 2006b), and for ethnographic accounts of deindustrialization in East Germany, see, for example, Ringel (2018, 2021).

2 Brandenburg Tours: Natur- und Erlebnisfahrten (home page), accessed July 3, 2019, http://www.brandenburg-tours.de.

3 The term in German is *nationale Naturlandschaften* and refers to a network of all nature reserves (*Grosschutzgebiete*) throughout Germany, including Brandenburg, that was founded in 2005, with the aim to represent Germany's national nature heritage (*nationales Naturerbe*). See LUA (2004).

4 For a history of the proliferation of wild boar in post–World War II Germany and Eastern Europe and their connection to industrial agriculture, anthropogenic land use, and climate change, see Fleischmann (2016, 2019) and Stoetzer (2014a, 2020b).

5 For a discussion of postunification unemployment rates in Brandenburg and the March Oder region, see chapter 5.

6 During the Brandenburg state election in 2019, the Social Democratic Party gained the highest percentage of votes, 26.2 percent, closely followed by the right-wing nationalist party AfD with 23.5 percent (Anker 2019). The Green Party gained 10.8 percent of the vote. In contrast, in the European parliament election that same year, the AfD was able to gain 21.1 percent, and thus the highest proportion of the vote in the region (see "Europawahl 2019: Märkisch-Oderland," Der Bundeswahlleiter, accessed December 31, 2019, https://www.bundeswahlleiter.de/europawahlen/2019/ergebnisse /bund-99/land-12/kreis-12064.html, for full election results).

7 The postunification privatization process was overseen by a single agency, the so-called Treuhand. Founded in the summer of 1990, the Treuhand took over 75 percent of the forest in East Germany to reestablish private and communal forest ownership. The agency also received massive criticism because it took control over 12,000 state-owned enterprises, shutting down many or selling them to shady profiteers, while laying off 2.5 million employees. Amid criticism and protests, especially in the steel industry, the chair of the Treuhand was murdered in 1991—allegedly by members of the left-wing organization RAF (Red Army Faction) (Wiederwald 2010).

8 Farmers and agricultural cooperatives often sell the maize as feed. After German unification, Brandenburg became one of the states with the highest percentage of genetically modified maize crops in Germany. In the March Oder region, environmental organizations repeatedly expressed concern about the proximity of genetically modified Bt maize to nature preserves and therefore called for regulatory measures to establish minimum-required distances to them. In the mid-2000s, numerous environmental activists organized so-called field liberation (*Feldbefreiung*) protests in Brandenburg, occupying GMO maize fields (*Berliner Zeitung* 2006). Since the 2010s, EU-level regulations around the authorization, labeling, and traceability of genetically modified crops have been initiated. While a ban on GMOs was subsequently implemented in Germany, the ban was not always fully enforced.

9   For a detailed history of the draining of the Oder marshes, see Blackbourn (2006, 19).

10 The Huguenots introduced the tobacco plant to the region in the seventeenth century. Thriving on Brandenburg's sandy soil, tobacco was also a popular crop during the socialist period because international supplies were limited (*MOZ* 2010a).

11 See also Eeden (2006) on leisure activities and images of colonial-style adventure connected to the Land Rover in African safari tourism. The image of the Land Rover as conquest technology over African landscapes, and its inherent binaries of culture/nature, male/female, white adventurer/native, is also cultivated on the company's website. "All-terrain vehicles" with names such as "Defender," "Freelander," or "Discovery" tackle all kinds of environments—rivers, deserts, steppe—and are "still going strong" after sixty years (see the brand's home page at https://www.landrover.com).

12 Local media, tourist brochures, and the state of Brandenburg's official tourist websites advertise exploring "Wild Brandenburg" via tours and "safaris." See, for example, https://www.reiseland-brandenburg.de/orte-regionen /nationale-naturlandschaften/, accessed May 29, 2022; Götting (2014); and *MOZ* (2011).

13 As Henrichsen (2000) points out, the so-called *Herrensafari*, or gentleman's safari, was established in the 1950s in Namibia. Almost exclusively available to white men, it was a display of motorized masculinity in which European men took both symbolic and physical control over supposedly unmapped, risky, and uncivilized land via four-wheel drive technology—and it also served as a display of white European power vis-à-vis Himba culture, which was imagined as traditional and static (161). In fact, the safari did not seek to encounter Indigenous communities but rather to legitimize European power over a supposedly "empty" landscape (179).

14 During her photo safaris in Kenya from the 1950s to the 1970s, Leni Riefenstahl sought to escape her reputation as a Nazi photographer. In his article "Riefenstahl on Safari," George Meiu (2008) argues that Riefenstahl's photographic depiction of East Africa transferred an aesthetic that was common among Nazi portrayals of the white body, masculine mastery, and pristine German landscapes both to images of bodily perfection and heroic endurance among Nuba men and to African landscapes (see also Sontag 1975). In addition, Riefenstahl's vision shared a broader aesthetic that is common throughout the West and that continues to shape a contemporary tourist gaze, specifically in its eroticized nostalgia for the popular cliché of the Maasai and the Samburu warrior as an antidote to civilization and a mythical return to nature.

15 On the history of marketing East African wildlife tourism and German fascination with the Serengeti, see Thomas Lekan (2020). In this book, Lekan traces the impact of documentary filmmaker and wildlife conservationist Bernhard Grzimek's work. Doing so, he shows how Europeans projected

Cold War anxieties around race, war, and environmental destruction onto African landscapes while seeking refuge from fascism and displacing imperial histories of environmental destruction.

16 For example, German translations of books such as James Fenimore Cooper's *The Pioneers* (1824) were popular among both émigrés and those who dreamt about the American West but were not able to go there (Adam 2005, 554–59). Adam (2005) also mentions the geographic fragmentation following the 1815 Vienna Congress as a major driving force behind European fascination with the American West.

17 The stories revolve around the friendship between Winnetou, an Apache chief, and Old Shatterhand, a white German settler. The stories include *Der Schatz im Silbersee* (1890; The treasure in Silver Lake), *Der Schwarze Mustang* (1897; The black mustang), *Der Sohn des Baerenjagers* (1890; The son of the bear hunter), *Winnetou I–III* (1963–65), and *Old Surehand I–II* (1893–96). May also wrote numerous stories about the same character traveling to the "Orient," although in these stories he was named Kara Ben Nemsi. These included *Durchs Wilde Kurdistan* (1892; Travels through wild Kurdistan), *Im Reiche des Silbernen Löwen* (1902–3; In the Realm of the Silver Lion), and *Von Baghdad nach Stambul* (1892; From Baghdad to Istanbul).

18 Blackbourn (2006, 9) points out that the early twentieth-century nature conservationists' rhetoric of expansion for the "homeland" was situated in a nationalist and racial framework, and that the term *green* often stood as synonym for German superiority—especially in relation to what was considered the Slav desert or wilderness.

19 Wilderness thus also always stood side-by-side with ideas about pastoral nature. Thomas Lekan argues that between 1885 and 1945, wilderness did not have much currency among German landscape preservationists. In the face of pervasive anthropogenic landscapes, preservationists focused on a notion of cultural landscapes (*Landschaft*) and *Heimat* (home) at the center of environmental concerns. This notion of a cultural landscape of home, unlike the American wilderness aesthetic, did not so much rely on the binary of civilization and nature, but rather saw landscape as a "cultivated garden that blends the natural, cultivated, and built environments in an aesthetically harmonious whole" (Lekan 2004, 15). Yet Landschaft, understood as both a "cultural and a natural space" (Lekan 2004, 15), also depended on a notion of a closed, national community. In fact, modern German environmentalism included a whole range of political positions, ranging from liberal to conservative to outright nationalist and racist positions in the Wilhelmine era to the blood and soil discourse in Nazi racism (Lekan 2004, 16). Lekan furthermore points out that despite Nazi goals to center nature and landscape preservation as part of a national revolution, "the Third Reich systematically subordinated environmental concern to economic recovery and war mobilization, threatening decades of preservation

efforts through Autobahn construction, rearmament, land reclamation, and dam building" (Lekan 2004, 14). See also Cronon (1996) on the wilderness debate in the United States; Blavascunas (2008, 2020) and Schwartz (2006) on the influence of the European pastoral tradition on nature preservation during the postsocialist period; and Cioc (1998) on different notions of wilderness in North American and German environmental history.

20 In their fascination with the wild, and especially with predators, Nazis were concerned with the near extinction of wolves, bears, bison, and wild horses, they therefore established many conservation and breeding programs and passed new hunting laws (Arluke and Sax 1995, 230–37).

21 In her work on the production of Wild West spaces across Europe, Ruth Ellen Gruber (2010) points out the multiple cross-cultural references in these productions. For example, the first Winnetou film she saw was in Poland, dubbed in Czech. She also recalls someone's memory of walking along the Berlin Wall during the Cold War and hearing someone whistle the *Bonanza* theme song on the other side.

22 In addition, country music was imported to Europe and Germany, especially after World War II, and thus was incorporated, too, into Wild West hobby cultures (Berger 1974).

23 For example, the Karl May Festival near Hamburg has been one of the most popular outdoor performances in Germany, attracting an average of 300,000 visitors each year.

24 The Karl May Museum based in Radebeul, Germany, refused Ojibwa tribal members' demands for years to return ancestral remains. In 2021, after years of debate, only a portion of the remains in the museum were returned.

25 Lorimer and Driessen (2016) have traced the historical spectrum and geopolitical implications of rewilding as a conservation paradigm and its relations to ecologies of national belonging in Germany and Europe. They illustrate how rewilding became a key strategy of annexation and exertion of German power over the East in the first half of the twentieth century. In this context, the term *wild* has been used to describe the anatomy, genomics, behavior, and ecology of animals; and it often was deeply entangled with ecologies of *Heimat*, race, and the nation.

26 Tracey Heatherington (2001) develops a similar argument: while rural Sardinians authenticate and ironize the notion of the backwardness of Sardinian central highlands, they seize nationalist tropes of time. Embracing "barbarian" ecological ideas and invoking the figure of the primitive, they mock global perspectives of modern environmentalism and conservation. While thus entering the political field, they nevertheless reinforce stereotypes of the Sardinian wilderness (302–3).

27 On nostalgia for the East and "Ostalgie," see my discussion in chapter 5.

28 Indeed, the right-wing anti-immigrant party AfD, which has widespread support throughout Brandenburg and was able to gain 23.5 percent of the vote in the 2019 state election, organized a controversial event in the

German parliament in late 2019 titled "Die Bilanz des deutschen Kolonial-ismus: Warum sich die Deutschen nicht für die Kolonialzeit entschuldigen müssen und erst recht nicht dafür bezahlen müssen!" (The results of German colonialism: Why Germans do not need to apologize or pay reparations for the colonial era). Inviting revisionist historian Bruce Gilley, their event triggered widespread criticism and debate, and yet it is indicative of a broader political climate that downplays or denies the harm that European colonialism inflicted on Indigenous communities and land (Georgi 2019).

29   For a discussion of the critiques of Germany's 2021 offer to pay 1.1 billion euros over thirty years in reparations for the colonial atrocities and geno-cide of people in Namibia, especially as these critiques have been voiced by the victims' descendants, see Cotterill (2022).

30   El-Tayeb (2020, 74) writes: "Our understanding of our past, thus, is always contested and malleable, depending on our contemporary conditions, while also shaping them. Usually, however, this process of creating historical narra-tives remains invisible, as history seems to unfold automatically and inevita-bly; the present necessarily follows a past that logically leads to exactly this here and now. Cracks in this process, its constructedness, become obvious when our perception of the present changes dramatically and abruptly, when the dominant logic of historical development collapses and it seems uncertain what will take its place."

31   For a more detailed discussion of the history of German forestry and the forestry school in Eberswalde, as well as its international impact, see Nel-son (2005) and Rajan (2006).

32   Despite their critique of pollution in the East, West German policies, ironi-cally, did not adhere to their own environmental standards. For example, West Germany disposed much of its garbage in East Germany before and after the fall of the Wall (Borneman 1991).

33   Within this network, national parks are categorized as areas with the least human influence. They include ecosystems in which native plants and animals are under protection, thus allowing their "own developmental dynamic." Nevertheless, sustainable tourism is allowed in these areas. In contrast, biosphere reserves are part of the UNESCO program "man and biosphere" seeking to protect, care for, and develop "internationally sig-nificant landscapes with a rich natural and cultural heritage." Nature parks are significant "cultural landscapes" that include a combination of nature reserves and areas suitable for sustainable tourism (MUGV 2011).

34   Nelson (2005, 187) points out the obvious contradictions of what counts as the "wild": "Many Germans perceive the modern, artificial, park-like forest as something both uniquely natural and expressive of the German spirit at once; the complex, never before seen close-to-nature forest is alien to the popular aesthetic. They also read the large game herd as evidence of wildness and nature, even though these animals are semidomesticated and block the emergence of a truly natural and German forest."

35 On seeing with the eyes of the former socialist state, see Scott's (1998) notion of "seeing like a state."

Mr. Jasinski's words are translated from my interview with him. The German original, spoken with a slight dialect, reads: "Da schaute keener mehr durch. Das ist nicht nachvollziehbar für einen normalen Menschen, und dann ist erstmal alles den Bach runtergegangen, das kann man wohl so sagen. Und wenig ist übriggeblieben."

36 See also Schama (1995) on the forest as mythical symbol of German national identity.

37 For a detailed discussion of the political economy of refugee camps in Germany, as well as the formal and informal economies of migration in them, see Pieper (2008, 319, 323).

38 With ostrich farming providing a new investment opportunity for entrepreneurs in Europe, African ostrich meat exports (from countries such as Botswana) to EU markets have risen (African Business 2002). Today, there are many ostrich farms in the region around Berlin and in Brandenburg; their numbers grew as people sought economic alternatives to the formal labor market. Yet animal rights groups have criticized the keeping of African ostriches on farms in Germany because the climate—especially long periods of rain, snow, and ice in the winter—is harsh and considered unsuitable for the animals (Wöhr 2005).

39 The so-called chipcard system in Germany has a longer history and goes back to asylum policy reforms and restrictions in the 1990s. Although it was temporarily abolished in early 2015, many states throughout Germany have since reinstituted it as part of the asylum system.

40 Since 2015, debates about corruption and too-lenient treatment of asylum cases have circulated in German news. See Gude and Wiedmann-Schmidt (2018), for example, on the city of Bremen. These debates often omit the corruption and racist bureaucratic treatments that refugees and advocacy networks have reported and criticized for years.

41 See also Ghassan Hage's (2017) analysis of dehumanization and what he calls the "becoming wolf" of Muslims in Europe.

REFERENCES

Ackerman, Diane. 2007. *The Zookeeper's Wife: A War Story*. New York: Norton.

Adam, Thomas, ed. 2005. *Germany and the Americas: Culture, Politics, and History; a Multidisciplinary Encyclopedia*. Santa Barbara: ABC Clio.

African Business. 2002. "Rise in Demand of Ostrich Meat." April 1.

Akademie der Künste der Welt. 2019. "Hotspots: Migration and the Sea." Accessed June 9, 2022. https://www.adkdw.org/en/article/1672_hotspots_migration_and _the_sea.

Alexandrakis, Othon. 2016. "Indirect Activism: Graffiti and Political Possibility in Athens, Greece." *Cultural Anthropology* 31 (2): 272–96.

Amrute, Sareeta. 2016. *Encoding Race, Encoding Class: Indian IT Workers in Berlin*. Durham, NC: Duke University Press.

Anand, Nikhil. 2017. *Hydraulic City: Water and the Infrastructures of Citizenship in Mumbai*. Durham, NC: Duke University Press.

Anderson, Kaye. 1998. "Animals, Science, and Spectacle in the City." In *Animal Geographies: Place, Politics, and Identity in the Nature-Culture Borderlands*, edited by Jennifer Wolch and Jody Emel, 27–50. London: Verso.

Anderson, Mark. 2009. *Black and Indigenous: Garifuna Activism and Consumer Activism in Honduras*. Minneapolis: University of Minnesota Press.

Anderson, Mark. 2013. "Ruth Benedict, Boasian Anthropology, and the Problem of the Colour Line." *History and Anthropology* 25 (3): 395–414.

Anderson, Mark. 2019. *From Boas to Black Power: Racism, Liberalism, and American Anthropology*. Stanford, CA: Stanford University Press.

Angelo, Hillary. 2021. *How Green Became Good: Urbanized Nature and the Making of Cities and Citizens*. Chicago: University of Chicago Press.

Anjaria, Jonathan Shapiro. 2011. "Ordinary States: Everyday Corruption and the Politics of Space in Mumbai." *American Ethnologist* 38 (1): 58–72.

Anjaria, Jonathan Shapiro. 2016. *The Slow Boil: Street Food, Rights, and Public Space in Mumbai*. Stanford, CA: Stanford University Press.

Anker, Jens. 2019. "Die Zeichen in Brandenburg stehen auf Kenia-Koalition." *Berliner Morgenpost*, September 3. https://www.morgenpost.de/brandenburg/article226972453/Wahlen-in-Brandenburg-Die-Zeichen-stehen-auf-Kenia-Koalition.html.

Anzaldúa, Gloria. 1999. *Borderlands/La Frontera: The New Mestiza*. San Francisco: Aunt Lute.

Arendt, Hannah. 1973. *The Origins of Totalitarianism*. New York: Harcourt.

Argun, Betigül Ercan. 2003. *Turkey in Germany: The Transnational Sphere of Deutschkei*. New York: Routledge.

Arluke, Arnold, and Boria Sax. 1995. "The Nazi Treatment of Animals and People." In *Reinventing Biology: Respect for Life and the Creation of Knowledge*, edited by Lynda Birke and Ruth Hubbard, 28–60. Bloomington: Indiana University Press.

Asad, Talal, ed. 1973. *Anthropology and the Colonial Encounter*. London: Ithaca.

Asad, Talal. 1997. "Brief Note on the Idea of an Anthropology of Europe." *American Anthropologist* 99 (4): 719–20.

Asad, Talal, James W. Fernandez, Michael Herzfeld, Andrew Lass, Susan Carol Rogers, Jane Schneider, and Katherine Verdery. 1997. "Provocations of European Ethnology." *American Anthropologist* 99 (4): 713–30.

Auhagen, A., and H. Sukopp. 1983. "Ziel, Begründung und Methoden des Naturschutzes im Rahmen der Stadtentwicklungspolitik in Berlin." *Natur und Landschaft* 68 (10): 491–526.

Ayim, May. 1997. *Grenzenlos und unverschämt*. Berlin: Orlanda Buchverlag.

Bachelard, Gaston. 1964. *The Psychoanalysis of Fire*. Boston: Beacon.

Balibar, Etienne. 1991. "Is There a 'Neo-Racism'?" In *Race, Nation, Class: Ambiguous Identities*, edited by Etienne Balibar and Immanuel Wallerstein, 17–28. London: Verso.

Balibar, Etienne. 2004. *We the People of Europe: Reflections on Transnational Citizenship*. Princeton, NJ: Princeton University Press.

Balibar, Etienne, and Immanuel Wallerstein. 1991. *Race, Nation, Class: Ambiguous Identities*. London: Verso.

BAMF (Bundesamt für Migration und Flüchtlinge). 2022. "Aktuelle Zahlen (05/2022)." Accessed May 25, 2022. https://www.bamf.de/DE/Themen/Statistik/Asylzahlen/AktuelleZahlen/aktuellezahlen-node.html.

Barad, Karen. 1998. "Getting Real: Technoscientific Practices and the Materialization of Reality." *differences: A Journal of Feminist Cultural Studies* 10 (2): 87–128.

Barua, Maan. 2021. "Feral Ecologies: The Making of Postcolonial Nature in London." *Journal of the Royal Anthropological Institute* 28 (3): 896–919.

Bassin, Mark. 2005. "Blood or Soil? The Völkisch Movement, the Nazis, and the Legacy of Geopolitik." In Brüggemeier, Cioc, and Zeller, *How Green Were the Nazis?*, 204–42.

Battles, Matthew. 2017. *Tree*. New York: Bloomsbury.

Bauche, Manuela. 2017. *Medizin und Herrschaft: Malariabekämpfung in Kamerun, Ostafrika und Ostfriesland (1890–1919)*. Frankfurt: Campus.

Bauer, Andrew, and Mona Bhan. 2016. "Welfare and the Politics and Historicity of the Anthropocene." *South Atlantic Quarterly* 115 (1): 61–85.

Baviskar, Amita. 2007. "Demolishing Delhi: Notes from a World-Class City-in-the-Making." In *The Urban Poor in Globalizing India*, edited by Lalit Batra, 39–44. Delhi: Vasudhaiva Kutumbakam.

Bechhaus-Gerst, Marianne. 2012. "German Colonial Rule." *Oxford Bibliographies Online*, last modified October 25, 2012. https://doi.org/10.1093/OBO/9780199846733-0020.

Behar, Ruth, and Deborah A. Gordon. 1995. *Women Writing Culture*. Berkeley: University of California Press.

Beliso-De Jesús, Aisha M., and Jemima Pierre. 2019. "Introduction: Anthropology of White Supremacy." *American Anthropologist* 122 (1): 65–75.

Bendixsen, Synnøve Kristine Nepstad. 2005. "Being Young, Muslim and Female: Creating Space of Belonging in Berlin." *Berliner Blätter: Ethnographische und ethnologische Beiträge* 37:88–98.

Benjamin, Walter. 2006. *Berlin Childhood around 1900*. Cambridge, MA: Harvard University Press.

Bennett, Jane. 2010. *Vibrant Matter: A Political Ecology of Things*. Durham, NC: Duke University Press.

Bennett, Michael. 1999. "Manufacturing the Ghetto: Anti-urbanism and the Spatialization of Race." In *The Nature of Cities: Ecocriticism and Urban Environments*, edited by Michael Bennett and David Teague, 169–88. Tucson: University of Arizona Press.

Bennett, Michael, and David Teague, eds. 1999. *The Nature of Cities: Ecocriticism and Urban Environments*. Tucson: University of Arizona Press.

Berdahl, Daphne. 1999. *Where the World Ended: Re-unification and Identity in the German Borderland*. Berkeley: University of California Press.

Berdahl, Daphne. 2010. *On the Social Life of Postsocialism: Memory, Consumption, Germany*. Bloomington: University of Indiana Press.

Berger, John. 1974. *A Seventh Man: Migrant Workers in Europe*. New York: Viking.

Bergner, Paul. 2008. *Befehl "Filigran": Auf den Spuren interessanter Bunker*. Basdorf: FB Verlag.

Berliner Morgenpost. 2008. "Kampf der Drogendealer um die Berliner Hasenheide." June 9.

Berliner Morgenpost. 2009. "Durchwachsenes Wetter mindert die Grill-Lust." May 17.

Berliner Zeitung. 2006. "Vandalism of GMO Crops." August 10.

Berliner Zeitung. 2007. "Lamas und Heidschnucken in der Hasenheide: Volkspark mit neuen Angeboten für Familien." December 20.

Berliner Zeitung. 2017. "Hohe Kriminalität: Polizei veröffentlicht Liste von gefährlichen Orten in Berlin." June 7. https://www.berliner-zeitung.de/berlin/polizei/hohe-kriminalitaet-polizei-veroeffentlicht-liste-der-gefaehrlichsten-orte-in-berlin-27755638.

Bevölkerungsbilanz MOL. 2009. Märkisch Oderland. http://www.maerkisch-oderland.de/cms/upload/pdf/statistik/31-12-2009/Bevoelkerungsbilanz2010.pdf.

Bhabha, Homi. 1992. "The World and the Home." *Social Text*, nos. 31–32, 141–53.

Bhambra, Gurminder K. 2009. "Postcolonial Europe, or Understanding Europe in Times of the Postcolonial." In *The SAGE Handbook of European Studies*, edited by Chris Rumford, 69–85. London: SAGE.

Bhambra, Gurminder K. 2017. "The Current Crisis of Europe: Refugees, Colonialism, and the Limits of Cosmopolitanism." *European Law Journal* 23 (5): 395–405.

Biallas, Jörg. 2018. "Koloniales Erbe im Fokus der AfD." *Deutscher Bundestag, Parlamentsnachrichten*, July 19. https://bundestag.de/presse/hib/564526-564526.

Biehl, João. 2013. "Ethnography in the Way of Theory." *Cultural Anthropology* 28 (4): 573–97.

Binder, Beate. 2001. "Capital under Construction: History and the Production of Locality in Contemporary Berlin." *Ethnologia Europaea* 31 (2): 19–40.

Binder, Beate. 2009. *Streitfall Stadtmitte: Der Berliner Schlossplatz; Reihe Kultur und Alltag*. Köln: Böhlau.

Bisky, Jens. 2009. "Die Fortsetzung der Berliner Hasenheide." *Süddeutsche Zeitung*, May 6.

Bize, Amiel. 2019. "Gleaning." Theorizing the Contemporary, *Fieldsights*, March 29. https://culanth.org/fieldsights/gleaning.

Blackbourn, David. 2006. *The Conquest of Nature: Water, Landscape, and the Making of Modern Germany*. New York: Norton.

Blavascunas, Eunice. 2008. "The Peasant and Communist Past in the Making of an Ecological Region: Podlasie, Poland." PhD diss., University of California at Santa Cruz.

Blavascunas, Eunice. 2020. *Foresters, Borders, and Bark Beetles: The Future of Europe's Last Primeval Forest*. Bloomington: Indiana University Press.

Bodenschatz, Harald. 1987. *Platz Frei fuer das Neue Berlin! Geschichte der Stadterneuerung in 'der grössten Mietskasernenstadt der Welt' seit 1871*. Berlin: Transit Schwarzenbach.

Book, Tommy. 1995. "The Urban Field of Berlin: Expansion-Isolation-Reconstruction." *Geografiska Annaler. Series B, Human Geography* 77 (3): 177–96.

Borneman, John. 1991. *Belonging in the Two Berlins: Kin, State, Nation*. Cambridge: Cambridge University Press.

Borneman, John. 1998. "*Grenzregime* (Border Regime): The Wall and Its Aftermath." In *Border Identities: Nation and State at International Frontiers*, edited by Thomas M. Wilson and Hastings Donnan, 162–90. Cambridge: Cambridge University Press.

Borneman, John, and Parvis Ghassem-Fachandi. 2017. "The Concept of *Stimmung*: From Indifference to Xenophobia in Germany's Refugee Crisis." *HAU: Journal of Ethnographic Theory* 7 (3): 105–35.

Botting, Douglas. 2005. *In the Ruins of the Reich*. Boston: Allen & Unwin.

Boyer, Dominic. 2001. "Yellow Sand of Berlin." *Ethnography* 2 (3): 421–39.

Boyer, Dominic. 2005. *Spirit and System: Media, Intellectuals, and the Dialectic in Modern German Culture*. Chicago: University of Chicago Press.

Boyer, Dominic. 2006. "Ostalgie and the Politics of the Future in Eastern Germany." *Public Culture* 18 (2): 361–81.

Boyer, Dominic. 2014. "Dominic Boyer on the Anthropology of Infrastructure." *Platypus: The CASTAC Blog.* http://blog.castac.org/2014/03/dominic-boyer-on -the-anthropology-of-infrastructure/.

Boym, Svetlana. 2001. *The Futures of Nostalgia.* New York: Basic Books.

Brantz, Dorothee. 2017. "The Urban Politics of Nature: Two Centuries of Green Spaces in Berlin 1800–2014." In *Green Landscapes in the European City,* edited by Peter Clark, Marjaana Niemi, and Catharina Nolin, 141–59. London: Routledge.

Brantz, Dorothee. 2022. *Slaughterhouse Cities: Paris, Berlin, and Chicago, 1780–1914.* Baltimore, MD: Johns Hopkins University Press.

Brantz, Dorothee, and Sonja Dümpelmann, eds. 2011. *Greening the City: Urban Landscapes in the Twentieth Century.* Charlottesville: University of Virginia Press.

Braun, Karl. 2004. "Der Thai-Treff im Preußenpark: Eine ethnographische Spurensuche." *Berliner Blätter: Ethnographische und ethnologische Beiträge* 33:9–19.

Breuer, Ascan, Ursula Hansbauer, and Wolfgang Konrad, dirs. 2005. *Forst.* sixpackfilm, in cooperation with Voice Refugee Forum. DVD.

Brown, Jacqueline. 2005. *Dropping Anchor, Setting Sail: Geographies of Race in Black Liverpool.* Princeton, NJ: Princeton University Press.

Brüggemeier, Franz-Josef, Marc Cioc, and Thomas Zeller, eds. 2005. *How Green Were the Nazis? Nature, Environment, and Nation in the Third Reich.* Athens: Ohio University Press.

Bruun Jensen, Casper, and Atsuro Morita. 2017. "Introduction: Infrastructures as Ontological Experiments." *Ethnos* 82 (4): 615–26.

Buck-Morss, Susan. 1991. *The Dialectics of Seeing: Walter Benjamin and the Arcades Project.* Cambridge, MA: MIT Press.

Buck-Morss, Susan. 1992. "Aesthetics and Anaesthetics: Walter Benjamin's Artwork Essay Reconsidered." *October* 62 (Autumn): 3–41.

Bui, Pipo. 2001. *Envisioning Vietnamese Migrants in Germany: Ethnic Stigma, Immigrant Origin Narratives and Partial Masking.* Münster: Lit Verlag.

Bundesverband deutscher Gartenfreunde e.V. 2006. *Miteinander Leben: Integration im Kleingarten.* Bonn: Bundesverband deutscher Gartenfreunde e.V.

Bunzl, Matti. 2005. "Between Anti-Semitism and Islamophobia: Thoughts on the New Europe." *American Ethnologist* 32 (4): 499–508.

Burton, Orisanmi. 2015. "Black Lives Matter: A Critique of Anthropology." Hot Spots, *Fieldsights,* June 29. https://culanth.org/fieldsights/black-lives-matter-a -critique-of-anthropology.

Cabot, Heath. 2014. *On the Doorstep of Europe: Asylum and Citizenship in Greece.* Philadelphia: University of Pennsylvania Press.

Cabot, Heath. 2017. "*Philia* and *Phagia:* Thinking with *Stimmungswechsel* through the Refugee Crisis in Greece." *HAU: Journal of Ethnographic Theory* 7 (3): 141–46.

Cabot, Heath. 2019. "The Business of Anthropology and the European Refugee Regime." *American Ethnologist* 46 (3): 261–75.

Çağlar, Ayse. 1995. "German Turks in Berlin: Social Exclusion and Strategies of Mobility." *New Community* 21 (3): 309–23.

Çağlar, Ayse. 2001. "Constraining Metaphors and the Transnationalization of Spaces in Berlin." *Journal of Ethnic and Migration Studies* 27 (4): 601–13.

Çağlar, Ayse, and Levent Soysal. 2003. "Introduction: Turkish Migration to Germany 40 Years After." *New Perspectives on Turkey* 29 (Spring/Fall): 1–18.

Caldwell, Melissa. 2004a. "Domesticating the French Fry: McDonald's and Consumerism in Moscow." *Journal of Consumer Culture* 4 (1): 5–26.

Caldwell, Melissa. 2004b. *Not by Bread Alone: Social Support in the New Russia.* Berkeley: University of California Press.

Caldwell, Melissa. 2010. *Dacha Idylls: Living Organically in Russia's Countryside.* Berkeley: University of California Press.

Caldwell, Wilber. 2005. *Searching for the Dixie Barbecue: Journeys into the Southern Psyche.* Sarasota: Pineapple.

Campt, Tina. 2004. *Other Germans: Black Germans and the Politics of Race, Gender, and Memory in the Third Reich.* Ann Arbor: University of Michigan Press.

Carastathis, Anna, and Myrto Tsilimpounidi. 2018. "Experts, Refugees, and Radicals: Borders and Orders in the Hotspot of Crisis." *Theory in Action* 11 (4): 1–21.

Carmesin, Ulrich. 1995. "Der Grosse Tiergarten: Eine Kulturstätte mit Symbolkräften." In *Denk-mal Tiergarten: Geschichte—Bedeutung—Gefahren—Hauptstadtbau,* edited by Lydia Schend, 29–44. Berlin: Edition Baumverlag.

Carse, Ashley. 2012. "Nature as Infrastructure: Making and Managing the Panama Canal Watershed." *Social Studies of Science* 42 (4): 539–63.

Casid, Jill H. 2005. *Sowing Empire: Landscape and Colonization.* Minneapolis: University of Minnesota Press.

Certeau, Michel de. 1984. *The Practice of Everyday Life.* Berkeley: University of California Press.

Chakrabarty, Dipesh. 2012. "Postcolonial Studies and the Challenges of Climate Change." *New Literary History* 43 (1): 1–18.

Chalfin, Brenda. 2014. "Public Things, Excremental Politics, and the Infrastructure of Bare Life in Ghana's City of Tema." *American Ethnologist* 41 (1): 92–109.

Chao, Sophie. 2022. *In the Shadow of the Palms: More-than-Human Becomings in West Papua.* Durham, NC: Duke University Press.

Chari, Sharad, and Katherine Verdery. 2009. "Thinking between the Posts: Postcolonialism, Postsocialism, and Ethnography after the Cold War." *Comparative Studies in Society and History* 51 (1): 6–34.

Chen, Mel. 2012. *Animacies: Biopolitics, Racial Mattering, and Queer Affect.* Durham, NC: Duke University Press.

Cherkaev, Xenia. 2019. "High Frequency Gleaning and Usufruct Freedom." Theorizing the Contemporary, *Fieldsights,* March 29. https://culanth.org/fieldsights/high-frequency-gleaning-and-usufruct-freedom.

Cherkaev, Xenia. 2020. "St. Xenia and the Gleaners of Leningrad." *American Historical Review* 125 (3): 906–14.

Choy, Timothy. 2011. *Ecologies of Comparison: An Ethnography of Endangerment in Hong Kong.* Durham, NC: Duke University Press.

Christoffel, Udo, ed. 1981. *Berlin Wilmersdorf: Ein StadtTeilBuch.* Berlin: Kunstamt Wilmersdorf.

Cioc, Marc. 1998. "The Impact of the Coal Age on the German Environment: A Review of the Historical Literature." *Environment and History* 4 (1): 105–24.

Clarke, Kamari, and Deborah Thomas. 2006. *Globalization and Race: Transformations in the Cultural Production of Blackness.* Durham, NC: Duke University Press.

Clifford, James. 1997. *Routes: Travel and Translation in the Late Twentieth Century.* Cambridge, MA: Harvard University Press.

Clifford, James, and George Marcus, eds. 1986. *Writing Culture: The Poetics and Politics of Ethnography.* Berkeley: University of California Press.

Cotterill, Joseph. 2022. "Battle for Namibia Reparations: German Deal Was 'Never about Us.'" *Financial Times*, April 29.

Cowles, Sarah. 2017. "Ruderal Aesthetics: Annual Meeting Proceedings." 105th ACSA (Association of Collegiate Schools of Architecture) Annual Meeting Proceedings. https://www.acsa-arch.org/proceedings/Annual%20 Meeting%20Proceedings/ACSA.AM.105/ACSA.AM.105.62.pdf.

Cronon, William. 1991. *Nature's Metropolis: Chicago and the Great West.* New York: Norton.

Cronon, William. 1996. "The Trouble with Wilderness: Or, Getting Back to the Wrong Nature." In *Uncommon Ground: Rethinking the Human Place in Nature*, edited by William Cronon, 69–90. New York: Norton.

Cupers, Kenny. 2016. "Bodenständigkeit: The Environmental Epistemology of Modernism." *Journal of Architecture* 21 (8): 1226–52.

Czollek, Max. 2018. *Desintegriert euch.* München: Hanser.

Dahinden, Janine. 2016. "A Plea for the 'De-migranticization' of Research on Migration and Integration." *Ethnic and Racial Studies* 39 (13): 2207–25.

Dave, Naisargi. 2017. "Something, Everything, Nothing; or, Cows, Dogs, and Maggots." *Social Text* 35 (1): 35–57.

Davies, Thom, and Arshad Isakjee. 2015. "Geography, Migration and Abandonment in the Calais Refugee Camp." *Political Geography* 49 (November): 93–95.

Davies, Thom, and Arshad Isakjee. 2019. "Ruins of Empire: Refugees, Race, and the Postcolonial Geographies of European Migrant Camps." *Geoforum* 102 (June): 214–17.

Davis, Angela. 1981. *Women, Race and Class.* New York: Random House.

Davis, Heather, and Zoe Todd. 2017. "On the Importance of a Date, or, Decolonizing the Anthropocene." *ACME: An International Journal for Critical Geographies* 16 (4): 761–80.

Davis, Mike. 2002. *Dead Cities: And Other Tales.* New York: New Press.

Davis, Mike. 2004. "Planet of Slums: Urban Involution and the Informal Proletariat." In *Cultural Theory: An Anthology*, edited by Imre Szeman and Timothy Kaposy, 318–31. Malden, MA: Wiley.

Dawdy, Shannon. 2010. "Clockpunk Anthropology and the Ruins of Modernity." *Current Anthropology* 51 (6): 761–93.

de Castro, Eduardo Vivieros. 2012. "Immanence and Fear: Stranger Events and Subjects in Amazonia." *HAU: Journal of Ethnographic Theory* 2 (1): 27–43.

De Genova, Nicholas. 2017. *The Borders of "Europe": Autonomy of Migration, Tactics of Bordering.* Durham, NC: Duke University Press.

De Genova, Nicholas. 2018. "The 'Migrant Crisis' as Racial Crisis: Do *Black Lives Matter* in Europe?" *Ethnic and Racial Studies* 41 (44): 1–18.

de la Cadena, Marisol. 2015. *Earth Beings: Ecologies of Practice across Andean Worlds.* Durham, NC: Duke University Press.

de la Cadena, Marisol. 2019. "Uncommoning Nature: Stories from the Anthropo-Not-Seen." In *Anthropos and the Material*, edited by Penny Harvey, Christian Krohn-Hansen, and Knut G. Nustad, 35–58. Durham, NC: Duke University Press.

de Leon, Jason. 2015. *The Land of Open Graves: Living and Dying on the Migrant Trail.* Berkeley: University of California Press.

Del Tredici, Peter. 2010. *Wild Urban Plants of the Northeast: A Field Guide.* Ithaca, NY: Cornell University Press.

Der Beauftragte des Senats für Integration und Migration. 2007. "Berlin: Hauptstadt der interkulturellen Gärten." Accessed October 10, 2012. http://www.berlin.de/lb/intmig/presse/archiv/20070824.1000.84088.html.

Derrida, Jacques. 2006. *Specters of Marx: The State of the Debt, the Work of Mourning, and the New International.* New York: Routledge.

Descola, Philippe. 2013. *Beyond Nature and Culture.* Chicago: University of Chicago Press.

Deutscher Städtetag, ed. 1979. *Hinweise zur Arbeit in sozialen Brennpunkten.* Köln: Deutscher Städtetag.

Deutsche Welle. 2009a. "Berlin's Former City Finance Chief Calls the Capital Too Stupid to Be Great." September 30. https://www.dw.com/en/berlins-former-city-finance-chief-calls-the-capital-too-stupid-to-be-great/a-4747455.

Deutsche Welle. 2009b. "Vietnamese Immigrants Face Deportation from Germany." June 8. http://www.dw-world.de/dw/article/0,,4306885,00.html.

Diefendorf, Jeffry. 1993. *In the Wake of War: The Reconstruction of German Cities after World War II.* New York: Oxford University Press.

Dierig, Sven, Jens Lachmund, and Andrew Mendelsohn, eds. 2003. *Osiris* 18 (Science and the City). Chicago: University of Chicago Press.

Dölfs, Guntram. 2003. "Bau der Moschee am Columbiadamm gestoppt." *Die Welt*, September 13.

Dominguez, Virginia. 1986. *White by Definition: Social Classification in Creole Louisiana.* New Brunswick, NJ: Rutgers University Press.

Doughan, Sultan. 2022. "Desiring Memorials: Jews, Muslims, and the Human of Citizenship." In *Jews and Muslims in Europe*, edited by Ben Gidley and Samuel Sami Everett, 46–70. Leiden: Brill.

Douglas, Mary. 2002. *Purity and Danger: An Analysis of Concepts of Pollution and Taboo.* New York: Routledge.

Dower, John. 1986. *War without Mercy: Race and Power in the Pacific War.* New York: Pantheon.

Du Bois, W. E. B. 2008. *The Souls of Black Folk.* Oxford: Oxford University Press.

Düll, Ruprecht, and Herbert Werner. 1955. "Pflanzensoziologische Studien im Stadtgebiet von Berlin." *Wissenschaftliche Zeitschrift der Humboldt-Universität zu Berlin* 5 (4): 321–31.

Dümpelmann, Sonja. 2019. *Seeing Trees: A History of Street Trees in New York City and Berlin*. New Haven, CT: Yale University Press.

Dunn, Elizabeth. 2004. *Privatizing Poland: Baby Food, Big Business, and the Remaking of Labor*. Ithaca, NY: Cornell University Press.

Düspohl, Martin. 2009. *Kleine Kreuzberggeschichte*. Berlin: Berlin-Story Verlag.

Ebron, Paulla, and Anna Tsing. 2017. "Feminism and the Anthropocene: Assessing the Field through Recent Books." *Feminist Studies* 43 (3): 658–83. https://www.jstor.org/stable/10.15767/feministstudies.43.3.0658.

Eeden, Jeanne Van. 2006. "Land Rover and Colonial Style Adventure: The Himba Advertisement." *International Feminist Journal of Politics* 8 (3): 343–69.

Elder, Glen, Jennifer Wolch, and Jody Emel. 1998. "*Le Pratique Savage*: Race, Place, and the Human-Animal Divide." In *Animal Geographies: Place, Politics, and Identity in the Nature-Culture Borderlands*, edited by Jennifer Wolch and Jody Emel, 72–90. New York: Verso.

El-Enany, Nadine. 2020. *(B)ordering Britain: Law, Race, and Empire*. Manchester: Manchester University Press.

El-Tayeb, Fatima. 2001. *Schwarze Deutsche: Der Diskurs um 'Rasse' und nationale Identität 1890–1933*. Translated by Andreas Eckert. Frankfurt: Campus.

El-Tayeb, Fatima. 2008. "'The Birth of a European Public': Migration, Postnationality, and Race in the Uniting of Europe." *American Quarterly* 60 (3): 649–70.

El-Tayeb, Fatima. 2011. *European Others: Queering Ethnicity in Postnational Europe*. Minneapolis: University of Minnesota Press.

El-Tayeb, Fatima. 2012. "'Gays Who Cannot Properly Be Gay': Queer Muslims in the Neoliberal European City." *European Journal of Women's Studies* 19 (1): 79–95.

El-Tayeb, Fatima. 2020. "The Universal Museum: How the New Germany Built Its Future on Colonial Amnesia." *Nka: Journal of Contemporary African Art*, no. 46, 72–82.

El-Tayeb, Fatima, and Vanessa E. Thompson. 2019. "Alltagsrassismus, staatliche Gewalt und koloniale Tradition: Ein Gespräch über Racial Profiling und intersektionale Widerstände in Europa." In *Racial Profiling: Struktureller Rassismus und antirassistischer Widerstand*, edited by Mohamed Wa Baile, Serena O. Dankwa, Tarek Naguib, Patricia Purtschert, and Sarah Schilliger, 311–28. Münster: Transcript Verlag.

Erman, Tahire. 2001. "The Politics of Squatter (*Gecekondu*) Studies in Turkey: The Changing Representations of Rural Migrants in the Academic Discourse." *Urban Studies* 38 (7): 983–1002. https://doi.org/10.1080/00420980120080131.

Esen, Orhan. 2005. "Learning from Istanbul: Die Stadt Istanbul; Materielle Produktion und Produktion des Diskurses." In *Self Service City: Istanbul*, edited by Orhan Esen and Stephan Lanz, 33–55. Berlin: B_books.

Ette, Ottmar. 2009. *Alexander von Humboldt und die Globalisierung: Das Mobile des Wissens*. Frankfurt am Main: Insel Verlag.

Fanon, Frantz. 2004. *The Wretched of the Earth*. New York: Grove.

Fassin, Didier. 2011. "Policing Borders, Producing Boundaries: The Governmentality of Immigration in Dark Times." *Annual Review of Anthropology* 40:213–26.

Fassin, Didier. 2014. "True Life, Real Lives: Revisiting the Boundaries between Ethnography and Fiction." *American Ethnologist* 41 (1): 40–55.

FAZ (Frankfurter Allgemeine Zeitung). 2007. "Der Berliner Guerilla-Garten." March 21.

Featherstone, Don, dir. 1986. *Babakiueria. Barbecue Area*. Australia: Australian Broadcasting Corporation.

Feldman, Gregory. 2011. *The Migration Apparatus: Security, Labor, and Policymaking in the European Union*. Stanford, CA: Stanford University Press.

FeMigra. 1994. "Wir, die Seiltänzerinnen. Politische Strategien von Migrantinnen gegen Ethnisierung und Assimilation." In *Gender Killer: Texte zu Feminismus und Politik*, edited by Cornelia Eichhorn and Sabine Grimm, 49–63. Amsterdam, Berlin: Edition ID-Archiv.

Fennell, Catherine. 2011. "'Project Heat' and Sensory Politics in Redeveloping Chicago Public Housing." *Ethnography* 12 (1): 40–64.

Fennell, Catherine. 2015. *Last Project Standing: Civics and Sympathy in Post-welfare Chicago*. Minneapolis: University of Minneapolis Press.

Fenner, Daniel. 2020. "How Cool Are Allotment Gardens? A Case Study of Nocturnal Air Temperature Differences in Berlin, Germany." *Atmosphere* 11 (5): 500.

Ferdinand, Malcom. 2020. "Why We Need a Decolonial Ecology (Interview with Aurore Chaillou and Louise Roblin)." *European Green Journal*, June 4. https://www.greeneuropeanjournal.eu/why-we-need-a-decolonial-ecology/.

Ferdinand, Malcom. 2022. *Decolonial Ecology: Thinking from the Caribbean World*. Cambridge: Polity.

Fernando, Mayanthi. 2013. "Save the Muslim Woman, Save the Republic. Ni Putes Ni Soumises and the Ruse of Neoliberal Sovereignty." *Modern & Contemporary France* 21 (2): 147–65.

Fernando, Mayanthi, and Cristiana Giordano, eds. 2016. "Refugees and the Crisis of Europe." Hot Spots, *Fieldsights*, June 28. https://culanth.org/fieldsights/series/refugees-and-the-crisis-of-europe.

Finney, Carolyn. 2014. *Black Faces, White Spaces: Reimagining the Relationship of African Americans to the Great Outdoors*. Chapel Hill: University of North Carolina Press.

Flamm, Stefanie. 2009. "Die Affäre Hammelbein." *Die Zeit*, August 20.

Fleischmann, Thomas. 2016. "'A Plague of Wild Boars': A New History of Pigs and People in Late 20th Century Europe." *Antipode* 49 (4): 1015–34.

Fleischmann, Thomas. 2019. "The Half-Life of State Socialism: What Radioactive Wild Boars Tell Us about the Environmental History of Reunified Germany." In *Ecologies of Socialisms: Germany, Nature, and the Left in History, Politics, and Culture*, edited by Sabine Mödersheim, Scott Moranda, and Eli Rubin, 227–50. Oxford: Peter Lang.

Fleischmann, Thomas. 2022. *Communist Pigs: An Animal History of East Germany's Rise and Fall*. Seattle: University of Washington Press.

Flüchtlingsrat Brandenburg. 2005. *UnHEIMliches Brandenburg*. Potsdam: Flüchtlingsrat Brandenburg.

Flüchtlingsrat Brandenburg. 2019. "Pressemitteilung: Polizeigewalt in Ausländerbehörde in Märkisch-Oderland." November 8. https://www.fluechtlingsrat

-brandenburg.de/pressemitteilung-polizeigewalt-in-auslaenderbehoerde-in
-maerkisch-oderland/.

Fontane, Theodor. 1971. *Wanderungen durch die Mark Brandenburg.* Frankfurt: Nymphenburger Verlagshandlung.

Fortun, Kim. 2012. "Ethnography in Late Industrialism." *Cultural Anthropology* 27 (3): 446–64.

Fortun, Kim. 2014. "From Latour to Late Industrialism." *HAU: Journal of Ethnographic Theory* 4 (1): 309‒29.

Foster, Laura. 2019. "Critical Perspectives on Plants, Race, and Colonialism: An Introduction." *Catalyst: Feminism, Theory, Technoscience* 5 (2): 1–6.

Freud, Sigmund. (1919) 1955. "The Uncanny." In *The Standard Edition of the Complete Psychological Works of Sigmund Freud*, vol. 17: *1917–1919*, edited by James Strachey, 219–54. London: Hogarth Press and the Institute of Psychoanalysis.

Fulbrook, Mary. 1991. *A Concise History of Germany.* Cambridge: Cambridge University Press.

Fülling, Thomas. 2011. "Müll im Tiergarten: Ignoriert und angepöbelt; Mit der Grill-Streife unterwegs." *Berliner Morgenpost*, October 10.

Gandy, Matthew. 2006. "Urban Nature and the Ecological Imaginary." In *In the Nature of Cities: Urban Political Ecology and the Politics of Urban Metabolism*, edited by Nik Heynen, Maria Kaika, and Erik Swyngedouw, 62–72. New York: Routledge.

Gandy, Matthew. 2013. "Marginalia: Aesthetics, Ecology, and Urban Wastelands." *Annals of American Geographers* 103 (6): 1301–6.

Gandy, Matthew. 2022. *Natura Urbana: Ecological Constellations in Urban Space.* Cambridge, MA: MIT Press.

Gandy, Matthew, dir., and Sandra Jasper, exec. producer. 2017. *Natura Urbana: The Brachen of Berlin.* https://www.naturaurbana.org/. DVD.

Geertz, Clifford. 1973. *The Interpretation of Cultures.* New York: Basic Books.

Geissler, Heiner. 2008. "Darf Sarrazin Arbeitslose folgenlos verhöhnen?" *Tagesspiegel*, February 13.

Gelbin, Cathy, Kader Konuk, and Peggy Piesche, eds. 1999. *AufBrüche: Kulturelle Produktionen von Migrantinnen, Schwarzen und jüdischen Frauen in Deutschland.* Königstein: Taunus Helmer.

Georgi, Oliver. 2019. "Danke für die Unterdrückung!" *Frankfurter Allgemeine Zeitung*, November 28. https://www.faz.net/aktuell/politik/inland/afd-und -deutsche-kolonialzeit-danke-fuer-die-unterdrueckung-16508136.html.

Gilman, Sander. 1982. *On Blackness without Blacks: Essays on the Image of the Black in Germany.* Boston: Hall.

Gilmore, Ruth Wilson. 2007. *Golden Gulag: Prisons, Surplus, Crisis, and Opposition in Globalizing California.* Berkeley: University of California Press.

Gilroy, Paul. 1987. *There Ain't No Black in the Union Jack: The Cultural Politics of Race and Nation.* London: Hutchinson.

Gilroy, Paul. 2004. *After Empire: Melancholia or Convivial Culture?* New York: Routledge.

Gilroy, Paul. 2006. *Postcolonial Melancholia.* New York: Columbia University Press.

Giordano, Cristiana. 2014. *Migrants in Translation: Caring and the Logics of Difference in Contemporary Italy*. Berkeley: University of California Press.

Glaeser, Andreas. 2002. *Divided in Unity: Identity, Germany, and the Berlin Police*. Chicago: University of Chicago Press.

Glick-Schiller, Nina. 2005. "Racialized Nations, Evangelizing Christianity, Police States, and Imperial Power: Missing in Action in Bunzl's New Europe." *American Ethnologist* 32 (4): 526–32.

Glick-Schiller, Nina, Ayse Çağlar, and Thaddeus Guldbrandsen. 2006. "Beyond the Ethnic Lens: Locality, Globality, and Born-Again Incorporation." *American Ethnologist* 33 (4): 612–33.

Glick-Schiller, Nina, Data Dea, and Markus Hoehne. 2005. *African Culture and the Zoo in the 21st Century: The "African Village" in the Augsburg Zoo and Its Wider Implications*. Report to the Max Planck Institute for Social Anthropology. http://www.eth.mpg.de/cms/en/people/d/mhoehne/pdf/zooCulture.pdf.

Gockel, Roland, and Rosie Koch, dirs. 2013. *Wildes Berlin*. Germany: rbb/NDR/arte.

Göktürk, Deniz, Levent Soysal, and Ipek Tureli, eds. 2010. *Orienting Istanbul: Cultural Capital of Europe?* New York: Routledge.

Goldstein, Donna M. 2013. *Laughter Out of Place: Race, Class, Violence, and Sexuality in a Rio Shantytown*. Berkeley: University of California Press.

Golley, Frank. 1993. *A History of the Ecosystem Concept in Ecology*. New Haven, CT: Yale University Press.

Gordillo, Gaston. 2014. *Rubble: The Afterlife of Destruction*. Durham, NC: Duke University Press.

Götting, Jörg. 2014. *Wildes Brandenburg: Brandenburgs Nationale Naturlandschaften*. Potsdam: Landesumweltamt Brandenburg.

Govindrajan, Rhadika. 2018. *Animal Intimacies: Interspecies Relatedness in India's Central Himalayas*. Chicago: University of Chicago Press.

Gravlee, Clarence C. 2009. "How Race Becomes Biology: Embodiment of Social Inequality." *American Journal of Physical Anthropology* 139 (1): 47–57.

Grebe, Rainald. 2005. "Brandenburg." In *Rainald Grebe und die Kapelle der Versöhnung*. Köln: WortArt.

Gregory, Steven. 1998. *Black Corona: Race and the Politics of Place in an Urban Community*. Princeton, NJ: Princeton University Press.

Griffith, Marcie, Jennifer Wolch, and Unna Lassiter. 2002. "Animal Practices and the Racialization of Filipinas in Los Angeles." *Society and Animals* 10 (3): 222–48.

Grime, Jo P. 1977. "Evidence for the Existence of Three Primary Strategies in Plants and Its Relevance to Ecological and Evolutionary Theory." *American Naturalist* 111 (982): 1169–94.

Grindel, Susanne. 2015. "Educating the Nation. German History Textbooks since 1900: Representations of Colonialism." *Mélanges de l'École française de Rome— Italie et Méditerranée modernes et contemporaines*, no. 127-2. https://journals.openedition.org/mefrim/2250.

Gröning, Gert, and Uwe Schneider. 1999. "Design versus Leisure: Social Implications of Functionalist Design Approaches in Urban Private Gardens in the

Twentieth Century." In *Leisure/Tourism Geographies: Practices and Geographical Knowledge*, edited by David Crouch, 149–63. London: Routledge.

Gröning, Gert, and Joachim Wolschke-Bulmahn. 1992. "Some Notes on the Mania for Native Plants in Germany." *Landscape Journal* 11 (2): 116–26.

Grossmann, Atina. 2009. *Jews, Germans, and Allies: Close Encounters in Occupied Germany.* Princeton, NJ: Princeton University Press.

Grove, Richard. 1995. *Green Imperialism: Colonial Expansion, Tropical Island Edens and the Origins of Environmentalism, 1600 1860.* Cambridge: Cambridge University Press.

Gruber, Ruth Ellen. 2010. "Sauerkraut Cowboys and Klezmer Cafes." Presentation, University of California at Santa Cruz, October 5.

Guarasci, Bridget, Amelia Moore, and Sarah Vaughn. 2021. "Intersectional Ecologies: Reimagining Anthropology and Environment." *Annual Review of Anthropology* 50 (1): 275–90.

Gude, Hubert, and Wolf Wiedmann-Schmidt. 2018. "1000 Euro: Schon klappte das Asylverfahren." *Spiegel*, May 18. http://www.spiegel.de/spiegel/bremen-so -kamen-fluechtlinge-an-asyl-bescheide-a-1208468.html.

Guettel, Jens-Uwe. 2010. "From the Frontier to German South-West Africa: German Colonialism, Indians, and American Westward Expansion." *Modern Intellectual History* 7 (3): 523–52.

Gülfirat, Suzan. 2005. "Wir sind die Grillweltmeister: Wie türkische Blätter über die Rauchschwaden im Tiergarten berichten." *Tagesspiegel*, May 30.

Günel, Gökçe, Saiba Varma, and Chika Watanabe. 2020. "A Manifesto for Patchwork Ethnography." Member Voices, *Fieldsights*, June 9. https://culanth.org /fieldsights/a-manifesto-for-patchwork-ethnography.

Gutiérrez Rodríguez, Encarnación. 1999. *Intellektuelle Migrantinnen— Subjektivitäten im Zeitalter der Globalisierung: Eine postkoloniale dekonstruktive Analyse von Biographien im Spannungsverhältnis von Ethnisierung und Vergeschlechtlichung.* Opladen: Leske & Budrich.

Gutiérrez Rodríguez, Encarnación. 2018. "The Coloniality of Migration and the Refugee Crisis." *Refuge* 34 (1): 16–28.

Gutiérrez Rodríguez, Encarnación, and Hito Steyerl. 2003. *Spricht die Subalterne Deutsch? Migration und Postkoloniale Kritik.* Münster: Unrast.

Ha, Noa. 2012. "Preußenpark: Community Picknick am Rande der Deutschen Parkordnung." In *Asiatisch Deutsche: Vietnamesische Diaspora and Beyond*, edited by Kien Nghi Ha, 271–77. Berlin/Hamburg: Assoziation A Verlag.

Ha, Noa. 2014. "Perspektiven urbaner Dekolonisierung: Die europäische Stadt als 'Contact Zone.'" *Sub\urban: Zeitschrift für kritische Stadtforschung* 2 (1): 27–48.

Hage, Ghassan. 2016. "État de Siege: A Dying Domesticating Colonialism." *American Ethnologist* 43 (1): 38–49.

Hage, Ghassan. 2017. *Is Racism an Environmental Threat?* Cambridge: Polity.

Hagemann, Anke. 2006. "Go East: On the Wild West Rhetoric of Shrinking Cities Projects." In *Shrinking Cities*, vol. 2: *Interventions*, edited by Philipp Oswalt, 421–25. Ostfildern: Hatje Kantz.

Hagen, Joel. 1992. *An Entangled Bank: The Origins of Ecosystem Ecology*. New Brunswick, NJ: Rutgers University Press.

Hakan, Ahmet. 2005. "Faşist cesareti." *Radikal*, July 29.

Halberstam, Jack. 2020. *Wild Things: The Disorder of Desire*. Durham, NC: Duke University Press.

Hale, Charles. 2005. "Neoliberal Multiculturalism: The Remaking of Cultural Rights and Racial Dominance in Central America." *Political and Legal Anthropology Review* 28 (1): 10–28.

Hall, Stuart. 1991. "Europe's Other Self." *Marxism Today* (August): 18–19.

Hall, Stuart. 1992. "New Ethnicities." In *"Race," Culture and Difference*, edited by James Donald and Ali Rattansi, 252–59. London: Sage.

Hannah, Dehlia, and Sara Krajewski. 2015. *Placing the Golden Spike: Landscapes of the Anthropocene*. Portland, OR: Publication Studio. Exhibition catalog.

Haraway, Donna. 1991. *Simians, Cyborgs, and Women: The Reinvention of Nature*. New York: Routledge.

Haraway, Donna. 1992. "Otherworldly Conversations; Terran Topics; Local Terms." *Science as Culture* 3 (1): 64–98.

Haraway, Donna. 2003. *The Companion Species Manifesto*. Chicago: Prickly Paradigm.

Haraway, Donna. 2008. *When Species Meet*. Minneapolis: University of Minnesota Press.

Haraway, Donna. 2015. "Anthropocene, Capitalocene, Plantationocene, Chthulucene: Making Kin." *Environmental Humanities* 6 (1): 159–65.

Haraway, Donna. 2016. *Staying with the Trouble: Making Kin in the Chthulucene*. Durham, NC: Duke University Press.

Haraway, Donna, Noboru Ishikawa, Scott F. Gilbert, Kenneth Olwig, Anna Tsing, and Nils Bubandt. 2016. "Anthropologists Are Talking—about the Anthropocene." *Ethnos* 81 (3): 535–64.

Harms, Erik. 2013. "Eviction Time in the New Saigon: Temporalities of Displacement in the Rubble of Development." *Cultural Anthropology* 28 (2): 344–68.

Harper, Krista. 2006. *Wild Capitalism: Environmental Activism and Post-socialist Political Ecology in Hungary*. New York: Columbia University Press.

Harrison, Faye. 1995. "The Persistent Power of Race in the Cultural and Political Economy of Racism." *Annual Review of Anthropology* 24:47–74.

Hartigan, John. 1999. *Racial Situations: Class Predicaments of Whiteness in Detroit*. Princeton, NJ: Princeton University Press.

Hartigan, John. 2015. "Plant Publics: Multispecies Relating in Spanish Botanical Gardens." *Anthropological Quarterly* 88 (2): 481–507.

Hartigan, John. 2017. *Care of the Species: Races of Corn and the Science of Plant Biodiversity*. Minneapolis: University of Minnesota Press.

Hasselmann, Joern. 2005. "Es ist angegrillt: Jetzt ziehen wieder dichte Rauchschwaden durch den Tiergarten. Doch die Kiezstreifen machen sich rar." *Tagesspiegel*, May 30.

Heatherington, Tracey. 2001. "Ecology, Alterity and Resistance in Sardinia." *Social Anthropology* 9 (3): 285–302.

Heatherington, Tracey. 2010. *Wild Sardinia: Indigeneity and the Global Dreamtimes of Environmentalism.* Seattle: University of Washington Press.

Heidegger, Martin. 1970. *What Is a Thing?* Translated by W. B. Barton and Vera Deutsch. Chicago: Henry Regnery.

Hein, Rainer. 2009. "Mitte droht mit Sperrung von Grillplätzen im Tiergarten." *Berliner Morgenpost,* April 17.

Heinrich, Michael. 2004. "Agenda 2010 und Hartz IV: Vom rot-grünen Neoliberalismus zum Protest." *PROKLA: Zeitschrift für kritische Sozialwissenschaft* 34 (136): 477–83.

Hell, Julia, and Andreas Schoenle, eds. 2010. *Ruins of Modernity.* Durham, NC: Duke University Press.

Helmreich, Stefan. 2005. "How Scientists Think; about 'Natives' for Example: A Problem of Taxonomy by Biologists of Alien Species in Hawaii." *Journal of the Royal Anthropological Institute* 11 (1): 107–28.

Helmreich, Stefan. 2009. *Alien Ocean: Anthropological Voyages in Microbial Seas.* Berkeley: University of California Press.

Helmreich, Stefan. 2014. "The Left Hand of Nature and Culture." *HAU: Journal of Ethnographic Theory* 4 (3): 373–81.

Helmreich, Stefan. 2016. Review of *The Mushroom at the End of the World: On the Possibility of Life in Capitalist Ruins,* by Anna Tsing. *American Ethnologist* 43 (3): 570–72.

Helmreich, Stefan. 2019. "Domesticating Waves in the Netherlands." *Bomb,* no. 146. https://bombmagazine.org/articles/domesticating-waves-in-the-netherlands/.

Hennecke, Stefanie. 2011. "German Ideologies of City and Nature: The Creation and Reception of Schiller Park in Berlin." In *Greening the City: Urban Landscapes in the Twentieth Century,* edited by Dorothee Brantz and Sonja Dümpelmann, 75–94. Charlottesville: University of Virginia Press.

Henrichsen, D. 2000. "Pilgrimages into Kaoko: Herrensafaris, 4×4s, and Settler Illusions." In *New Notes on Kaoko: The Northern Kunene Region in Texts and Photographs,* edited by Giorgio Miescher and Dag Henrichsen, 159–85. Basel: Basler Afrika Bibliographien.

Herzfeld, Michael. 2010. *Anthropology through the Looking-Glass: Critical Ethnography on the Margins of Europe.* New York: Cambridge University Press.

Hess, Sabine, and Bernd Kasparek. 2019. "The Post-2015 European Border Regime. New Approaches in a Shifting Field." *Archivio Antropologico Mediterraneo* 21 (2). http://journals.openedition.org/aam/1812.

Hess, Sabine, Vassilis Tsianos, and Serhat Karakayali. 2009. "Transnational Migration: Theory and Method of an Ethnographic Analysis of Border Regimes." Working Paper No. 55. Institut für Volkskunde/Europäische Ethnologie, University of Munich, April.

Heynen, Nik, Maria Kaika, and Erik Swyngedouw, eds. 2006. *In the Nature of Cities: Urban Political Ecology and the Politics of Urban Metabolism.* New York: Routledge.

Hilbrandt, Hanna. 2021. *Housing in the Margins: Negotiating Urban Formalities in Berlin's Allotment Gardens.* Newark, NJ: Wiley.

Hillman, Felicitas. 2005. "Riders on the Storm: Vietnamese in Germany's Two Migration Systems." In *Asian Migrants and European Labour Market Patterns and Processes of Immigrant Labor Market Insertion in Europe*, edited by Ernst Spaan, Felicitas Hillman, and A. L. van Naerssen, 80–100. New York: Routledge.

Hinchliffe, Steven, Matthew B. Kearnes, Monica Degen, and Sarah Whatmore. 2005. "Urban Wild Things: A Cosmopolitical Experiment." *Environment and Planning D: Society and Space* 23 (5): 643–58.

Hinchliffe, Steven, and Sarah Whatmore. 2006. "Living Cities: Toward a Politics of Conviviality." *Science as Culture* 15 (2): 123–38.

Holmes, Seth M., and Heide Castañeda. 2016. "Representing the European Refugee Crisis in Germany and Beyond: Deservingness and Difference, Life and Death." *American Ethnologist* 43 (1): 12–24. https://anthrosource.onlinelibrary.wiley.com /doi/abs/10.1111/amet.12259.

hooks, bell. 1992. *Black Looks: Race and Representation.* Boston: South End.

Horte. 2019. "Analyse von Rechten Straftaten in 2018 in Märkisch-Oderland der Ag Borg." May 9. https://horte-srb.de/analyse-von-rechten-straftaten-in-2018-in -maerkisch-oderland-der-ag-borg/.

Howe, Cymene, Jessica Lockrem, Hannah Appel, Edward Hackett, Dominic Boyer, Randal Hall, Matthew Schneider-Mayerson, et al. 2016. "Paradoxical Infrastructures: Ruins, Retrofit, and Risk." *Science, Technology, and Human Values* 41 (3): 1–19.

Howell-Ardila, Deborah. 1998. "Berlin's Search for a 'Democratic' Architecture: Post–World War II and Post-unification." *German Politics and Society* 16 (3): 62–85.

Hu, Shiu Ying. 1979. "Ailanthus." *Arnoldia* 39 (2): 29–50.

Hügel, Ika, Chris Lange, May Ayim, Ilona Bubeck, Gülsen Aktas, and Dagmar Schultz, eds. 1993. *Entfernte Verbindungen: Rassismus, Antisemitismus, Klassenunterdrückung.* Berlin: Orlanda Frauenverlag.

Humphrey, Caroline. 2002. "Does the Category Postsocialism Still Make Sense?" In *Postsocialism: Ideals, Ideologies, and Practices in Eurasia*, edited by C. M. Hann, 12–14. London: Routledge.

Hürriyet. 2002. "Yesil aday, Turklere davullu zurnali mangal partisi verdi." August 27. https://www.hurriyet.com.tr/gundem/yesil-aday-turklere-davullu -zurnali-mangal-partisi-verdi-38407906.

Hustak, Carla, and Natasha Myers. 2012. "Involutionary Momentum: Affective Ecologies and the Science of Plant-Insect Encounters." *differences: A Journal of Feminist Cultural Studies* 25 (5): 74–118.

Huyssen, Andreas. 1997. "Voids of Berlin." *Critical Inquiry* 24 (1): 57–81.

Huyssen, Andreas. 2006. "Nostalgia for Ruins." *Grey Room*, no. 23, 6–21.

Ingold, Tim. 2011. *Being Alive: Essays on Movement, Knowledge and Description.* New York: Routledge.

Ismet, Berkan. 2006. "Istanbul köyü." *Radikal*, January 17.

Ivy, Marilyn. 1995. *Discourses of the Vanishing: Modernity, Phantasm, Japan.* Chicago: University of Chicago Press.

Jackisch, Barry. 2009. "Green Germania? Green Space and Urban Planning in Berlin 1900–1945." In *Topography and Literature: Berlin and Modernism*, edited by Richard Zachau, 51–68. Göttingen: V&R Unipress.

Jegathesan, Mythri. 2021. "Black Feminist Plots before the Plantationocene and Anthropology's 'Regional Closets.'" *Feminist Anthropology* 2 (1): 78–93.

Jentsch, Ernst. (1906) 1996. "On the Psychology of the Uncanny." *Angelaki* 2 (1): 7–21.

Jerolmack, Colin. 2007. "Animal Practices, Ethnicity, and Community: The Turkish Pigeon Handlers of Berlin." *American Sociological Review* 72 (6): 874–94.

Jobson, Ryan Cecil. 2020. "The Case for Letting Anthropology Burn: Sociocultural Anthropology in 2019." *American Anthropologist* 122 (2): 259–71.

Johnson, Andrew. 2013. "Progress and Its Ruins: Ghosts, Migrants, and the Uncanny in Thailand." *Cultural Anthropology* 28 (2): 299–319.

Joinda, Fridoon, dir. 2019. *Moria 35.* Joinda Productions.

Jordan, Jennifer A. 2006. *Structures of Memory: Understanding Urban Change in Berlin and Beyond.* Stanford, CA: Stanford University Press.

July, Robert W. 1997. *A History of the African People.* Long Gove, IL: Waveland.

Kaselow, Gerhild. 1999. *Die Schaulust am exotischen Tier: Studien zur Darstellung des zoologischen Gartens in der Malerei des 19. und 20. Jahrhunderts.* Hildeshieim: Georg Olms Verlag.

Kasparek, Bernd. 2021. *Europa Als Grenze: Eine Ethnographie der Grenzschutzagentur Frontex.* Bielefeld: Transcript Verlag.

Keiderling, Gerhard. 1999a. "Berlin ist endlich trümmerfrei." *Probleme/Projekte/Prozesse* 3:39–43. https://berlingeschichte.de/bms/bmstxt99/9903prog.htm.

Keiderling, Gerhard. 1999b. "'Mindestens 20 Jahre': Der Beginn der Enttrümmerung Berlins." *Probleme/Projekte/Prozesse* 1:36–39. https://berlingeschichte.de/bms/bmstxt99/9901prog.htm.

Kelly, Natasha. 2019. *Millis Erwachen: Schwarze Frauen, Kunst und Widerstand/Milli's Awakening: Black Women, Art and Resistance.* Berlin: Orlanda.

Kimmelman, Michael. 2007. "In Germany, Wild for Winnetou." *New York Times*, September 12. https://nyti.ms/2k91NF6.

Kimmerer, Robin Wall. 2015. *Braiding Sweetgrass: Indigenous Wisdom, Scientific Knowledge, and the Teachings of Plants.* Minneapolis: Milkweed.

Kimmerer, Robin Wall. 2020. "The Serviceberry: An Economy of Abundance." *Emergence Magazine*, December. Accessed April 1, 2022. https://emergencemagazine.org/essay/the-serviceberry/.

Kırıkkanat, Mine. 2005. "Halkımız Eğleniyor." *Radikal*, July 27.

Kirksey, Eben, and Stefan Helmreich. 2010. "The Emergence of Multispecies Ethnography." *Cultural Anthropology* 25 (4): 545–76.

Kleinman, Julie. 2019. *Adventure Capital: Migration and the Making of an African Hub in Paris.* Berkeley: University of California Press.

Klima, Alan. 2002. *The Funeral Casino: Meditation, Massacre, and Exchange with the Dead in Thailand.* Princeton, NJ: Princeton University Press.

Knecht, Michi. 1999. *Die andere Seite der Stadt: Armut und Ausgrenzung in Berlin.* Vienna: Böhlau Verlag.

Koçal, Ece. 2005. "Caddebostan'da şenlik var." *Sabah*, July 28.

Kohn, Eduardo. 2007. "How Dogs Dream: Amazonian Natures and the Politics of Transspecies Engagement." *American Ethnologist* 34 (1): 3–24.

Kohn, Eduardo. 2013. *How Forests Think: Toward an Anthropology beyond the Human*. Berkeley: University of California Press.

Kos, Alfred. 2004. "Lois und Franziska Weinberger." Exhibition text, evn sammlung. Accessed 2018. http://www. evn-sammlung.at/asp/asp/showwerk2.asp?lang=en &werkid=91&persid=49.

Kosnick, Kira. 2007. *Migrant Media: Turkish Broadcasting and Multicultural Politics in Berlin*. Bloomington: Indiana University Press.

Kowarik, Ingo. 1992. "Stadtnatur—Annäherung an die 'wahre Natur' der Stadt." In *Ansprüche an Freiflächen im urbanen Raum*, edited by Jürgen Gill, 63–81. Mainz: Stadt Mainz.

Kowarik, Ingo. 1995. *Dynamik und Konstanz: Festschrift für Herbert Sukopp*. Schriftenreihe für Vegetationskunde, Bd. 27. Bonn-Bad Godesberg: Bundesamt für Naturschutz.

Kowarik, Ingo. 2005. "Welche Natur wollen wir schützen und welche sind wir bereit zuzulassen? Ein Plädoyer für ein offenes Naturschutzkonzept." In *Die Erfindung von Natur und Landschaft*, edited by Albert Schmidt, 46–55. Denkanstösse, Bd. 3. Mainz: Stiftung Natur und Umwelt Rheinland-Pfalz.

Kowarik, Ingo, and Ina Säumel. 2007. "Biological Flora of Central Europe: Ailanthus altissima (Mill.) Swingle." *Perspectives in Plant Ecology, Evolution, and Systematics* 8 (4): 207–37.

Kreh, Wilhelm. 1955. "Das Ergebnis der Vegetationsentwicklung auf dem Stuttgarter Trümmerschutt." *Mitteilungen der Floristisch-Soziologischen Arbeitsgemeinschaft* 5:69–75.

Kropp, Cordula. 2005. "River Landscaping in Second Modernity." In *Making Things Public: Atmospheres of Democracy*, edited by Bruno Latour and Peter Weibel, 486–91. Cambridge, MA: MIT Press; Karlsruhe: ZKM.

LabourNet Germany ARCHIV! n.d. "Kampagne zur Abschaffung der Residenzpflicht: Den Apartheidgesetzen in Deutschland." Accessed February 15, 2018. http://archiv.labournet.de/diskussion/grundrechte/asyl/resiweg.html.

Lachmund, Jens. 2003. "Exploring the City of Rubble: Botanical Fieldwork in Bombed Cities in Germany after World War II." *Osiris* 18 (Science and the City): 234–54.

Lachmund, Jens. 2004a. "Knowing the Urban Wastelands: Ecological Expertise as Local Process." In *Earthly Politics: Local and Global in Environmental Governance*, edited by Sheila Jasanoff and Marybeth Long Martello, 241–61. Cambridge, MA: MIT Press.

Lachmund, Jens. 2004b. "Mapping Urban Nature: Bio-ecological Expertise and Urban Planning." In *Experts in Science and Society*, edited by Elke Kurz-Milcke and Gerd Gigerenzer, 231–48. New York: Springer.

Lachmund, Jens. 2007. "Ecology in a Walled City: Researching Urban Wildlife in Post-war Berlin." *Endeavour* 31 (2): 78–82.

Lachmund, Jens. 2013. *Greening Berlin: The Co-production of Science, Politics, and Urban Nature*. Cambridge, MA: MIT Press.

Lack, Walter. 2002. "Botanische Handbücher für die deutschen Kolonien in Afrika." In *Kolonialmetropole Berlin: Eine Spurensuche*, edited by Ulrich van der Heyden and Joachim Zeller, 112–14. Berlin: Berlin Edition.

Ladd, Brian. 1997. *Ghosts of Berlin: Confronting German History in the Urban Landscape*. Chicago: University of Chicago Press.

Lampland, Martha. 1995. *The Object of Labor: Commodification of Agrarian Life in Hungary*. Chicago: University of Chicago Press.

Land Brandenburg. 2022. "Brandenburgs Agrar und Umwelt in Daten und Zahlen." Accessed May 25, 2022. https://mluk.brandenburg.de/mluk/de/service/daten-und-fakten/.

Landratsamt Märkisch Oderland. 2022. *Landkreis Märkisch Oderland Statistischer Jahresbericht 2021*. Seelow: Landkreis Märkisch-Oderland.

Lange, Katrin. 2011. "Mitte beschliesst Grillverbot im Tiergarten." *Berliner Zeitung*, November 18.

Lanz, Stephan. 2005. "If You Make It in Istanbul, You Can Make It Anywhere: On Urbanites and Anti-urbanites, Village and Metropolis." In *Self Service City: Istanbul*, edited by Orhan Esen and Stephan Lanz. Berlin: B_books.

Lanz, Stephan. 2007. *Berlin aufgemischt: Abendländisch—multikulturell—kosmopolitisch? Die politische Konstruktion einer Einwanderungsstadt*. Bielefeld: Transcript Verlag.

Larkin, Brian. 2013. "The Politics and Poetics of Infrastructure." *Annual Review of Anthropology* 42:327–43.

LASV (Landesamt für Soziales und Versorgung des Landes Brandenburg). 2011. "Brandenburger Sozialindikatoren 2011." Accessed December 20, 2020. http://www.lasv.brandenburg.de/sixcms/detail.php/bb1.c.172281.de.

LASV (Landesamt für Soziales und Versorgung des Landes Brandenburg). 2021. "Brandenburger Sozialindikatoren 2021." Accessed May 25, 2022. https://lasv.brandenburg.de/lasv/de/soziales/sozialberichterstattung/publikationen/#aktuelles.

Latour, Bruno. 2004. *Politics of Nature: How to Bring the Sciences into Democracy*. Cambridge, MA: Harvard University Press.

Latour, Bruno. 2013. *Modes of Existence: An Anthropology of the Moderns*. Cambridge, MA: Harvard University Press.

Latour, Bruno, and Peter Weibel. 2005. "The Parliament of Nature." In *Making Things Public: Atmospheres of Democracy*, edited by Bruno Latour and Peter Weibel, 458–59. Cambridge, MA: MIT Press.

Laurance, William F., Henrique E. M. Nascimento, Susan G. Laurance, Ana Andrade, Robert M. Ewers, Kyle E. Harms, Regina C. C. Luizao, and José E. Ribeiro. 2007. "Habitat Fragmentation, Variable Edge Effects, and the Landscape-Divergence Hypothesis." *PLoS One* 2 (10): e1017.

Lauser, Andrea. 2004. *"Ein guter Mann ist harte Arbeit": Eine ethnographische Studie zu philippinischen Heiratsmigrantinnen*. Bielefeld: Transcript Verlag.

Lawton, Philip, Karen E. Till, Sandra Jasper, Alexander Vasudevan, Sonja Dümpelmann, Michael Flitner, Matthew Beach, Catherine Nash, and Matthew Gandy. 2019. Review of *Natura Urbana: The Brachen of Berlin*, directed by Matthew Gandy. *AAG Review of Books* 7 (3): 214–27.

Lee, Erica Violet. 2016. "In Defense of the Wastelands: A Survival Guide." *Guts*, no. 7. http://gutsmagazine.ca/wastelands/.

Lefebvre, Henri. 1996. *Writings on Cities*. Translated and edited by Eleonore Kaufman and Elizabeth Lebas. Oxford: Blackwell.

Le Guin, Ursula. 1989. *Dancing at the Edge of the World: Thoughts on Words, Women, Places*. New York: Grove.

Lekan, Thomas. 2004. *Imagining the Nation in Nature: Landscape Preservation and German Identity 1885–1945*. Cambridge, MA: Harvard University Press.

Lekan, Thomas. 2020. *Our Gigantic Zoo: A German Quest to Save the Serengeti*. Oxford: Oxford University Press.

Lepselter, Susan. 2005. "Why Rachel Isn't Buried at Her Grave: Ghosts, UFOs, and a Place in the West." In *Histories of the Future*, edited by Daniel Rosenberg and Susan Harding, 255–80. Durham, NC: Duke University Press.

Lettre International. 2009. "Klasse statt Masse: Von der Hauptstadt der Transferleistungen zur Metropole der Eliten." Thilo Sarrazin im Gespräch mit Frank Berberich. *Lettre International*, no. 86. https://www.lettre.de/content/frank -berberich_klasse-statt-masse.

Lewis, Diane. 1973. "Anthropology and Colonialism." *Current Anthropology* 14 (5): 581–602.

Li, Tanya Murray, and Pujo Semedi. 2021. *Plantation Life: Corporate Occupation in Indonesia's Oil Palm Zone*. Durham, NC: Duke University Press.

Liboiron, Max. 2021. *Pollution Is Colonialism*. Durham, NC: Duke University Press.

Light, Andrew. 1999. "Boyz in the Woods: Urban Wilderness in American Cinema." In *The Nature of Cities: Ecocriticism and Urban Environments*, edited by Michael Bennett and David Teague, 137–56. Tucson: University of Arizona Press.

Light, Jennifer. 2009. *The Nature of Cities: Ecological Visions and the American Urban Professions, 1920–1960*. Baltimore, MD: Johns Hopkins University Press.

Limón, José. 1994. *Dancing with the Devil: Society and Cultural Poetics in Mexican American South Texas*. Madison: University of Wisconsin Press.

Lindqvist, Sven. 2001. *A History of Bombing*. New York: New Press.

Linke, Uli. 1999a. *Blood and Nation: The European Aesthetics of Race*. Philadelphia: University of Pennsylvania Press.

Linke, Uli. 1999b. "Formations of White Public Space: Racial Aesthetics, Body Politics and the Nation." *Transforming Anthropology* 8 (1): 129–61.

Linke, Uli. 1999c. *German Bodies: Race and Representation after Hitler*. London: Routledge.

Linke, Uli. 2014. "Racializing Cities, Naturalizing Space: The Seductive Appeal of Iconicities of Dispossession." *Antipode* 46 (5): 1222–39.

Linke, Uli. 2015. "Mobile Imaginaries, Portable Signs: Global Consumption and Representations of Slum Life." In *Tourism and the Geographies of Inequality: The New Global Slumming Phenomenon*, edited by Fabian Frenzel and Ko Koens, 100–125. New York: Routledge.

Liu, Roseann, and Savannah Shange. 2018. "Toward Thick Solidarity: Theorizing Empathy in Social Justice Movements." *Radical Historical Review*, no. 131, 189–98.

Lorbek, Maja, and Milena Martinsen. 2015. "Allotment Garden Dwellings: Exploring Tradition and Legal Framework." *Urbani Izziv* 26:98–113.

Lorimer, Jamie, and Clemens Driessen. 2016. "From 'Nazi Cows' to Cosmopolitan 'Ecological Engineers': Specifying Rewilding through a History of Heck Cattle." *Annals of the American Association of Geographers* 106 (3): 631–52.

LUA (Landesumweltamt Brandenburg). 2004. *Grosschutzgebiete. Modellregionen für Schutz und Nutzung Brandenburger Landschaften: Eine Sozio-ökonomische Analyse.* Potsdam: Landesumweltamt Brandenburg.

Lüneburg, Anja. 2006. "Gesundheitliche Situation und zukünftiger Versorgungsbedarf von älteren türkischen Arbeitsmigranten." MA thesis, Hamburg University of Applied Sciences.

MacCormack, Carol, and Marilyn Strathern, eds. 1980. *Nature, Culture and Gender.* Cambridge: Cambridge University Press.

MacDonogh, Giles. 1997. *Berlin: A Portrait of Its History, Architecture, and Society.* New York: St. Martin's.

Maestri, Gaja. 2017. "The Contentious Sovereignties of the Camp: Political Contention among State and Non-state Actors in Italian Roma Camps." *Political Geography* 60 (September): 213–22.

Malkki, Liisa. 1992. "National Geographic: The Rooting of Peoples and the Territorialization of National Identity among Scholars and Refugees." *Cultural Anthropology* 7 (1): 22–44.

Malkki, Liisa. 1995. "Refugees and Exile: From Refugee Studies to the National Order of Things." *Annual Review of Anthropology* 24:495–523.

Mallwitz, Gudrun. 2013. "Brandenburg hat 73% mehr Flüchtlinge als vor einem Jahr." *Berliner Morgenpost,* June 29.

Malter, Bettina. 2014. "Vietnamesen in Berlin: Der Nord-Süd-Konflikt." *Tagesspiegel,* October 2. https://www.tagesspiegel.de/berlin/vietnamesen-in-berlin-der-nord-sued-konflikt/10786964.html.

Mandel, Ruth. 1996. "A Place of Their Own: Contesting and Defining Places in Berlin's Migrant Community." In *Making Muslim Space in North America and Europe,* edited by Barbara Metcalf, 147–66. Berkeley: University of California Press.

Mandel, Ruth. 2008. *Cosmopolitan Anxieties: Turkish Challenges to Citizenship and Belonging in Germany.* Durham, NC: Duke University Press.

Marcus, George. 1995. "Ethnography in/of the World System: The Emergence of Multi-sited Ethnography." *Annual Review of Anthropology* 24:95–117.

Marcuse, Peter. 2006. "The Down Side Dangers in the Social City Program: Contradictory Potentials in German Social Policy." *German Politics and Society* 24 (4): 122–30.

Masco, Joseph. 2005. "A Notebook on Desert Modernism: From the Nevada Test Site to Liberace's 200-Pound Suit." In *Histories of the Future,* edited by Susan Harding and David Rosenberg, 19–49. Durham, NC: Duke University Press.

Masco, Joseph. 2006. *Nuclear Borderlands: The Manhattan Project in Post–Cold War New Mexico.* Princeton, NJ: Princeton University Press.

Masco, Joseph. 2008. "Survival Is Your Business: Engineering Ruins and Affect in Nuclear America." *Cultural Anthropology* 22 (2): 361–98.

Masco, Joseph. 2014. *The Theater of Operations: National Security Affect from the Cold War to the War on Terror*. Durham, NC: Duke University Press.

Masco, Joseph. 2017. "The Crisis in Crisis." *Current Anthropology* 58 (S15): S65–76. https://doi.org/10.1086/688695.

Mathews, Andrew. 2003. "Suppressing Fire and Memory: Environmental Degradation and Political Restoration in the Sierra Juárez of Oaxaca, 1887–2001." *Environmental History* 8 (1): 77–108.

Mbembe, Achille. 2001. *On the Postcolony*. Berkeley: University of California Press.

Mbembe, Achille. 2003. "Necropolitics." *Public Culture* 15 (1): 11–40.

Mbembe, Achille. 2020. "The Universal Right to Breathe." Translated by Carolyn Shread. *Critical Inquiry* (blog), April 13. https://critinq.wordpress.com/2020/04/13/the-universal-right-to-breathe/.

McGrane, Sally. 2009. "Berlin's Poverty Protects It from Downturn." *Spiegel Online*, March 4. https://www.spiegel.de/international/germany/can-t-even-afford-a-crisis-berlin-s-poverty-protects-it-from-downturn-a-611086.html.

McNeur, Catherine. 2018. "The Tree That Still Grows in Brooklyn, and Almost Everywhere Else." *The Gotham Center for New York City History* (blog), January 4. https://www.gothamcenter.org/blog/the-tree-that-still-grows-in-brooklyn-and-almost-everywhere-else.

Meiu, George Paul. 2008. "Riefenstahl on Safari: Embodied Contemplation in East Africa." *Anthropology Today* 24 (2): 18–22.

Merxmüller, Hermann. 1952. "Änderungen des Florenbildes am Münchener Südbahnhof." *Berichte der Bayerischen Botanischen Gesellschafr zur Erforschung der heimischen Flora* 29:37–47.

Meyer-Renschhausen, Elisabeth, and Anne Holl, eds. 2000. *Die Wiederkehr der Gärten: Kleinlandwirtschaft im Zeitalter der Globalisierung*. Innsbruck: Studien Verlag.

Micosse-Aikins, Sandrine. 2017. "Vorwärtsgehen ohne Zurück zu Blicken: Eine kolonialismuskritische aktivistische Perspektive auf das Humboldtforum." In *Decolonize the City! Zur Kolonialität der Stadt—Gespräche, Aushandlungen, Perspektiven*, edited by Zwischenraum Kollektiv, 119–33. Münster: Unrast Verlag.

Miliyet. 2000. "Berlin Duvarı'na Turkish kondu." Accessed July 25, 2020. http://www.milliyet.com.tr/2000/02/27/haber/hab03.html.

Mitchell, Don. 2003. *The Right to the City: Social Justice and the Fight for Public Space*. New York: Guilford.

Mitchell, Timothy. 2002. *Rule of Experts*. Berkeley: University of California Press.

Mitchell, William John Thomas. 1994. "Imperial Landscape." In *Landscape and Power*, edited by William John Thomas Mitchell, 5–34. Chicago: University of Chicago Press.

Mitman, Gregg. 1992. *The State of Nature: Ecology, Community, and American Social Thought, 1900–1950*. Chicago: University of Chicago Press.

MLUK (Ministerium f. Landwirtschaft, Umwelt und Klimaschutz). 2021. "Bürgerbewegung für ländliche Räume." Accessed June 7, 2022. https://mluk.brandenburg

.de/mluk/de/aktuelles/presseinformationen/detail/~04-11-2021-unser-dorf-hat
-zukunft.

Moore, Donald, Jake Kosek, and Anand Pandian, eds. 2003. *Race, Nature, and the Politics of Difference*. Durham, NC: Duke University Press.

Moore, Donald, Anand Pandian, and Jake Kosek. 2003. "The Cultural Politics of Race and Nature: Terrains of Power and Practice." In *Race, Nature, and the Politics of Difference*, edited by Donald Moore, Jake Kosek, and Anand Pandian, 1–70. Durham, NC: Duke University Press.

Moss, Timothy. 2020. *Remaking Berlin: A History of the City through Infrastructure, 1920–2020*. Cambridge, MA: MIT Press.

Mosse, George. 1985. *Toward the Final Solution: A History of European Racism*. Madison: University of Wisconsin Press.

MOZ. 2010a. "Uckermärkischem Tabakanbau droht das Aus." *Märkische Oderzeitung* magazine, October 12.

MOZ. 2010b. "Weniger Arbeitslose." *Märkische Oderzeitung* magazine, September 30.

MOZ. 2011. "Wildes Brandenburg." *Märkische Oderzeitung* magazine. Accessed May 30, 2011. http://www.moz.de/themen/wildes-brandenburg/.

MUGV. 2011. "Nationale Naturlandschaften Brandenburgs." Ministerium für Umwelt-, Gesundheit- und Verbraucherschutz. http://www.mugv.brandenburg.de.

Müller, Christa. 2000. "Wurzeln Schlagen in der Migration." *Das Parlament* 3–4:11.

Müller, Christa. 2007. "Interkulturelle Gärten: Urbane Orte der Subsistenzproduktion und der Vielfalt." *Deutsche Zeitschrift für Kommunalwissenschaften* 1:5–67.

Müller, Christa. 2009. "Die neuen Gärten in der Stadt." In *Mind the Park: Planungsräume, Nutzersichten, Kunstvorfälle*, edited by Thomas Kästle, 84–89. Oldenburg: Frühwerk Verlag.

Müller, K. 1950. "Beiträge zur Kenntnis der eingeschleppten Pflanzen Württembergs." *Mitteilungshefte des Verein für Naturwissenschaft und Mathematik, Ulm e. V.* 23:86–116.

Munn, Nancy D. 1992. *The Fame of Gawa: A Symbolic Study of Value Transformation in a Massim (Papua New Guinea) Society*. Durham, NC: Duke University Press.

Myers, Natasha. 2017a. "From the Anthropocene to the Planthroposcene: Designing Gardens for Plant/People Involution." *History and Anthropology* 28 (3): 297–301.

Myers, Natasha. 2017b. "Ungrid-able Ecologies: Decolonizing the Ecological Sensorium in a 10,000 Year-Old NaturalCultural Happening." *Catalyst: Feminism, Theory, Technoscience* 3 (2): 1–24.

Myers, Natasha. 2019. "From Edenic Apocalypse to Gardens against Eden: Plants and People in and after the Anthropocene." In *Infrastructure, Environment, and Life in the Anthropocene*, edited by Kregg Hetherington, 115–48. Durham, NC: Duke University Press.

Myers, Natasha. 2020. "After the Fires, Are We Invited into Moral Community with Trees?" Interview by Waleed Aly and Scott Stephens. *The Minefield* (podcast), ABC National Radio, January 29. Audio, 43:47. https://www.abc.net.au/radionational/programs/theminefield/after-the-fires,-are-we-invited-to-moral-community-with-trees/11901494.

Naranch, Bradley, and Geoff Eley, eds. 2014. *German Colonialism in a Global Age*. Durham, NC: Duke University Press.

Navaro-Yashin, Yael. 2012. *The Make-Believe Space: Affective Geography in a Postwar Polity*. Durham, NC: Duke University Press.

Nelson, Arvid. 2005. *Cold War Ecology: Forests, Farms, and People in the East German Landscape, 1945–1989*. New Haven, CT: Yale University Press.

Nghi Ha, Kien. 2006. "Inside Out: Integration as Politics of Postcolonial Exclusion." *Shedhalle-Zeitung, Zürich, Rote Fabrik* (Winter): 16–17.

Nghi Ha, Kien. 2010. "Integration as Colonial Pedagogy of Postcolonial Immigrants and People of Color: A German Case Study." In *Decolonizing European Sociology: Transdisciplinary Approaches*, edited by Encarnación Gutiérrez Rodríguez, Manuela Boatcă, and Sérgio Costa, 161–78. Farnham, UK: Ashgate.

Nghi Ha, Kien, ed. 2012. *Asiatisch Deutsche: Vietnamesische Diaspora and Beyond*. Berlin: Assoziation A Verlag.

Niendorf, Jörg. 2008. "Baracke mit Weltruhm." *Berliner Morgenpost*, June 10.

Nishime, Leilani, and Kim D. Hester Williams, eds. 2018. *Racial Ecologies*. Seattle: University of Washington Press.

Nixon, Rob. 2011. *Slow Violence and the Environmentalism of the Poor*. Cambridge, MA: Harvard University Press.

Njoh, Ambe. 1997. "Colonial Spatial Development Policies, Economic Instability, and Urban Public Transportation in Cameroon." *Cities* 14 (3): 133–43.

Oguntoye, Katharina. 1997. *Eine afro-deutsche Geschichte: Zur Lebenssituation von Afrikanern und Afro-Deutschen in Deutschland von 1884 bis 1950*. Berlin: HoHo Verlag.

Oguntoye, Katharina. 2004. "Afrikanische Zuwanderung nach Deutschland 1884–1945." Bundeszentrale für politische Bildung, July 30. https://www.bpb.de/gesellschaft/migration/afrikanische-diaspora/59383/zuwanderung-1884-1945?p=0.

Ong, Aihwa. 1996. "Cultural Citizenship as Subject Making: Immigrants Negotiate Racial and Cultural Boundaries in the United States." *Current Anthropology* 37(5): 737–62.

Ong, Aihwa, and Ananya Roy. 2011. *Worlding Cities: Asian Experiments and the Art of Being Global*. London: Wiley.

Onken, Henning. 2008. "Sarrazin: So sollten Arbeitslose einkaufen." *Tagesspiegel*, February 11.

Opitz, May, May Ayim, Katharina Oguntoye, and Dagmar Schultz, eds. 1992. *Showing Our Colors: Afro-German Women Speak Out*. Amherst: University of Massachusetts Press.

Orlow, Dietrich. 1999. *A History of Modern Germany: 1871 to Present*. Upper Saddle River, NJ: Prentice Hall.

Oswalt, Philipp. 2006a. *Atlas of Shrinking Cities*. Ostfildern: Hatje Kantz.

Oswalt, Philipp, ed. 2006b. *Shrinking Cities, Vols. 1 and 2*. Ostfildern: Hatje Kantz.

Otyakmaz, Özlem Berrin. 1995. *Auf allen Stühlen: Das Selbstverständnis junger türkischer Migrantinnen in Deutschland*. Köln: ISP.

Özkan, Derya. 2008. "The Misuse Value of Space: Spatial Practices and the Production of Space in Istanbul." PhD diss., University of Rochester.

Özkök, Ertugrul. 2005. "Who Is Right? Mine or Ahmet?" *Hürriyet*, August 3.

Özyürek, Esra. 2014. *Being German, Becoming Muslim: Race, Religion, and Conversion in the New Europe*. Princeton, NJ: Princeton University Press.

Parreñas, Juno. 2018. *Decolonizing Extinction: The Work of Care in Orangutan Rehabilitation*. Durham, NC: Duke University Press.

Partridge, Damani. 2012. *Hypersexuality and Headscarves: Race, Sex, and Citizenship in the New Germany*. Bloomington: Indiana University Press.

Pasch, Nele. 2013. "Viel Gedränge um wenig Platz." *Der Tagesspiegel*, May 5.

Pataya, Ruenkaew. 2003. *Heirat nach Deutschland: Motive und Hintergründe thailändisch-deutscher Eheschliessungen*. Frankfurt: Campus.

Pataya, Ruenkaew. 2009. "Female Transnational Migration from Thailand: Like Thirty Years Before?" *Pacific News* 32 (July–August): 22–24.

Paxson, Heather. 2013. *The Life of Cheese: Crafting Food and Value in America*. Berkeley: University of California Press.

Pécoud, Antoine. 2002. "Cosmopolitanism and Business among German Turks in Berlin." *Journal of the Society for the Anthropology of Europe* 2 (1): 2–12.

Pfeiffer, H. 1957. "Pflanzliche Gesellschaftsbildung auf dem Trümmerschutt ausgebombter Städte." *Vegetatio* 7 (5–6): 301–20.

Phillips, Denise. 2003. "Friends of Nature: Urban Sociability and Regional Natural History in Dresden 1800–1850." *Osiris* 18 (Science and the City): 43–59.

Picker, Giovanni, Margaret Greenfields, and David Smith. 2015. "Colonial Refractions: The 'Gypsy Camp' as Spatio-Racial Political Technology." *City* 19 (5): 741–52.

Pieper, Tobias. 2008. *Die Gegenwart der Lager*. Münster: Westfälisches Dampfboot.

Piesche, Peggy, ed. 2012. *"Euer Schweigen schützt Euch nicht": Audre Lorde und die Schwarze Frauenbewegung in Deutschland*. Berlin: Orlanda-Frauenverlag.

Piesche, Peggy. 2017. "Der 'Fortschritt' der Aufklärung: Kants 'Race' und die Zentrierung des weißen Subjekts." In *Mythen, Masken und Subjekte: Kritische Weissseinsforschung in Deutschland*, edited by Susan Arndt, Maureen Maisha Eggers, Grada Kilomba, and Peggy Piesche, 30–40. Münster: Unrast Verlag.

Povinelli, Elizabeth. 2002. *The Cunning of Recognition: Indigenous Alterities and the Making of Australian Multiculturalism*. Durham, NC: Duke University Press.

Pratt, Mary Louise. 1992. *Imperial Eyes: Travel Writing and Transculturation*. New York: Routledge.

Pred, Allan. 2000. *Even in Sweden: Racisms, Racialized Spaces, and the Popular Geographic Imagination*. Berkeley: University of California Press.

PRO ASYL. 2011. "PRO ASYL zur Asylstatistik 2010." Press release, January 17. https://www.proasyl.de/pressemitteilung/pro-asyl-zur-asylstatistik-2010/.

PRO ASYL. 2020. "Tod an Europas Außengrenzen." https://www.proasyl.de/thema/tod-an-den-aussengrenzen/.

Proglio, Gabriele, Camilla Hawthorne, Ida Danewid, P. Khalil Saucier, Giuseppe Grimaldi, Angelica Pesarini, Timothy Raeymaekers, Giulia Grechi, and Vivian Gerrand. 2021. *The Black Mediterranean: Bodies, Borders, and Citizenship*. London: Palgrave Macmillan.

Puff, Helmut. 2010. "Ruins as Models: Displaying Destruction in Postwar Germany." In *Ruins of Modernity*, edited by Julia Hell and Andreas Schoenle, 253–69. Durham, NC: Duke University Press.

Puig de la Bellacasa, María. 2017. *Matters of Care: Speculative Ethics in More than Human Worlds*. Minneapolis: University of Minnesota Press.

Pundt, Hermann. 1972. *Schinkel's Berlin: A Study in Environmental Planning*. Cambridge, MA: Harvard University Press.

Rada, Uwe. 1997. *Hauptstadt der Verdrängung: Berliner Zukunft zwischen Kiez und Metropole*. Berlin: Verlag Schwarze Risse.

Rada, Uwe. 2004. *Zwischenland: Europäische Geschichten aus dem deutsch-polnischen Grenzgebiet*. Berlin-Brandenburg: BeBra.

Rademacher, Anne, and K. Sivaramakrishnan, eds. 2013. *Ecologies of Urbanism in India*. Hong Kong: Hong Kong University Press.

Raffles, Hugh. 2002. *In Amazonia: A Natural History*. Princeton, NJ: Princeton University Press.

Raffles, Hugh. 2010. *Insectopedia*. New York: Pantheon Books.

Raffles, Hugh. 2012. "Twenty-Five Years Is a Long Time." *Cultural Anthropology* 27 (3): 526–34.

Rajan, Ravi. 2006. *Modernizing Nature: Forestry and Imperial Eco-Development 1800–1950*. Oxford: Oxford University Press.

RBB. 2010. "Brandenburg schrumpft weiter." RBB, May 12. http://www.rbb-online. de/nachrichten/politik/2010_05/brandenburg_schrumpft.html.

Red Haircrow, dir. 2018. *Forget Winnetou! Loving in the Wrong Way*. United States: Flying with Red Haircrow Productions.

Reichow, H. B. 1948. *Organische Stadtbaukunst: Von der Grossstadt zur Stadtlandschaft*. Braunschweig: Westermann.

Reidl, Konrad. 2005. "Ruderalflächen." In *Handbuch Naturschutz und Landschaftspflege: Kompendium zu Schutz und Entwicklung von Lebensräumen und Landschaften*, edited by Werner Konold, Reinhard Böcker, and Ulrich Hampicke, 1–9. Landsberg: Ecomed.

Reuters. 2009. "Garden Blooms in Shade of Berlin Wall." *Today's Zaman*, August 20.

Richter, Christine. 1999. "Liepelt freut sich über den Grill." *Berliner Zeitung*, August 7.

Riechelmann, Cord. 2004. *Wilde Tiere in der Grosstadt*. Berlin: Nicolaische Verlagsbuchhandlung.

Ringel, Felix. 2018. *Back to the Postindustrial Future: An Ethnography of Germany's Fastest Shrinking City*. New York: Berghahn Books.

Ringel, Felix. 2021. "Postsocialist Dialectics or Postindustrial Critique? On Discomfort in a Former Socialist Model City in East Germany." *Europe Asia Studies* 73 (9): 1748–67.

Rink, Dieter. 2009. "Wilderness: The Nature of Urban Shrinkage? The Debate on Urban Restructuring and Restoration in Eastern Germany." *Nature and Culture* 4 (3): 275–92.

Rittner, Marianne. 2005. "Grillverbot bleibt bestehen." *Berliner Morgenpost*, June 11.

Rofel, Lisa. 1994. "Yearnings: Televisual Love and Melodramatic Politics in Contemporary China." *American Ethnologist* 21 (4): 700–722.

Rofel, Lisa. 1999. *Other Modernities: Gendered Yearnings in China after Socialism.* Berkeley: University of California Press.

Rofel, Lisa. 2007. *Desiring China: Experiments in Neoliberalism, Sexuality, and Public Culture.* Durham, NC: Duke University Press.

Ronneberger, Klaus, and Vassilis Tsianos. 2009. "Panische Räume: Das Ghetto und die Parallelgesellschaft." In *No Integration?! Kulturwissenschaftliche Beiträge zur Integrationsdebatte in Europa,* edited by Sabine Hess, Jana Binder, and Johannes Moser, 137–52. Bielefeld: Transcript Verlag.

Rosaldo, Renato. 1989. "Imperialist Nostalgia." *Representations,* no. 26, 107–22.

Rosaldo, Renato. 1993. *Culture and Truth: The Remaking of Social Analysis.* Boston: Beacon.

Rose, Deborah Bird. 2004. *Reports from a Wild Country: Ethics for Decolonization.* Sydney: University of New South Wales Press.

Rosol, Marit. 2006. "Gemeinschaftsgärten in Berlin: Eine qualitative Untersuchung zu Potentialen und Risiken bürgerschaftlichen Engagements im Grünflächenbereich vor dem Hintergrund von Staat und Planung." PhD diss., Humboldt University, Berlin.

Rosol, Marit. 2012. "Community Volunteering as Neoliberal Strategy? Green Space Production in Berlin." *Antipode* 44 (1): 239–57.

Ross, Andrew. 1999. "The Social Claim on Urban Ecology." In *The Nature of Cities: Ecocriticism and Urban Environments,* edited by Michael Bennett and David Teague, 15–30. Tucson: University of Arizona Press.

Roth, Jenni. 2008. "Arbeitslose zeigen wie man für 4.33 Euro satt wird." *Die Welt,* February 16. http://www.welt.de/politik/article3211600/.

Roy, Ananya, and Nezar Al Sayyad, eds. 2004. *Urban Informality: Transnational Perspectives from the Middle East, Latin America, and South Asia.* Lanham, MD: Lexington Books.

Roy, Ananya, and Aihwa Ong, eds. 2011. *Worlding Cities: Asian Experiments and the Art of Being Global.* London: Wiley.

Rubin, Eli. 2016. *Amnesiopolis: Modernity, Space, and Memory in East Germany.* Oxford: Oxford University Press.

Sarrazin, Thilo. 2010. *Deutschland schafft sich ab.* München: DVA.

Satsuka, Shiho. 2015. *Nature in Translation: Freedom, Subjectivity, and Japanese Tourism Encounters in Canada.* Durham, NC: Duke University Press.

Sawyer, Lena. 2006. "Racialization, Gender, and the Negotiation of Power in Stockholm's African Dance Courses." In *Globalization and Race: Transformations in the Cultural Production of Blackness,* edited by Kamari Clarke and Deborah Thomas, 316–34. Durham, NC: Duke University Press.

Sax, Boria. 1997. "What Is a 'Jewish Dog'? Konrad Lorenz and the Cult of Wildness." *Society and Animals* 5 (1): 3–21.

Sax, Boria. 2000. *Animals in the Third Reich: Pets, Scapegoats, and the Holocaust.* London: Continuum.

Schama, Simon. 1995. *Landscape and Memory.* New York: Alfred Knopf.

Schicks, Reiner. 1995. "Leben im Tiergarten." In *Denk-mal Tiergarten: Geschichte, Bedeutung, Gefahren, Hauptstadtbau*, edited by Lydia Schend, 7–16. Berlin: Edition Baumverlag.

Schiebinger, Londa. 2004. *Plants and Empire: Colonial Bioprospecting in the Atlantic World*. Cambridge, MA: Harvard University Press.

Schildt, Axel. 2002. "Urban Reconstruction and Urban Development in Germany after 1945." In *Towards an Urban Nation: Germany since 1780*, edited by Friedrich Lenger, 141–61. Oxford: Berg.

Schilp, Susanne. 2014. "Kleingartenkolonie an der Togostrasse wird nach jahrelangem Streit umbenannt." *Berliner Woche*, August 25.

Schleich, Christa. 2011. "Die Trümmerfrauen des Waldes." Frauen im Forstbereich e.V. http://www.forstfrauen.de.

Schmiemann, Brigitte, and Katrin Schoelkopf. 2009. "Müll in Parks—Buschkowsky gibt Tiergarten verloren." *Berliner Morgenpost*, April 15.

Schnitzler, Antina. 2013. "Traveling Technologies: Infrastructure, Ethical Regimes, and the Materiality of Politics in South Africa." *Cultural Anthropology* 28 (4): 670–93.

Scholz, Hildemar. 1956. "Die Ruderalvegetation Berlins." PhD diss., Freie Universität Berlin.

Schomaker, Gilbert. 2008. "Sarrazin entwickelt Speiseplan für Hartz-IV-Empfänger." *Berliner Morgenpost*, February 9.

Schwanhäußer, Anja. 2010. *Kosmonauten des Underground: Ethnografie einer Berliner Szene*. Frankfurt: Campus.

Schwartz, Katrina. 2006. *Nature and National Identity after Communism: Globalizing the Ethnoscape*. Pittsburg: University of Pittsburg Press.

Schwenkel, Christina. 2013. "Post/Socialist Affect: Ruination and Reconstruction of the Nation in Urban Vietnam." *Cultural Anthropology* 28 (2): 252–77.

Scott, James. 1998. *Seeing like a State: How Certain Schemes to Improve the Human Condition Have Failed*. New Haven, CT: Yale University Press.

Sebald, W. G. 2004. *On the Natural History of Destruction*. New York: Modern Library.

Seidel-Pielen, Eberhard. 2007. "The Billion-Mark Coup." In *Germany in Transit: Nation and Migration 1955–2005*, edited by Deniz Göktürk, David Gramling, and Anton Kaes, 452–55. Berkeley: University of California Press.

SenStadt (Senatsverwaltung für Stadtentwicklung). 2004. *Grillen in Berlin* (brochure). Berlin.

SenStadt (Senatsverwaltung für Stadtentwicklung). 2009. *Das Grüne Berlin. Green Berlin* (brochure). Berlin.

SenStadt (Senatsverwaltung für Stadtentwicklung). 2012. *Kleingärten in Berlin* (brochure). Berlin.

SenStadt (Senatsverwaltung für Stadtentwicklung). 2014. *Strategie Stadtlandschaft Berlin: natürlich, urban, produktiv* (brochure). Berlin

SenUVK (Senatsverwaltung für Umwelt, Mobilität, Verbraucher- und Klimaschutz). 2022a. "Kleingärten." Accessed May 12, 2022. https://www.berlin.de/sen/uvk/natur-und-gruen/stadtgruen/geschichte/kleingaerten/.

SenUVK (Senatsverwaltung für Umwelt, Mobilität, Verbraucher- und Klimaschutz). 2022b. "Kleingartenentwicklungsplan Berlin 2030." Accessed May 8,
2022. https://www.berlin.de/sen/uvk/natur-und-gruen/stadtgruen/gaertnern-in
-der-stadt/kleingaerten/kleingartenentwicklungsplan/..

SenUVK (Senatsverwaltung für Umwelt, Mobilität, Verbraucher- und Klimaschutz). 2022c. "Öffentliche Grün- und Erholungsanlagen." Accessed April 1,
2022. https://www.berlin.de/sen/uvk/natur-und-gruen/stadtgruen/daten-und
-faktcn/gruenflaecchen gruenanlagen/.

SenUVK (Senatsverwaltung für Umwelt, Mobilität, Verbraucher- und Klimaschutz). 2022d. "Stadtgrün." Accessed April 1, 2022. https://www.berlin.de
/sen/uvk/natur-und-gruen/stadtgruen/geschichte/stadtgruen/.

Shange, Savannah. 2019a. "Black Girl Ordinary: Flesh, Carcerality, and the Refusal
of Ethnography." *Transforming Anthropology* 27(1): 3–21.

Shange, Savannah. 2019b. *Progressive Dystopia: Abolition, Anti-Blackness, and School-
ing in San Francisco*. Durham, NC: Duke University Press.

Sharpe, Christina. 2016. *In the Wake: On Blackness and Being*. Durham, NC: Duke
University Press.

Shaw, Martin. 2006. "War/Krieg." In *Atlas of Shrinking Cities: Atlas der schrumpfen-
den Städte*, edited by Philipp Oswalt, 52–53. Ostfilern: Hatje Kantz.

Shoshan, Nitzan. 2016. *The Management of Hate: Nation, Affect, and the Governance
of Right-Wing Extremism in Germany*. Princeton, NJ: Princeton University Press.

Sieg, Katrin. 2002. *Ethnic Drag: Performing Race, Nation, Sexuality in West Germany*.
Ann Arbor: University of Michigan Press.

Silverstein, Paul A. 2004. *Algeria in France: Transpolitics, Race, and Nation*. Bloomington: Indiana University Press.

Silverstein, Paul A. 2005. "Immigrant Racialization and the New Savage Slot: Race,
Migration, and Immigration in the New Europe." *Annual Review of Anthropology* 34:363–84.

Silverstein, Paul A. 2006. "Guerilla Capitalism and Ghettocentric Cosmopolitanism
on the French Urban Periphery." In *Frontiers of Capital: Ethnographic Reflections
on the New Economy*, edited by Melissa Fisher and Greg Downey, 282–304.
Durham, NC: Duke University Press.

Simmel, Georg. 1983. *Philosophische Kultur*. Berlin: Klaus Wagenbach.

Simonds, Merilyn. 2008. "Guns and Roses." *The Walrus*, February.

Simone, AbdouMaliq. 2004. *For the City Yet to Come: Changing African Life in Four
Cities*. Durham, NC: Duke University Press.

Simone, AbdouMaliq. 2010. *City Life from Jakarta to Dakar: Movements at the Crossroads*. New York: Routledge.

Simone, AbdouMaliq. 2016. "The Uninhabitable? In Between Collapsed and Yet
Still Rigid Distinctions." *Cultural Politics* 12 (2): 135–54.

Simpson, Audra. 2007. "On Ethnographic Refusal: Indigeneity, 'Voice,' and Colonial Citizenship." *Junctures*, no. 9, 67–80.

Simpson, Audra. 2014. *Mohawk Interruptus: Political Life across the Borders of Settler
States*. Durham, NC: Duke University Press.

Small, Ernest. 2006. *Culinary Herbs*. Ottawa: National Research Council Canada.

Smith, Betty. 1943. *A Tree Grows in Brooklyn*. New York: Harper and Brothers.

Smith, Linda Tuhawei. 1999. *Decolonizing Methodologies: Research and Indigenous Peoples*. New York: Zed Books.

Sontag, Susan. 1975. "Fascinating Fascism." *New York Review of Books*, February 6.

Soysal, Levent. 2001. "Diversity of Experience, Experience of Diversity: Turkish Migrant Youth Culture in Berlin." *Cultural Dynamics* 13 (1): 5–28.

Spiegel International. 2008. "Berlin's Poor Should Catch Rats, Says Politician." December 16. https://www.spiegel.de/international/germany/pied-piper-proposal-berlin-s-poor-should-catch-rats-says-politician-a-596705.html.

Spiegel International. 2009. "Former Finance Minister Slams Berlin's Underclass." October 1. http://www.spiegel.de/international/germany/0,1518,652582,00.html.

Star, Susan Leigh. 1999. "The Ethnography of Infrastructure." *American Behavioral Scientist* 43 (3): 377–91.

Statistisches Bundesamt (Destatis). 2022. *Bevölkerung und Erwerbstätigkeit: Ausländische Bevölkerung—Ergebnisse des Ausländerzentralregisters* 1 (2). Accessed May 21, 2022. https://www.destatis.de/DE/Themen/Gesellschaft-Umwelt/Bevoelkerung/Migration-Integration/Publikationen/Downloads-Migration/auslaend-bevoelkerung-2010200217005.html.

Staudinger, Angelika. 1995. "Das Schöne mit dem Nützlichen Verbinden, Volkspark Tiergarten." In *Denk-mal Tiergarten: Geschichte—Bedeutung—Gefahren—Hauptstadtbau*, edited by Lydia Schend, 45–63. Berlin: Edition Baumverlag.

Stein, Hartwig. 2000. *Inseln im Häusermeer: Eine Kulturgeschichte des deutschen Kleingar tenwesens bis zum Ende des Zweiten Weltkriegs Reichsweite Tendenzen und Gross-Hamburger Entwicklung*. Frankfurt am Main: Peter Lang.

Stern, Lesley. 2017. "A Garden or a Grave?" In *Arts of Living on a Damaged Planet: Ghosts of the Anthropocene*, edited by Anna Tsing, Heather Swanson, Elaine Gan, and Nils Bubandt, 17–29. Minneapolis: University of Minnesota Press.

Stern, Lesley. 2020. *Diary of a Detour*. Durham, NC: Duke University Press.

Stewart, Kathleen. 1996. *A Space on the Side of the Road: Cultural Poetics in an "Other" America*. Princeton, NJ: Princeton University Press.

Stewart, Kathleen. 2007. *Ordinary Affects*. Durham, NC: Duke University Press.

Steyerl, Hito. 2001. "Europe's Dream." *Springerin* 2 (1). https://www.springerin.at/en/2001/2/europas-traum/.

Stoetzer, Bettina. 2004. *InDifferenzen: Feministische Theorie in der antirassistischen Kritik*. Hamburg: Argument.

Stoetzer, Bettina. 2011. "At the Forest Edges of the City: Nature, Race, and National Belonging in Berlin." PhD diss., University of California at Santa Cruz.

Stoetzer, Bettina. 2014a. "Boar." In *To See Once More the Stars: Living in a Post-Fukushima World*, edited by Daisuke Naito, Ryan Sayre, Heather Swanson, and Satsuki Takahashi, 15–19. Santa Cruz, CA: New Pacific.

Stoetzer, Bettina. 2014b. "A Path through the Woods: Remediating Affective Environments in Documentary Asylum Worlds." *Transit* 9 (2): 1–23. https://escholarship.org/uc/item/4qk4p516.

Stoetzer, Bettina. 2014c. "Wild Barbecuing: Urban Citizenship and the Politics of (Trans-)Nationality in Berlin's Tiergarten." In *Transnationalism and the German*

City, edited by Jeffry Diefendorf and Janet Ward, 73–86. London: Palgrave Macmillan.

Stoetzer, Bettina. 2018. "Ruderal Ecologies: Rethinking Nature, Migration, and the Urban Landscape in Berlin." *Cultural Anthropology* 33 (2): 295–323.

Stoetzer, Bettina. 2019. "Wildes Brandenburg: Engaging 'Unruly Nature' in Berlin's Peripheries." In *Ecologies of Socialisms: Germany, Nature, and the Left in History, Politics and Culture*, edited by Sabine Mödersheim, Scott Moranda, and Eli Rubin, 295 315. Bern: Peter Lang.

Stoetzer, Bettina. 2020a. "*Ailanthus altissima*: The Botanical Afterlives of European Power." In *The Botanical City*, edited by Matthew Gandy and Sandra Jasper, 82–90. Berlin: Jovis.

Stoetzer, Bettina. 2020b. "Pigs, Viruses, and Humans Co-evolve in a Deadly Dance." In *Feral Atlas: The More-than-Human Anthropocene*, edited by Anna Tsing, Jennifer Deger, Alder Keleman, and Feifei Zhou. Stanford, CA: Stanford University Press. https://feralatlas.supdigital.org/poster/pigs-viruses-and -humans-co-evolve-in-a-deadly-dance.

Stolcke, Verena. 1995. "Talking Culture: New Boundaries, New Rhetorics of Exclusion in Europe." *Current Anthropology* 16 (1): 1–23.

Stoler, Ann Laura. 1995. *Race and the Education of Desire: Foucault's History of Sexuality and the Colonial Order of Things*. Durham, NC: Duke University Press.

Stoler, Ann Laura. 2004. "Affective States." In *A Companion to the Anthropology of Politics*, edited by David Nugent and Joan Vincent, 4–20. Malden, MA: Blackwell.

Stoler, Ann Laura. 2008. "Imperial Debris: Reflections on Ruins and Ruination." *Cultural Anthropology* 23 (2): 191–219.

Stoler, Ann Laura, ed. 2013. *Imperial Debris: On Ruins and Ruination*. Durham, NC: Duke University Press.

Stoler, Ann Laura. 2016. *Duress: Imperial Durabilities in Our Time*. Durham, NC: Duke University Press.

Sukopp, Herbert. 1958. "Vergleichende Untersuchungen der Vegetation Berliner Moore unter Berücksichtigung der anthropogenen Veränderungen." PhD diss., Freie Universität Berlin.

Sukopp, Herbert. 1971. "Beiträge zur Ökologie von *Chenopodium botrys L.*: Pt. I: Verbreitung und Vergesellschaftung." *Verhandlungen des Botanischen Vereins der Provinz Brandenburg* 108:3–25.

Sukopp, Herbert. 1980. *Naturschutz in der Grossstadt* (brochure). Berlin: Senator fuer Bau- und Wohnungswesen.

Sukopp, Herbert. 1998. "Urban Ecology: Scientific and Practical Aspects." In *Urban Ecology*, edited by Jürgen Breuste, Hildegard Feldmann, and Ogari Uhlmann, 3–16. Berlin: Springer.

Sukopp, Herbert. 2003a. "Flora and Vegetation Reflecting the Urban History of Berlin." *Die Erde* 134 (3): 295–316.

Sukopp, Herbert. 2003b. *Rückeroberung? Natur im Grossstadtbereich*. Vienna: Wiener Vorlesungen/Picus.

Sukopp, Herbert. 2007. "Rückeroberung? Natur in der Grosstadt." In *Wildschweine in Berlin, Füchse in Zürich*, edited by Michael Steinhaus, 57–70. Denkanstösse, Bd. 5. Mainz: Stiftung Natur und Umwelt Rheinland-Pfalz.

Sukopp, Herbert. 2008. "On the Early History of Urban Ecology in Europe." In *Urban Ecology: An International Perspective on the Interaction between Humans and Nature*, edited by John Marzluff, 79–97. Berlin: Springer.

Sukopp, Herbert, Slavomil Hejny, and Ingo Kowarik, eds. 1990. *Urban Ecology*. The Hague: SPB Academic Publishers.

Sukopp, Herbert, and Barbara Markstein. 1989. "Changes of the Reed Beds along the Berlin Havel, 1962–1987." *Aquatic Botany* 35:27–39.

Sukopp, Herbert, and Angelika Wurzel. 2003. "The Effects of Climate Change on the Vegetation of Central European Cities." *Urban Habitats* 1 (1): 66–86.

Suzuki, Yuka. 2016. *The Nature of Whiteness: Race, Animals, and Nation in Zimbabwe*. Seattle: University of Washington Press.

Szczygielska, Marianna, and Olga Cielemecka. 2019. "Introduction." In "Plantarium: Human-Vegetal Ecologies," edited by Marianna Szczygielska and Olga Cielemecka, special section, *Catalyst: Feminism, History, Technoscience* 5 (2): 1–12.

Tadiar, Neferti. 2009. *Things Fall Away: Philippine Historical Experience and the Makings of Globalization*. Durham, NC: Duke University Press.

Tagesschau. 2013. "Flüchtlinge in Deutschland." August 21.

TallBear, Kim. 2011. "Why Interspecies Thinking Needs Indigenous Standpoints." *Fieldsights*, November 18. https://culanth.org/fieldsights/why-interspecies -thinking-needs-indigenous-standpoints.

Taussig, Michael. 1987. *Shamanism, Colonialism, and the Wild Man: A Study in Terror and Healing*. Chicago: University of Chicago Press.

Tazzioli, Martina. 2017. "Containment through Mobility: Migrants' Spatial Disobediences and the Reshaping of Control through the Hotspot System in the Mediterranean." *Journal of Ethnic and Migration Studies* 44 (16): 2764–79.

Tazzioli, Martina. 2019. *The Making of Migration: The Biopolitics of Mobility at Europe's Borders*. Thousand Oaks: Sage.

Telegraf. 1949. "Die Linde am Großen Stern." March 18.

Thomas, Deborah. 2019. *Political Life in the Wake of the Plantation: Sovereignty, Witnessing, Repair*. Durham, NC: Duke University Press.

Thompson, Vanessa. 2018a. "Commentary on David Goldberg's Conversation with Achille Mbembe." *Theory, Culture & Society*, July 24. https://www .theoryculturesociety.org/blog/responses-vanessa-thompson-commentary-on -david-goldbergs-conversation-with-achille-mbembe.

Thompson, Vanessa E. 2018b. "'Hey, Sie da!': Postkolonial-feministische Kritik der Polizei am Beispiel von Racial Profiling." In *Kritik der Polizei*, edited by Daniel Loick, 197–219. Frankfurt: Campus.

Thrift, Nigel. 2004. "Intensities of Feeling: Towards a Spatial Politics of Affect." *Geografiska Annaler: Series B, Human Geography* 86 (1): 57–78.

Ticktin, Miriam. 2011. *Casualties of Care: Immigration and the Politics of Humanitarianism in France*. Berkeley: University of California Press.

Ticktin, Miriam. 2016. "What's Wrong with Innocence." Hot Spots, *Fieldsights*, June 28. https://culanth.org/fieldsights/whats-wrong-with-innocence.

Till, Karen. 2005. *The New Berlin: Memory, Politics, Place*. Minneapolis: University of Minnesota Press.

TIP Redaktion. 2017. "Abenteuer Brandenburg." TIP Berlin, June 12. https://www.tip-berlin.de/abenteuer-brandenburg/.

Tironi, Manuel, and Israel Rodríguez-Giralt. 2017. "Healing, Knowing, Enduring: Care and Politics in Damaged Worlds." *Sociological Review* 65 (2): 89–109.

Todd, Zoe. 2016. "An Indigenous Feminist Take on the Ontological Turn." *Journal of Historical Sociology* 29 (1): 4–21.

Treitel, Corinna. 2017. *Eating Nature in Modern Germany: Food, Agriculture and Environment, c.1870 to 2000*. Cambridge: Cambridge University Press.

Troesser, Julia. 2008. "Sarrazins Speiseplan. Der Dritte Tag: Teure Tomaten und Lust auf mehr." *Die Welt*, March 3.

Trouillot, Michel-Rolph. 1995. *Silencing the Past: Power and the Production of History*. Boston: Beacon.

Tsing, Anna. 1993. *In the Realm of the Diamond Queen: Marginality in an Out-of-the-Way Place*. Princeton, NJ: Princeton University Press.

Tsing, Anna. 2012. "Contaminated Diversity in Slow Disturbance: Potential Collaborators for a Livable Earth." *Rachel Carson Center Perspectives* 2012 (9): 95–97.

Tsing, Anna. 2014. "Blasted Landscapes (and the Gentle Arts of Mushroom Picking)." In *Multispecies Salon*, edited by Eben Kirksey, 87–109. Durham, NC: Duke University Press.

Tsing, Anna. 2015. *The Mushroom at the End of the World: On the Possibility of Life in Capitalist Ruins*. Princeton, NJ: Princeton University Press.

Tuck, Eve. 2009. "Suspending Damage: A Letter to Communities." *Harvard Educational Review* 79 (3): 409–27.

Tuck, Eve, and K. Wayne Yang. 2012. "Decolonization Is Not a Metaphor." *Decolonization: Indigineity, Education and Society* 1 (1): 1–40.

Tuck, Eve, and K. Wayne Yang. 2014a. "R-Words: Refusing Research." In *Humanizing Research: Decolonizing Qualitative Inquiry with Youth and Communities*, edited by Django Paris and Maisha T. Winn, 223–48. Thousand Oaks, CA: Sage.

Tuck, Eve, and K. Wayne Yang. 2014b. "Unbecoming Claims: Pedagogies of Refusal in Qualitative Research." *Qualitative Inquiry* 20 (6): 811–18.

Twardawa, Susanne. 2006. *Der Tiergarten in Berlin: Das Abenteuer liegt um die Ecke*. Berlin: Motzbuch.

van der Heyden, Ulrich, and Joachim Zeller. 2002. *Kolonialmetropole Berlin: Eine Spurensuche*. Berlin: Berlin Edition.

Verdery, Katherine. 1996. *What Was Socialism and What Comes Next?* Princeton, NJ: Princeton University Press.

Verdery, Katherine. 1997. "The New Eastern Europe in an Anthropology of Europe." *American Anthropologist* 99 (4): 715–17.

Verdery, Katherine. 2003. *The Vanishing Hectare: Property and Value in Postsocialist Transylvania*. Ithaca, NY: Cornell University Press.

Vick, Karl. 2005. "On Istanbul's Beaches, an Altered Social Fabric: Class Divisions Seen in Swimsuit Uproar." *Washington Post*, September 21.

Virilio, Paul. 1994. *Bunker Archeology*. New York: Princeton Architectural Press.

Visweswaran, Kamala. 1994. *Fictions of Feminist Ethnography*. Minneapolis: University of Minnesota Press.

Visweswaran, Kamala. 1998. "Race and the Culture of Anthropology." *American Anthropologist* 100 (1): 70–83.

Wacquant, Loïc. 2008. *Urban Outcasts: A Comparative Sociology of Advanced Marginality*. Cambridge: Polity.

Ward, Janet. 2010. "Recapitalizing Berlin." Paper presented at the Annual Meeting of the German Studies Association, Oakland, CA, October 2010.

Warnes, Andrew. 2008. *Savage Barbecue: Race, Culture, and the Invention of America's First Food*. Athens: University of Georgia Press.

Weisspflug, Hainer. 1999. "Das Landeswaldgesetz wird erlassen." *Berlinische Monatsschrift* 1:47–49 (Luisenstadt edition).

Werner, Karin. 2008. "Interkulturelle Gärten als Sozialräume der Mikro-Integration." *Skripte zur Migration und Nachhaltigkeit, Nr. 6*. München: Stiftung Interkultur.

Weston, Kath. 2017. *Animate Planet: Making Visceral Sense of Living in a High-Tech Ecologically Damaged World*. Durham, NC: Duke University Press.

Wiederwald, Rupert. 2010. "Treuhand Took the Heat for Privatization of East German Economy." *Deutsche Welle*, September 20. http://www.dw-world.de/dw/article/0,,5985015,00.html.

Wilkens, Katrin. 2009. *50 einfache Dinge die typisch deutsch sind*. Frankfurt: Westend.

Williams, Raymond. 1973. *The Country and the City*. Oxford: Oxford University Press.

Willis, William. 1972. "Skeletons in the Anthropological Closet." In *Reinventing Anthropology*, edited by Dell Hymes, 121–52. New York: Random House.

Wilmanns, Otti, and Jochen Bammert. 1965. "Zur Besiedlung der Freiburger Trümmerflächen: Eine Bilanz nach zwanzig Jahren." *Berichte der Naturforschenden Gesellschaft zu Freiburg* 55:399–411.

Wilson, Ara. 2004. *The Intimate Economies of Bangkok: Tomboys, Tycoons, and Avon Ladies in the Global City*. Berkeley: University of California Press.

Wimmer, Clemens Alexander. 2001. "Die Fiktion des deutschen Nationalgartens im 19. Jahrhundert." In *Gartenkultur und nationale Identität: Strategien nationaler und regionaler Identitätsstiftung in der deutschen Gartenkultur*, edited by Gert Gröning and Uwe Schneider, 35–51. Worms: Wernersche Verlagsgesellschaft.

Wise, N., and E. M. Wise. 2004. "Staging an Empire." In *Things That Talk: Object Lessons from Art and Science*, edited by Lorraine Daston, 101–45. New York: Zone Books.

Wöhr, A. C. 2005. "Animal Welfare Aspects regarding the Raising of Breeding Ostriches in Germany." *Deutsche Tierärztliche Wochenzeitschrift* 112 (3): 87–91.

Wolch, Jennifer. 1998. "Zoopolis." In *Animal Geographies: Place, Politics, and Identity in the Nature-Culture Borderlands*, edited by Jody Emel and Jennifer Wolch, 119–38. New York: Verso.

Wolch, Jennifer. 2002. "Anima Urbis." *Progress in Human Geography* 26 (6): 721–42.

Wolf, Andre Christian. 2008. "Kleine bunte Gärten: Bürgerengagement und Integration in Kleingärtnervereinen." *PNDonline* 1.

Wolf, Eric. 1994. *Europe and the People without History*. Berkeley: University of California Press.

Wolff, Larry. 1994. *Inventing Eastern Europe: The Map of Civilization on the Mind of the Enlightenment*. Stanford, CA: Stanford University Press.

Wolschke Bulmahn, Joachim. 2005. "Violence as the Basis of National Socialist Landscape Planning in the 'Annexed Eastern Areas.'" In Brüggemeier, Cioc, and Zeller, *How Green Were the Nazis?*, 243–56.

Worster, Donald. 1985. *Nature's Economy: A History of Ecological Ideas*. Cambridge: Cambridge University Press.

Yanagisako, Sylvia, and Carol Delaney, eds. 1995. *Naturalizing Power: Essays in Feminist Cultural Analysis*. New York: Routledge.

Yildiz, Armanc. 2017. "Fear Makes the Soul: Racialized Sex Panics from Colonial Germany to the Cologne Attacks." Paper presented at the 116th Annual Meeting of the American Anthropological Association, Washington, DC, November.

Yildiz, Armanc. 2020. "Racism Is Never Here: The United States as a Discursive Trope in Racism Discussions in Germany." Echoes. https://keywordsechoes
.com/armanc-yildiz-racism-is-never-here.

Yoneyama, Lisa. 1999. *Hiroshima Traces: Time, Space, and the Dialectics of Memory*. Berkeley: University of California Press.

Yusoff, Kathryn. 2018. *A Billion Black Anthropocenes or None*. Minneapolis: University of Minnesota Press.

Zeller, Thomas. 1996. "Ganz Deutschland (s)ein Garten? Ideologie und Praxis des Prinzips der bodenständigen Bepflanzung beim Bau der Reichsautobahnen." In *Kontinuität oder Brüche? Werkstattberichte zur Landespflege der Nachkriegszeit*, edited by C. Valentien, 7–29. Munich: Lehrstuhl für Landschaftsarchitektur und Entwerfen.

Zeller, Thomas. 2005. "Molding the Landscape in Nazi Environmentalism: Alwin Seifert and the Third Reich." In Brüggemeier, Cioc, and Zeller, *How Green Were the Nazis?*, 147–70.

Zepernick, Bernhard. 2002. "Die Botanische Zentralstelle für die Kolonien." In *Kolonialmetropole Berlin: Eine Spurensuche*, edited by Ulrich van der Heyden and Joachim Zeller, 107–11. Berlin: Berlin Edition.

Zeybek, Ozan. 2006. "Republican Swimming: Modernity and Culture in Turkey." *Uninvited Guest* 42, November 10. http://www.uninvitedguest.net/index.
php/2006/11/10/republican-swimming-modernity-and-culture-in-turkey/.

Žižek, Slavoj. 2010. "A Permanent Economic Emergency." *New Left Review* (July–August): 85–95.

Zwischenraum Kollektiv, ed. 2017. *Decolonize the City! Zur Kolonialität der Stadt— Gespräche, Aushandlungen, Perspektiven*. Münster: Unrast Verlag.

INDEX

barbecuing, 30, 106, 140–42, 147, 151–58, 162, 167–70, 269nn7–10; colonial imaginations of, 146, 167; etymology of, 167; German fascination with, 270n13; in public parks, 27, 81, 122, 140, 147–48, 150–52, 161, 241, 269n5; in Turkey, 160, 163–65. *See also* Thai Park (Preußen Park)/Thai Picnic; wild barbecuing
Benedict, Ruth, 10, 247n14
Bennett, Michael, 75, 262n18
Berlin airlift, 43, 45, 144, 263n36
Berliners, 3, 21, 43, 62–63, 71, 100, 104, 210, 220; barbecuing and, 139, 150, 163; collapse of socialism and, 106; of color, 78; elderly, 61; forests and, 250n30; gardening and, 40, 70; integration of, 83; March Oder region and, 205; migrant, 2, 78; Tiergarten and, 144–47; Turkish, 2, 89–90, 139, 142, 250n33; urban nature and, 5, 75
Berlin Wall, 1–2, 4, 12–13, 19, 42, 110–11; botanists and, 47; countryside and, 252n42; forests and, 227; Kreuzberg and, 76–77; March Oder region and, 179; migration and the fall of, 70, 109; Tiergarten and, 145, 147
Blackbourn, David, 217, 277n9, 278n18
black locust tree (*Robinia pseudoacacia*), 20, 48–49, 53
blasted landscapes, 4, 35, 54, 58, 61, 256n27
blood and soil ideology, 41, 74, 254n12, 279n19
Bodenständigkeit, 41, 254n14
bombings, 38–39, 41, 45, 254n6, 254n11, 256n25
borders, 52, 169, 177, 210; collaborations across political, 47; Europe's 12–13, 16–17, 22, 24–25, 158, 163, 167–68, 175, 239–40; German, 6, 48, 113; March Oder region and, 178–79, 183, 187, 201; national, 24, 72, 142, 158, 163, 166, 219 (*see also* barbecuing); political, 179; refugee deaths at EU, 12–13; smoke and, 170; the *unheimlich* and, 176
Bosporus, 163–66
botanists, 4, 29, 36–37, 46–57, 59, 241, 256n25, 257n32, 257n34; Nazi-era, 259n43
botany, 4, 58; history of colonial, 70; German, 254n8; post–World War II, 6,

46–48; of ruderal plants, 48–50. *See also* phytosociology
Brandenburg, 17, 30, 47, 173, 178–82, 195, 204–7, 216–17, 222, 252n42; AfD in, 207, 276n6, 279–80n28; African refugees in, 261n13; asylum seekers in, 23, 273n19; forestry in, 223, 250n30; forests, 227; GMO agriculture in, 207, 276–77n8; ostrich farms in, 229, 281n38; protected nature and landscape area in, 272n11, 276n3; refugee homes in, 229; state election of 2019, 276n6; tobacco and, 277n10; tourism and, 220; tourist brochures, 191, 277n12; unemployment in, 180, 272n14, 276n5; as *unheimlich*, 188, 201; wild, 212, 214, 236, 238, 277n12; wilderness, 210, 213. *See also* Grebe, Rainald; March Oder region; Märkische Schweiz Nature Park
Brown, Jacqueline, 24, 79, 272n8
built environments, 8, 59–60, 206, 278n19

capitalism, 10, 24, 31, 58, 137; anesthesia and, 254n10; Berlin's ecology and, 18; gambling and, 121; ghettos and, 263n27; *longue durée* of, 14; postsocialism and, 247n15; promises of, 202; ruins of, 17, 37, 219; socialism and, 175, 220, 235–36, 268n27; street vendors and, 135; subjectivities produced by, 107; urban life and, 4, 7; wildness of, 226
climate change, 5, 8, 54, 59, 219, 222, 242, 259n47, 276n4; ruderal plants and, 53; sticky goosefoot and, 37
cognitive dissonance, 30, 175–76, 188, 192, 202, 271n4
Cold War, 19, 130, 202; allotment gardens and, 74; Berlin Wall and, 252n42, 279n21; March Oder and, 179; rise of, 42; rubble and, 43; ruins of, 30; Teufelsberg and, 255n21; Vietnamese migration during, 109; West Berlin during, 266n13
colonialism, 7, 192–93, 217, 219; anthropology and, 10–11; European, 12–13, 167, 202, 279–80n28; German, 41, 73, 182, 192, 214, 218, 248n22, 279–80n28; legacies of, 16, 60; *longue durée* of, 14–15; ruins of, 17; settler, 246n9, 247n14; urban nature and, 270n12; white settler, 146, 208
colonial mimicry, 216

colonization, 10, 15, 20, 146, 180; of Africa, 215; of the Americas, 214; Anthropocene and, 246n9; Fanon on, 202; Nazi ideas about, 216, 273n15; refugees and, 193; urban nature and, 5; wildness and, 208, 226, 234

conservation, 226, 258n40, 280n26; African Americans and, 261n9; alternative, 225; areas, 179; biotope, 259n42; botanical gardens as sites for, 72; environmental, 19; nature, 47, 56f, 179; Nazis and, 279n20; policies, 54, 55, 75; programs, 62; rewilding and, 279n25; strategy, 206

conservationists, 62, 226, 278n18; Nazi, 217

cultural critique: anthropology and, 7, 10, 12, 28, 31, 57, 246n8; rubble of twenty-first-century Europe and, 12, 31, 57; ruderal worlds and, 57; in a time of destruction, 12; in a time of rubble, 7, 10

cultural difference, 12, 15, 78, 136

cultural hybridity, 17, 24–25

culture, 8–9, 11, 29, 71, 99; assumptions about Turkish, 30; barbecuing and, 147, 152–53, 156, 166; car, 215; European, 96; gardens and, 138, 141; German conceptions of, 217, 251n37, 267n25; Islamic, 79; material, 200, 272n7; nature and, 7, 9–10, 20, 36, 57, 70, 98, 175, 277n11; political, 157, 168; popular, 125, 183, 200, 214, 216, 274n22; of poverty, 112; race and, 10–12; ruderal ecologies and, 241; technical, 51; vending, 104 (see also Thai Park (Preußen Park)/ Thai Picnic)

Davis, Heather, 12, 246n9

decolonization, 15, 193, 208; in Berlin, 248n22; cities and, 16, 24; ecology and, 12, 60; ethnographic writing and, 195; Europe and, 14

deer, 39–40, 143, 191, 205, 212, 269n3

displacement, 20, 132, 136, 177, 194, 202, 227, 240–42; aesthetics of urban wastelands and, 24; affect and, 272n7; of the asylum system, 234; Berlin and, 266n13; blasted landscapes and, 4; capitalism and, 235; the East as temporal, 275n33; everyday experiences of, 142; gentrification and, 80; long-term effects of, 272n6; of migrants, 98–99, 209; mushrooms and, 131;

nostalgia and, 200, 226; plants and, 71; refugee, 13, 193, 230, 273n17; ruderals and, 38, 57–58; the unheimlich (uncanny) and, 30; the unhomely and, 176

dispossession, 10, 176, 190, 216, 218, 234, 238; Bodenständigkeit and, 254n14; economies of, 243; ghettos and, 263n27; of land, 15; plants and, 14; settler colonial, 27

East Berlin, 42–43, 213, 256n26; botanists, 47; migrants in, 109; rubble and, 43, 255n18

East Germany, 207, 210, 213, 216, 224, 266n8; allotment gardens in, 74; deindustrialization in, 275n1; forests and, 256n22, 276n7; Hartz measures and, 112; March Oder region and, 179; as a neo-Nazi space, 273n16; refugees from, 268n27; rural, 23, 181, 205, 227; Vietnamese migrants in, 109–10, 113, 186; West German garbage dumped in, 280n32. See also German Democratic Republic (GDR)

ecological care, 25, 71

ecologies, 4–5, 10, 71, 272n7; affective, 57; of belonging, 28, 279n25; Berlin's, 6, 19, 26, 50–51, 54, 93; Brandenburg's, 206; of buildings, 95; of gardens, 100; intersectional, 12, 24; local, 225–26, 236; of migration, 25, 38, 76, 79; of the nation, 176; racialized, 24, 25, 30, 79, 141, 177, 190, 272n8; of race, 25, 279n25; of racialization, 24–25, 38, 76; rubble, 48; ruderal, 25, 36; of ruderal plants, 53; of ruination, 9, 31, 203 (see also unheimlich, the); socialist, 31, 208; of urban life, 240. See also ruderal ecologies; urban ecologies

ecology, 6, 51, 57, 59–60, 203; of animals, 279n25; Berlin's, 17–18, 20, 24; of blasted landscapes, 256n27; blood and soil ideology and, 41; of cities, 51–52; colonial encounter and, 6; decolonization of, 12, 60; garden, 3, 93; of March Oder region, 206; Nazism and, 259n43; of place, 272n8; of plant-insect relations, 259n44; of racialized fears, 81 (see also Sarrazin, Thilo); of rubble spaces, 46; ruderal, 3, 91; ruderal worlds and, 5; of sticky goosefoot, 50; of Thai Park, 107; of Tiergarten, 142; urban, 4, 18, 22, 37, 56, 88, 94, 253n4, 258n36; of urban life, 16 edge effects, 4, 245n4

El-Tayeb, Fatima, 13, 15–16, 21, 78

environmental destruction, 26, 38, 58, 216, 241, 246n8, 277–78n15

environmental discourse, 223, 272n10; fascist, 41

environmentalism, 152–53, 272n13, 280n26; German, 279n19

environmental justice, 31, 242

ethnography, 6, 27, 121, 128, 226; as gleaning practice, 5–7, 25–28, 60; multisited, 26; multispecies, 7; patchwork, 252n47

European Union (EU): asylum and immigration policies, 13, 181, 202; borders, 12, 181, 183, 247n17; expansion, 247n16; GMOs and, 277n8; governments, 13; integration projects of, 21; markets, 281n38; nations, 239; Poland and, 178–79, 230; political cohesion, 14; Social City program of, 68; Turkey and, 163

exclusion, 14, 23, 37, 63, 93, 100, 264n41, 266n13; barbecuing and, 162; of food production, 106; geographies of, 204; landscape practices and, 28; nationalist, 58; practices of, 31; racial, 180; racialized, 16, 228; refugee, 13; sites of, 18, 29; social, 167

exploitation, 7, 11, 100, 216, 234, 252n44; asylum system and, 238; capitalist, 5, 59; colonial, 10–11; of labor, 46, 93; plantation agriculture and, 72. See also race; racialization; racism

extinction. See species extinction

extraction, 27, 60, 234; capitalist, 5, 7, 12, 24, 38, 60, 219, 241; histories of, 5–6; of labor, 238; land, 242

Fanon, Frantz, 93, 146, 202–3, 237

fascism, 17–18, 24, 29, 178, 212, 229n49; Africa and, 277–78n15; demographic categories and, 250n33; history of, 274n26; legacy of, 247n11; numbing of the senses after, 40; refugees of, 273n17; ruination and, 53; trauma of, 37

Finney, Carolyn, 70, 261n9

fire, 30, 39, 58, 81, 138–39, 154, 170, 245n3; danger of, 21, 63, 147, 158, 169. See also barbecuing

Fontane, Theodor, 179, 209, 217

foresters, 25, 32, 62, 223, 235

forestry, 223, 250n30; close-to-nature, 206, 224; German, 272n10; 280n31; monocultural, 52, 226; socialist, 209, 236

forests, 6, 40–41, 217, 241, 257n29; asylum shelters in, 23, 177; Berlin's, 5, 18–20, 23, 62, 161, 250n30; 258n41; Brandenburg's, 23, 227; close-to-nature, 207, 214; collectivization of, 222; domestication of, 143; Germany's, 175, 240, 256n22; March Oder region's, 178–79, 183, 206, 209; monocultural, 224; mushroom picking in, 104, 130, 136, 268n29; rubble and, 144; urban, 5, 19, 45, 63

Freud, Sigmund, 175–76, 192, 271n4. See also unheimlich, the

frontiers, 217–18, 235; colonial, 220, 236; imaginaries of, 273n15

gambling, 103, 107, 117, 120–21, 267n23. See also hi-lo

Gandy, Matthew, 18, 56, 259n43

garbage, 265n1, 280n32; barbecuing and, 30, 154–55, 166, 168; by the Berlin Wall, 1; collection, 114; in parks, 21, 81, 104, 150, 152, 267n25; racial meanings of, 154

gardening, 68–69, 71, 87, 99–100; British practices of, 261n11; immigrants and, 22; multicultural, 29, 100; national and colonial legacies of, 74; Nazi "Germanization" efforts and, 74, 254n12; urban, 6, 29, 72, 75, 80

gardens, 5–6, 22–23, 29, 53, 63, 67, 72–76, 82, 88, 105, 258n41; allotment, 5, 19, 67–68, 70, 73–74, 88, 260nn1–4; courtyard, 241; intercultural, 5, 68–69, 260n4, 260n7; makeshift, 92–93, 99–100; multicultural, 5, 22, 68, 70–71, 85, 87–88; Nazis and, 41, 74, 262n16; private, 145, 158; rubble and, 255n19; ruins and, 10; sticky goosefoot and, 35, 50; tree-of-heaven and, 49; urban, 27, 73, 75

gecekondu, 2, 97–98, 164, 245n2

Geertz, Clifford, 125

gender: exchange in Thai Park and, 124, 126, 128, 137; formations, 248n20; inequalities, 6, 72, 242, 249n29; performance of, 29

genocide, 20, 38, 218–19, 274n26, 280n29

gentrification, 24, 80, 98, 100, 114, 241

German Democratic Republic (GDR), 2, 109,
196, 199–200, 252n42
Gestapo headquarters, 61, 255n20
ghettos, 38, 63, 70, 78, 80, 164; Jewish, 263n27
giant goldenrod (*Solidago gigantea*), 48,
83, 84*f*
Gilroy, Paul, 157, 237, 265n42
gleaning, 5–7, 25–28, 60
governance, 125, 245n6; human, 57; of nature,
16; state, 124; urban, 4, 8, 55, 71–72, 124,
158, 168; urban nature and, 55, 105
Grebe, Rainald, 180, 212
greening, 37, 58, 87; anesthetic, 93; design,
55; policies, 224; of rubble, 44–46; of
ruins, 42
green spaces, 6, 17, 22, 44–45, 62–63, 77–78,
80–81, 105, 114, 139; artificially created,
258n40; barbecuing and, 164; benefits of,
265n2; civic engagement in, 75
grilling, 30, 152, 155, 161, 165–66, 270n11.
See also barbecuing
Grunewald, 19, 45, 61, 161
guest workers, 76, 90, 97

Ha, Noa, 16, 105
Hage, Ghassan, 158, 219, 236, 281n41
Hartz IV: benefits, 110–12, 133–34, 266n12,
267n18; diet, 115, 117, 137; menu, 114–16,
137, 267n19; recipients, 112–16, 135, 266n11,
267n18
Hasenheide, 61, 82, 89, 92*f*
Heim, the, 173, 177, 182–83, 185*f*, 186–96, 201,
203, 229–30, 232–35, 271n2, 274nn23–24
Heimat, 21, 74, 208, 240, 250–51n35, 254n13,
262n15, 278n19; ecologies of, 279n25
hi-lo, 119–21, 126–27, 129, 132, 136, 267n20,
267n22
Holocaust, 15, 259n50, 263n27, 274n26,
275n33
hot spots (*Brennpunkte*), 22, 76, 78, 80–81,
202, 262n26; social, 63, 70; urban, 155,
240

immigration, 52, 90, 136, 155, 245–46n6;
law, 251n37, 263n28; in the March Oder
region, 232; policies, 13, 109, 116, 180–81,
227; racism and, 10
informal economies, 28–29, 78, 110, 113,
134–35, 281n37

infrastructure, 7–9, 59, 206, 247n12; anthropological scholarship on, 8; Berlin's, 19,
134; border, 3; clearance, 46; local, 214;
of nature, 45; socialist, 236; for tourism,
227; transportation, 42, 211; urban, 25, 54,
73, 113, 249n28; urban green-space, 100;
water, 2
integration, 22, 68–71, 79, 81, 83, 85, 88, 97,
100, 147, 232–34, 247n14, 260n5; allotment gardens and, 260n4; environmental
consciousness and, 152, 168; EU projects
of, 21; failed, 98, 153; framework of, 107;
imagined, 151; lack of, 90, 96; lived, 150;
as neocolonial violence, 168; practices of,
99; resistance to, 78; rhetoric of, 238; self-
help and, 114; social, 18, 68, 105; as tool of
political control, 79
Integration Summit, 79, 233, 236, 238
Intercultural Foundation (Stiftung Interkultur), 69, 261n7
intimate economies, 107, 128, 136; mushrooms
and, 129, 267–68n26; of Thai Park, 29,
106, 128, 135–37
Islamophobia, 14–15
Istanbul, 3, 97, 270–71nn19–20; barbecuing
and, 141–42, 160, 163–68, 170; sticky
goosefoot and, 35, 49

Jobson, Ryan Cecil, 10, 27

Kalın, Osman, 1–2, 245n1; garden of, 4, 91;
gecekondu/treehouse (*Baumhaus*) of, 3,
14, 91, 98, 245n1
kinship, 29, 126, 128, 249n25, 272n13; networks, 109; ties, 267–68n26
Kırıkkanat, Mine, 164–65
Klima, Alan, 120–21, 267n24
Kosek, Jake, 75, 262n17
Kottbusser Gate (Kotti), 77, 79, 98
Kreuzberg, 1, 69, 75–79, 97–98, 245n1; barbecuing and, 269n15; Muslims in, 264n36;
squatting in, 262n19

Lachmund, Jens, 18, 44, 55, 255n19, 256n26
landscape architects, 37, 74, 144
landscaping, 45, 53; British, 261n11; ideals, 146;
imperial practices of, 72; Nazi, 41, 254n12;
river, 224–25; rubble and, 255n18
Lanz, Stephan, 166, 263n28, 264n40, 270n19

ness and, 156; wilderness and, 52–53; wildness and, 258n37, 279n20; work camps of, 18. *See also* Gestapo headquarters; Riefenstahl, Leni

Nelson, Arvid, 223, 280n31, 280n34

neo-Nazis, 193, 204, 207, 273n16, 274n29

Neukölln, 61, 75–89, 94, 97, 113, 140, 148, 269n9; Muslims in, 264n36; North, 79–80

Nghi Ha, Kien, 79, 167–68

9/11 attacks, 75, 78, 158

no-go areas/zones, 89, 180–81, 201, 264n39

nonhumans, 25–26, 37; displacement of, 240; modernist planning and, 55; racial formations and, 272n7

nonnative plants, 36, 48, 53–54, 257n34

nostalgia, 45, 58, 92, 100, 160, 196, 226, 237; colonial, 218; eroticized, 278n14; imperial(ist), 8, 41, 214, 240; nuclear, 241; for socialist objects, 200, 279n27; for the wild, 216

oikos, 74, 135, 203

otherness, 75, 147, 166; consumption of animal meat and, 168, 270n12; cultural, 151, 155; images of, 228; of the March Oder region, 211; racialized, 153, 218, 270n12; sites of, 79; Wild East as space of, 218. *See also* barbecuing; Thai Park (Preußen Park)/Thai Picnic

Pandian, Anand, 75, 262n17

parallel societies, 70, 78, 98

parallel worlds, 20, 62–63, 240

phytosociology, 52, 257–58n34

planners, 22, 43, 48, 70, 113, 224, 265n2, 266n13; city, 37; diversity and, 81; Nazi, 53; urban, 42, 68, 93, 105, 112, 255n16

postsocialism, 17, 247n15, 249n24

postsocialist transition, 177–80, 206, 208–9, 272n13

privatization, 166, 207, 221, 227, 276n7

Prussia, 73, 211, 214, 217, 221; East, 210; German refugees from East, 222; immigrants from East, 76; Muslims in, 264n36

public parks, 70, 105, 265n2; barbecuing in, 27, 148, 161, 163, 166

Pyramid Garden, 82–83, 84f, 86f, 89, 98–99

Quartiersmanagement, 68, 79, 83, 85, 87

rabbits, 25, 32, 94–96, 98, 119, 143–44, 271n21

race, 24, 218, 249n29; anthropology and, 11, 15; Cold War anxieties around, 277–78n15; culture and, 10–11; ecologies of, 25, 279n25; geographies of, 24; German, 273n15; German notions of, 252n42; inequalities of, 72; national anxieties about, 75; nature and, 6, 156–57; Nazi discourse of, 270n11, 273n15; performance of, 29; place and, 156, 218; politics of, 7, 15, 71, 209; practices of exchange in Thai Park and, 126; private property and, 158; scholarship on, 248n20, 249n25; as social construction, 11, 248n20, 252n43; urban nature and, 270n12

racial geographies, 79, 263n35, 272n8

racialization, 6–7, 18, 25, 27, 208, 238; barbecuing and, 147; of citizenship in Germany, 264n41; ecologies of, 6, 31, 38, 76; ghettos and, 263n27; human-animal relations and, 270n12; migrants and, 71, 93, 155, 248n21; nature and, 157; of Muslims, 158; of the outdoors, 261n9; the *unheimlich* and, 31, 192; of urban nature, 25, 76–82; urban space and, 82

racial politics, 6–7, 23

racial profiling, 21, 78, 265n1

racism, 10–12, 15–16, 23–24, 31, 58–60, 192, 195, 202, 208, 252n44, 263n31, 279; anti-Black, 158, 250n32; biological, 10, 12, 15, 24; economic crisis and, 114; in environmental narratives, 28; erasure of, 238; everyday, 30, 193; integration and, 247n14; *longue durée* of, 15, 240; migration and, 78–79; nationalism and, 248n20, 248n23; Nazi, 10, 41, 279n19; new, 12, 15, 78, 82; no-go area as space of, 264n39; people-plant relations and, 70; protests against, 252n43; refugees and, 234; ruderal ecologies and, 241; ruins of, 7, 10, 12, 93; spatial dimensions of, 248n23; urban conflicts around, 20; urban green space and, 142; urban nature and, 5; violence of, 217; wildness of, 193, 209. *See also* cultural difference; Nazis/Nazism; Sarrazin, Thilo

reconstruction, 17, 39–46, 52, 58; national, 45, 48, 146; symbolic, 249n25; of the Tiergarten, 144; urban, 255n16